Pinocchio
Vampire Slayer

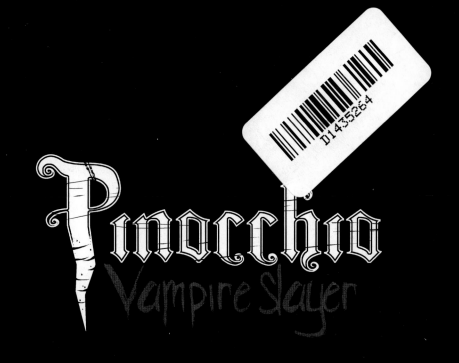

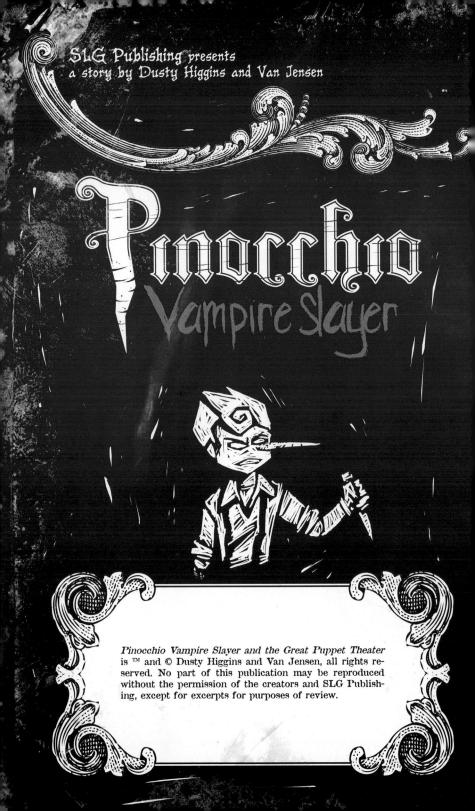

SLG Publishing presents
a story by Dusty Higgins and Van Jensen

Pinocchio
Vampire Slayer

and the GREAT PUPPET THEATER

Published by
SLG Publishing
P.O. Box 26427
San Jose, CA 95159
www.slgcomic.com

First Printing: October 2010
ISBN 978-1-59362-203-9
Printed in Indonesia

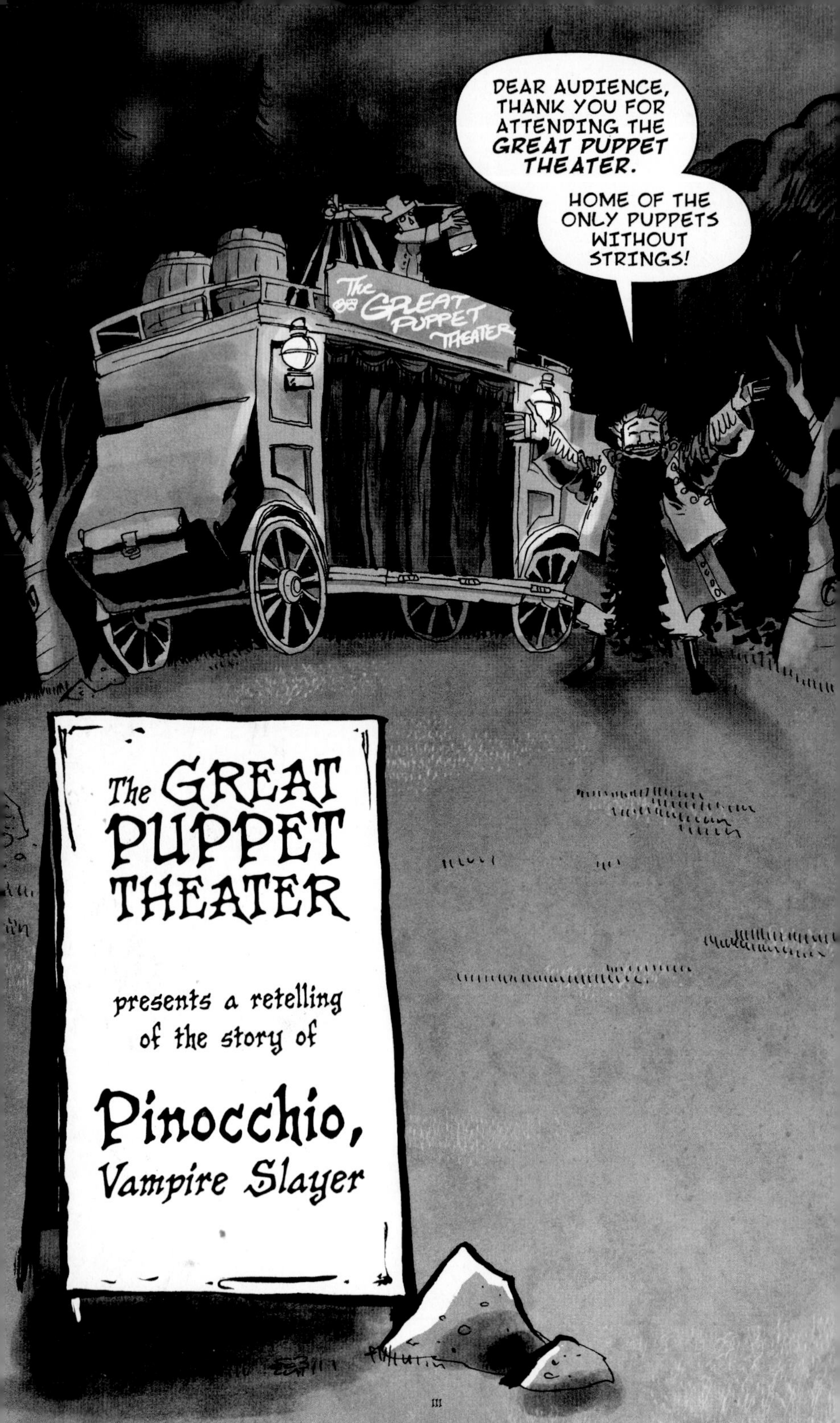
DEAR AUDIENCE, THANK YOU FOR ATTENDING THE GREAT PUPPET THEATER.
HOME OF THE ONLY PUPPETS WITHOUT STRINGS!
The GREAT PUPPET THEATER
The GREAT PUPPET THEATER
presents a retelling of the story of
Pinocchio, Vampire Slayer

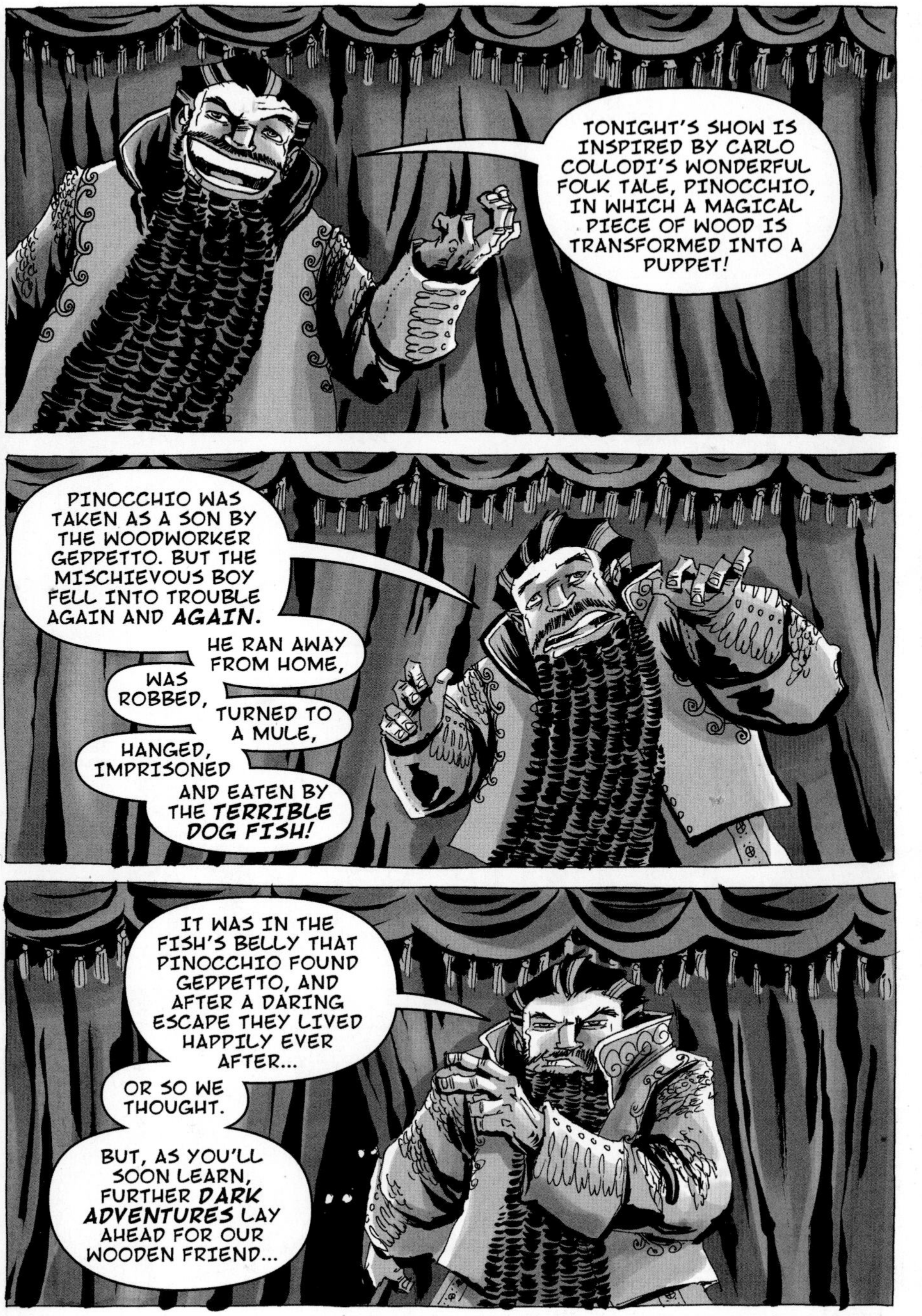
TONIGHT'S SHOW IS INSPIRED BY CARLO COLLODI'S WONDERFUL FOLK TALE, PINOCCHIO, IN WHICH A MAGICAL PIECE OF WOOD IS TRANSFORMED INTO A PUPPET!
PINOCCHIO WAS TAKEN AS A SON BY THE WOODWORKER GEPPETTO. BUT THE MISCHIEVOUS BOY FELL INTO TROUBLE AGAIN AND **AGAIN**.
HE RAN AWAY FROM HOME,
WAS ROBBED,
TURNED TO A MULE,
HANGED, IMPRISONED
AND EATEN BY THE ***TERRIBLE DOG FISH!***
IT WAS IN THE FISH'S BELLY THAT PINOCCHIO FOUND GEPPETTO, AND AFTER A DARING ESCAPE THEY LIVED HAPPILY EVER AFTER...
OR SO WE THOUGHT.
BUT, AS YOU'LL SOON LEARN, FURTHER ***DARK ADVENTURES*** LAY AHEAD FOR OUR WOODEN FRIEND...

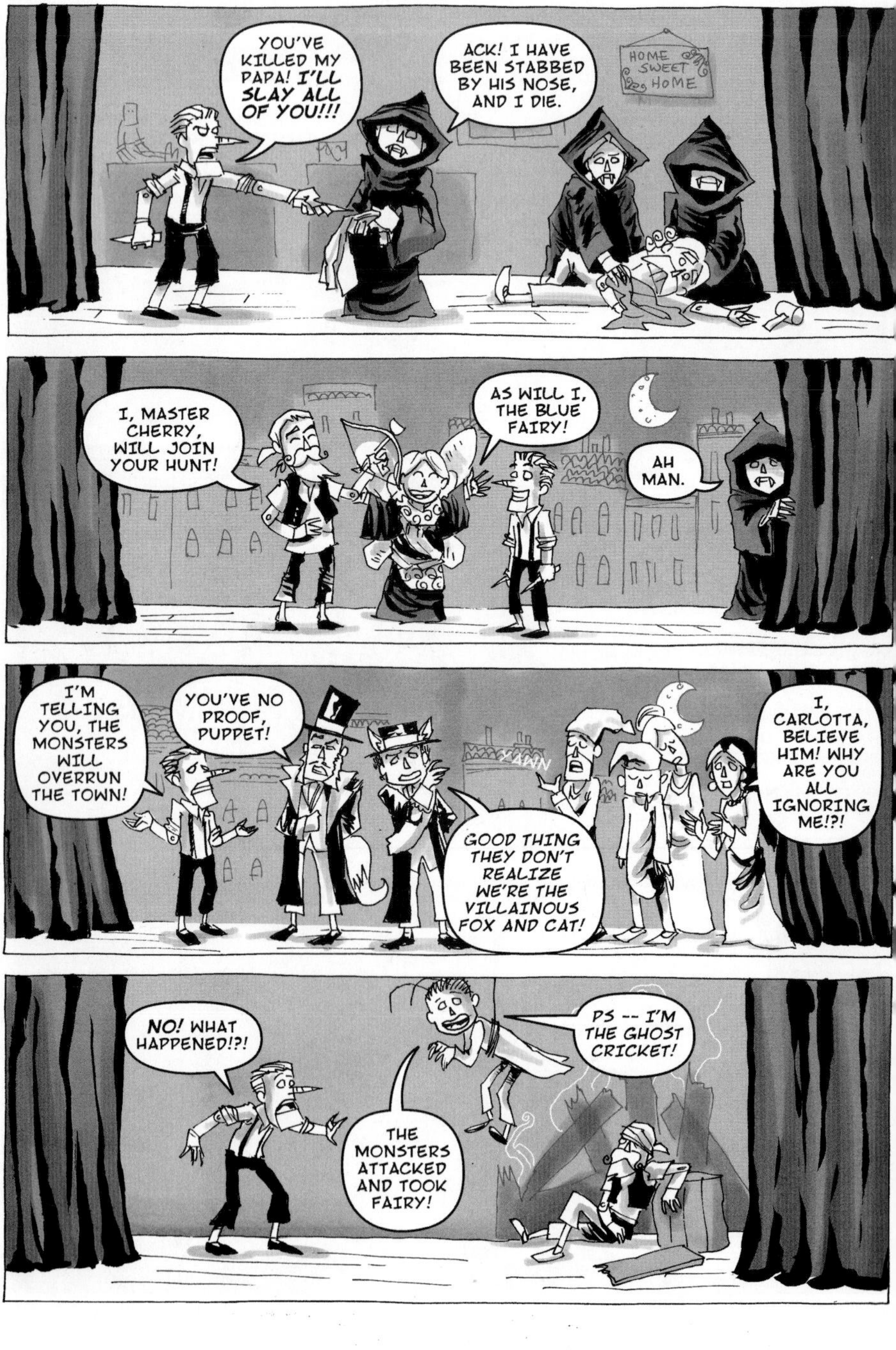
YOU'VE KILLED MY PAPA! I'LL SLAY ALL OF YOU!!!
ACK! I HAVE BEEN STABBED BY HIS NOSE, AND I DIE.
HOME SWEET HOME
I, MASTER CHERRY, WILL JOIN YOUR HUNT!
AS WILL I, THE BLUE FAIRY!
AH MAN.
I'M TELLING YOU, THE MONSTERS WILL OVERRUN THE TOWN!
YOU'VE NO PROOF, PUPPET!
GOOD THING THEY DON'T REALIZE WE'RE THE VILLAINOUS FOX AND CAT!
YAWN
I, CARLOTTA, BELIEVE HIM! WHY ARE YOU ALL IGNORING ME!?!
NO! WHAT HAPPENED!?!
THE MONSTERS ATTACKED AND TOOK FAIRY!
PS -- I'M THE GHOST CRICKET!

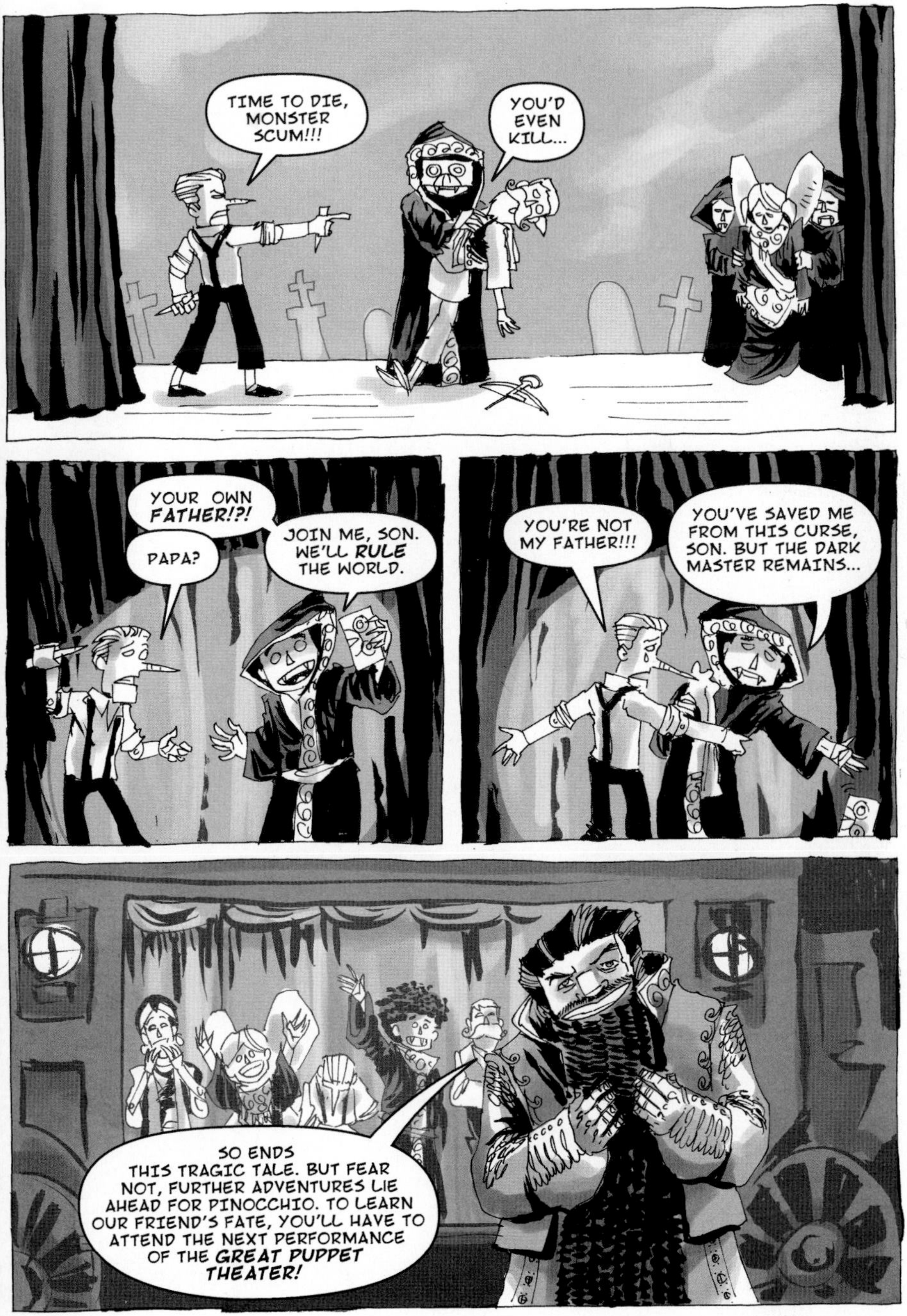

TIME TO DIE, MONSTER SCUM!!!
YOU'D EVEN KILL...
YOUR OWN FATHER!?!
PAPA?
JOIN ME, SON. WE'LL RULE THE WORLD.
YOU'RE NOT MY FATHER!!!
YOU'VE SAVED ME FROM THIS CURSE, SON. BUT THE DARK MASTER REMAINS...
SO ENDS THIS TRAGIC TALE. BUT FEAR NOT, FURTHER ADVENTURES LIE AHEAD FOR PINOCCHIO. TO LEARN OUR FRIEND'S FATE, YOU'LL HAVE TO ATTEND THE NEXT PERFORMANCE OF THE GREAT PUPPET THEATER!

There was once
upon a time a
piece of wood...

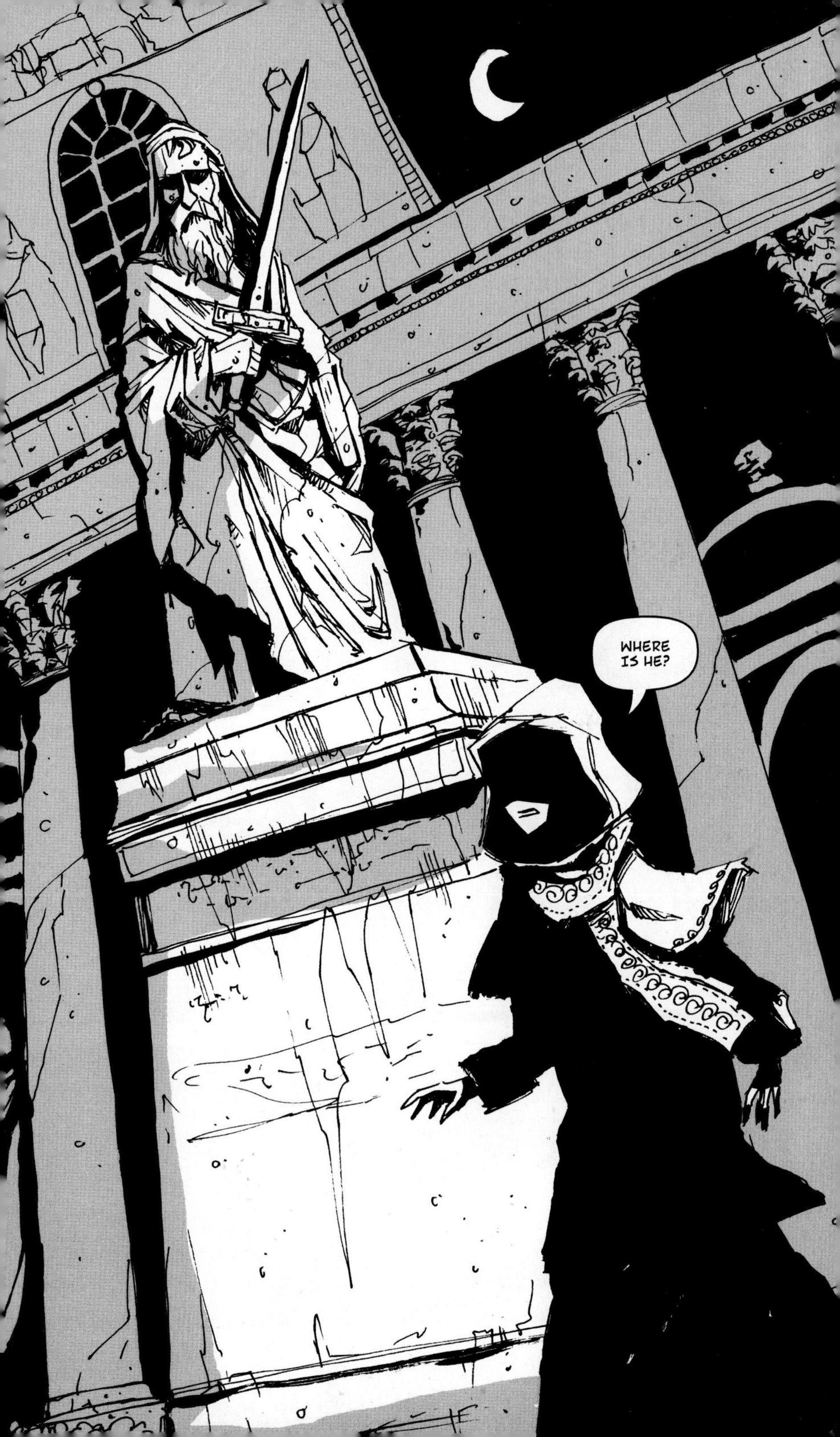
WHERE IS HE?

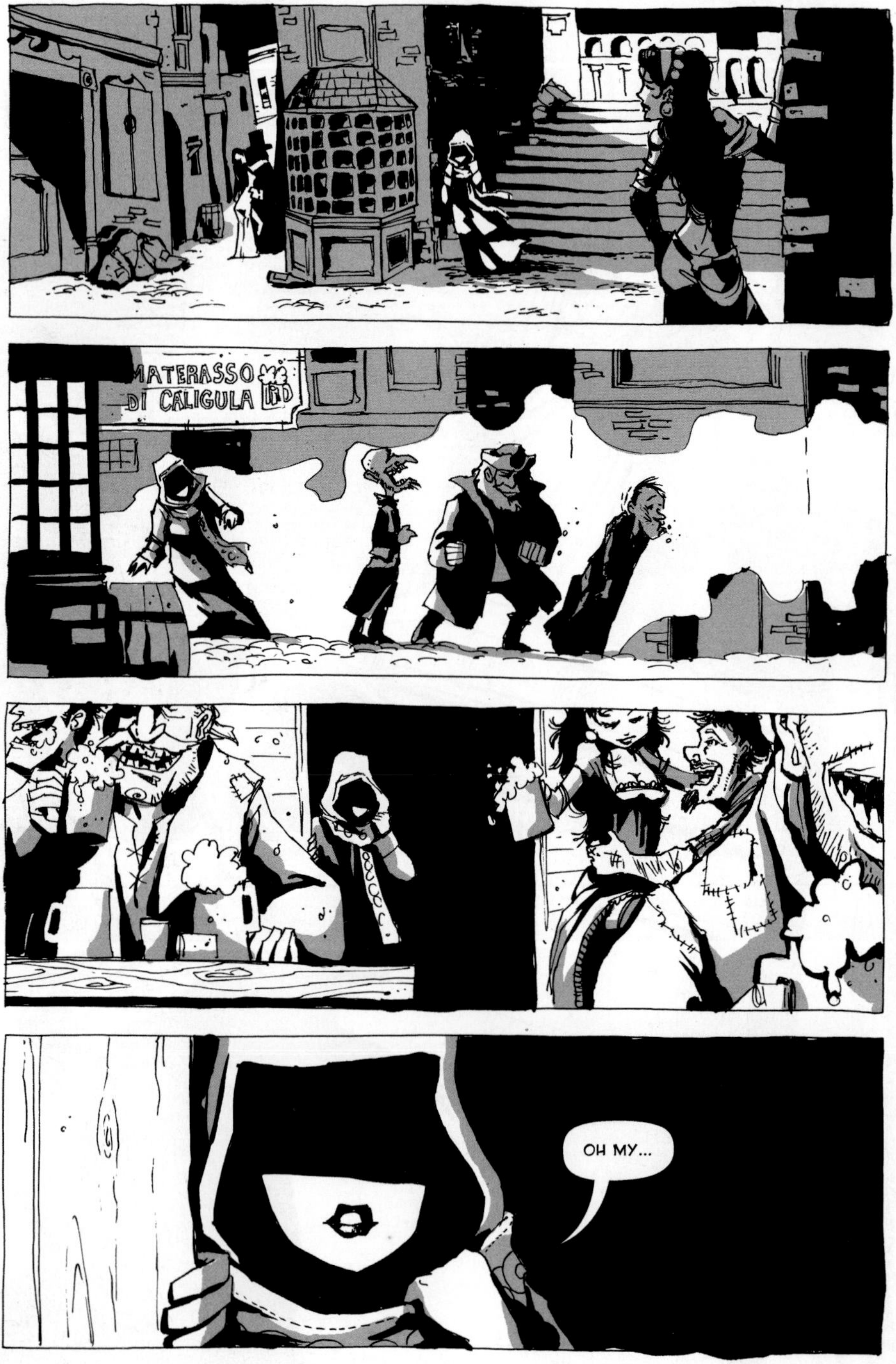
MATERASSO
DI CALIGULA
OH MY...

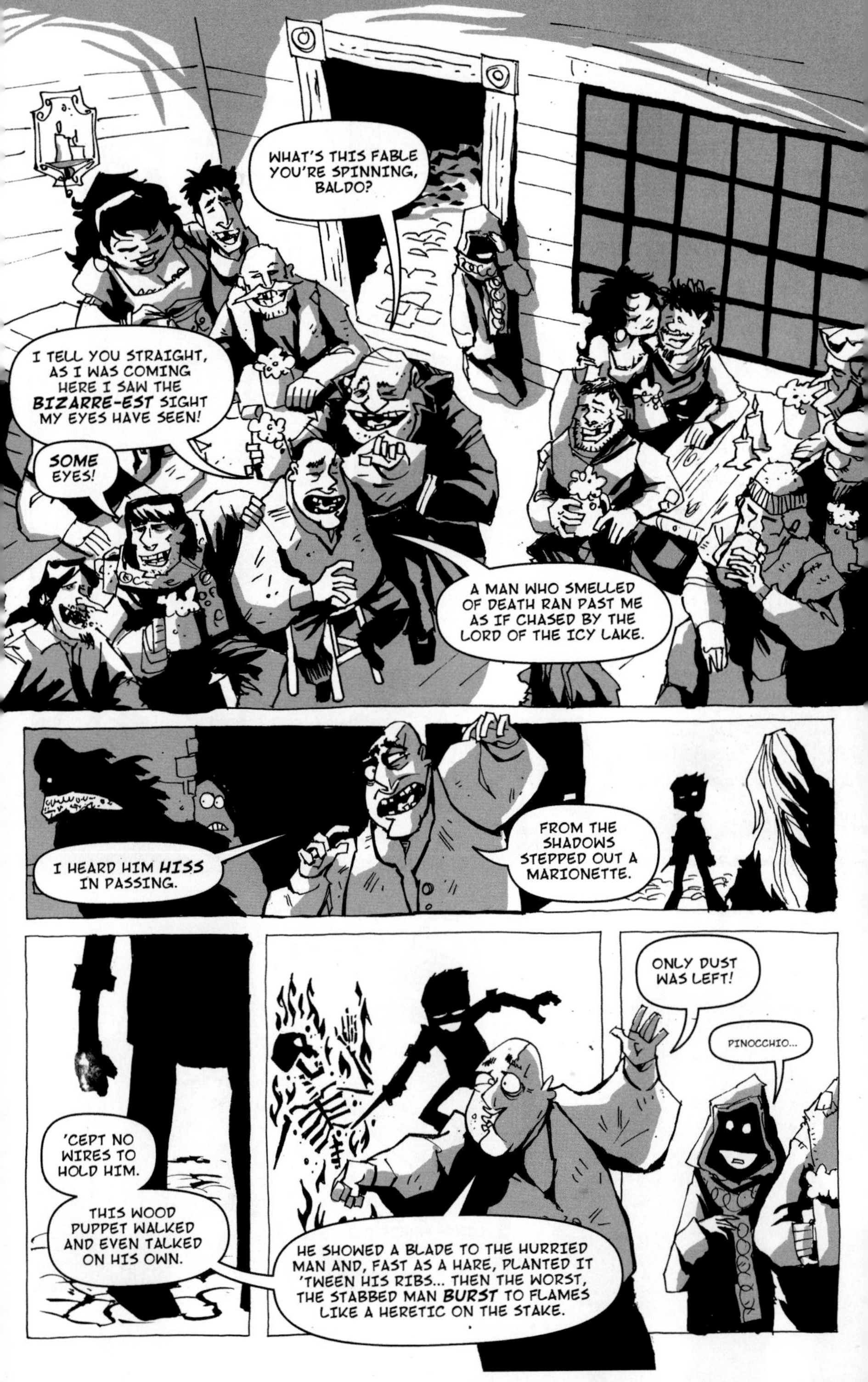
WHAT'S THIS FABLE YOU'RE SPINNING, BALDO?
I TELL YOU STRAIGHT, AS I WAS COMING HERE I SAW THE BIZARRE-EST SIGHT MY EYES HAVE SEEN!
SOME EYES!
A MAN WHO SMELLED OF DEATH RAN PAST ME AS IF CHASED BY THE LORD OF THE ICY LAKE.
I HEARD HIM HISS IN PASSING.
FROM THE SHADOWS STEPPED OUT A MARIONETTE.
'CEPT NO WIRES TO HOLD HIM.
THIS WOOD PUPPET WALKED AND EVEN TALKED ON HIS OWN.
HE SHOWED A BLADE TO THE HURRIED MAN AND, FAST AS A HARE, PLANTED IT 'TWEEN HIS RIBS... THEN THE WORST, THE STABBED MAN BURST TO FLAMES LIKE A HERETIC ON THE STAKE.
ONLY DUST WAS LEFT!
PINOCCHIO...

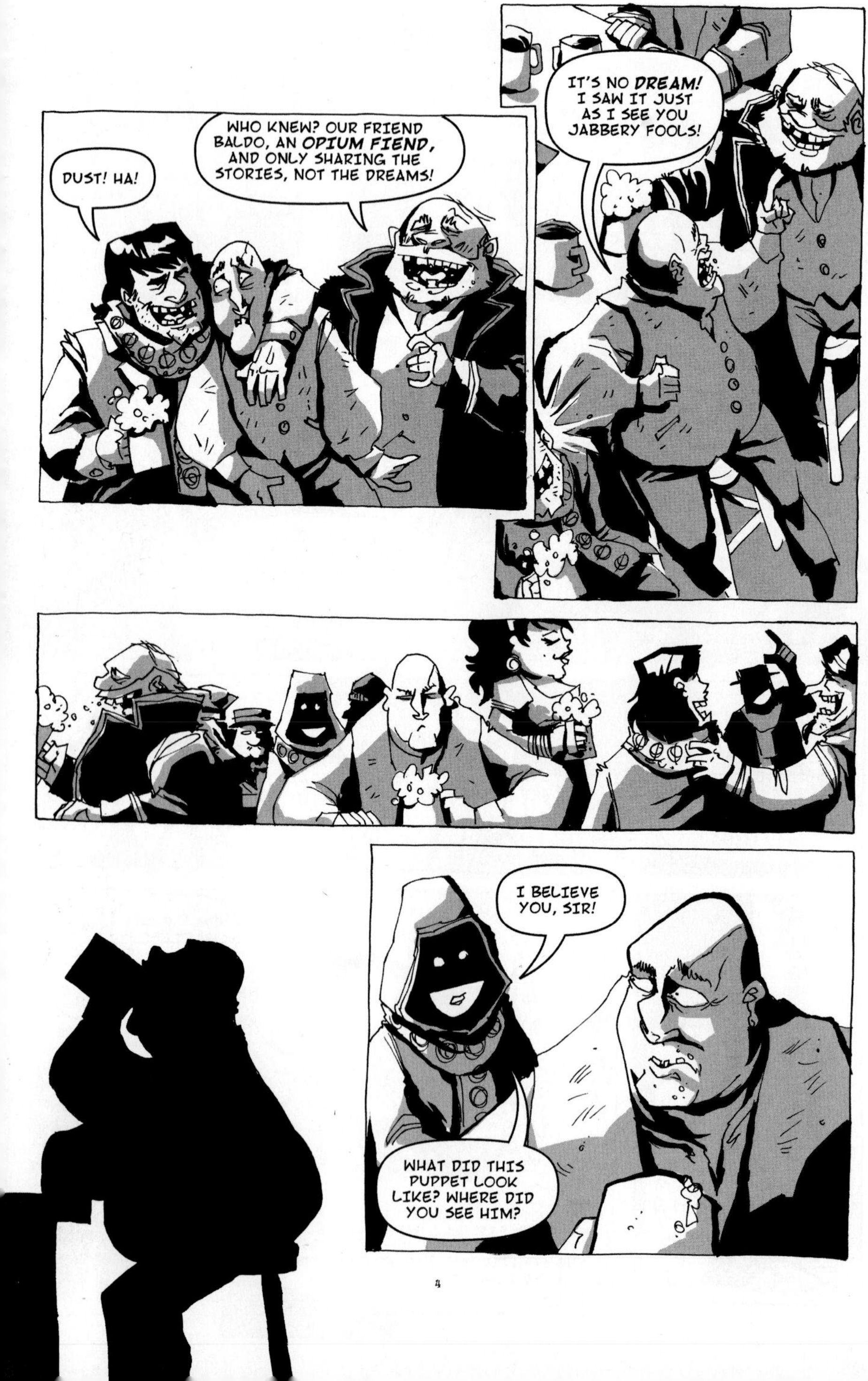
DUST! HA!
WHO KNEW? OUR FRIEND BALDO, AN OPIUM FIEND, AND ONLY SHARING THE STORIES, NOT THE DREAMS!
IT'S NO DREAM! I SAW IT JUST AS I SEE YOU JABBERY FOOLS!
I BELIEVE YOU, SIR!
WHAT DID THIS PUPPET LOOK LIKE? WHERE DID YOU SEE HIM?

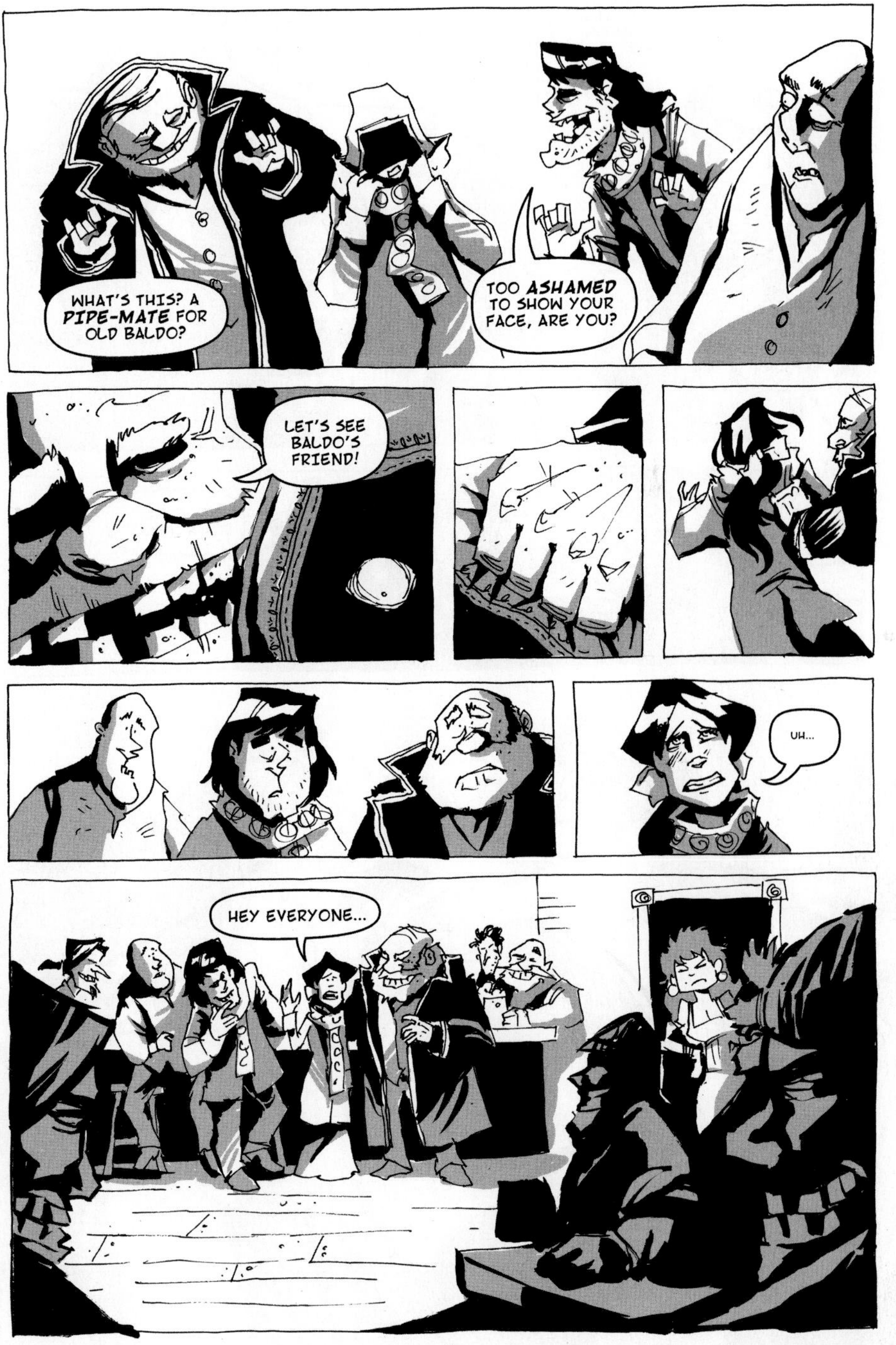
WHAT'S THIS? A PIPE-MATE FOR OLD BALDO?
TOO ASHAMED TO SHOW YOUR FACE, ARE YOU?
LET'S SEE BALDO'S FRIEND!
UH...
HEY EVERYONE...

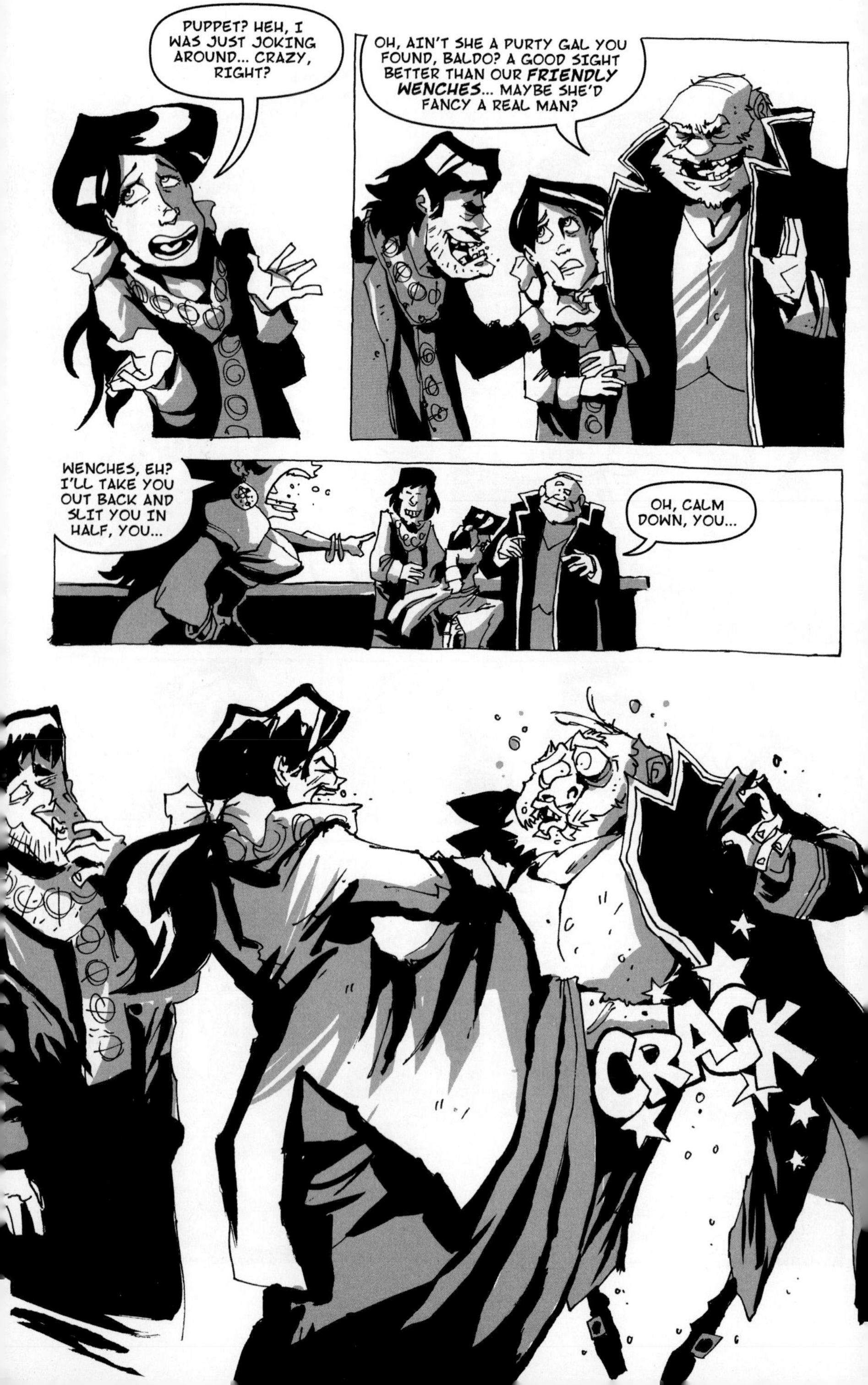
PUPPET? HEH, I WAS JUST JOKING AROUND... CRAZY, RIGHT?
OH, AIN'T SHE A PURTY GAL YOU FOUND, BALDO? A GOOD SIGHT BETTER THAN OUR FRIENDLY WENCHES... MAYBE SHE'D FANCY A REAL MAN?
WENCHES, EH? I'LL TAKE YOU OUT BACK AND SLIT YOU IN HALF, YOU...
OH, CALM DOWN, YOU...
CRACK

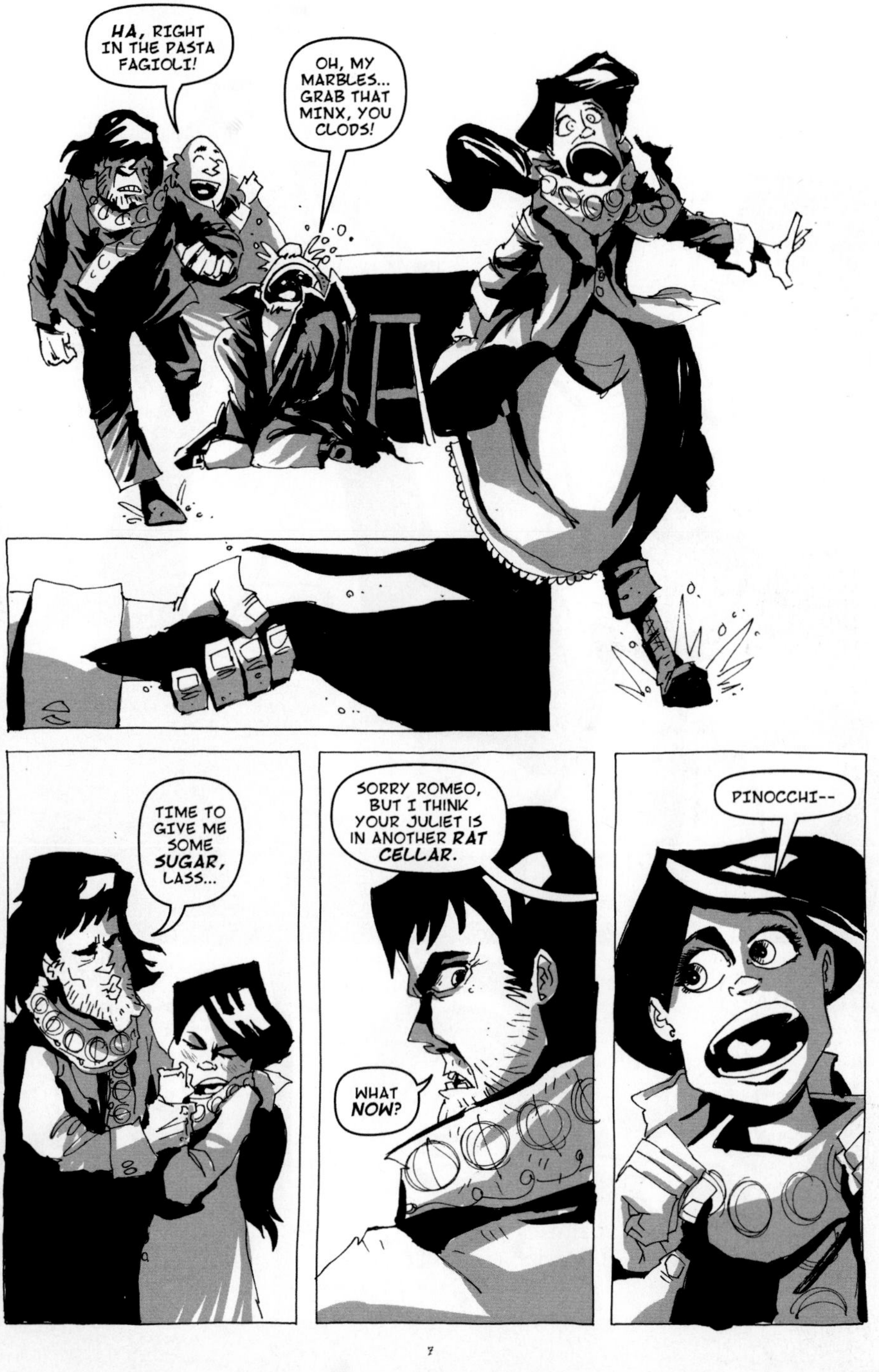
HA, RIGHT IN THE PASTA FAGIOLI!
OH, MY MARBLES... GRAB THAT MINX, YOU CLODS!
TIME TO GIVE ME SOME SUGAR, LASS...
SORRY ROMEO, BUT I THINK YOUR JULIET IS IN ANOTHER RAT CELLAR.
WHAT NOW?
PINOCCHI--

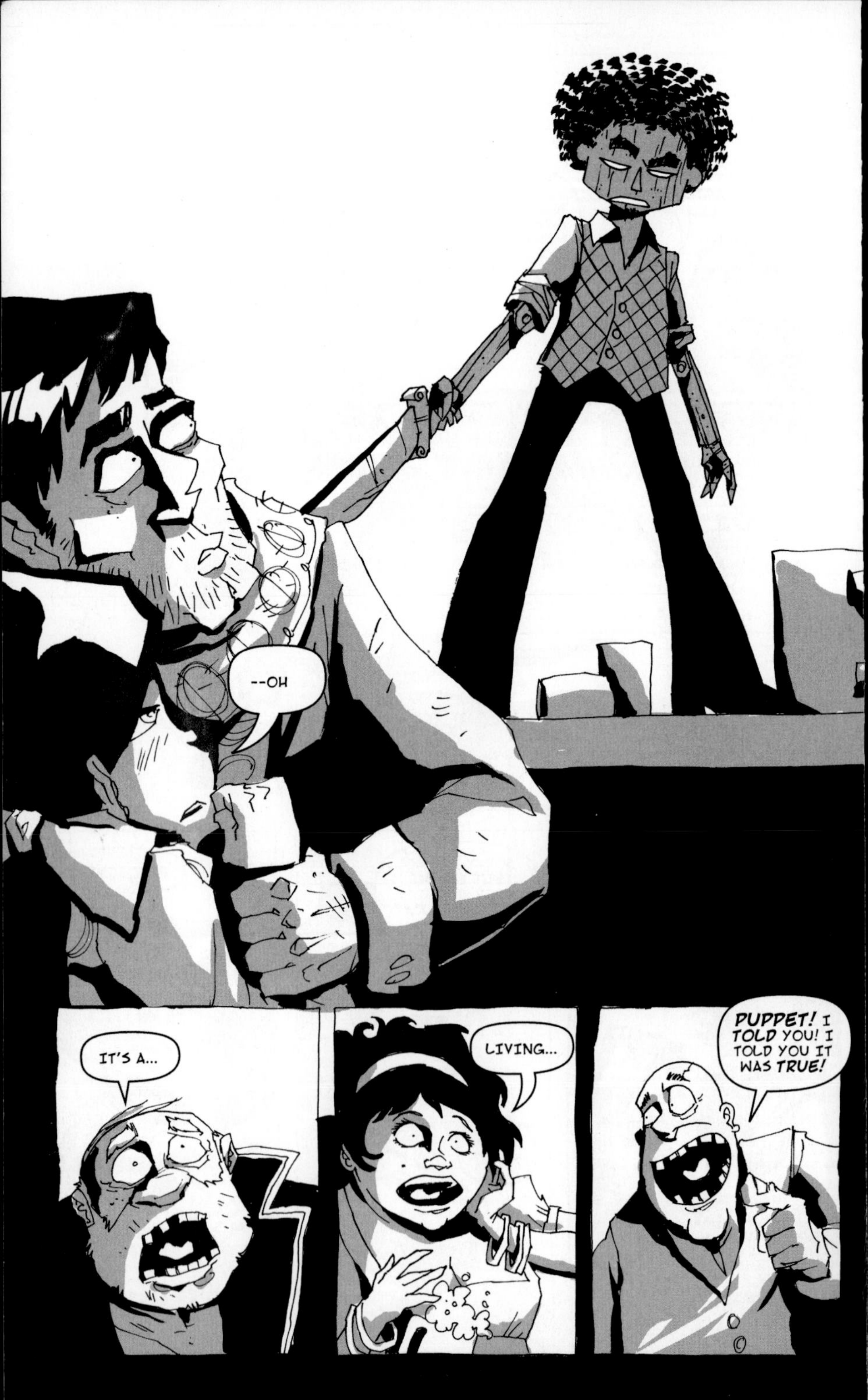
--OH
IT'S A...
LIVING...
PUPPET! I TOLD YOU! I TOLD YOU IT WAS TRUE!

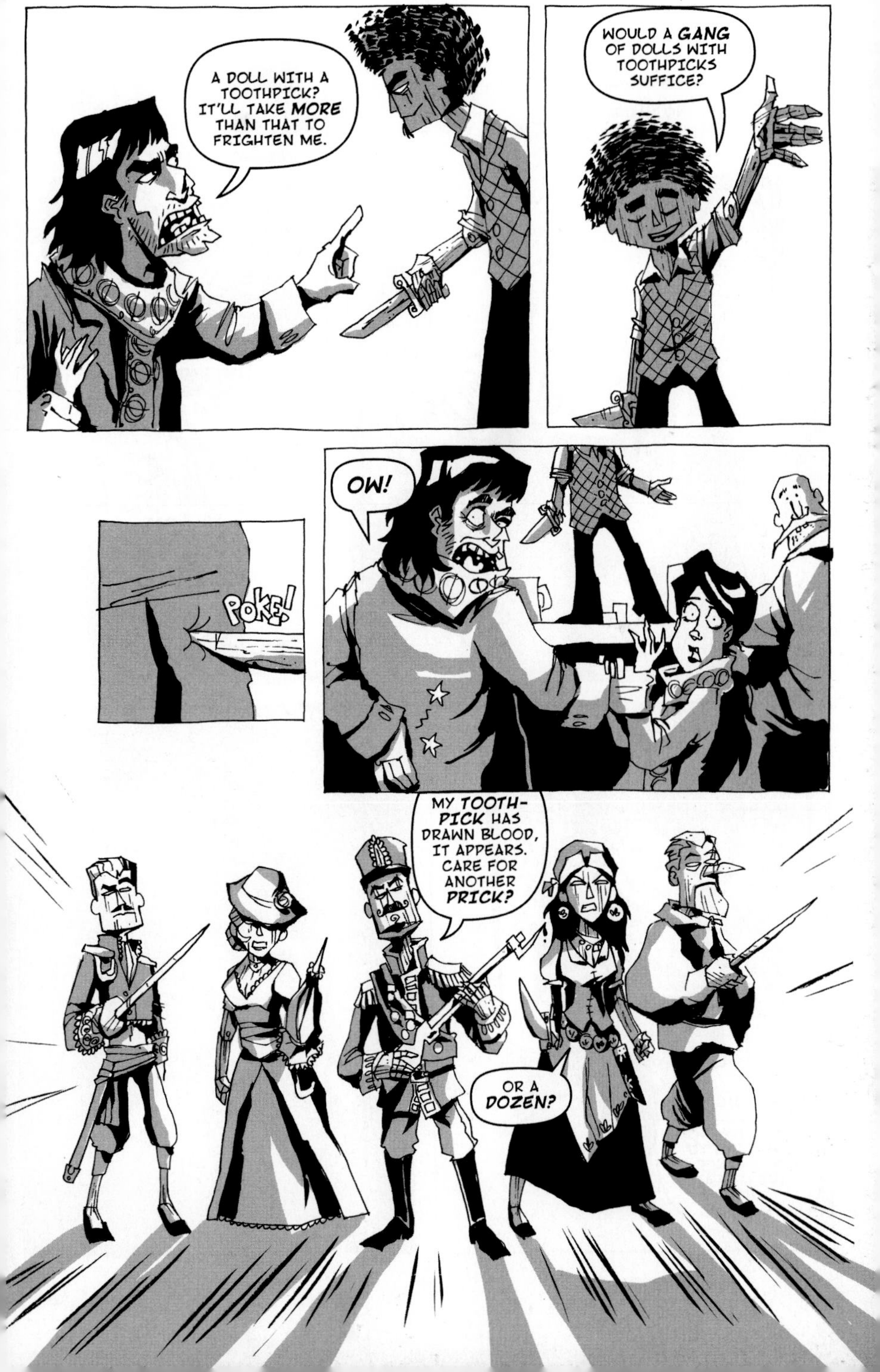
A DOLL WITH A TOOTHPICK? IT'LL TAKE **MORE** THAN THAT TO FRIGHTEN ME.
WOULD A **GANG** OF DOLLS WITH TOOTHPICKS SUFFICE?
POKE!
OW!
MY ***TOOTH-PICK*** HAS DRAWN BLOOD, IT APPEARS. CARE FOR ANOTHER ***PRICK?***
OR A ***DOZEN?***

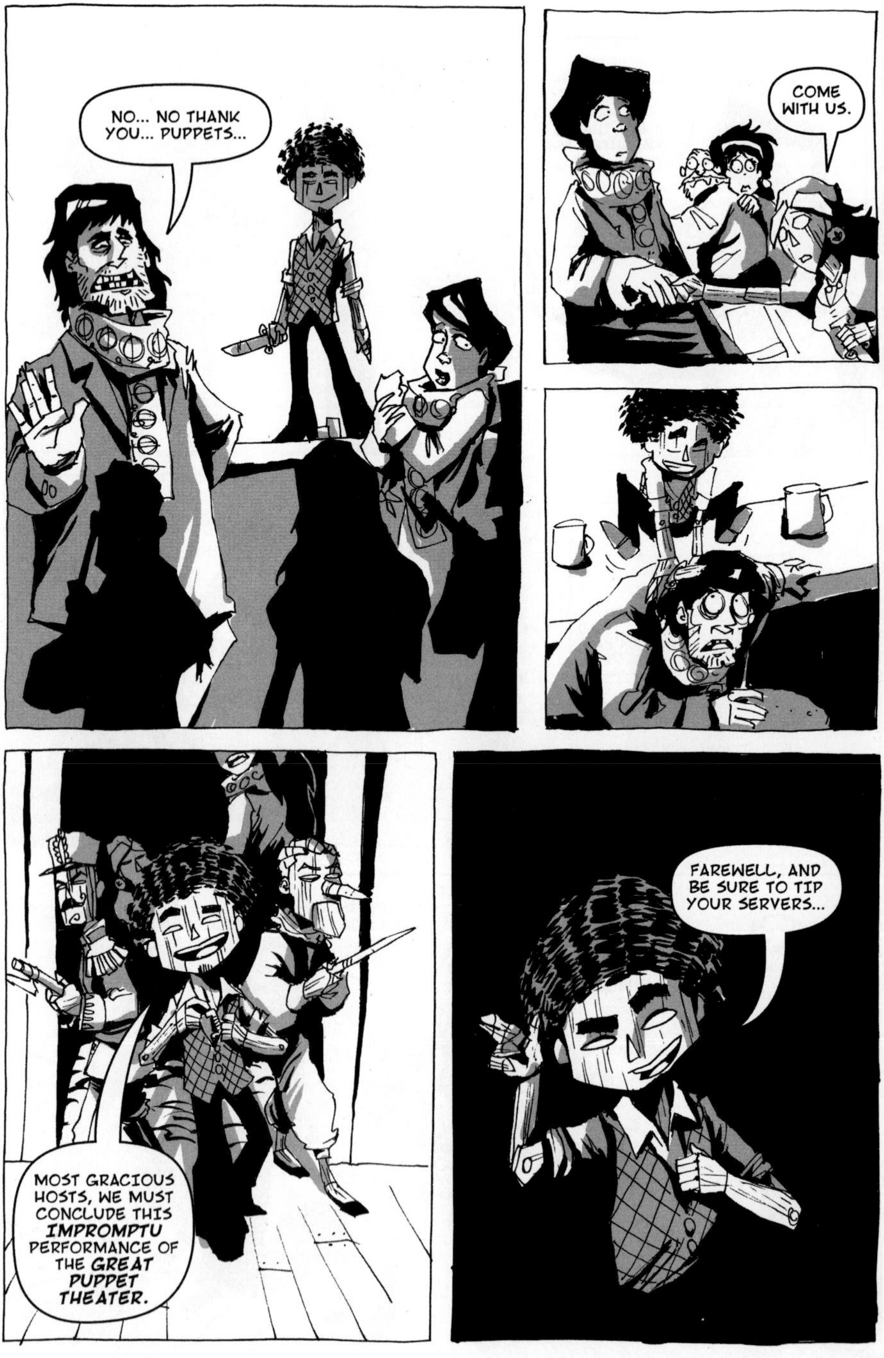
NO... NO THANK YOU... PUPPETS...
COME WITH US.
MOST GRACIOUS HOSTS, WE MUST CONCLUDE THIS *IMPROMPTU* PERFORMANCE OF THE *GREAT PUPPET THEATER.*
FAREWELL, AND BE SURE TO TIP YOUR SERVERS...

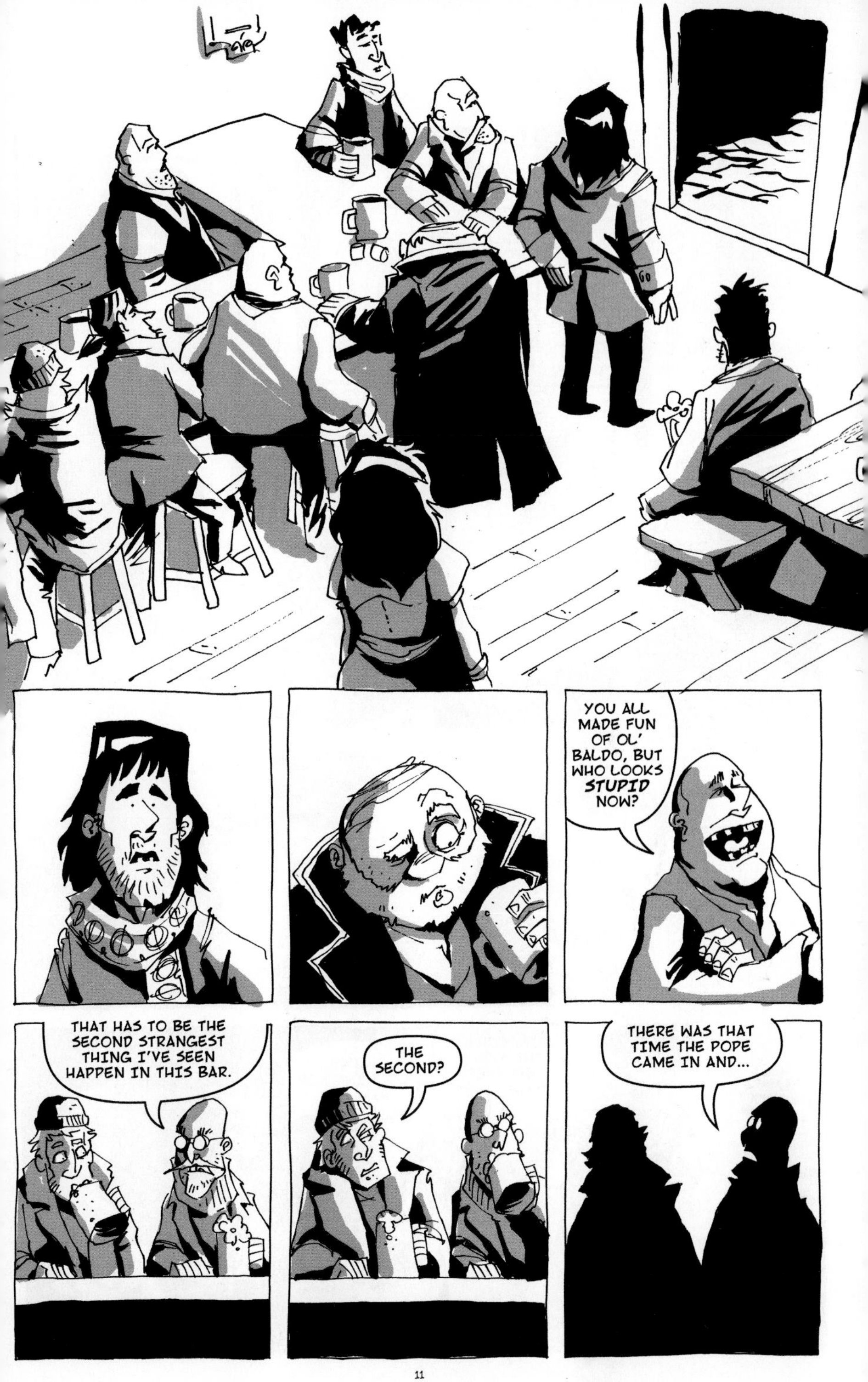
YOU ALL MADE FUN OF OL' BALDO, BUT WHO LOOKS **STUPID** NOW?
THAT HAS TO BE THE SECOND STRANGEST THING I'VE SEEN HAPPEN IN THIS BAR.
THE SECOND?
THERE WAS THAT TIME THE POPE CAME IN AND...

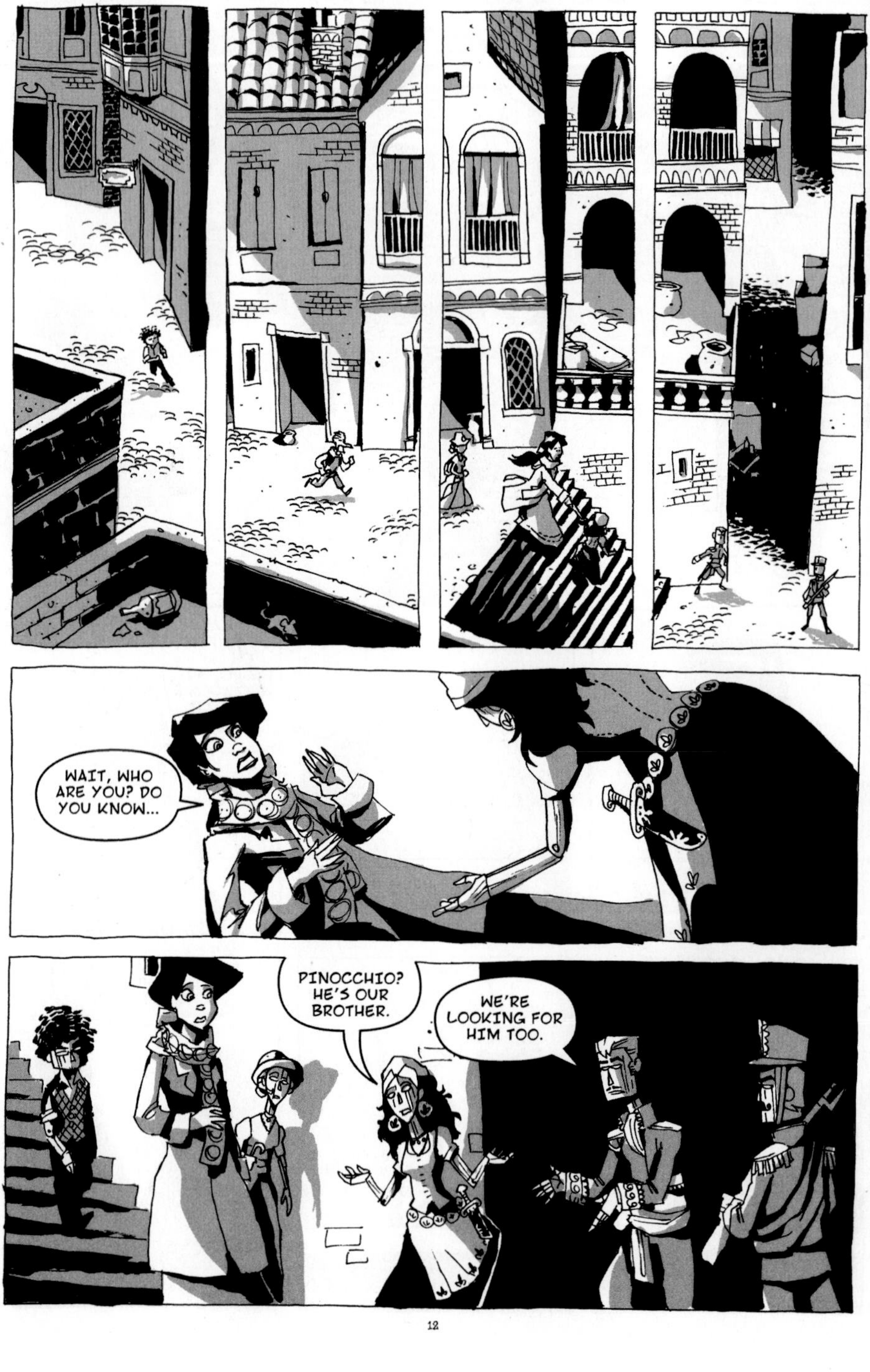
WAIT, WHO ARE YOU? DO YOU KNOW...
PINOCCHIO? HE'S OUR BROTHER.
WE'RE LOOKING FOR HIM TOO.

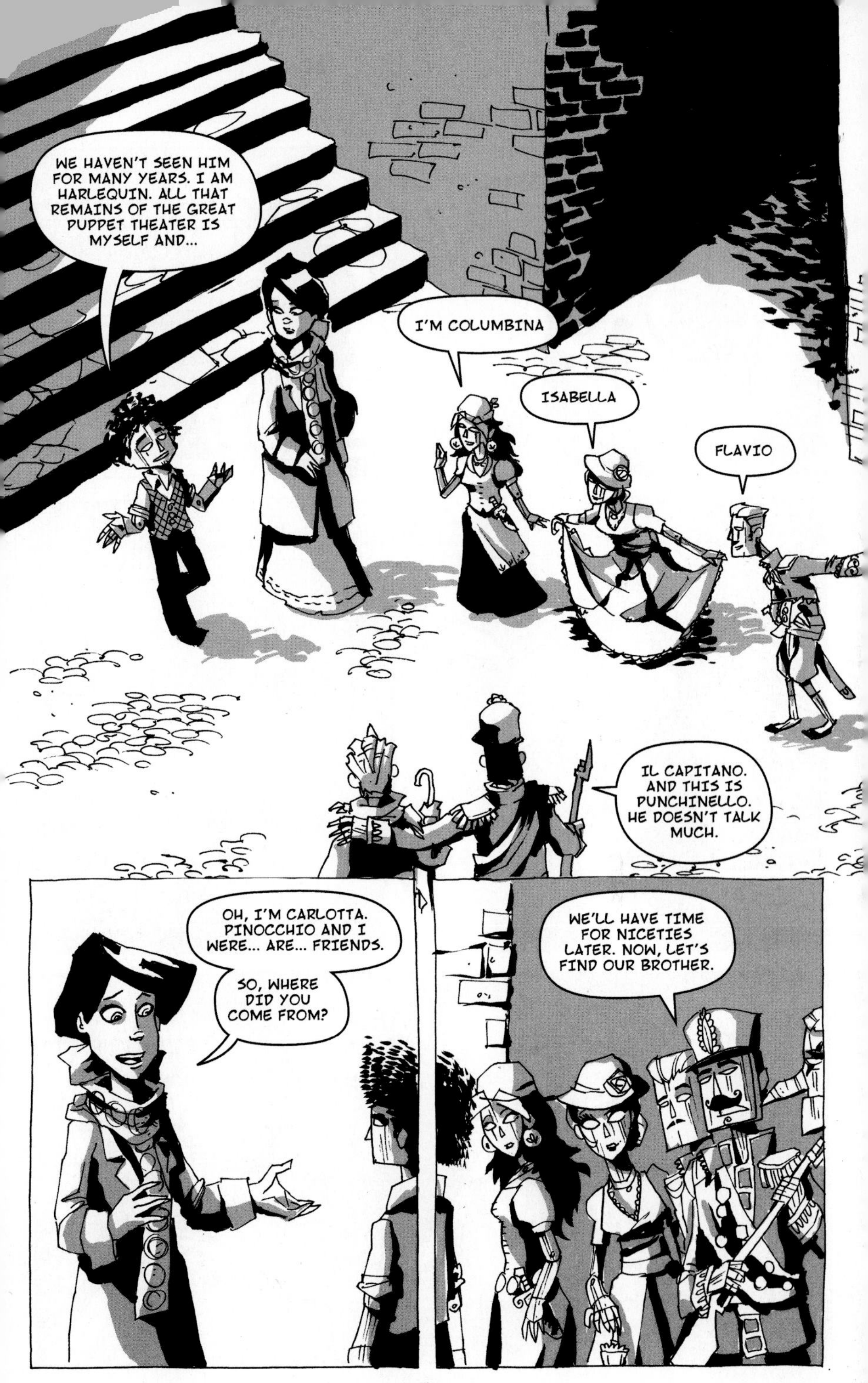
WE HAVEN'T SEEN HIM FOR MANY YEARS. I AM HARLEQUIN. ALL THAT REMAINS OF THE GREAT PUPPET THEATER IS MYSELF AND...
I'M COLUMBINA
ISABELLA
FLAVIO
IL CAPITANO. AND THIS IS PUNCHINELLO. HE DOESN'T TALK MUCH.
OH, I'M CARLOTTA. PINOCCHIO AND I WERE... ARE... FRIENDS.
SO, WHERE DID YOU COME FROM?
WE'LL HAVE TIME FOR NICETIES LATER. NOW, LET'S FIND OUR BROTHER.

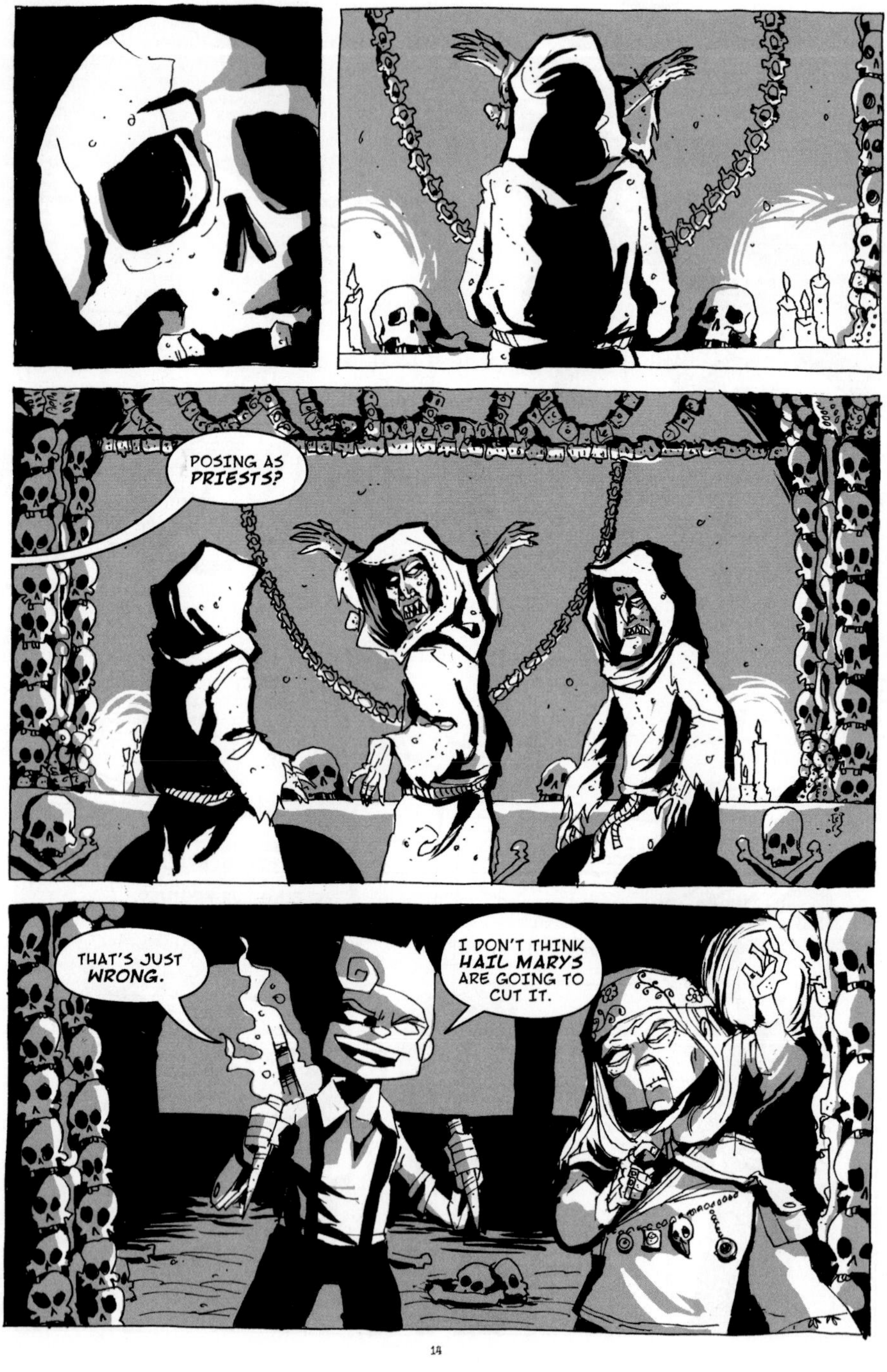
POSING AS PRIESTS?
THAT'S JUST WRONG.
I DON'T THINK HAIL MARYS ARE GOING TO CUT IT.

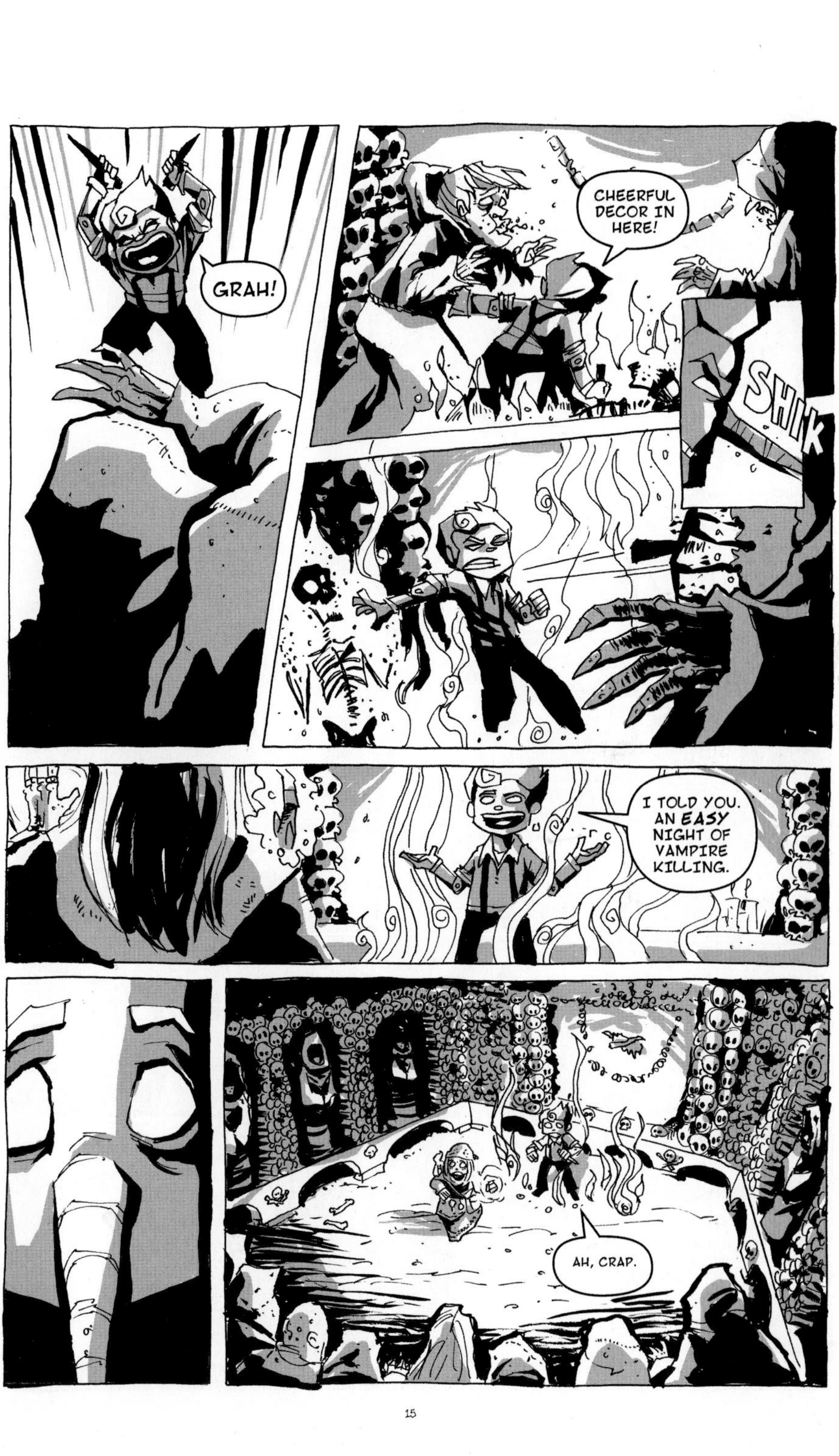
GRAH!
CHEERFUL DECOR IN HERE!
SHIK
I TOLD YOU. AN EASY NIGHT OF VAMPIRE KILLING.
AH, CRAP.

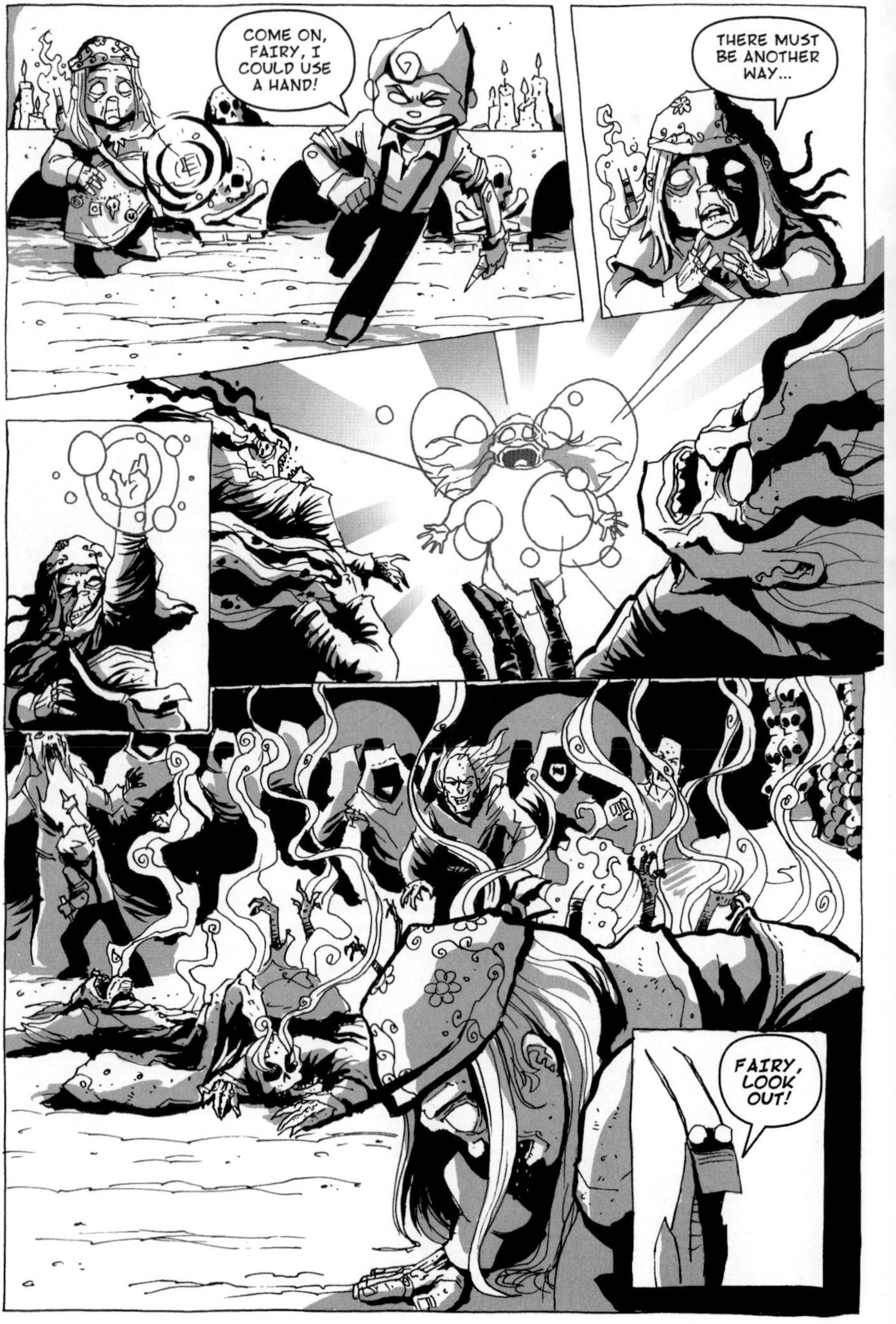
COME ON, FAIRY, I COULD USE A HAND!
THERE MUST BE ANOTHER WAY...
FAIRY, LOOK OUT!

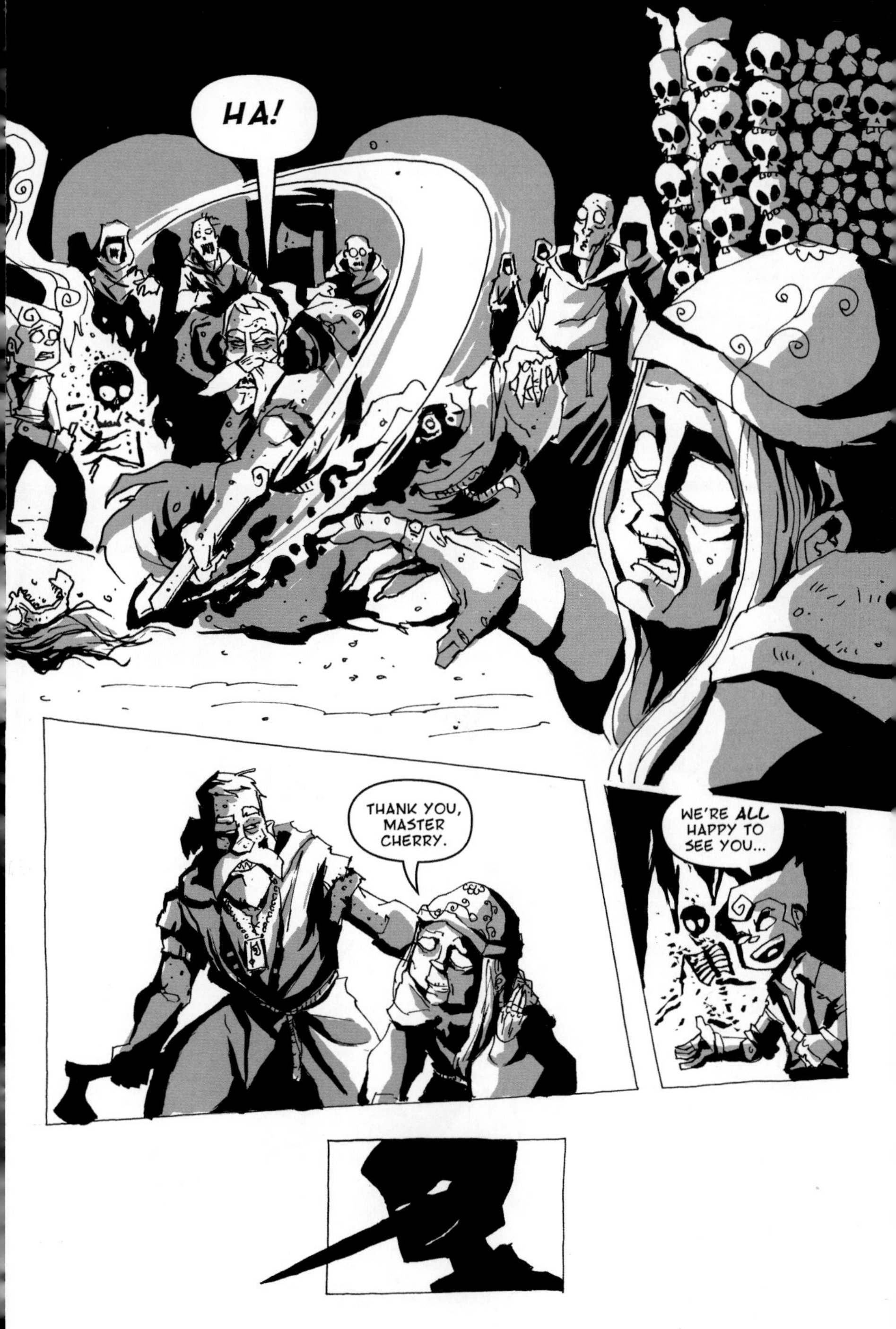
HA!
THANK YOU, MASTER CHERRY.
WE'RE ALL HAPPY TO SEE YOU...

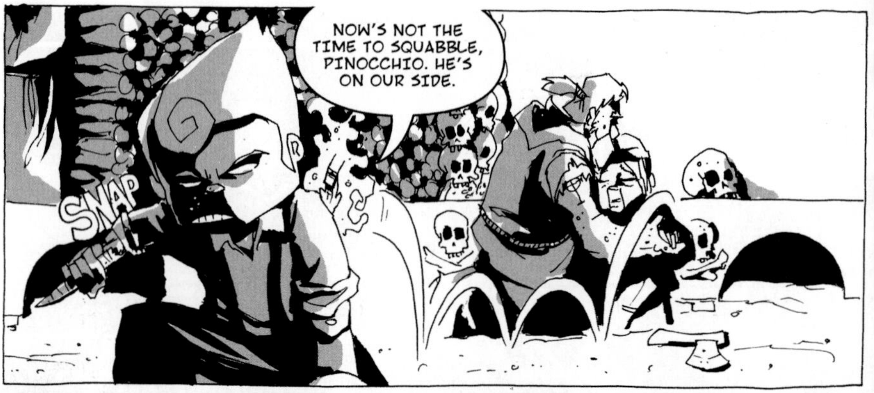
NOW'S NOT THE TIME TO SQUABBLE, PINOCCHIO. HE'S ON OUR SIDE.
SNAP
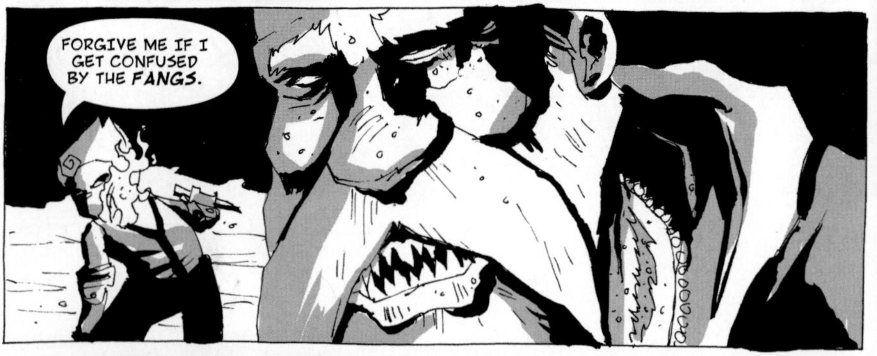
FORGIVE ME IF I GET CONFUSED BY THE FANGS.
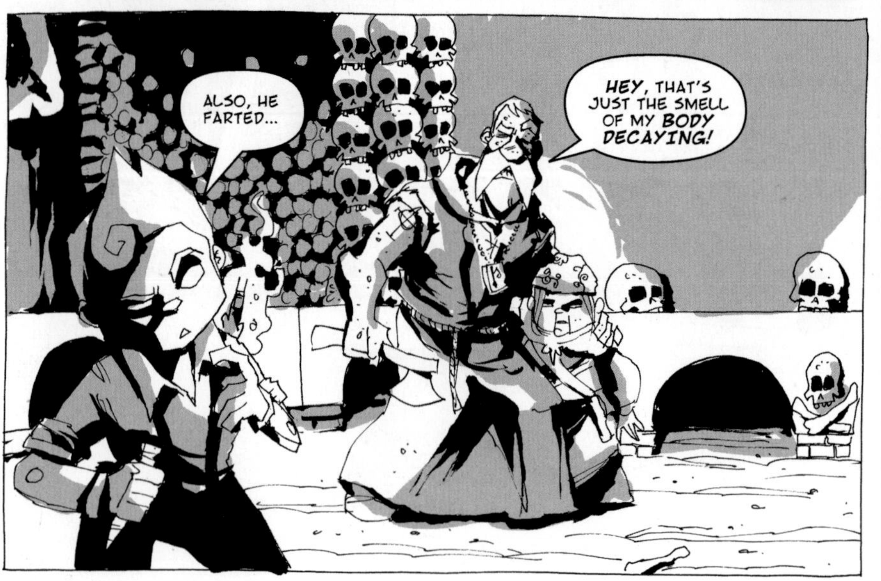
ALSO, HE FARTED...
HEY, THAT'S JUST THE SMELL OF MY BODY DECAYING!

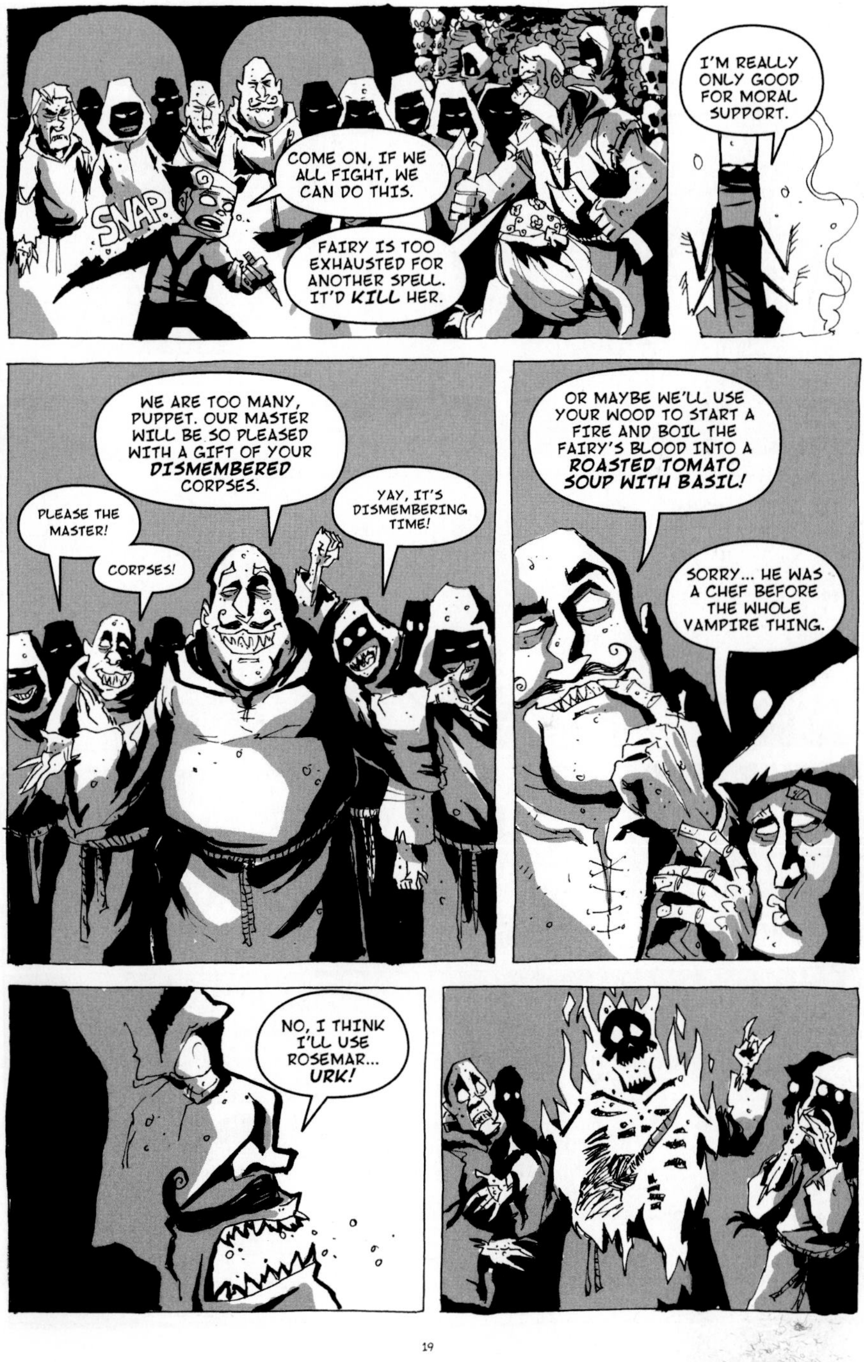
SNAP.
COME ON, IF WE ALL FIGHT, WE CAN DO THIS.
FAIRY IS TOO EXHAUSTED FOR ANOTHER SPELL. IT'D KILL HER.
I'M REALLY ONLY GOOD FOR MORAL SUPPORT.
WE ARE TOO MANY, PUPPET. OUR MASTER WILL BE SO PLEASED WITH A GIFT OF YOUR DISMEMBERED CORPSES.
PLEASE THE MASTER!
CORPSES!
YAY, IT'S DISMEMBERING TIME!
OR MAYBE WE'LL USE YOUR WOOD TO START A FIRE AND BOIL THE FAIRY'S BLOOD INTO A ROASTED TOMATO SOUP WITH BASIL!
SORRY... HE WAS A CHEF BEFORE THE WHOLE VAMPIRE THING.
NO, I THINK I'LL USE ROSEMAR... URK!

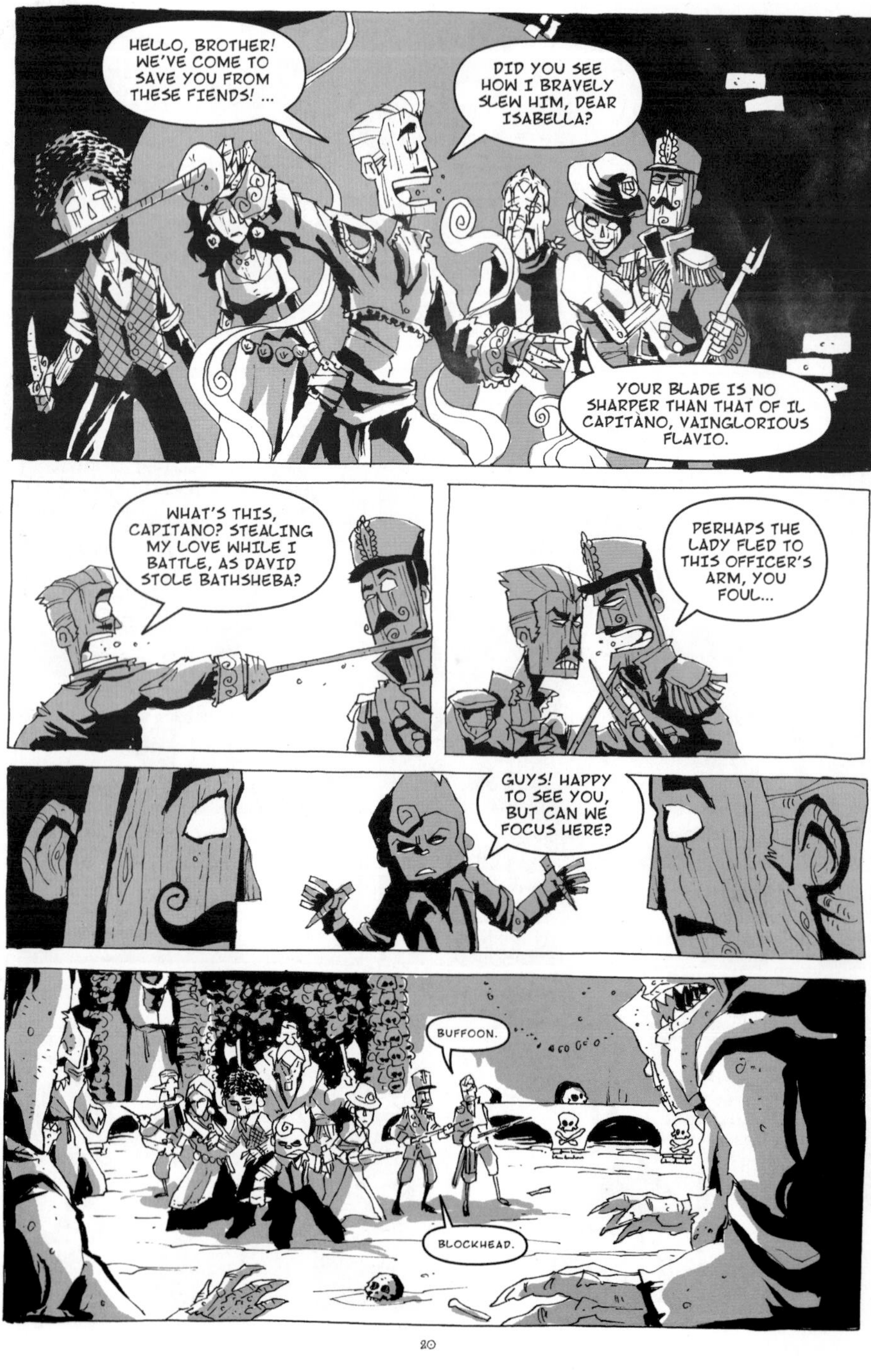
HELLO, BROTHER! WE'VE COME TO SAVE YOU FROM THESE FIENDS! ...
DID YOU SEE HOW I BRAVELY SLEW HIM, DEAR ISABELLA?
YOUR BLADE IS NO SHARPER THAN THAT OF IL CAPITÀNO, VAINGLORIOUS FLAVIO.
WHAT'S THIS, CAPITANO? STEALING MY LOVE WHILE I BATTLE, AS DAVID STOLE BATHSHEBA?
PERHAPS THE LADY FLED TO THIS OFFICER'S ARM, YOU FOUL...
GUYS! HAPPY TO SEE YOU, BUT CAN WE FOCUS HERE?
BUFFOON.
BLOCKHEAD.

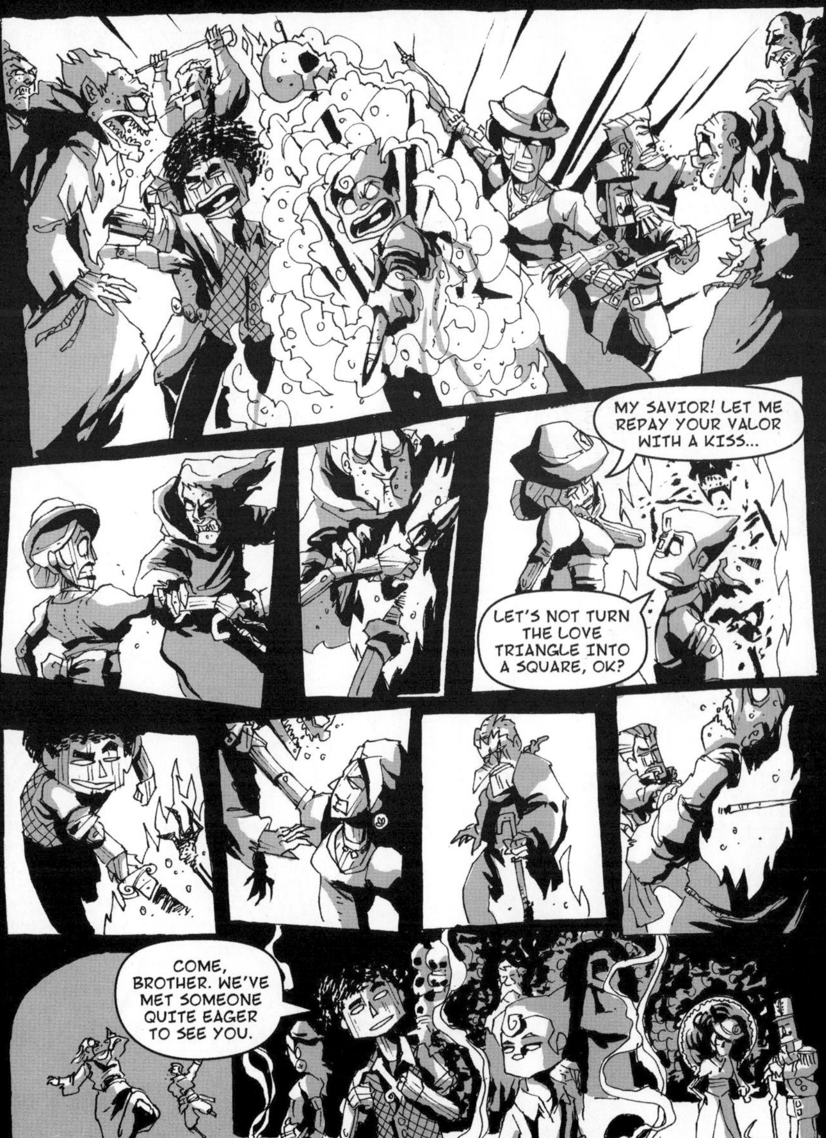
MY SAVIOR! LET ME REPAY YOUR VALOR WITH A KISS...
LET'S NOT TURN THE LOVE TRIANGLE INTO A SQUARE, OK?
COME, BROTHER. WE'VE MET SOMEONE QUITE EAGER TO SEE YOU.

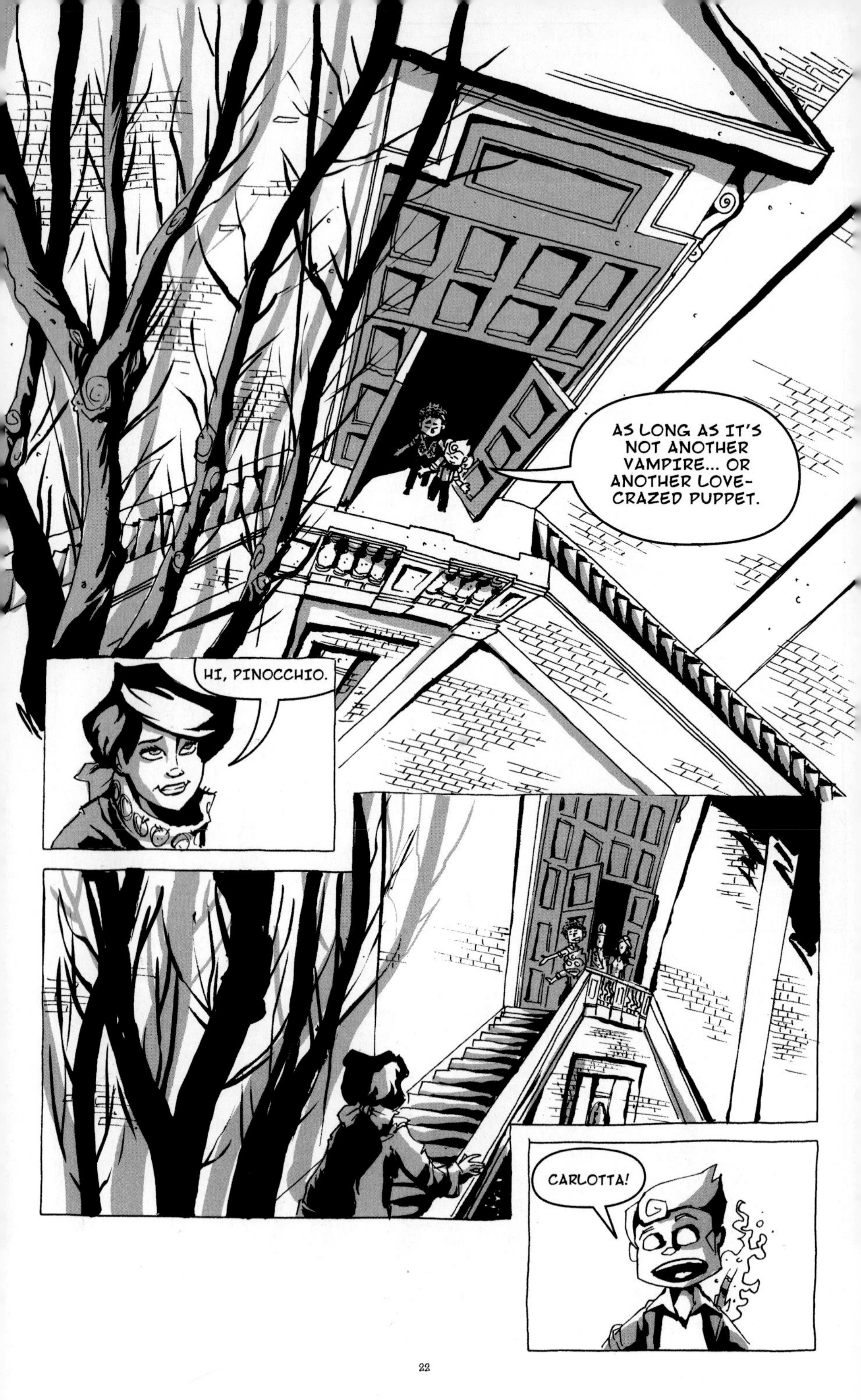
AS LONG AS IT'S NOT ANOTHER VAMPIRE... OR ANOTHER LOVE-CRAZED PUPPET.
HI, PINOCCHIO.
CARLOTTA!

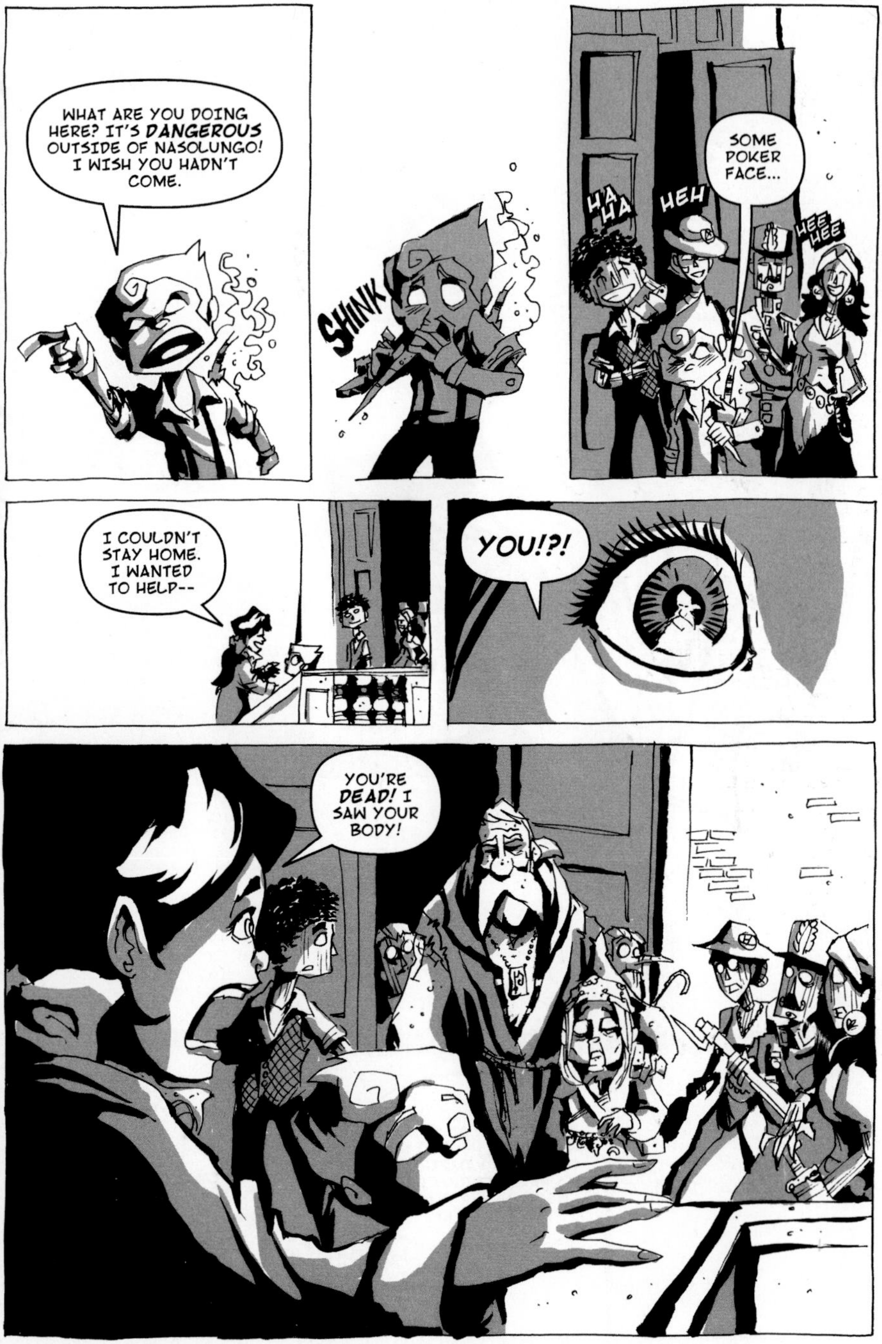

WHAT ARE YOU DOING HERE? IT'S DANGEROUS OUTSIDE OF NASOLUNGO! I WISH YOU HADN'T COME.
SHINK
HA HA
HEH
SOME POKER FACE...
HEE HEE
I COULDN'T STAY HOME. I WANTED TO HELP--
YOU!?!
YOU'RE DEAD! I SAW YOUR BODY!

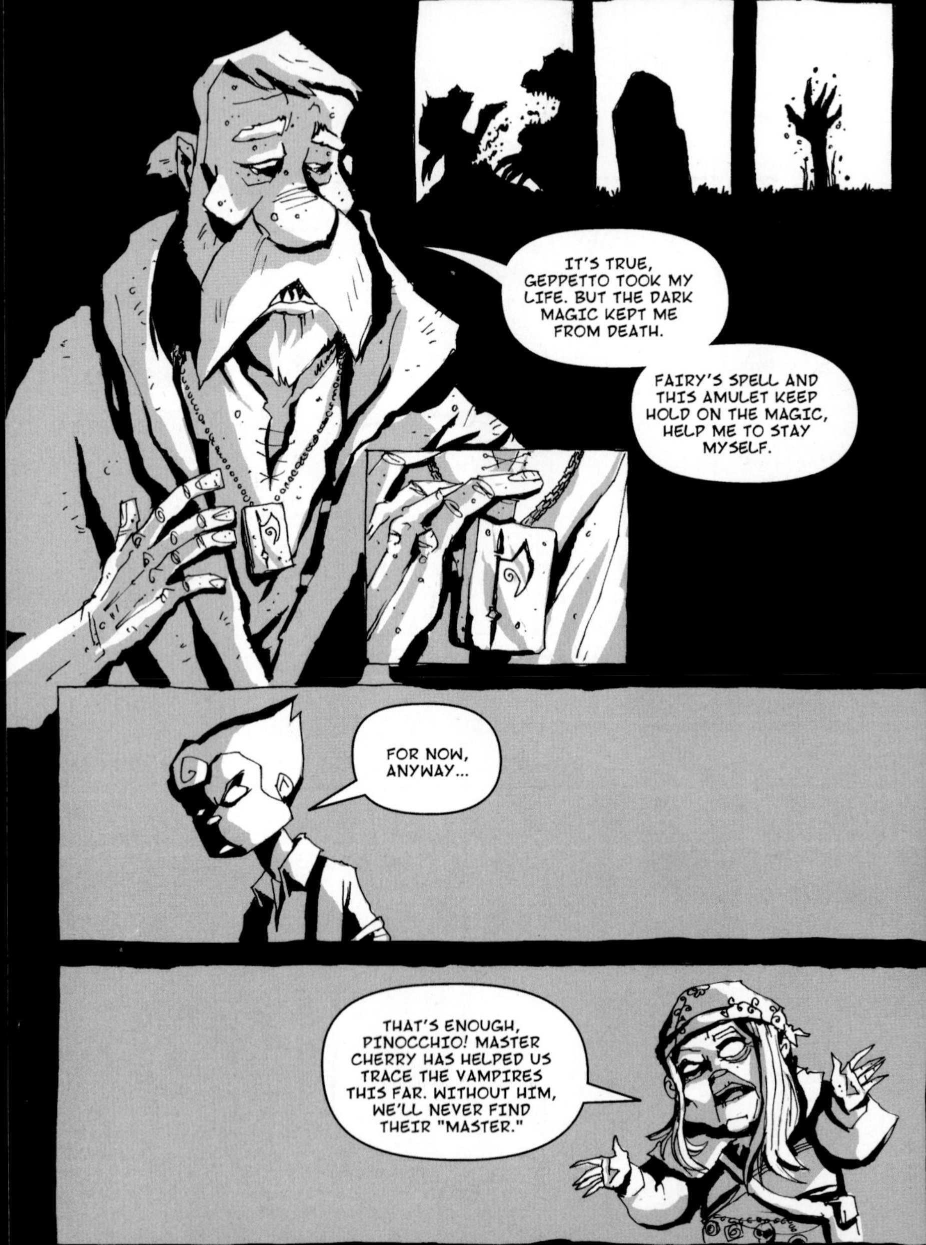
IT'S TRUE, GEPPETTO TOOK MY LIFE. BUT THE DARK MAGIC KEPT ME FROM DEATH.
FAIRY'S SPELL AND THIS AMULET KEEP HOLD ON THE MAGIC, HELP ME TO STAY MYSELF.
FOR NOW, ANYWAY...
THAT'S ENOUGH, PINOCCHIO! MASTER CHERRY HAS HELPED US TRACE THE VAMPIRES THIS FAR. WITHOUT HIM, WE'LL NEVER FIND THEIR "MASTER."

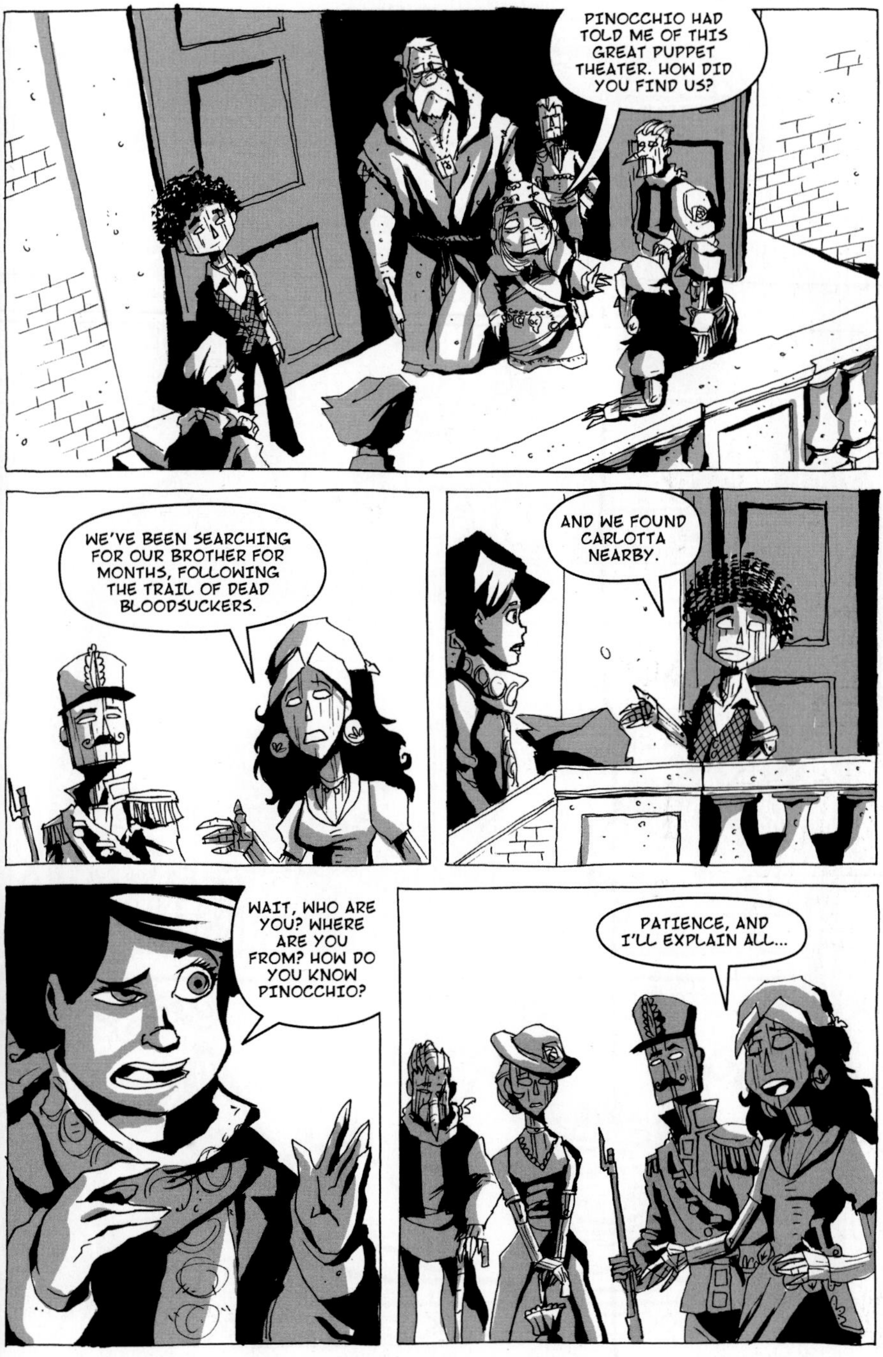
PINOCCHIO HAD TOLD ME OF THIS GREAT PUPPET THEATER. HOW DID YOU FIND US?
WE'VE BEEN SEARCHING FOR OUR BROTHER FOR MONTHS, FOLLOWING THE TRAIL OF DEAD BLOODSUCKERS.
AND WE FOUND CARLOTTA NEARBY.
WAIT, WHO ARE YOU? WHERE ARE YOU FROM? HOW DO YOU KNOW PINOCCHIO?
PATIENCE, AND I'LL EXPLAIN ALL...

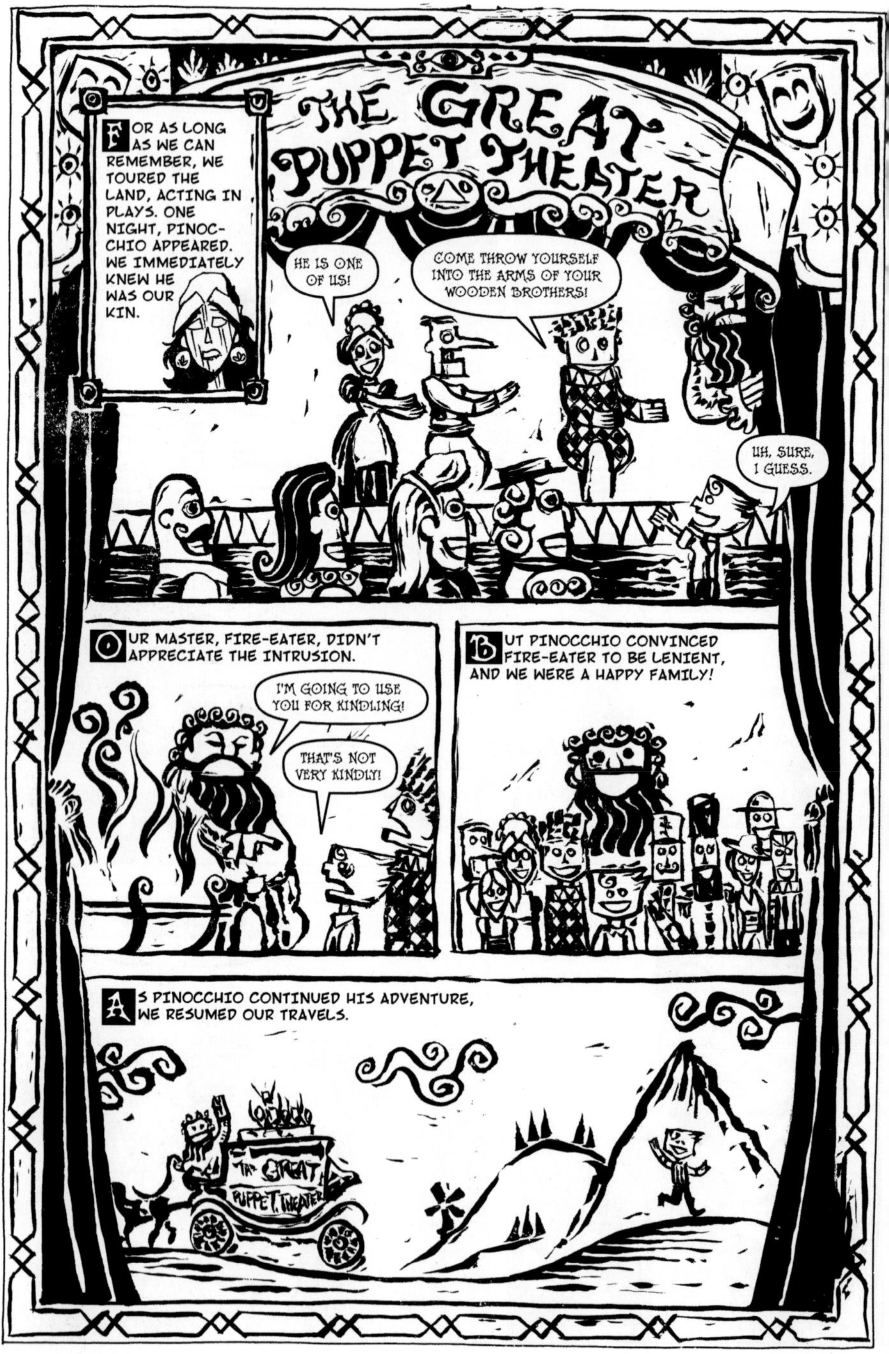
THE GREAT PUPPET THEATER
FOR AS LONG AS WE CAN REMEMBER, WE TOURED THE LAND, ACTING IN PLAYS. ONE NIGHT, PINOCCHIO APPEARED. WE IMMEDIATELY KNEW HE WAS OUR KIN.
HE IS ONE OF US!
COME THROW YOURSELF INTO THE ARMS OF YOUR WOODEN BROTHERS!
UH, SURE, I GUESS.
OUR MASTER, FIRE-EATER, DIDN'T APPRECIATE THE INTRUSION.
I'M GOING TO USE YOU FOR KINDLING!
THAT'S NOT VERY KINDLY!
BUT PINOCCHIO CONVINCED FIRE-EATER TO BE LENIENT, AND WE WERE A HAPPY FAMILY!
AS PINOCCHIO CONTINUED HIS ADVENTURE, WE RESUMED OUR TRAVELS.
THE GREAT PUPPET THEATER

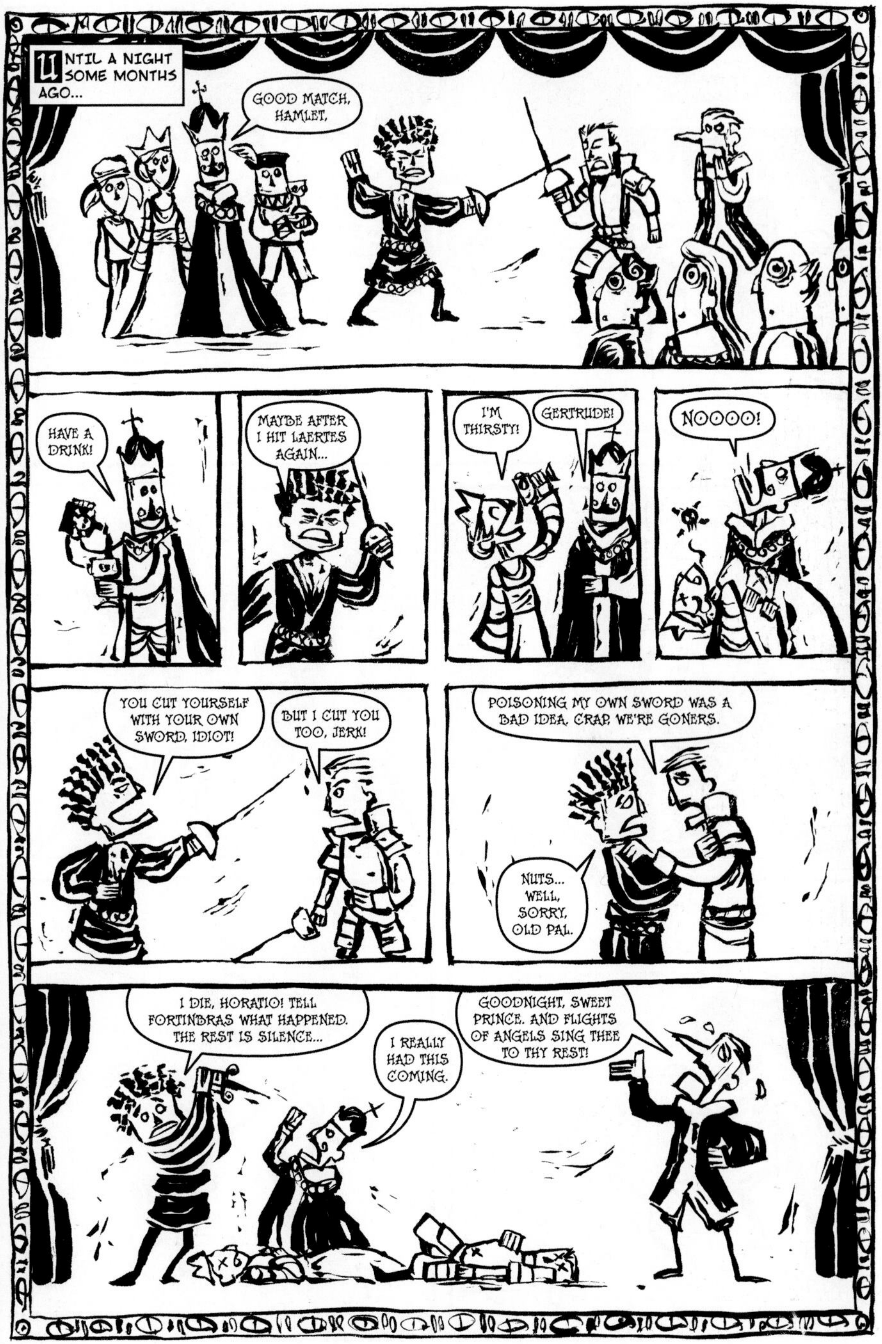
UNTIL A NIGHT SOME MONTHS AGO...
GOOD MATCH, HAMLET.
HAVE A DRINK!
MAYBE AFTER I HIT LAERTES AGAIN...
I'M THIRSTY!
GERTRUDE!
NOOOO!
YOU CUT YOURSELF WITH YOUR OWN SWORD, IDIOT!
BUT I CUT YOU TOO, JERK!
POISONING MY OWN SWORD WAS A BAD IDEA. CRAP, WE'RE GONERS.
NUTS... WELL, SORRY, OLD PAL.
I DIE, HORATIO! TELL FORTINBRAS WHAT HAPPENED. THE REST IS SILENCE...
I REALLY HAD THIS COMING.
GOODNIGHT, SWEET PRINCE. AND FLIGHTS OF ANGELS SING THEE TO THY REST!

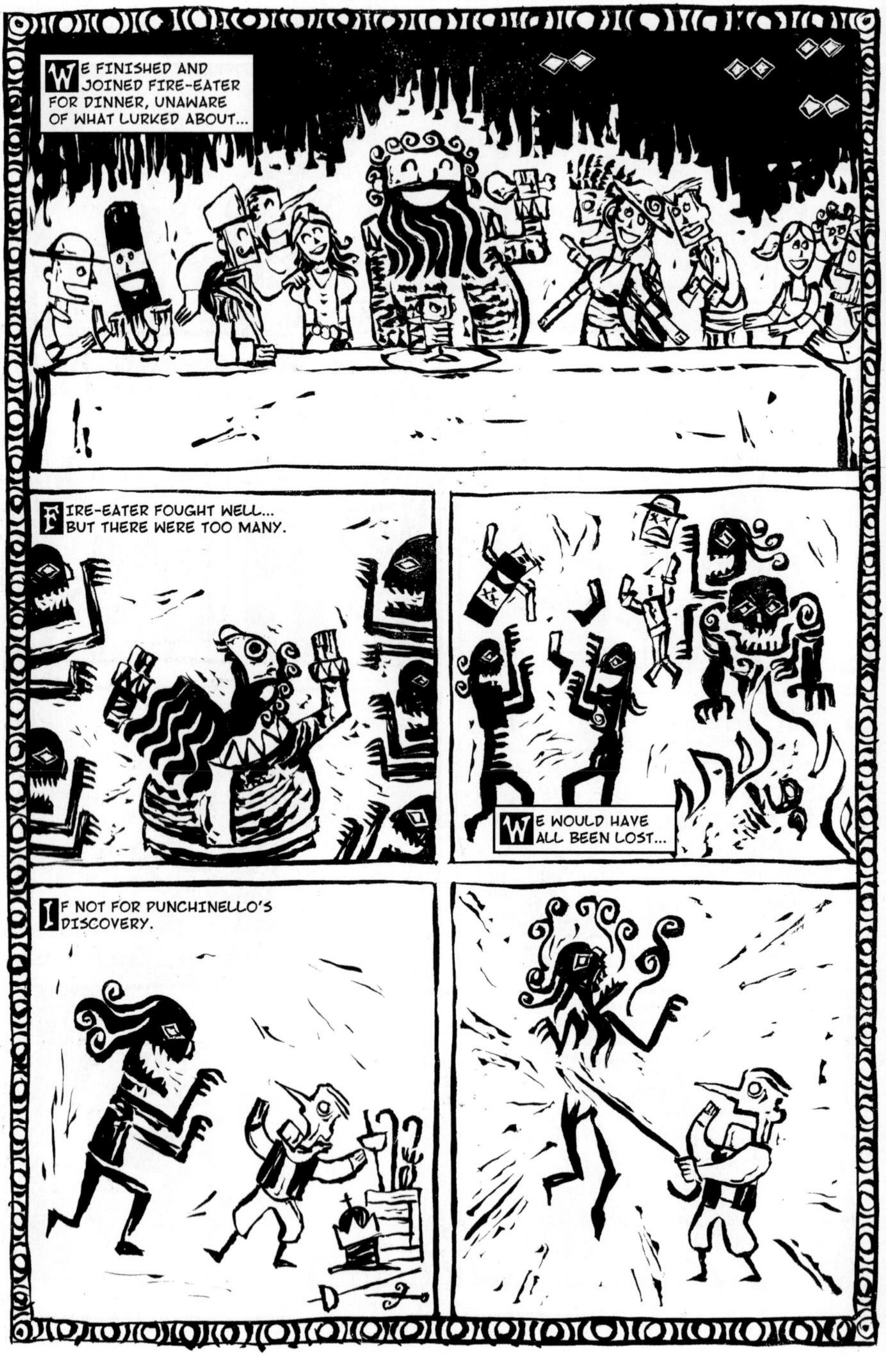
WE FINISHED AND JOINED FIRE-EATER FOR DINNER, UNAWARE OF WHAT LURKED ABOUT...
FIRE-EATER FOUGHT WELL... BUT THERE WERE TOO MANY.
WE WOULD HAVE ALL BEEN LOST...
IF NOT FOR PUNCHINELLO'S DISCOVERY.

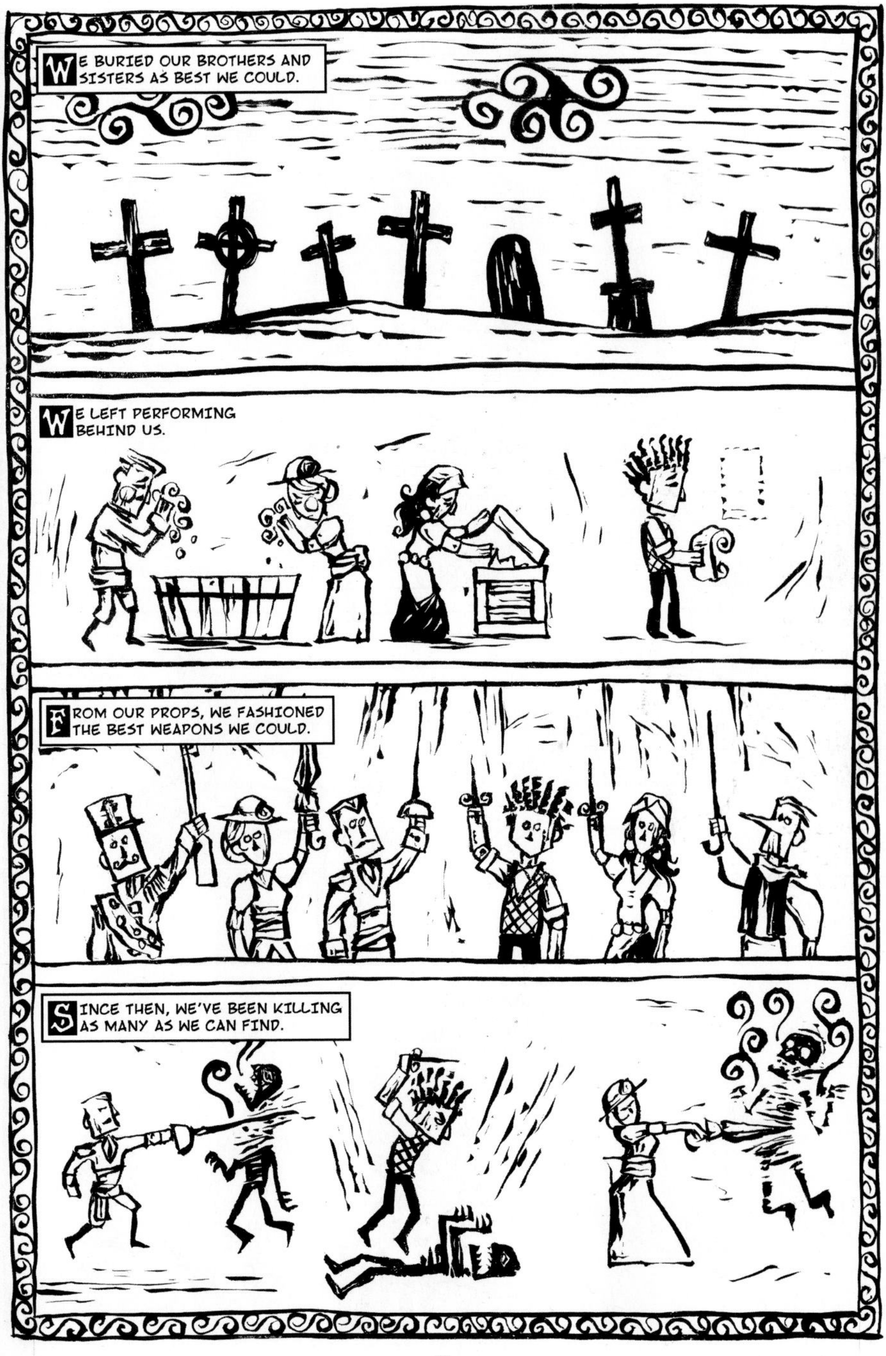
WE BURIED OUR BROTHERS AND SISTERS AS BEST WE COULD.
WE LEFT PERFORMING BEHIND US.
FROM OUR PROPS, WE FASHIONED THE BEST WEAPONS WE COULD.
SINCE THEN, WE'VE BEEN KILLING AS MANY AS WE CAN FIND.

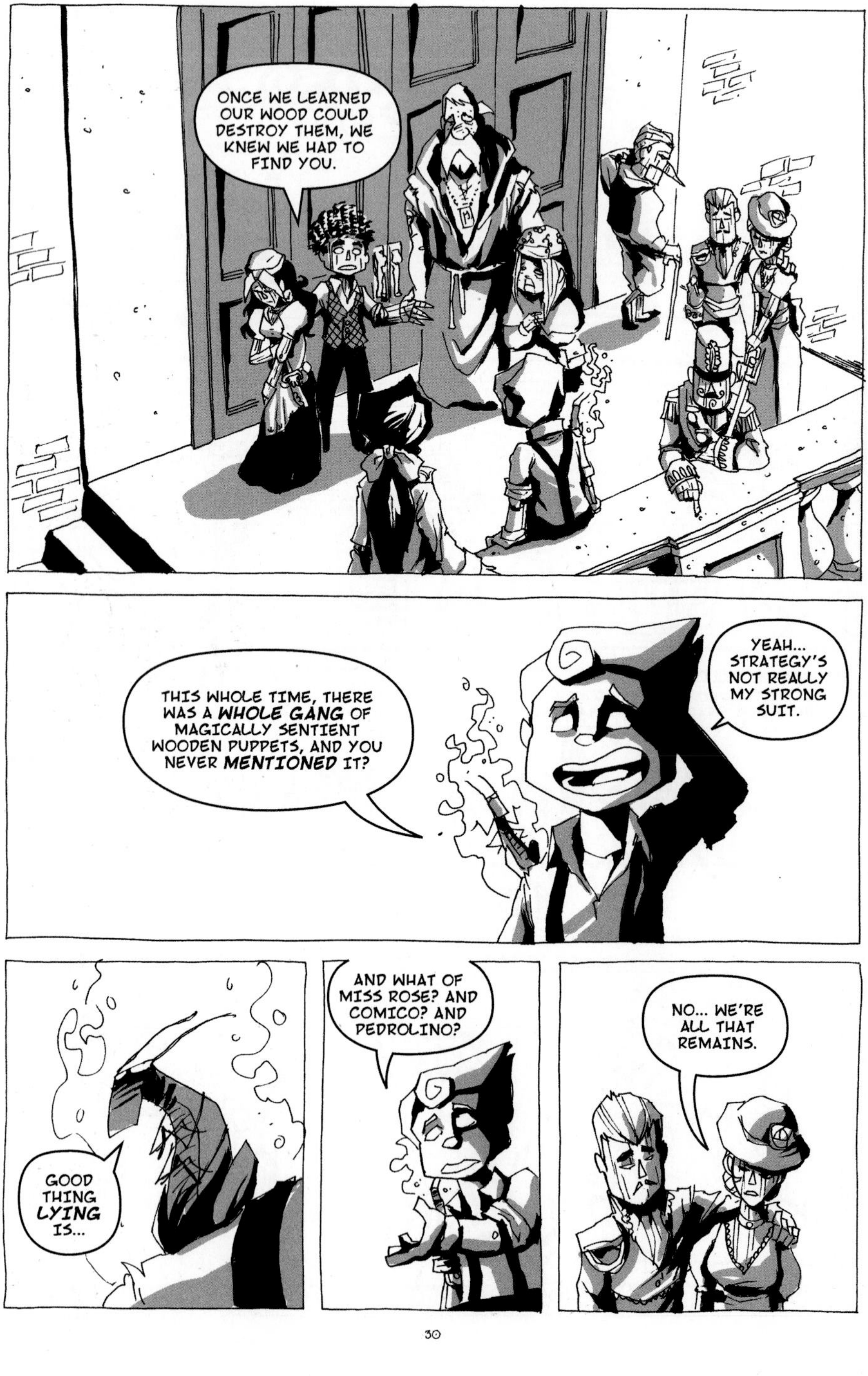
ONCE WE LEARNED OUR WOOD COULD DESTROY THEM, WE KNEW WE HAD TO FIND YOU.
THIS WHOLE TIME, THERE WAS A WHOLE GANG OF MAGICALLY SENTIENT WOODEN PUPPETS, AND YOU NEVER MENTIONED IT?
YEAH... STRATEGY'S NOT REALLY MY STRONG SUIT.
GOOD THING LYING IS...
AND WHAT OF MISS ROSE? AND COMICO? AND PEDROLINO?
NO... WE'RE ALL THAT REMAINS.

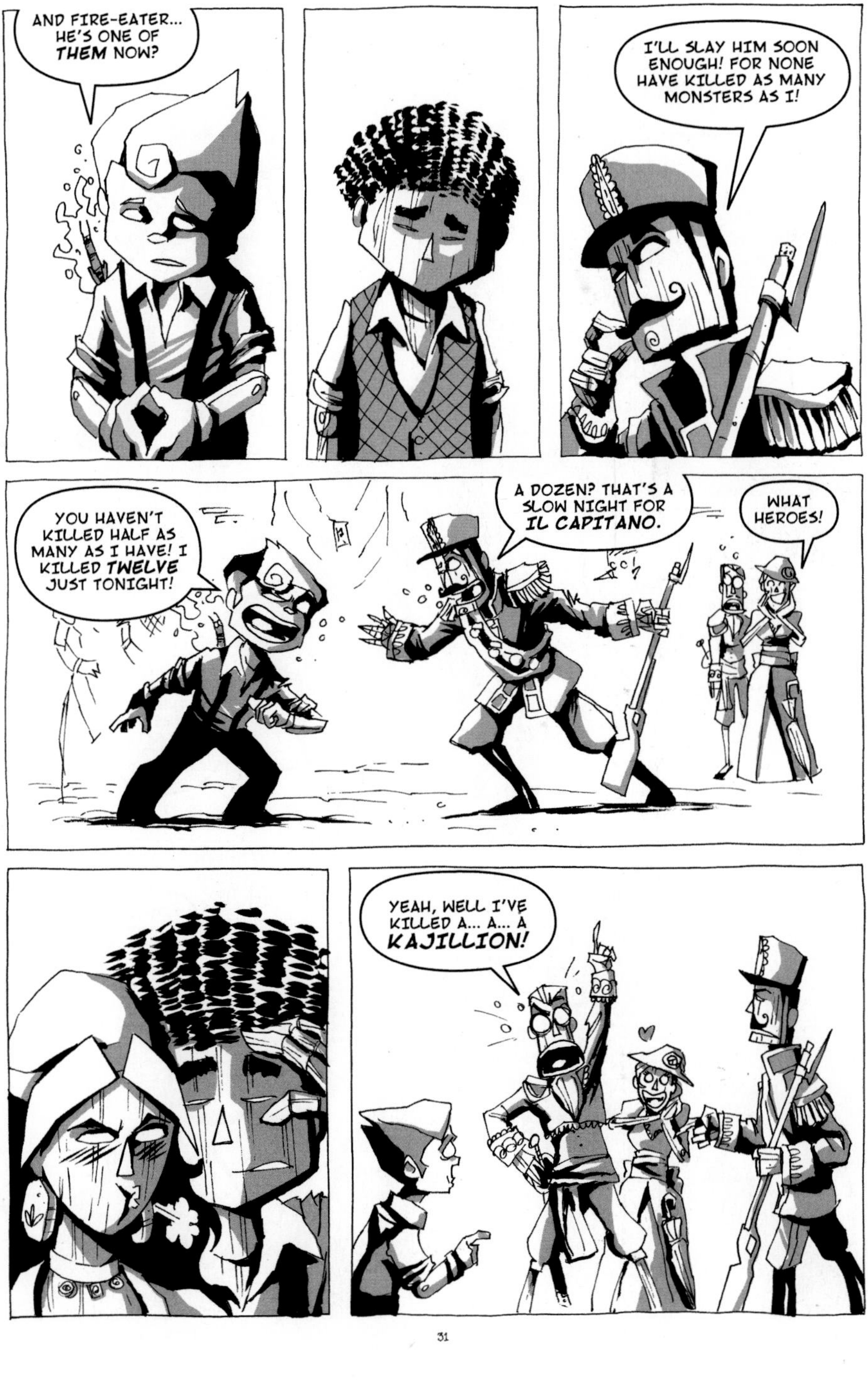
AND FIRE-EATER... HE'S ONE OF **THEM** NOW?
I'LL SLAY HIM SOON ENOUGH! FOR NONE HAVE KILLED AS MANY MONSTERS AS I!
YOU HAVEN'T KILLED HALF AS MANY AS I HAVE! I KILLED **TWELVE** JUST TONIGHT!
A DOZEN? THAT'S A SLOW NIGHT FOR **IL CAPITANO.**
WHAT HEROES!
YEAH, WELL I'VE KILLED A... A... A **KAJILLION!**

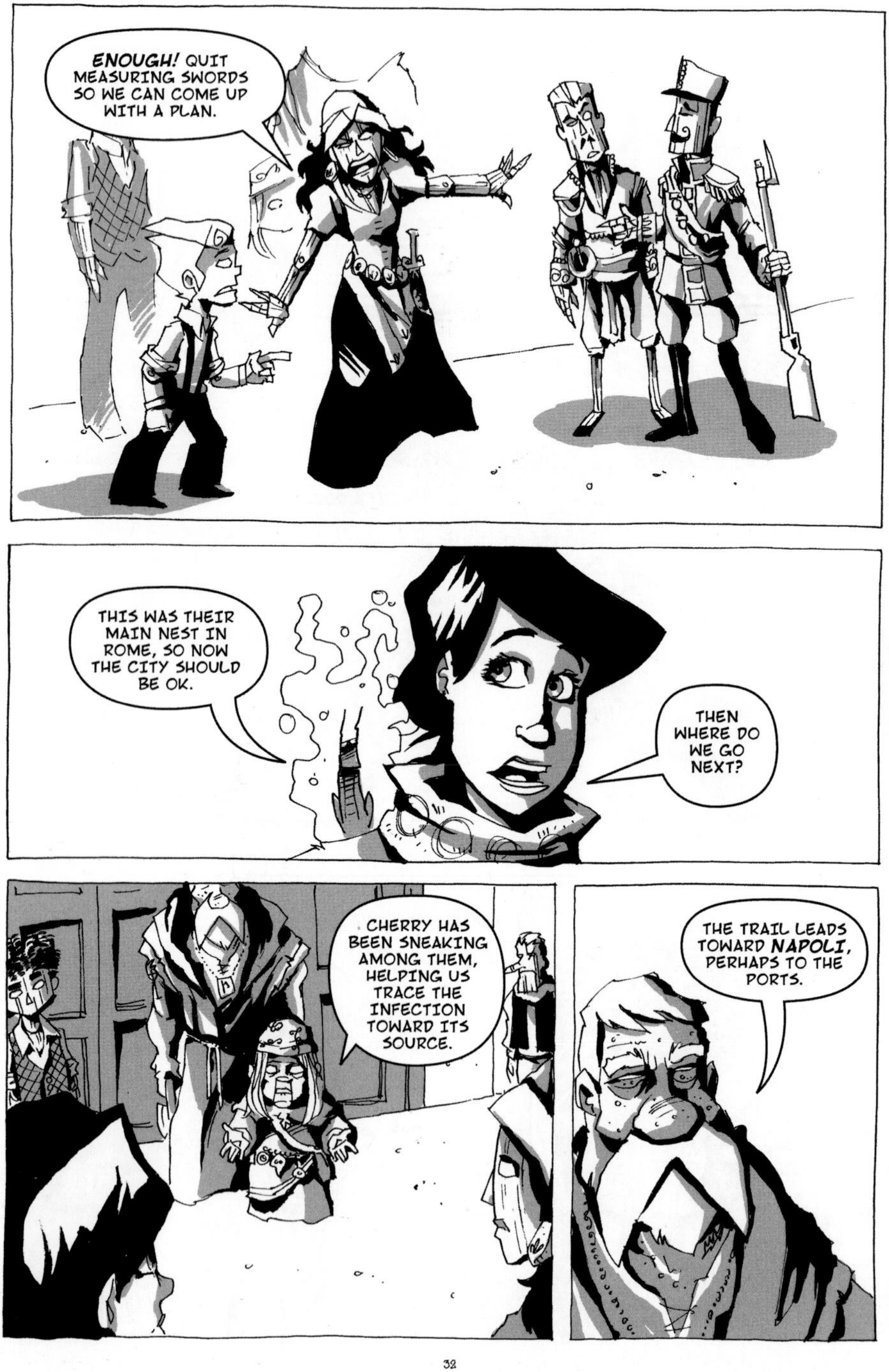

ENOUGH! QUIT MEASURING SWORDS SO WE CAN COME UP WITH A PLAN.
THIS WAS THEIR MAIN NEST IN ROME, SO NOW THE CITY SHOULD BE OK.
THEN WHERE DO WE GO NEXT?
CHERRY HAS BEEN SNEAKING AMONG THEM, HELPING US TRACE THE INFECTION TOWARD ITS SOURCE.
THE TRAIL LEADS TOWARD NAPOLI, PERHAPS TO THE PORTS.

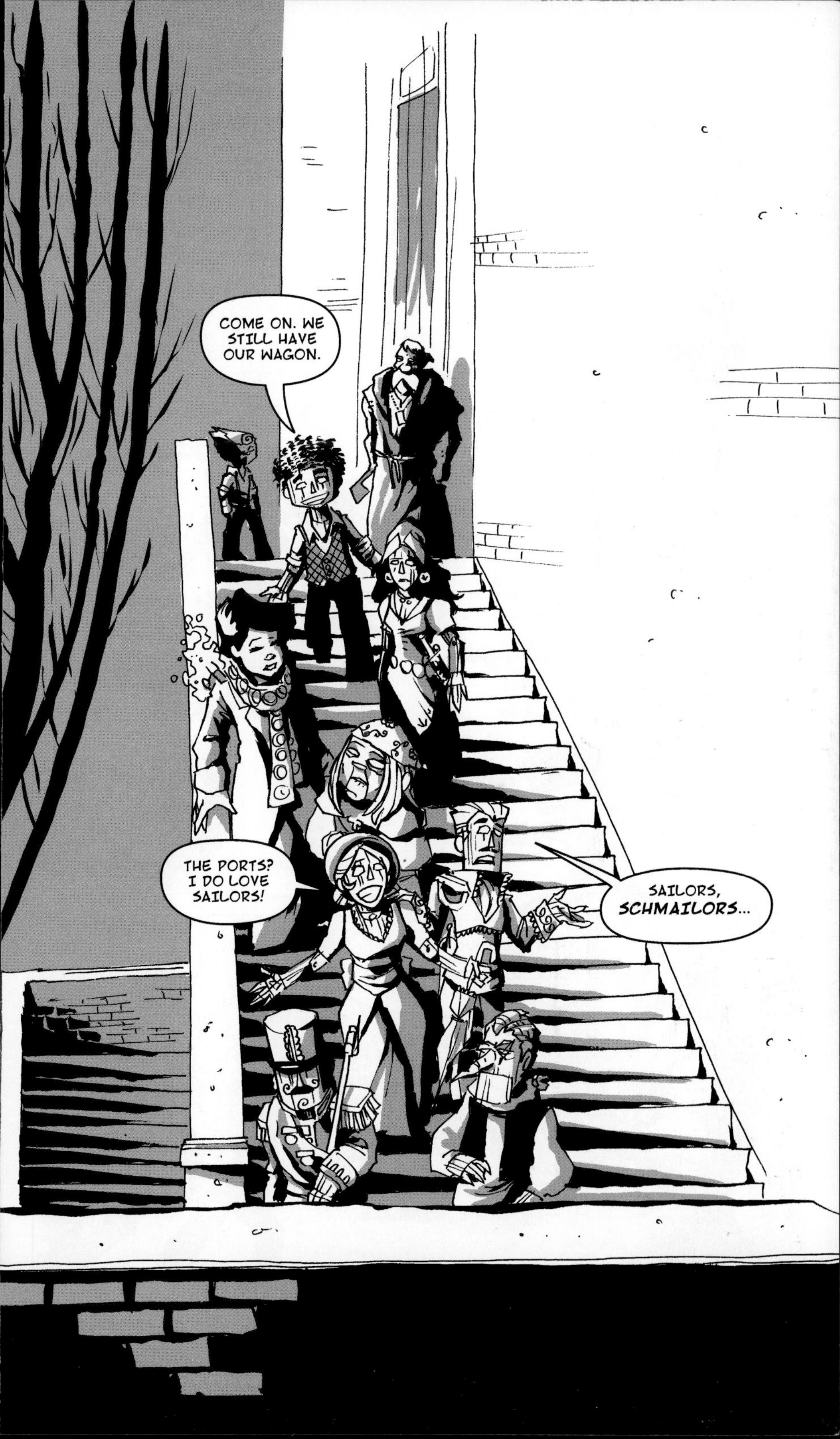
COME ON. WE STILL HAVE OUR WAGON.
THE PORTS? I DO LOVE SAILORS!
SAILORS, SCHMAILORS...

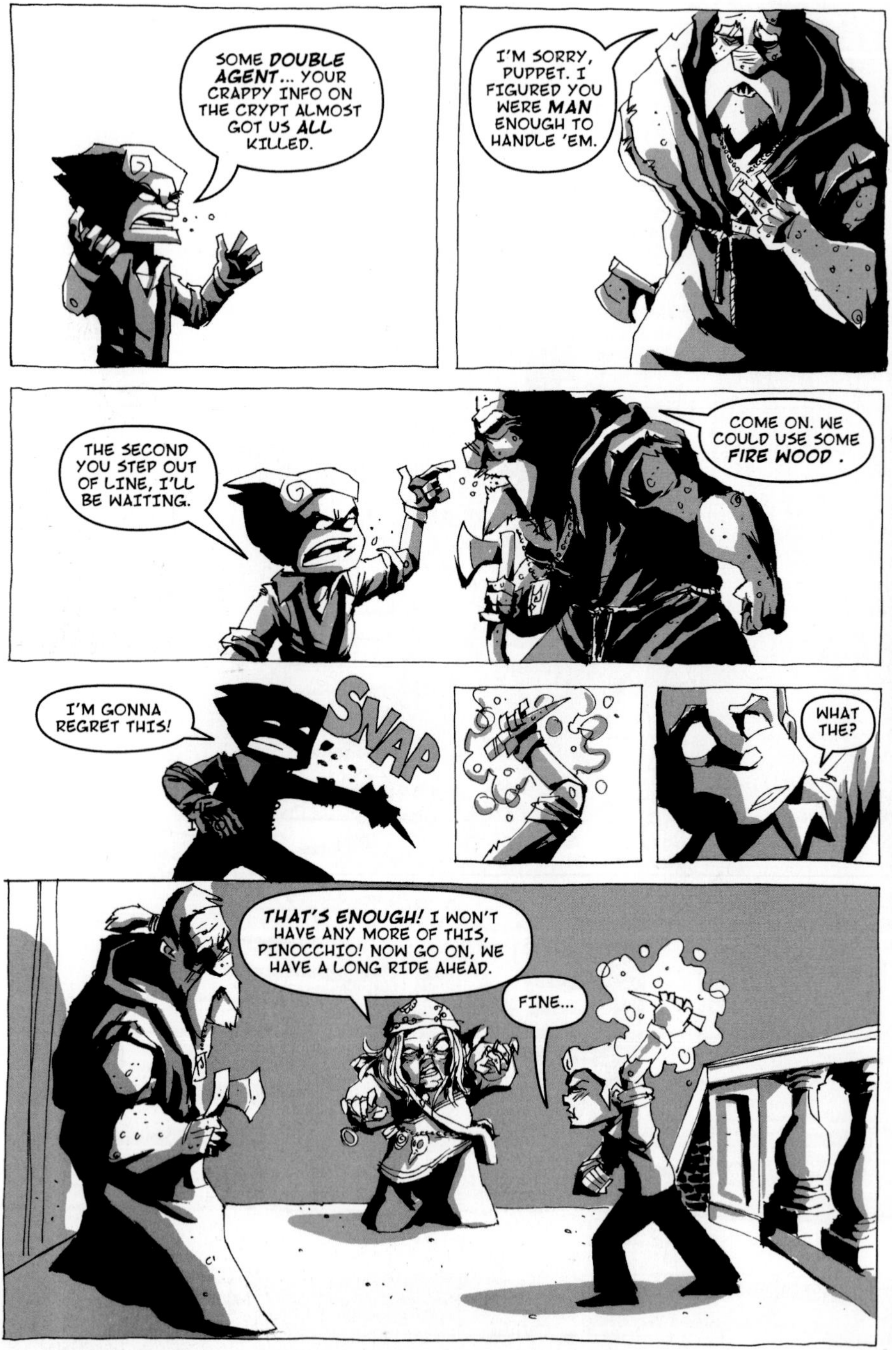
SOME DOUBLE AGENT... YOUR CRAPPY INFO ON THE CRYPT ALMOST GOT US ALL KILLED.
I'M SORRY, PUPPET. I FIGURED YOU WERE MAN ENOUGH TO HANDLE 'EM.
THE SECOND YOU STEP OUT OF LINE, I'LL BE WAITING.
COME ON. WE COULD USE SOME FIRE WOOD .
I'M GONNA REGRET THIS!
SNAP
WHAT THE?
THAT'S ENOUGH! I WON'T HAVE ANY MORE OF THIS, PINOCCHIO! NOW GO ON, WE HAVE A LONG RIDE AHEAD.
FINE...

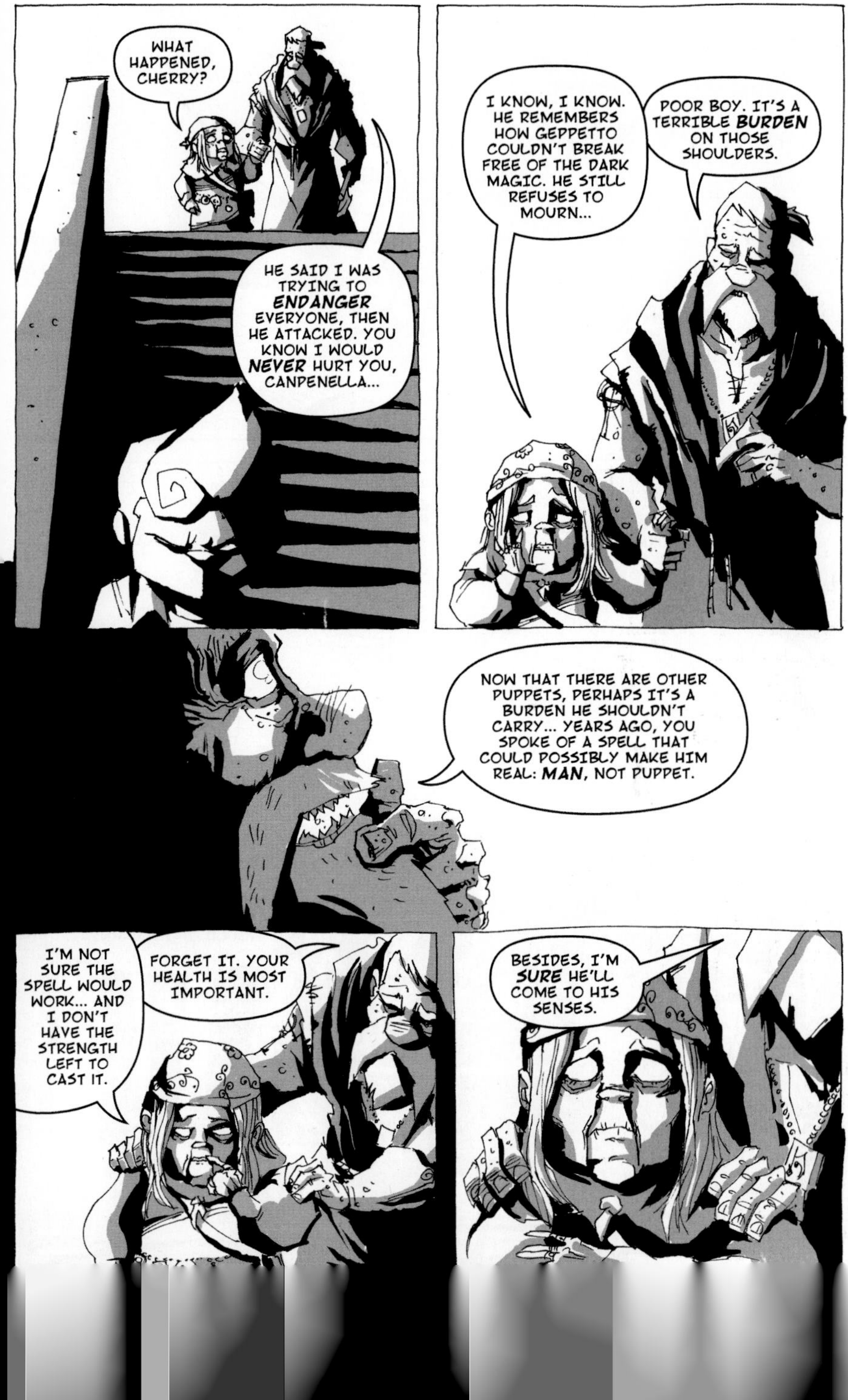
WHAT HAPPENED, CHERRY?
HE SAID I WAS TRYING TO **ENDANGER** EVERYONE, THEN HE ATTACKED. YOU KNOW I WOULD **NEVER** HURT YOU, CANPENELLA...
I KNOW, I KNOW. HE REMEMBERS HOW GEPPETTO COULDN'T BREAK FREE OF THE DARK MAGIC. HE STILL REFUSES TO MOURN...
POOR BOY. IT'S A TERRIBLE **BURDEN** ON THOSE SHOULDERS.
NOW THAT THERE ARE OTHER PUPPETS, PERHAPS IT'S A BURDEN HE SHOULDN'T CARRY... YEARS AGO, YOU SPOKE OF A SPELL THAT COULD POSSIBLY MAKE HIM REAL: **MAN**, NOT PUPPET.
I'M NOT SURE THE SPELL WOULD WORK... AND I DON'T HAVE THE STRENGTH LEFT TO CAST IT.
FORGET IT. YOUR HEALTH IS MOST IMPORTANT.
BESIDES, I'M **SURE** HE'LL COME TO HIS SENSES.

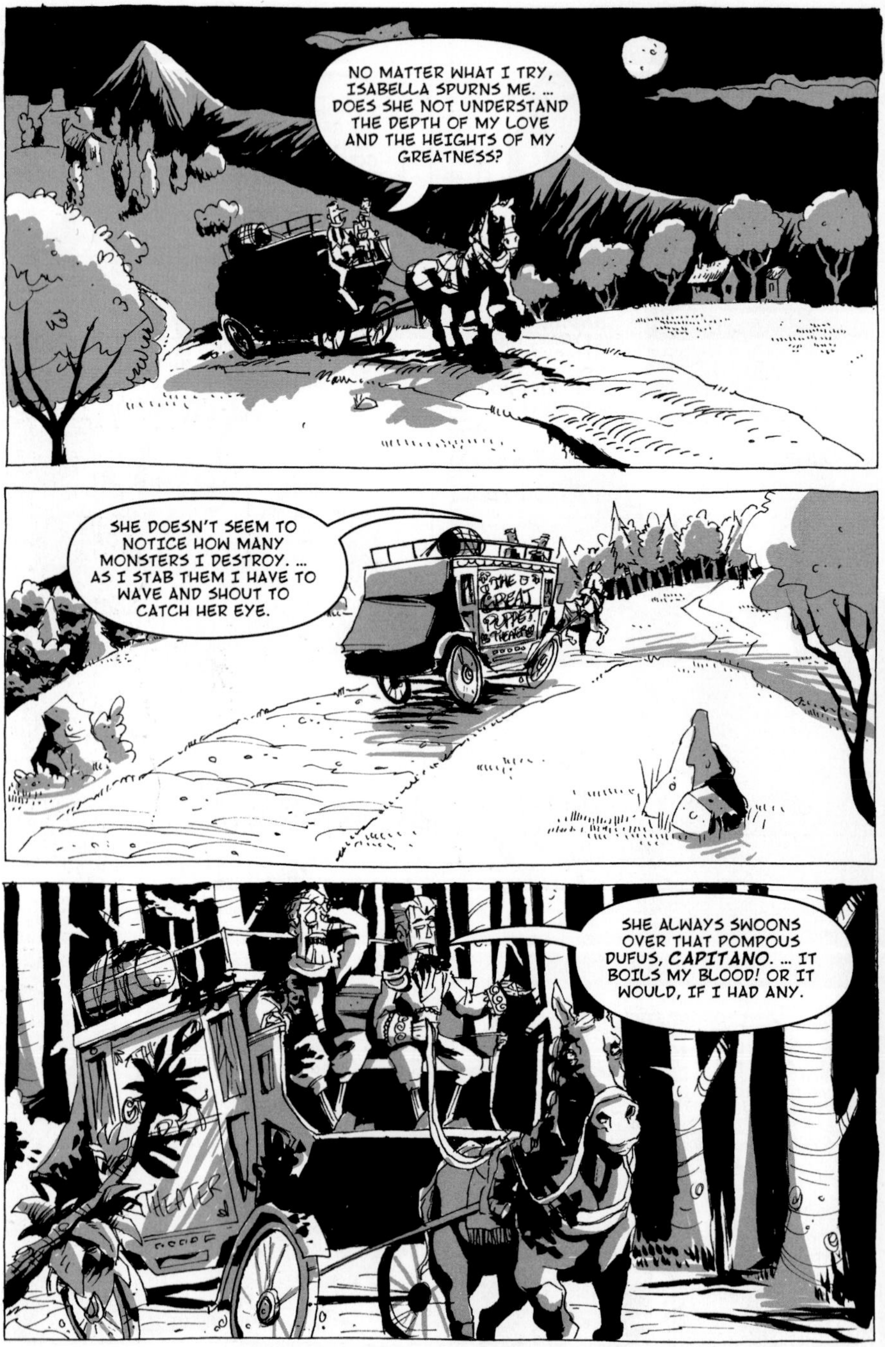
NO MATTER WHAT I TRY, ISABELLA SPURNS ME. ... DOES SHE NOT UNDERSTAND THE DEPTH OF MY LOVE AND THE HEIGHTS OF MY GREATNESS?
SHE DOESN'T SEEM TO NOTICE HOW MANY MONSTERS I DESTROY. ... AS I STAB THEM I HAVE TO WAVE AND SHOUT TO CATCH HER EYE.
THE GREAT PUPPET THEATER
SHE ALWAYS SWOONS OVER THAT POMPOUS DUFUS, **CAPITANO**. ... IT BOILS MY BLOOD! OR IT WOULD, IF I HAD ANY.
THEATER

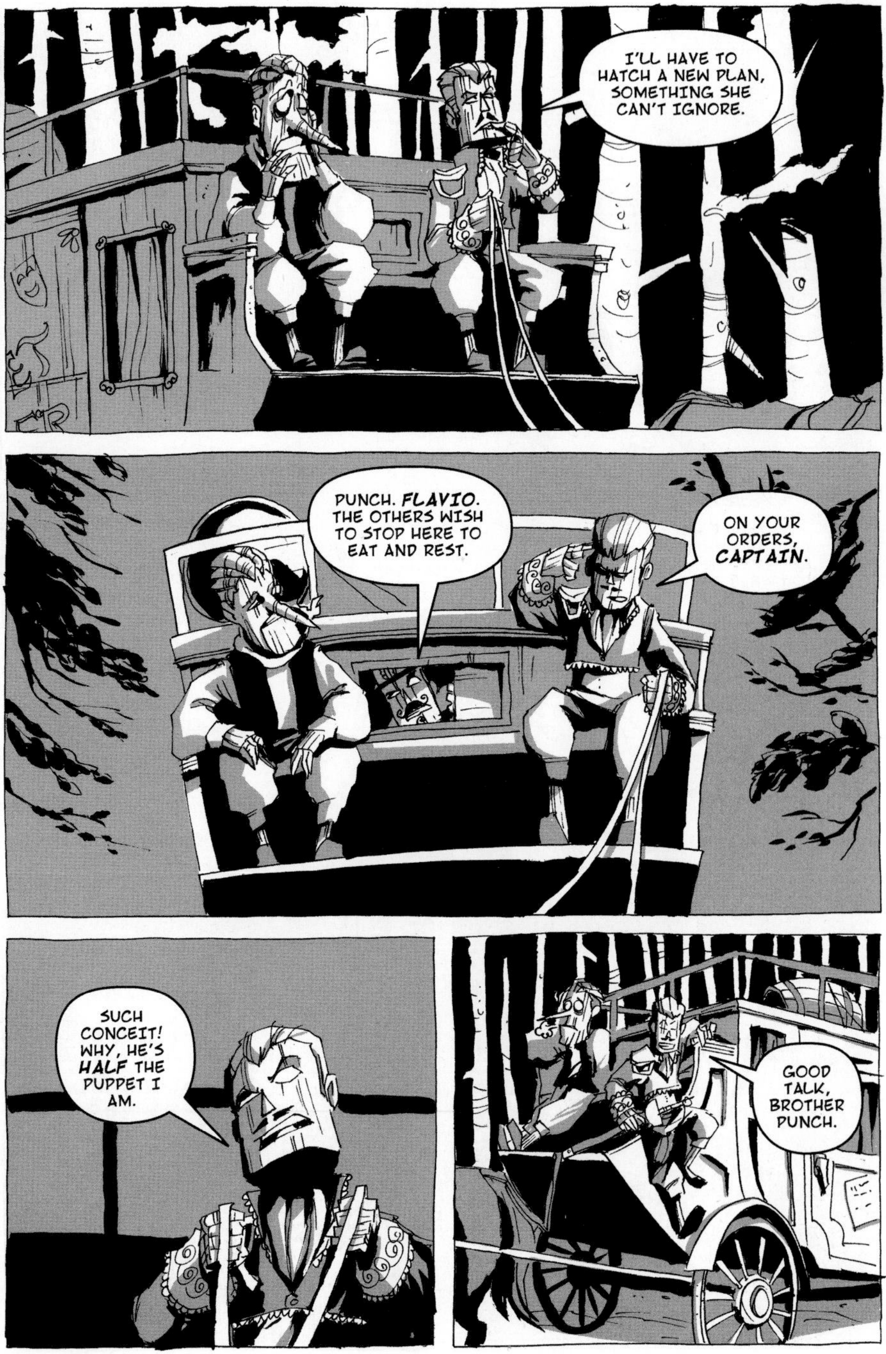
I'LL HAVE TO HATCH A NEW PLAN, SOMETHING SHE CAN'T IGNORE.
PUNCH. FLAVIO. THE OTHERS WISH TO STOP HERE TO EAT AND REST.
ON YOUR ORDERS, CAPTAIN.
SUCH CONCEIT! WHY, HE'S HALF THE PUPPET I AM.
GOOD TALK, BROTHER PUNCH.

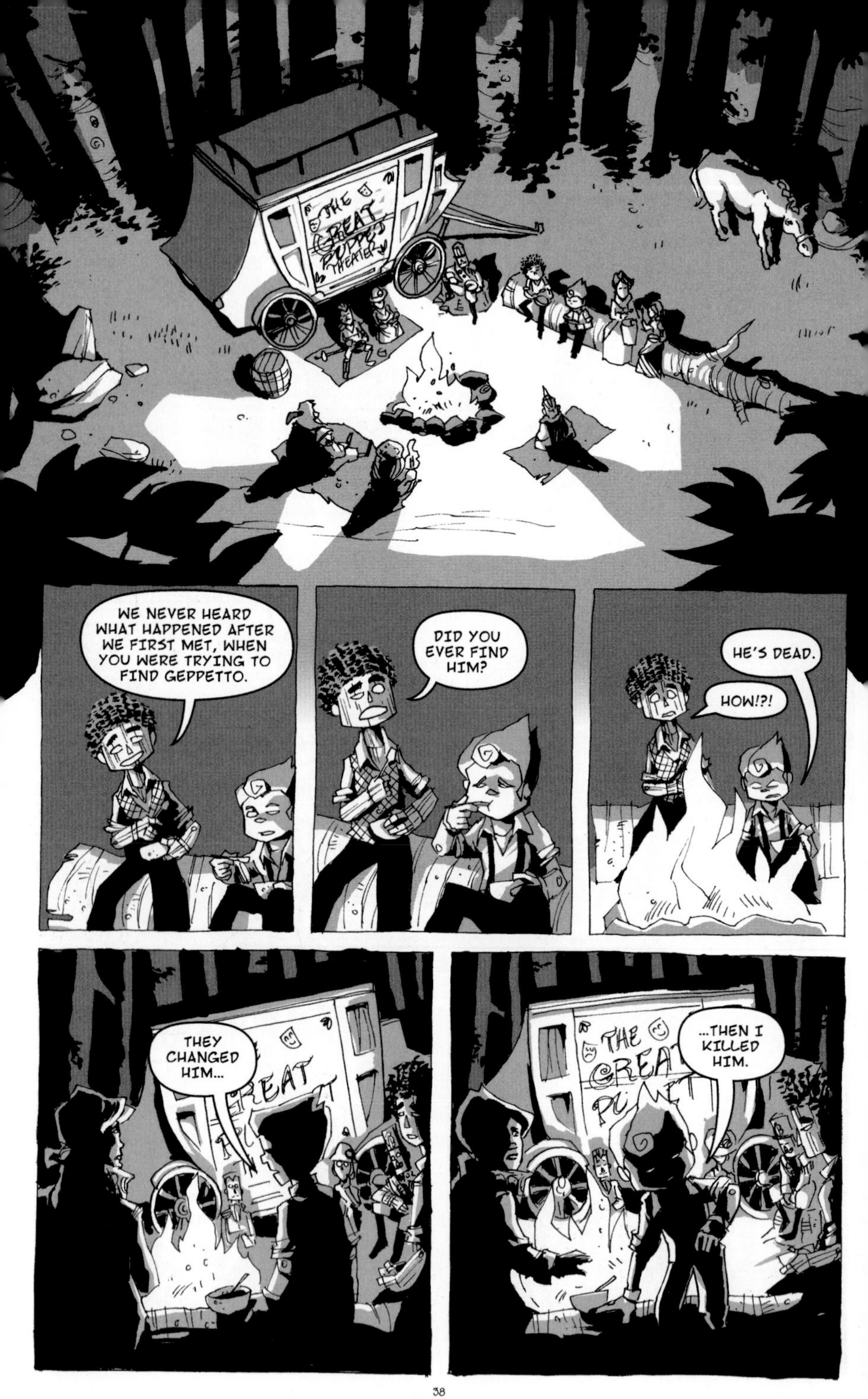
THE GREAT PUPPET THEATER
WE NEVER HEARD WHAT HAPPENED AFTER WE FIRST MET, WHEN YOU WERE TRYING TO FIND GEPPETTO.
DID YOU EVER FIND HIM?
HE'S DEAD.
HOW!?!
THEY CHANGED HIM...
...THEN I KILLED HIM.

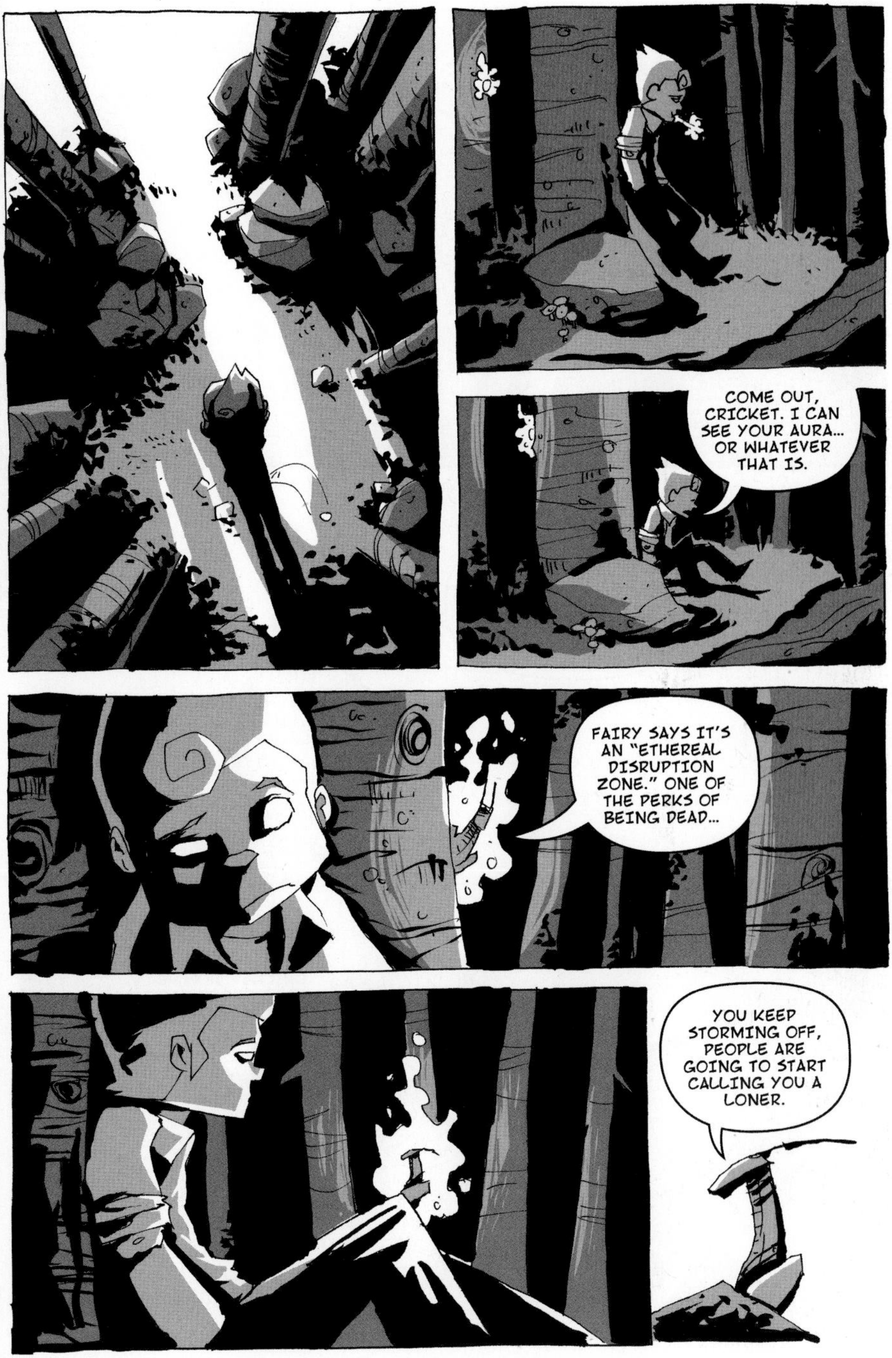
COME OUT, CRICKET. I CAN SEE YOUR AURA... OR WHATEVER THAT IS.
FAIRY SAYS IT'S AN "ETHEREAL DISRUPTION ZONE." ONE OF THE PERKS OF BEING DEAD...
YOU KEEP STORMING OFF, PEOPLE ARE GOING TO START CALLING YOU A LONER.

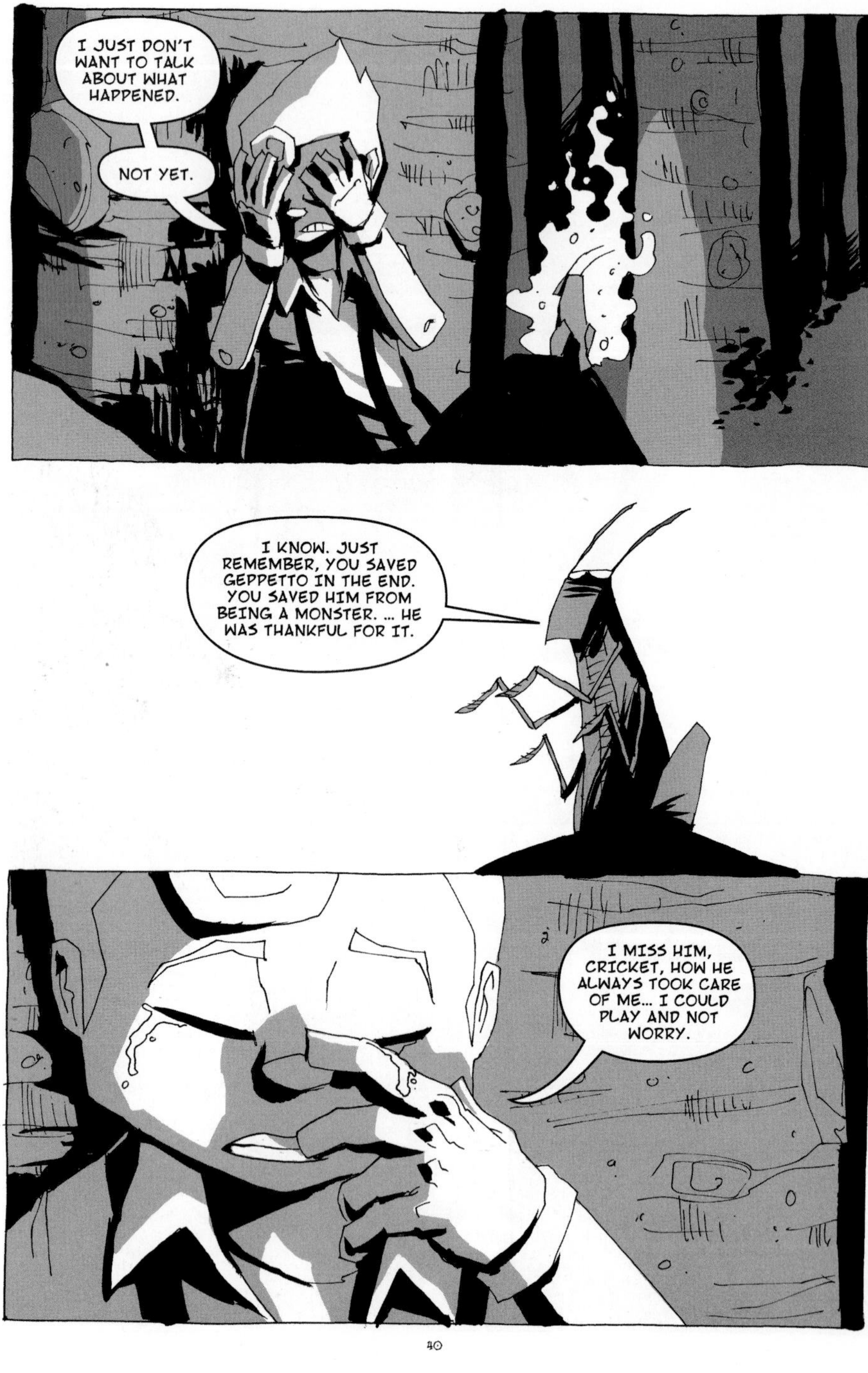
I JUST DON'T WANT TO TALK ABOUT WHAT HAPPENED.
NOT YET.
I KNOW. JUST REMEMBER, YOU SAVED GEPPETTO IN THE END. YOU SAVED HIM FROM BEING A MONSTER. ... HE WAS THANKFUL FOR IT.
I MISS HIM, CRICKET, HOW HE ALWAYS TOOK CARE OF ME... I COULD PLAY AND NOT WORRY.

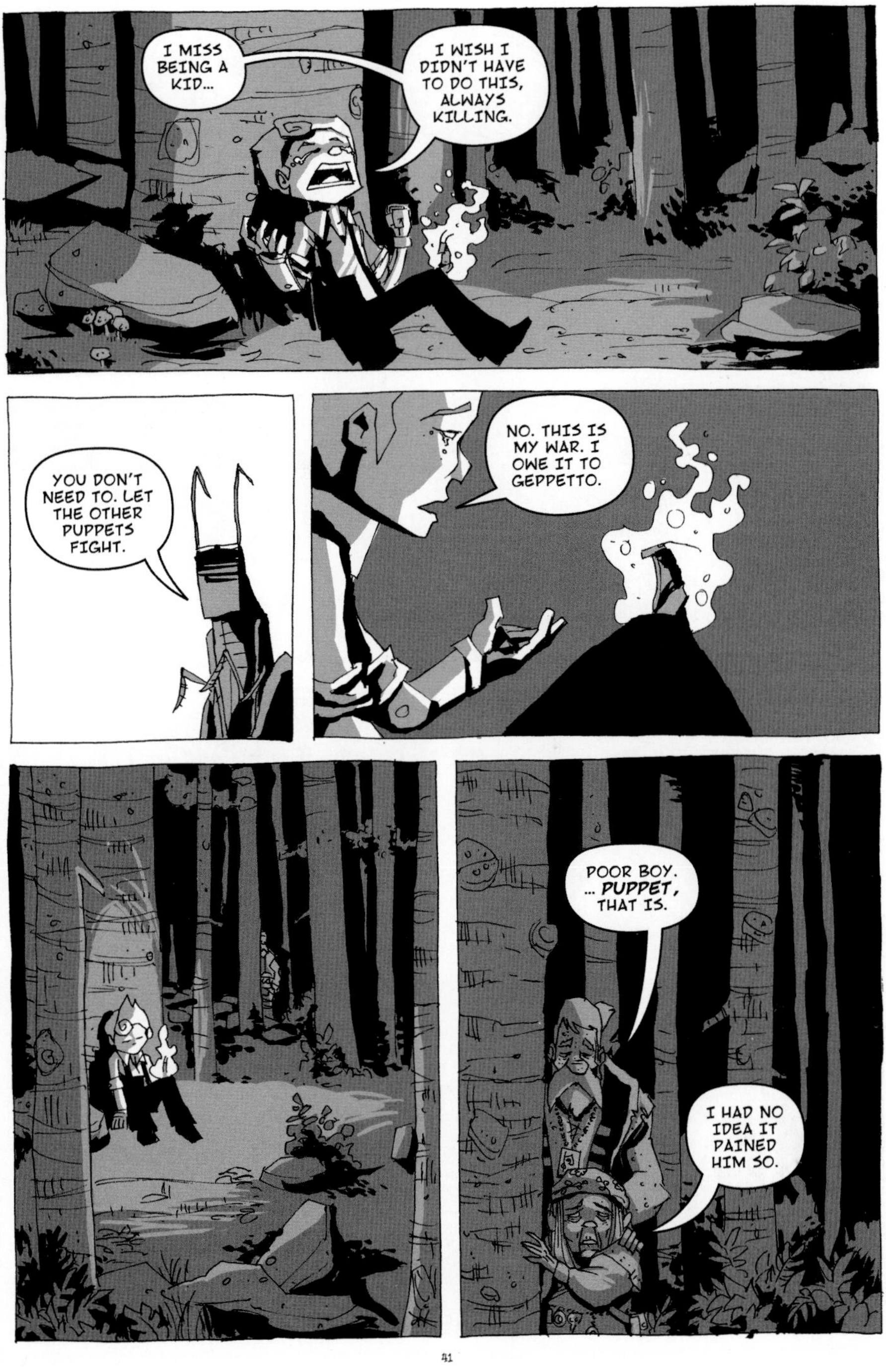
I MISS BEING A KID...
I WISH I DIDN'T HAVE TO DO THIS, ALWAYS KILLING.
YOU DON'T NEED TO. LET THE OTHER PUPPETS FIGHT.
NO. THIS IS MY WAR. I OWE IT TO GEPPETTO.
POOR BOY. ... *PUPPET*, THAT IS.
I HAD NO IDEA IT PAINED HIM SO.

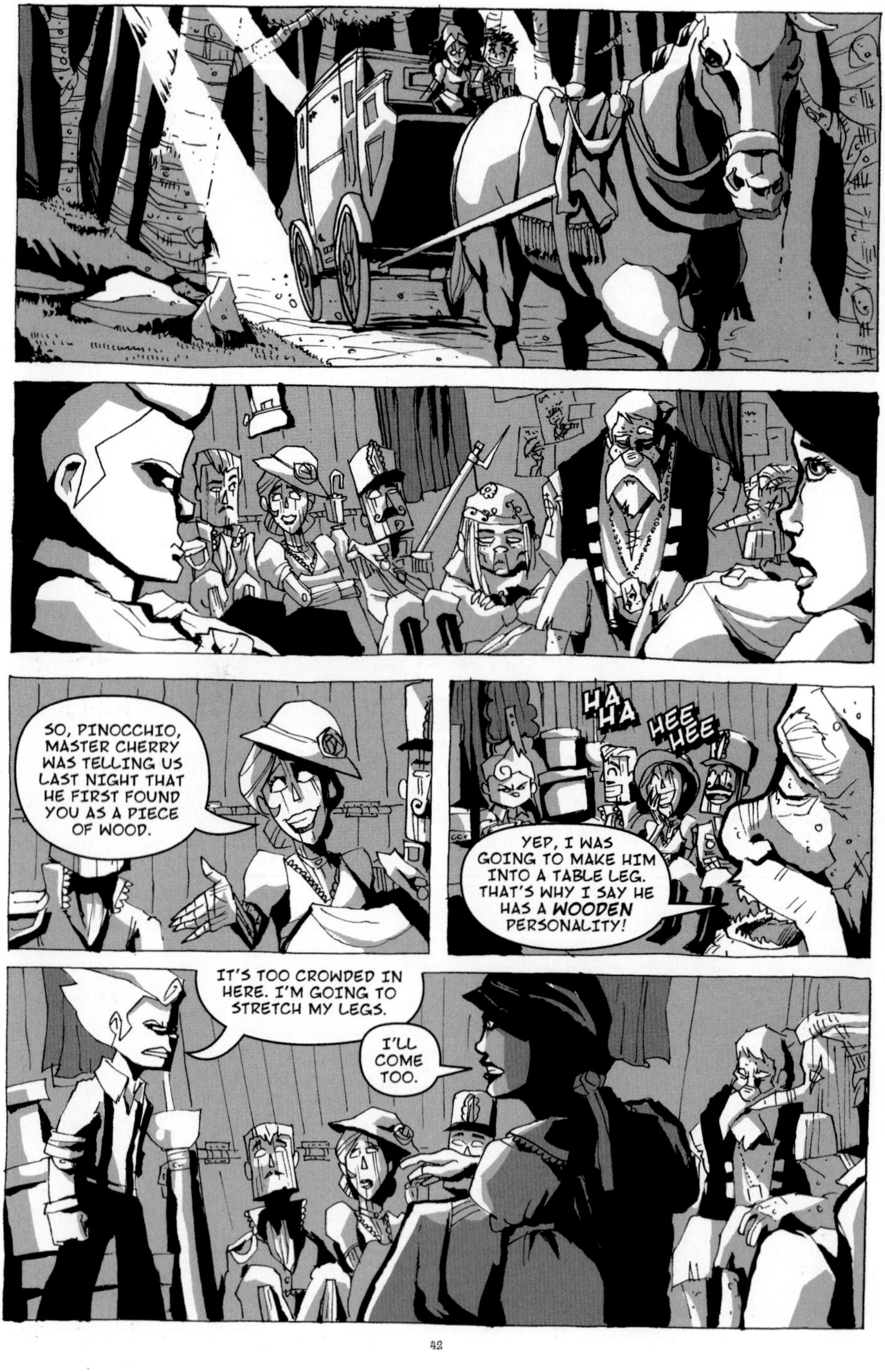
SO, PINOCCHIO, MASTER CHERRY WAS TELLING US LAST NIGHT THAT HE FIRST FOUND YOU AS A PIECE OF WOOD.
HA HA
HEE HEE
YEP, I WAS GOING TO MAKE HIM INTO A TABLE LEG. THAT'S WHY I SAY HE HAS A **WOODEN** PERSONALITY!
IT'S TOO CROWDED IN HERE. I'M GOING TO STRETCH MY LEGS.
I'LL COME TOO.

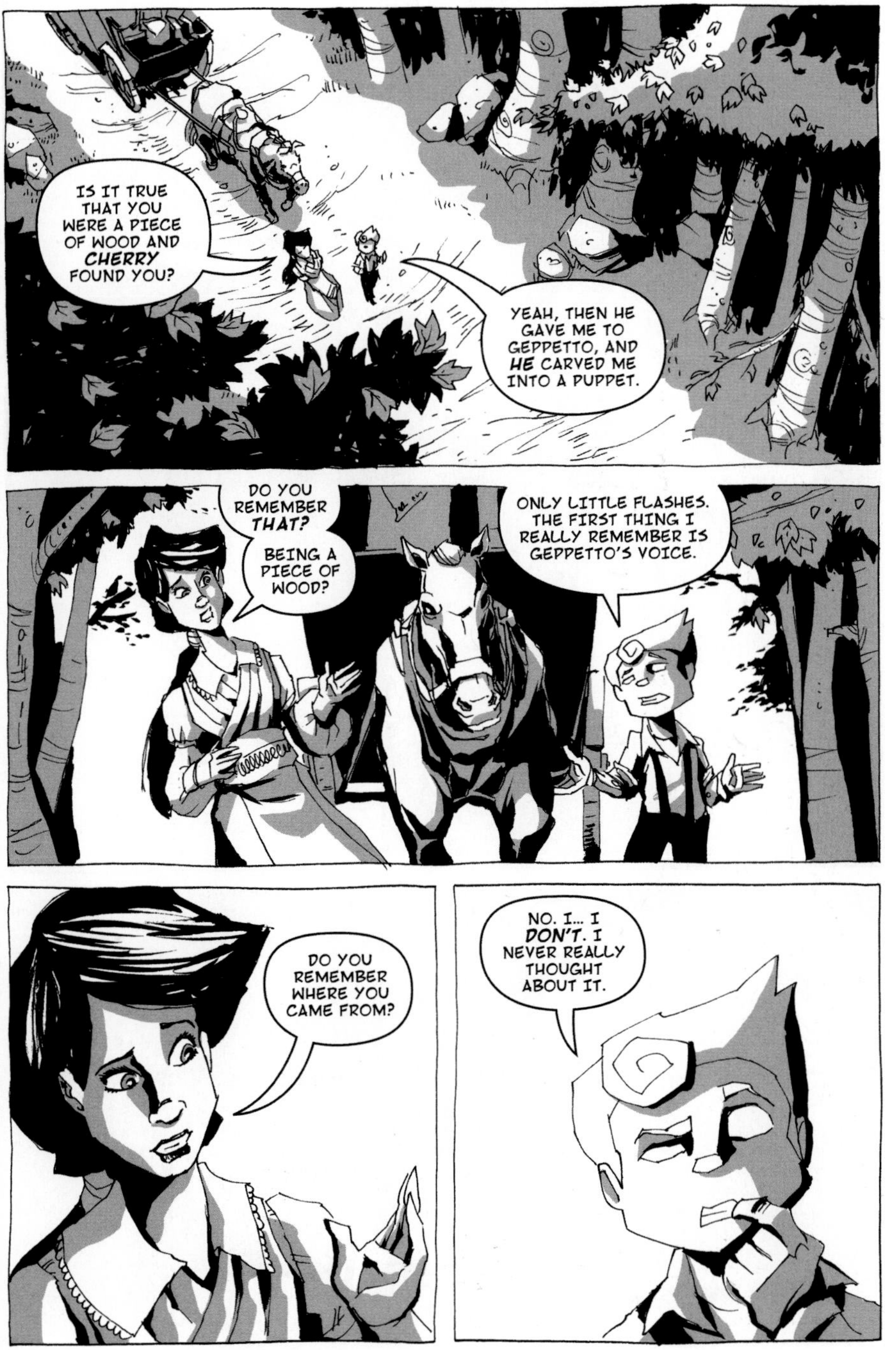

IS IT TRUE THAT YOU WERE A PIECE OF WOOD AND *CHERRY* FOUND YOU?
YEAH, THEN HE GAVE ME TO GEPPETTO, AND *HE* CARVED ME INTO A PUPPET.
DO YOU REMEMBER *THAT?*
BEING A PIECE OF WOOD?
ONLY LITTLE FLASHES. THE FIRST THING I REALLY REMEMBER IS GEPPETTO'S VOICE.
DO YOU REMEMBER WHERE YOU CAME FROM?
NO. I... I *DON'T*. I NEVER REALLY THOUGHT ABOUT IT.

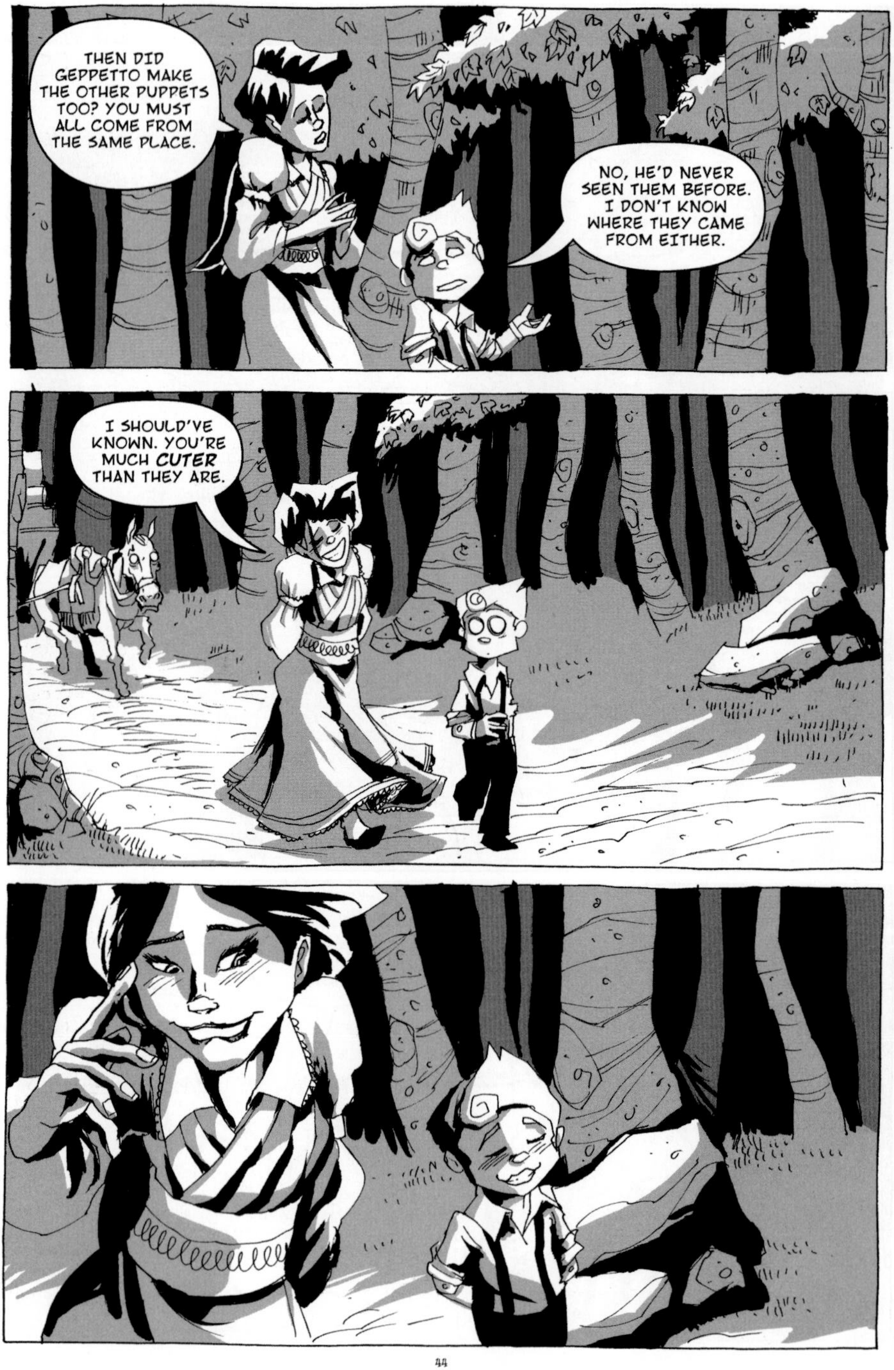
THEN DID GEPPETTO MAKE THE OTHER PUPPETS TOO? YOU MUST ALL COME FROM THE SAME PLACE.
NO, HE'D NEVER SEEN THEM BEFORE. I DON'T KNOW WHERE THEY CAME FROM EITHER.
I SHOULD'VE KNOWN. YOU'RE MUCH CUTER THAN THEY ARE.

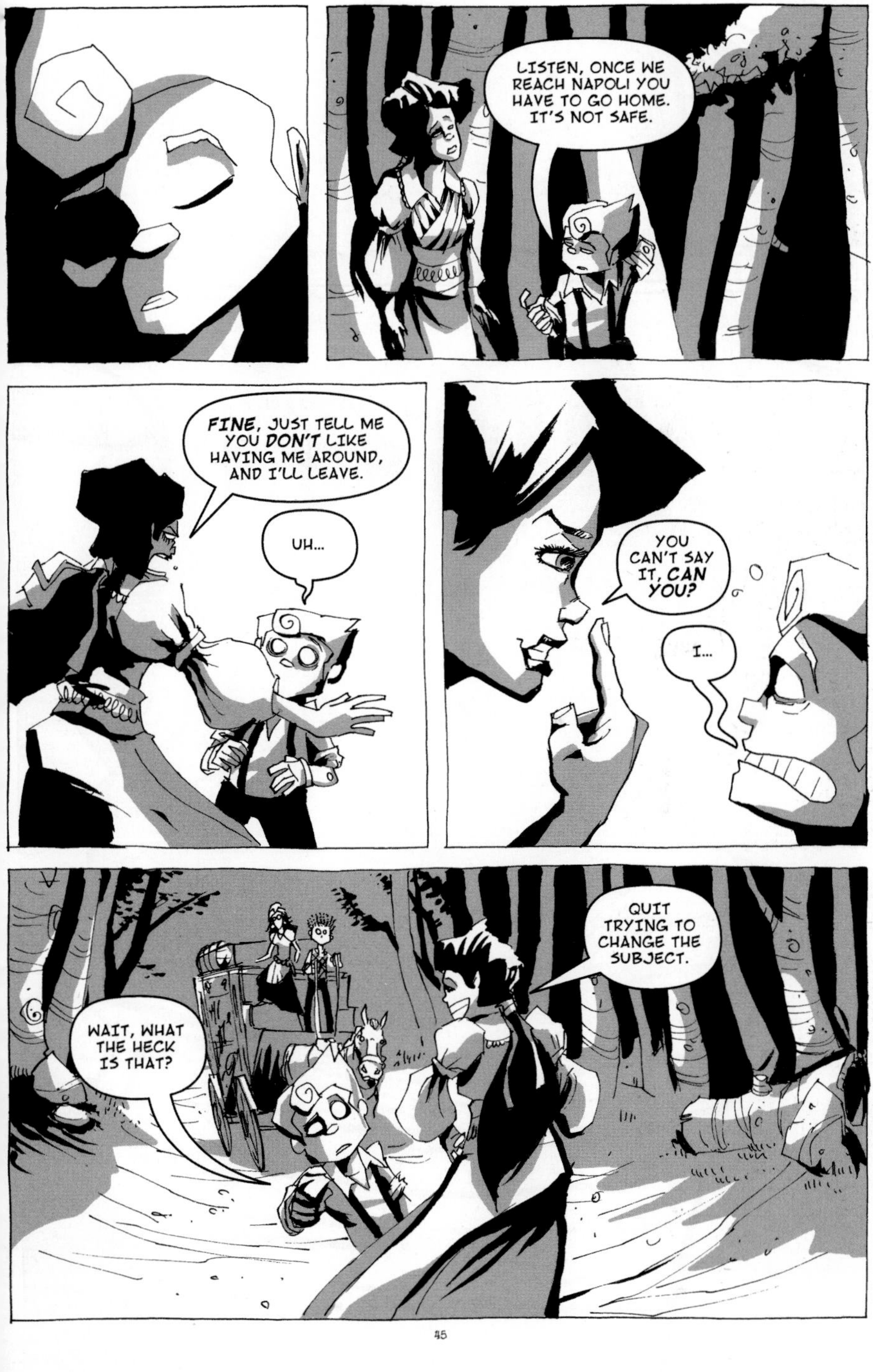
LISTEN, ONCE WE REACH NAPOLI YOU HAVE TO GO HOME. IT'S NOT SAFE.
FINE, JUST TELL ME YOU DON'T LIKE HAVING ME AROUND, AND I'LL LEAVE.
UH...
YOU CAN'T SAY IT, CAN YOU?
I...
QUIT TRYING TO CHANGE THE SUBJECT.
WAIT, WHAT THE HECK IS THAT?

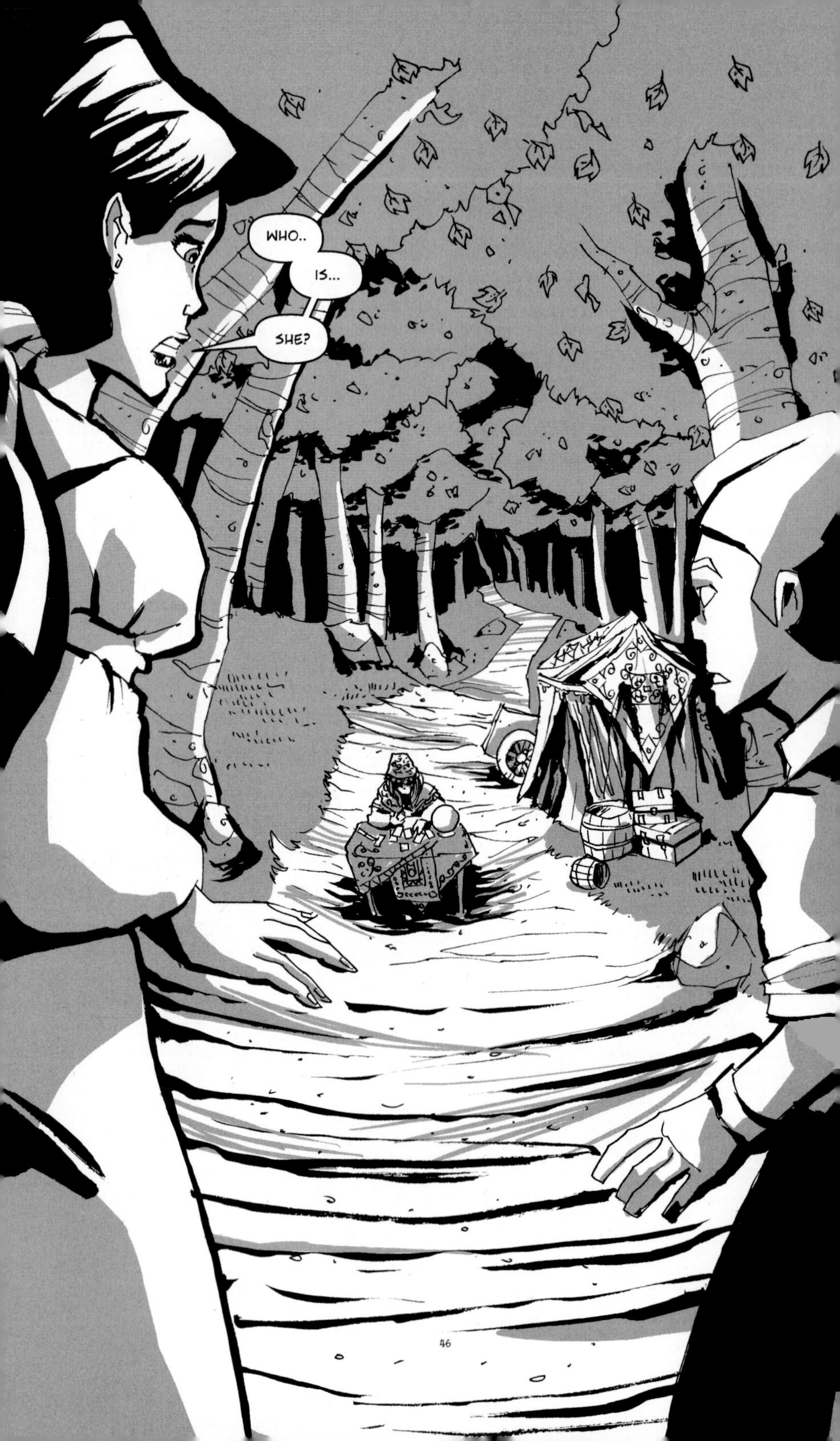
WHO..
IS...
SHE?

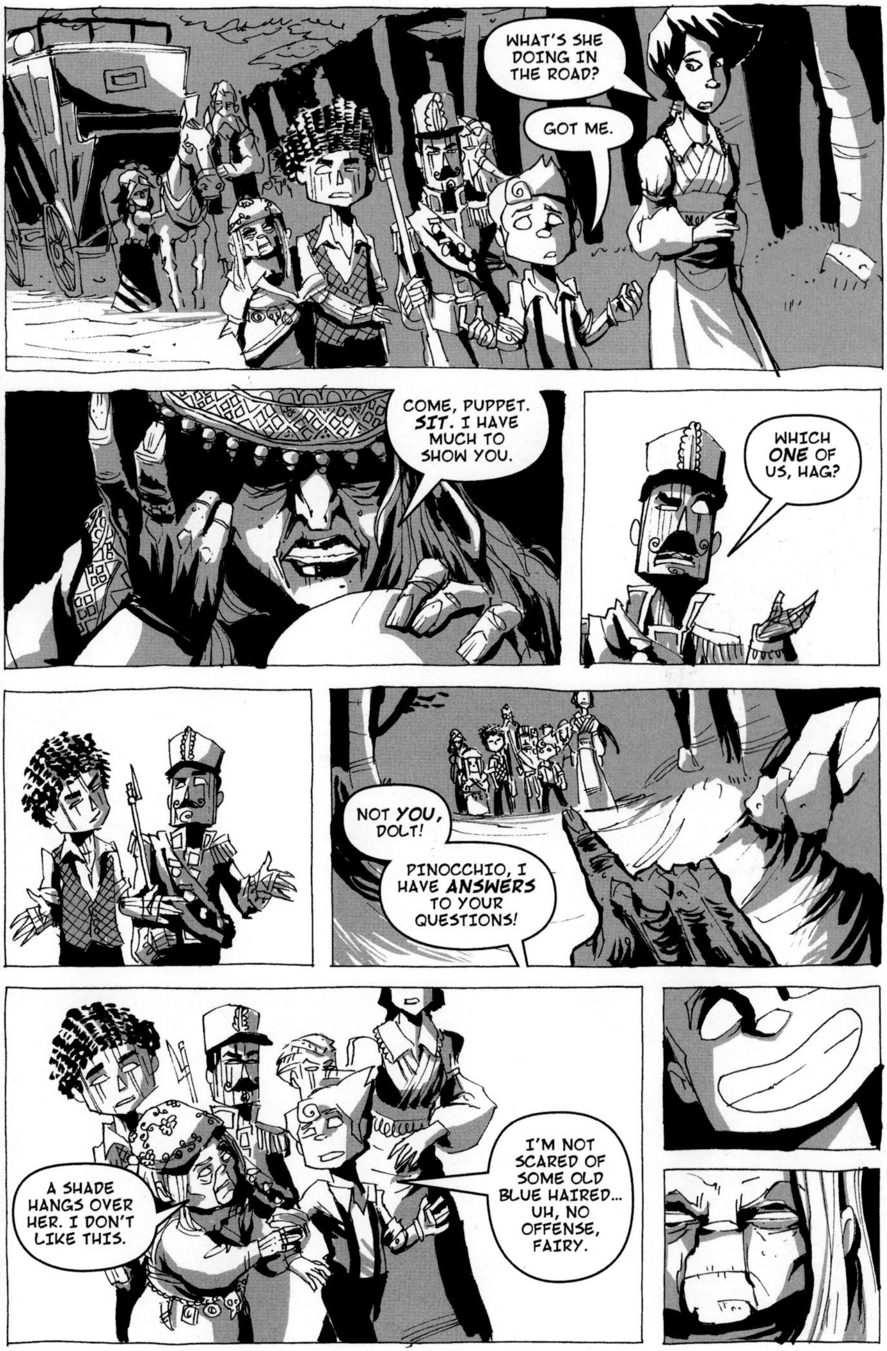
WHAT'S SHE DOING IN THE ROAD?
GOT ME.
COME, PUPPET. SIT. I HAVE MUCH TO SHOW YOU.
WHICH ONE OF US, HAG?
NOT YOU, DOLT!
PINOCCHIO, I HAVE ANSWERS TO YOUR QUESTIONS!
A SHADE HANGS OVER HER. I DON'T LIKE THIS.
I'M NOT SCARED OF SOME OLD BLUE HAIRED... UH, NO OFFENSE, FAIRY.

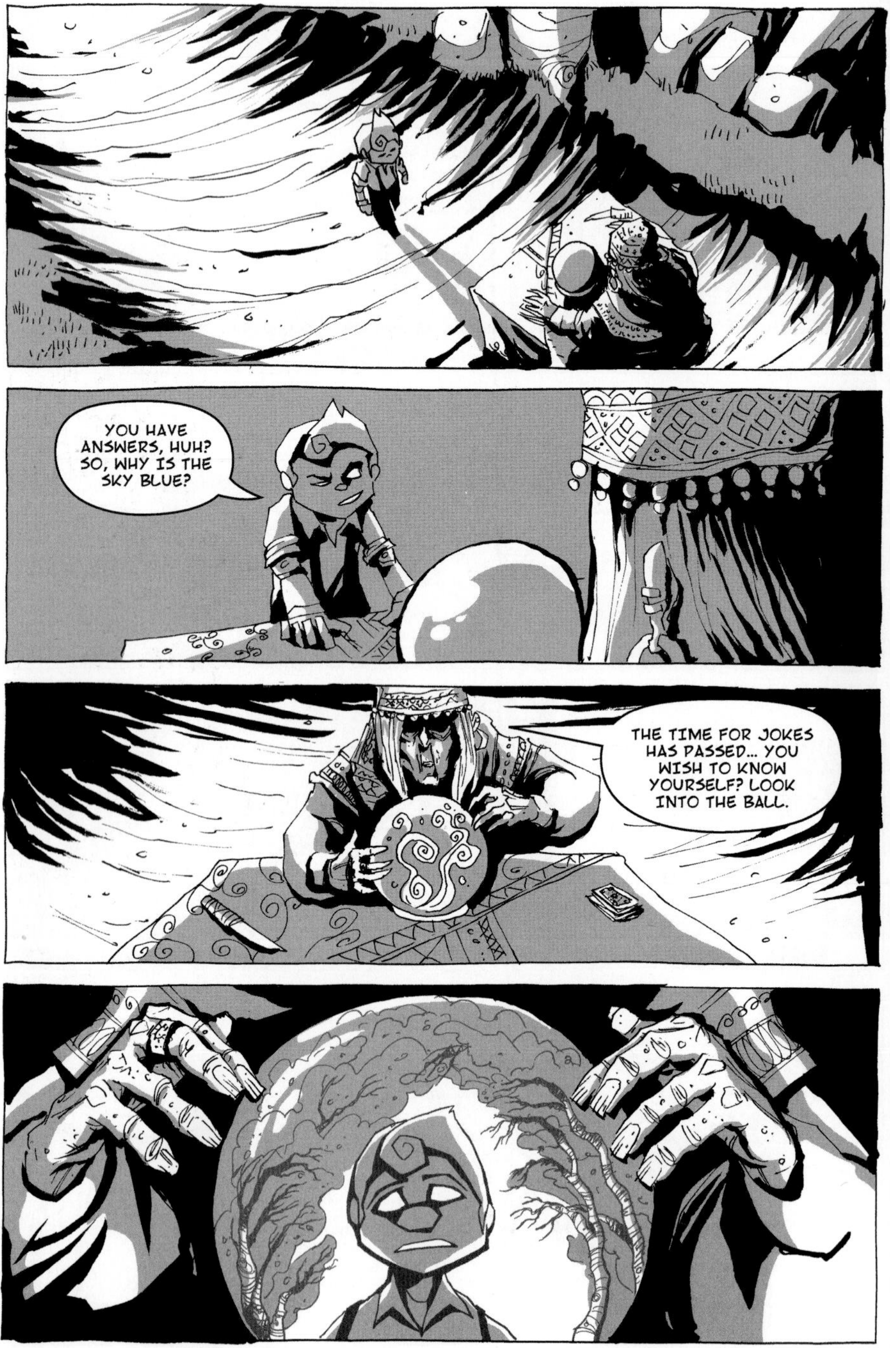
YOU HAVE ANSWERS, HUH? SO, WHY IS THE SKY BLUE?
THE TIME FOR JOKES HAS PASSED... YOU WISH TO KNOW YOURSELF? LOOK INTO THE BALL.

IT BEGINS WITH THE TREES, YES. *OLD MAGIC* FROM DEEP IN THE EARTH.

A DRYAD, FREED OF ROOTS, REMADE IN MAN'S IMAGE.

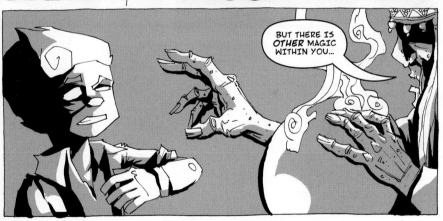

BUT THERE IS *OTHER* MAGIC WITHIN YOU...

IT IS THAT WHICH THREATENS THE *DARK ONE.*

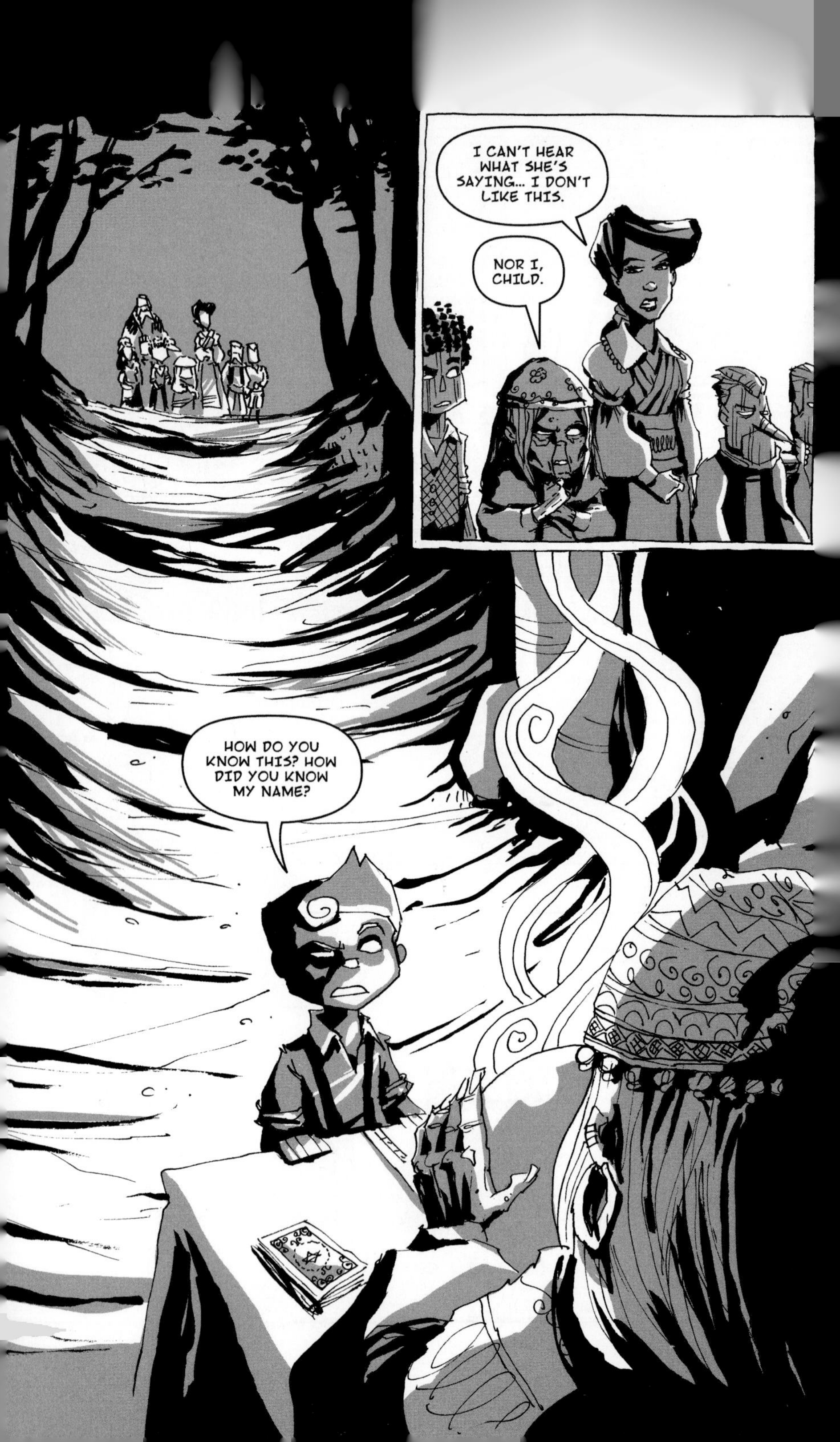
I CAN'T HEAR WHAT SHE'S SAYING... I DON'T LIKE THIS.
NOR I, CHILD.
HOW DO YOU KNOW THIS? HOW DID YOU KNOW MY NAME?

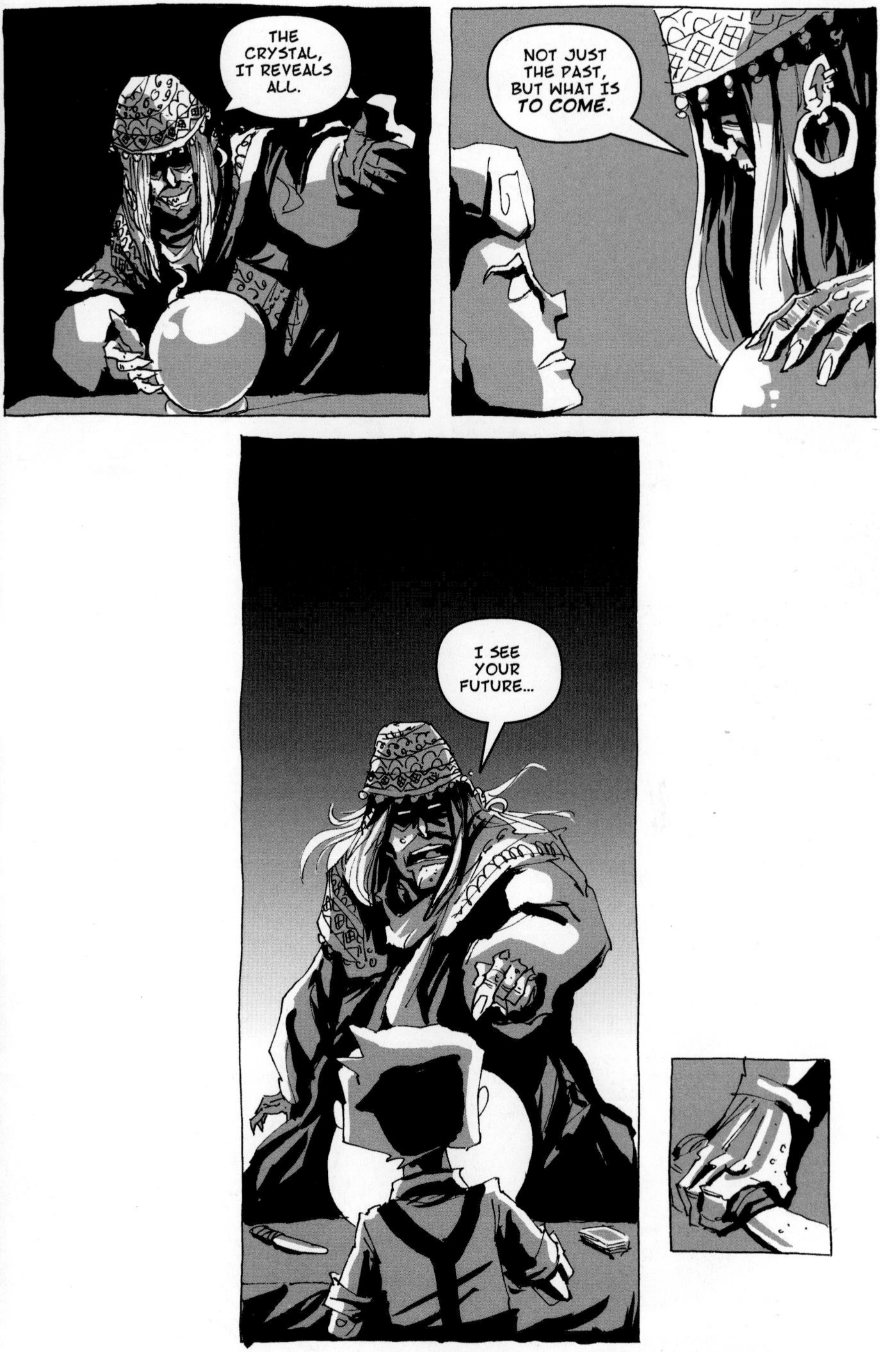
THE CRYSTAL, IT REVEALS ALL.
NOT JUST THE PAST, BUT WHAT IS *TO COME*.
I SEE YOUR FUTURE...

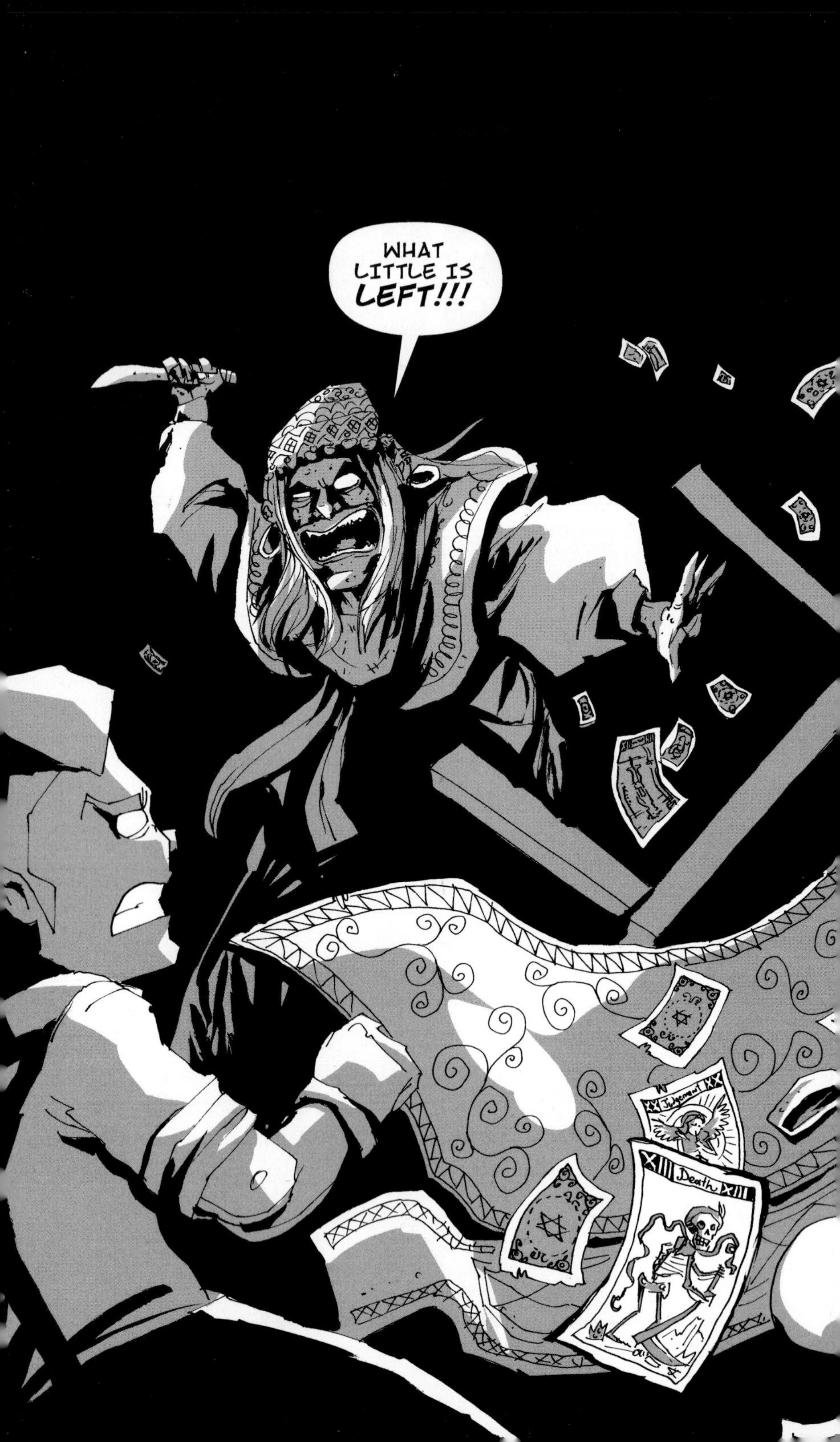
WHAT LITTLE IS LEFT!!!
Judgement
Death

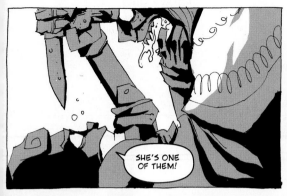

SHE'S ONE OF THEM!

I KNEW SHE WAS TROUBLE!

YOU'LL SAVE HIM, WON'T YOU, *CAPITANO?*

COME *ON*, IT'S ONE OLD HAG! THAT'S NOTHING!

LET'S SEE HIM SINGLE-HANDEDLY BEAT A WHOLE...

GANG...

OF...

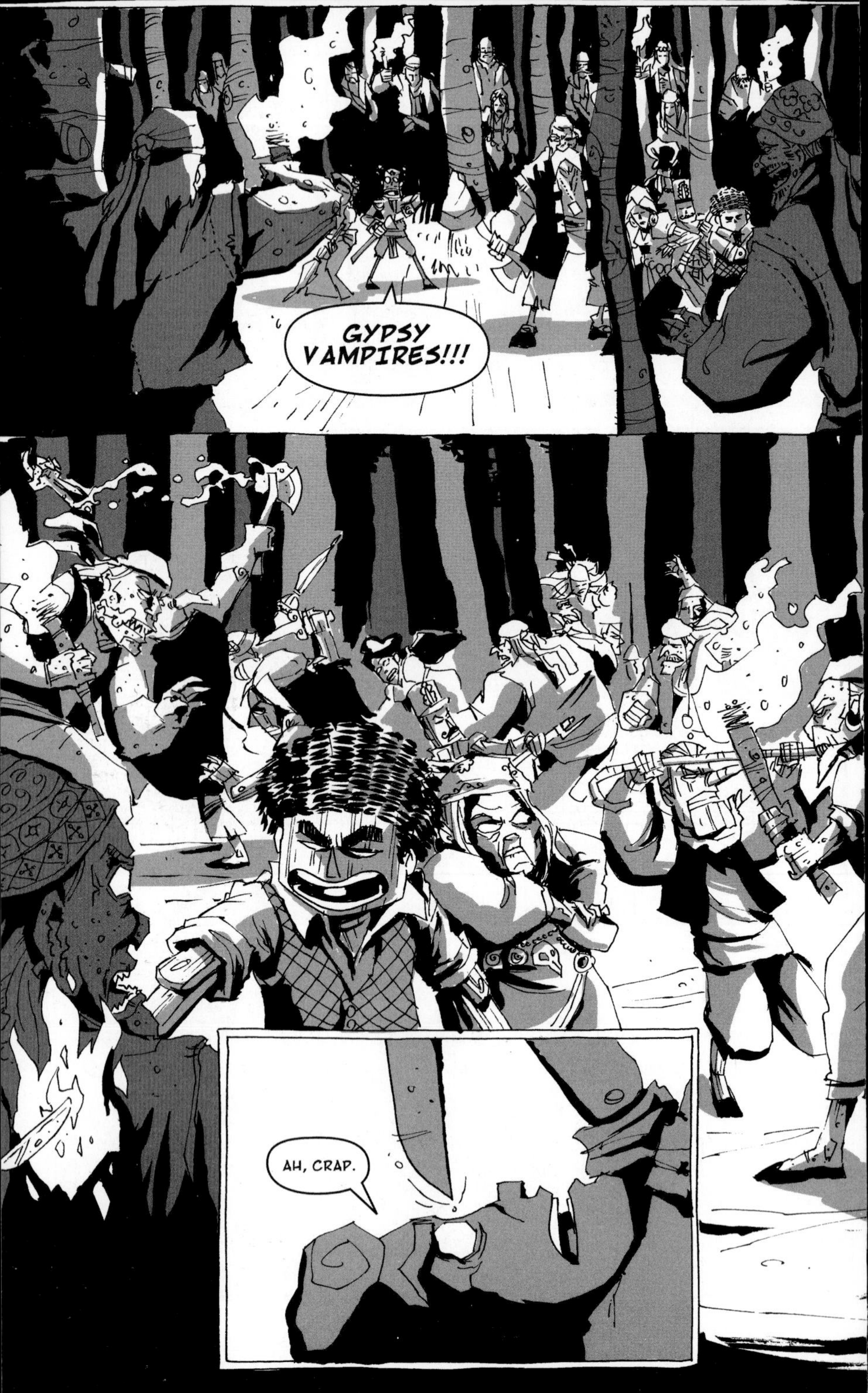
GYPSY VAMPIRES!!!
AH, CRAP.

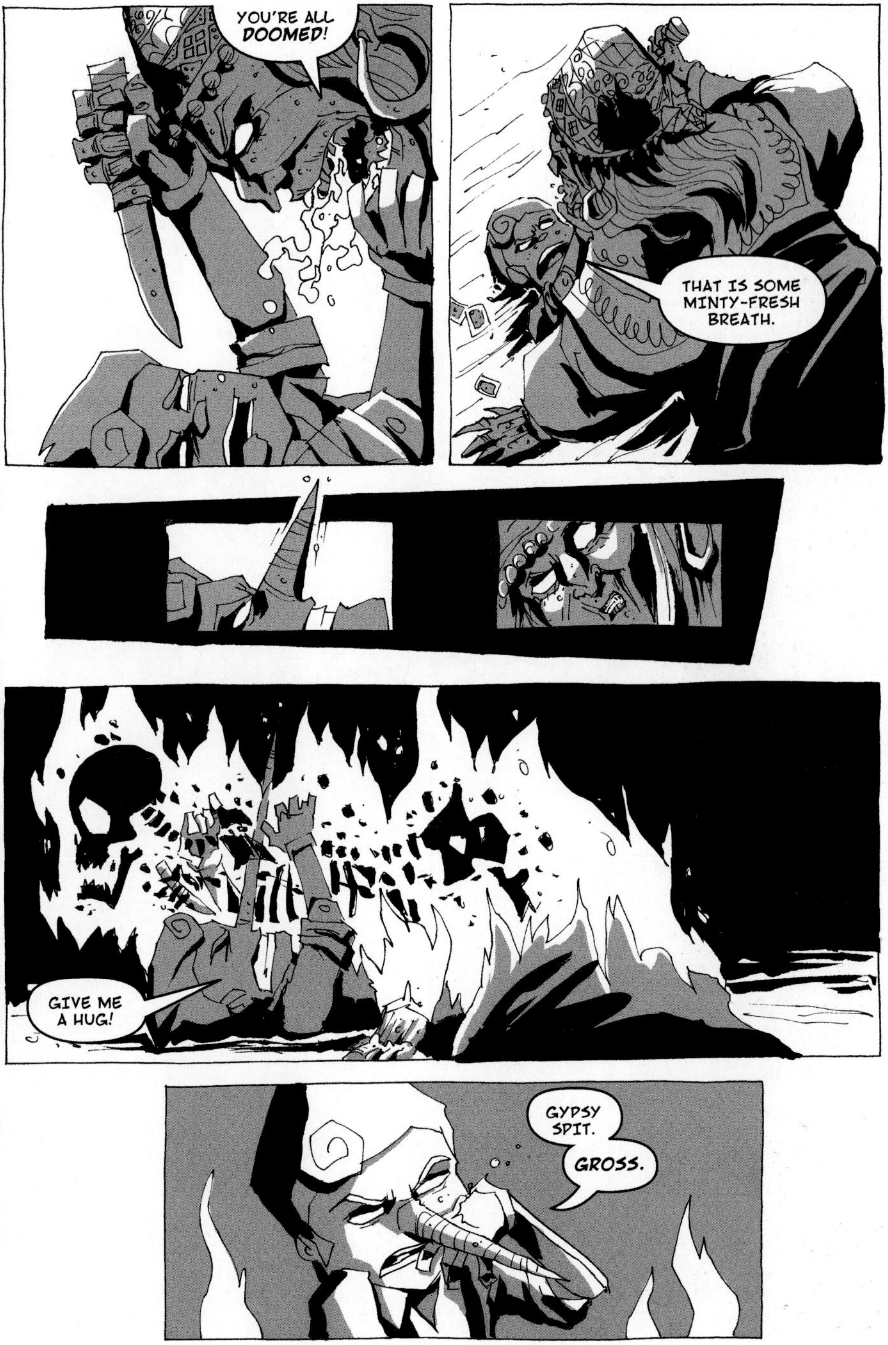
YOU'RE ALL DOOMED!
THAT IS SOME MINTY-FRESH BREATH.
GIVE ME A HUG!
GYPSY SPIT.
GROSS.

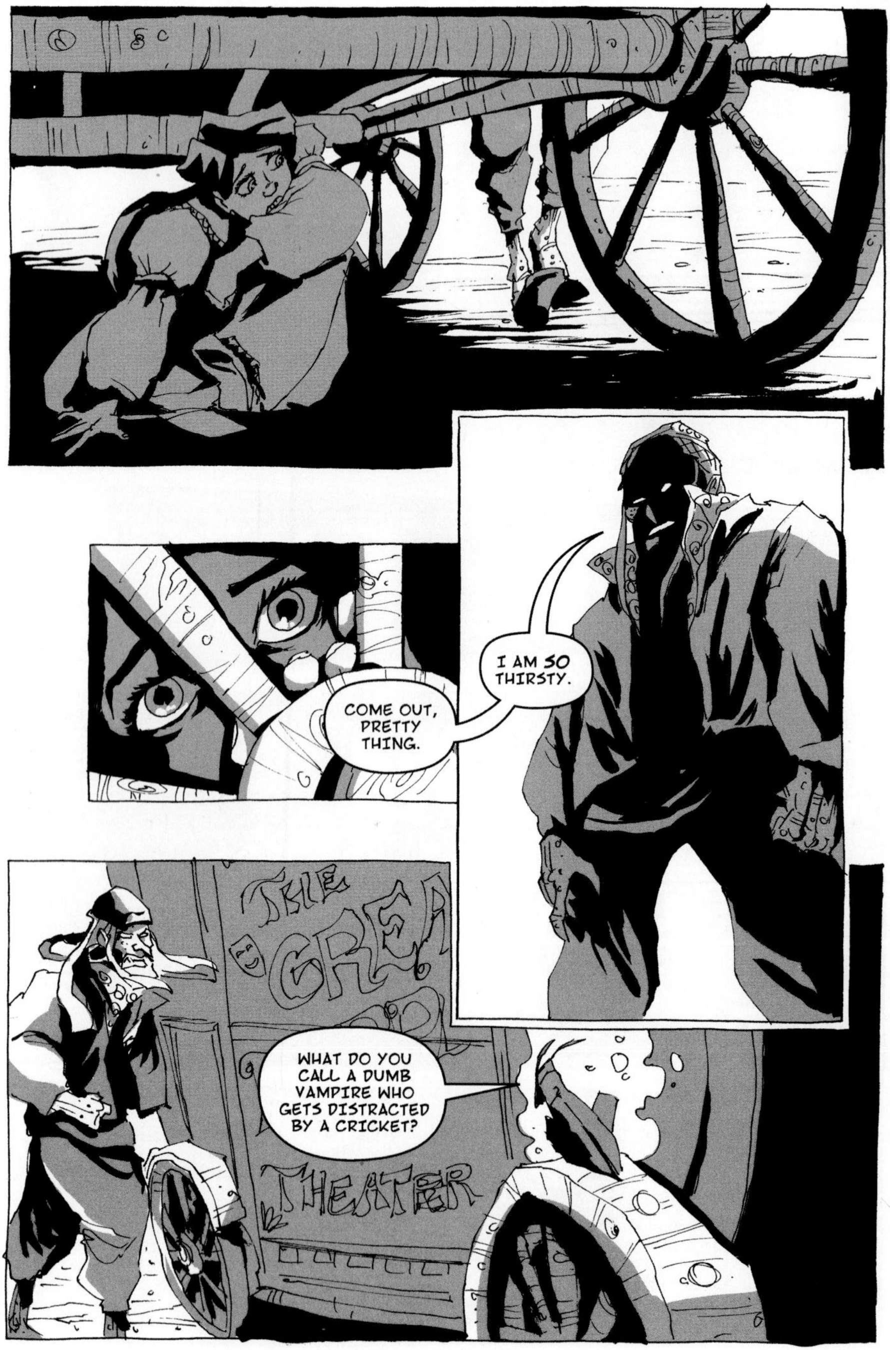
I AM SO THIRSTY.
COME OUT, PRETTY THING.
THE GREAT
THEATER
WHAT DO YOU CALL A DUMB VAMPIRE WHO GETS DISTRACTED BY A CRICKET?

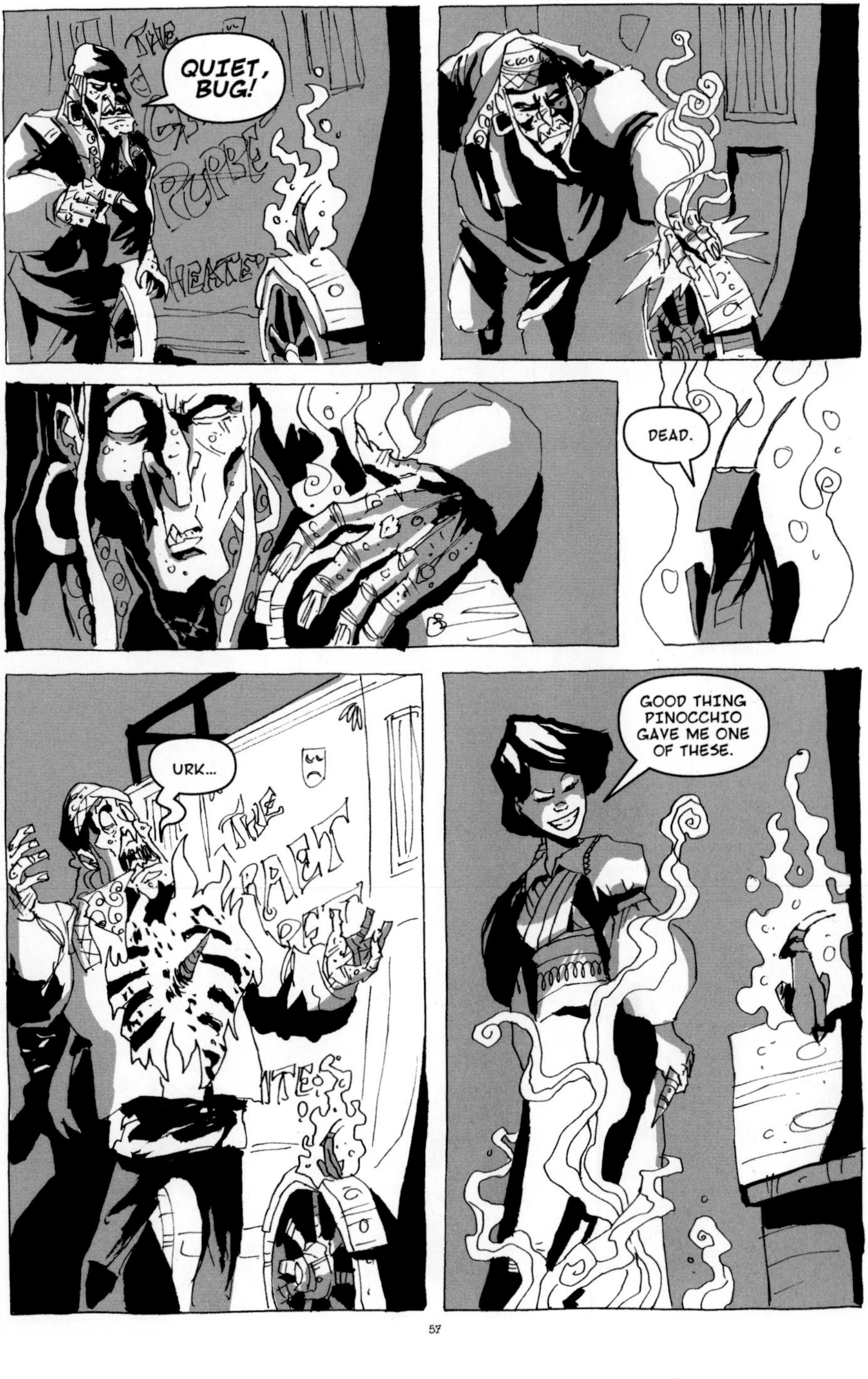
QUIET, BUG!
DEAD.
URK...
GOOD THING PINOCCHIO GAVE ME ONE OF THESE.

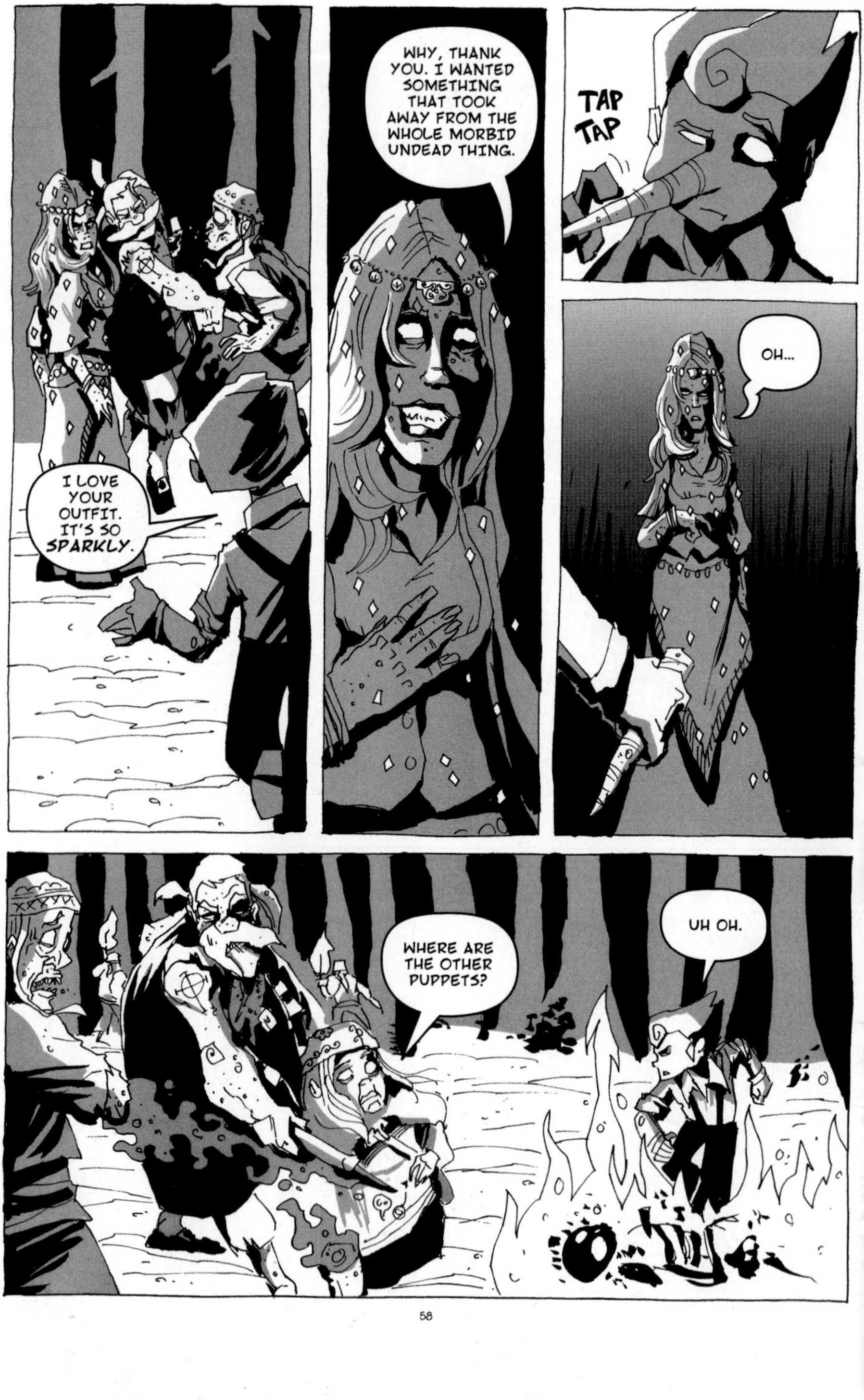
I LOVE YOUR OUTFIT. IT'S SO SPARKLY.
WHY, THANK YOU. I WANTED SOMETHING THAT TOOK AWAY FROM THE WHOLE MORBID UNDEAD THING.
TAP TAP
OH...
WHERE ARE THE OTHER PUPPETS?
UH OH.

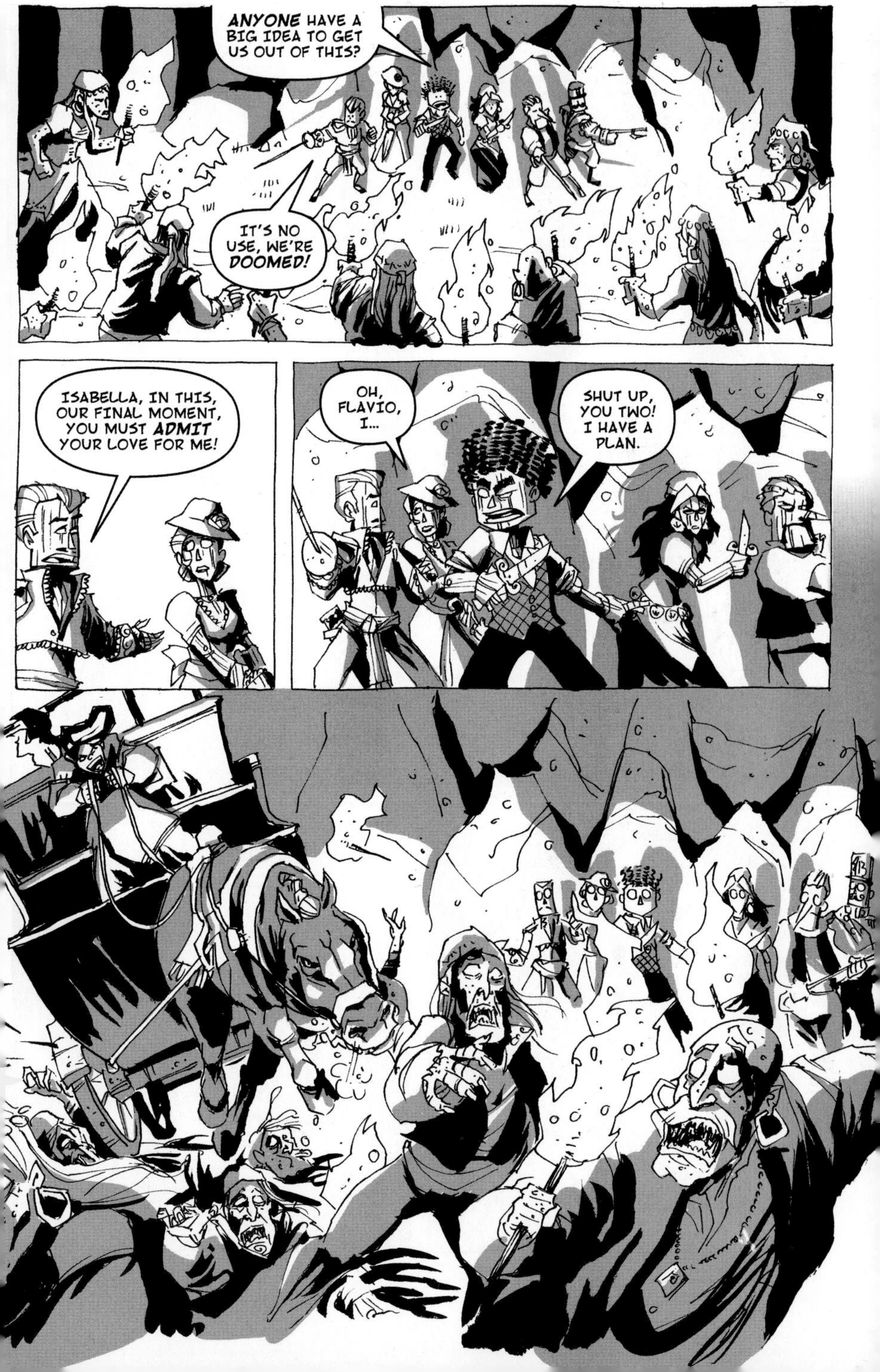
ANYONE HAVE A BIG IDEA TO GET US OUT OF THIS?
IT'S NO USE, WE'RE DOOMED!
ISABELLA, IN THIS, OUR FINAL MOMENT, YOU MUST ADMIT YOUR LOVE FOR ME!
OH, FLAVIO, I...
SHUT UP, YOU TWO! I HAVE A PLAN.

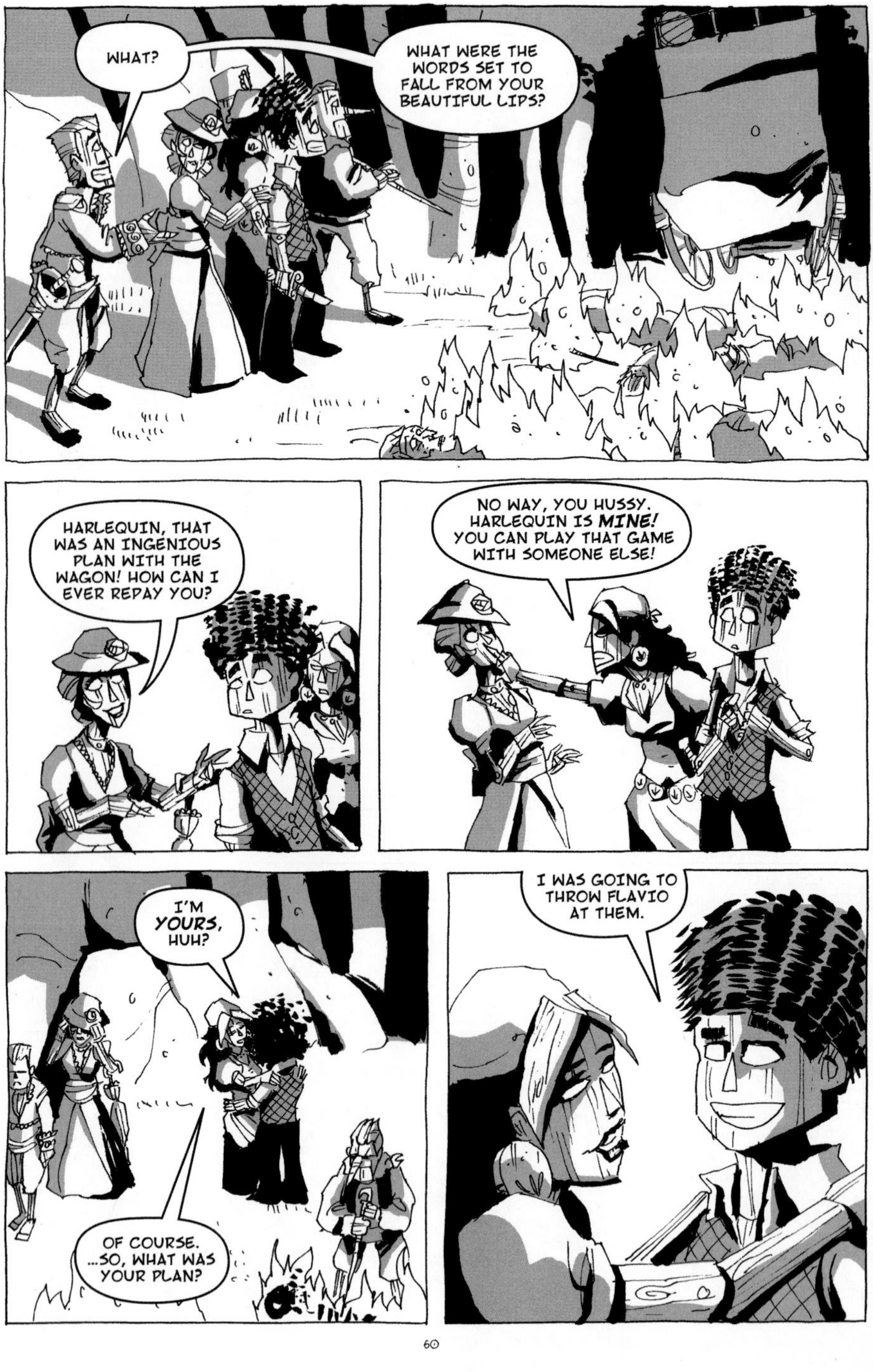
WHAT?
WHAT WERE THE WORDS SET TO FALL FROM YOUR BEAUTIFUL LIPS?
HARLEQUIN, THAT WAS AN INGENIOUS PLAN WITH THE WAGON! HOW CAN I EVER REPAY YOU?
NO WAY, YOU HUSSY. HARLEQUIN IS *MINE!* YOU CAN PLAY THAT GAME WITH SOMEONE ELSE!
I'M *YOURS,* HUH?
OF COURSE. ...SO, WHAT WAS YOUR PLAN?
I WAS GOING TO THROW FLAVIO AT THEM.

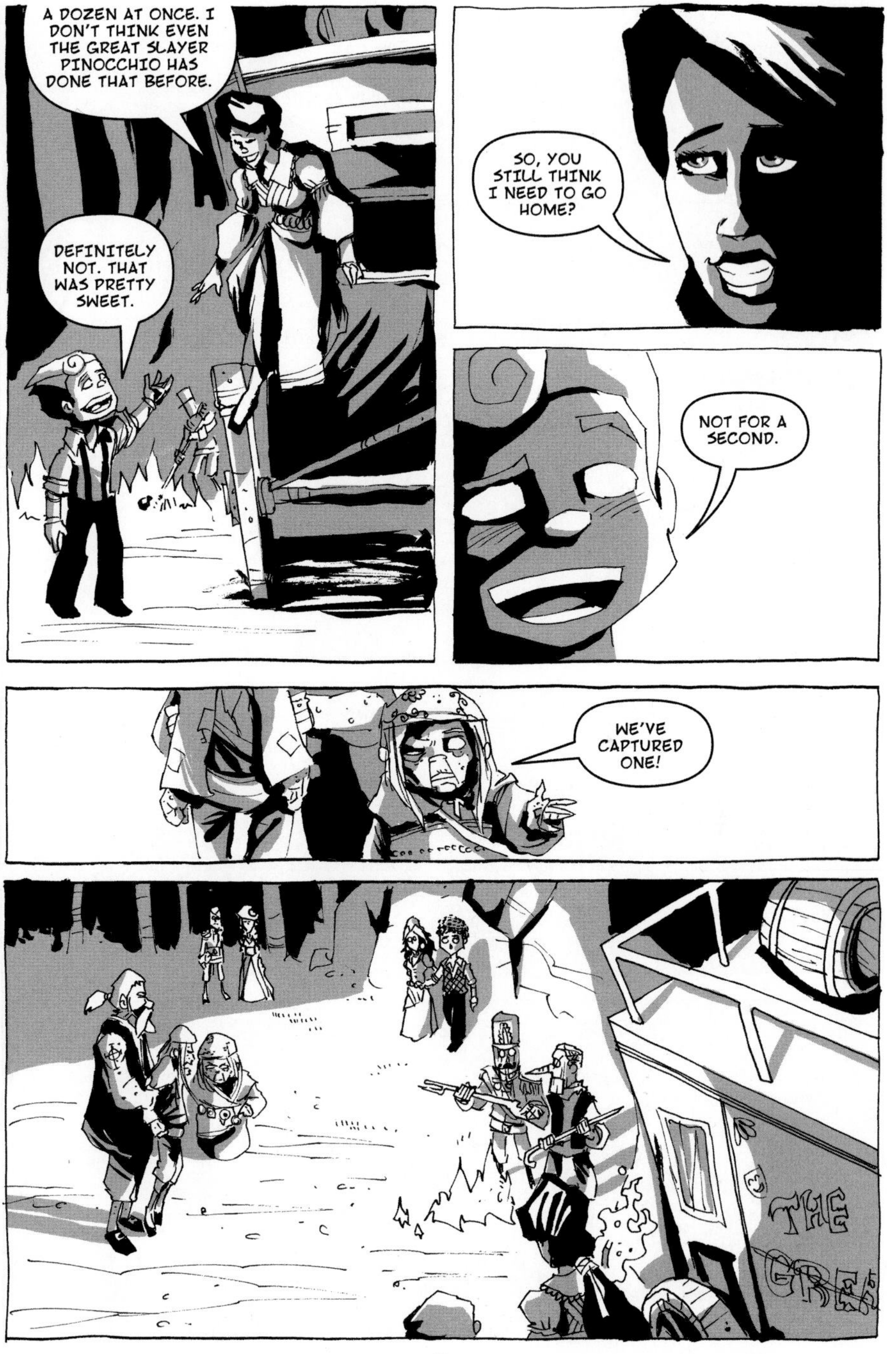
A DOZEN AT ONCE. I DON'T THINK EVEN THE GREAT SLAYER PINOCCHIO HAS DONE THAT BEFORE.
DEFINITELY NOT. THAT WAS PRETTY SWEET.
SO, YOU STILL THINK I NEED TO GO HOME?
NOT FOR A SECOND.
WE'VE CAPTURED ONE!
THE

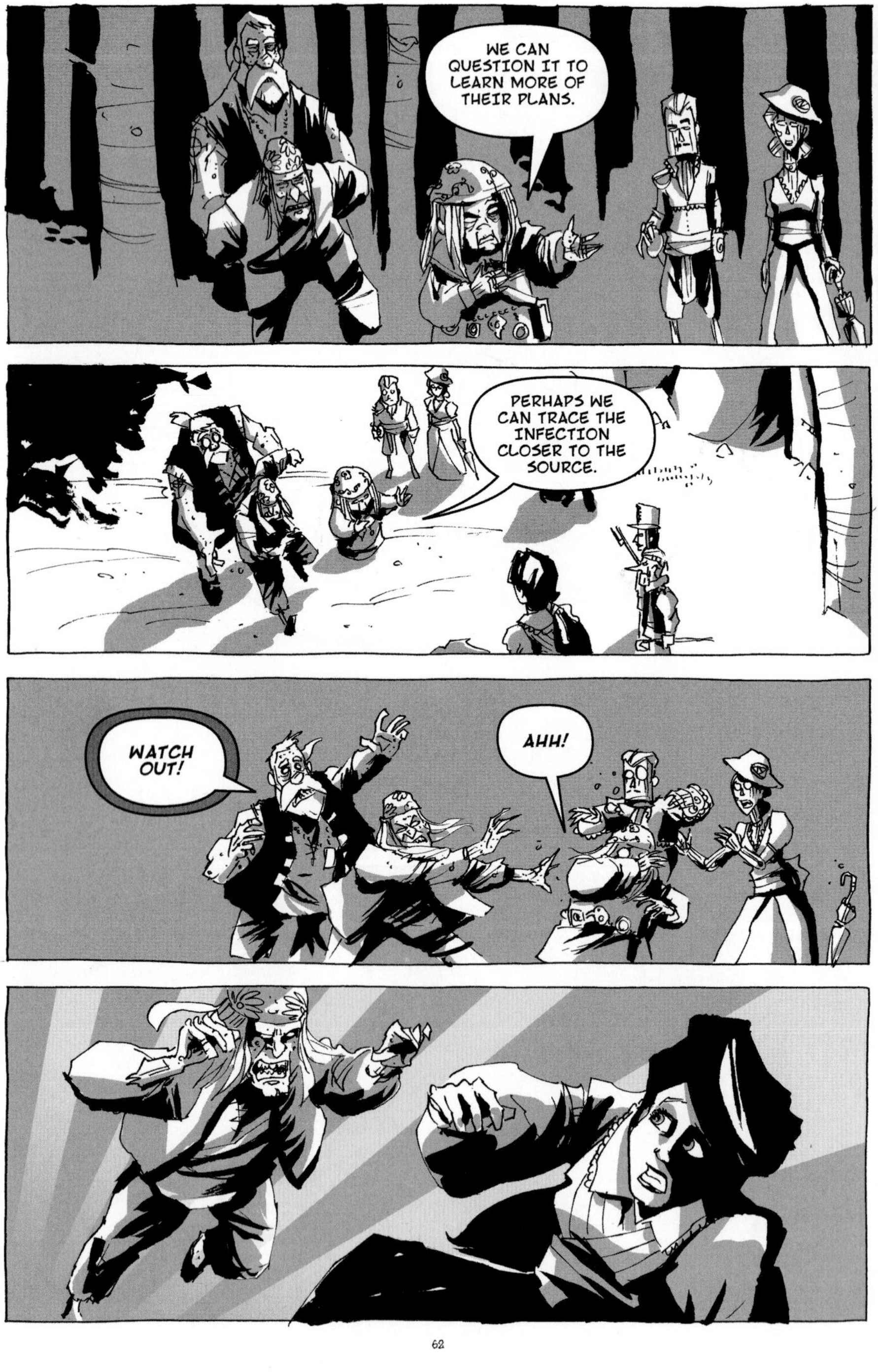
WE CAN QUESTION IT TO LEARN MORE OF THEIR PLANS.
PERHAPS WE CAN TRACE THE INFECTION CLOSER TO THE SOURCE.
WATCH OUT!
AHH!

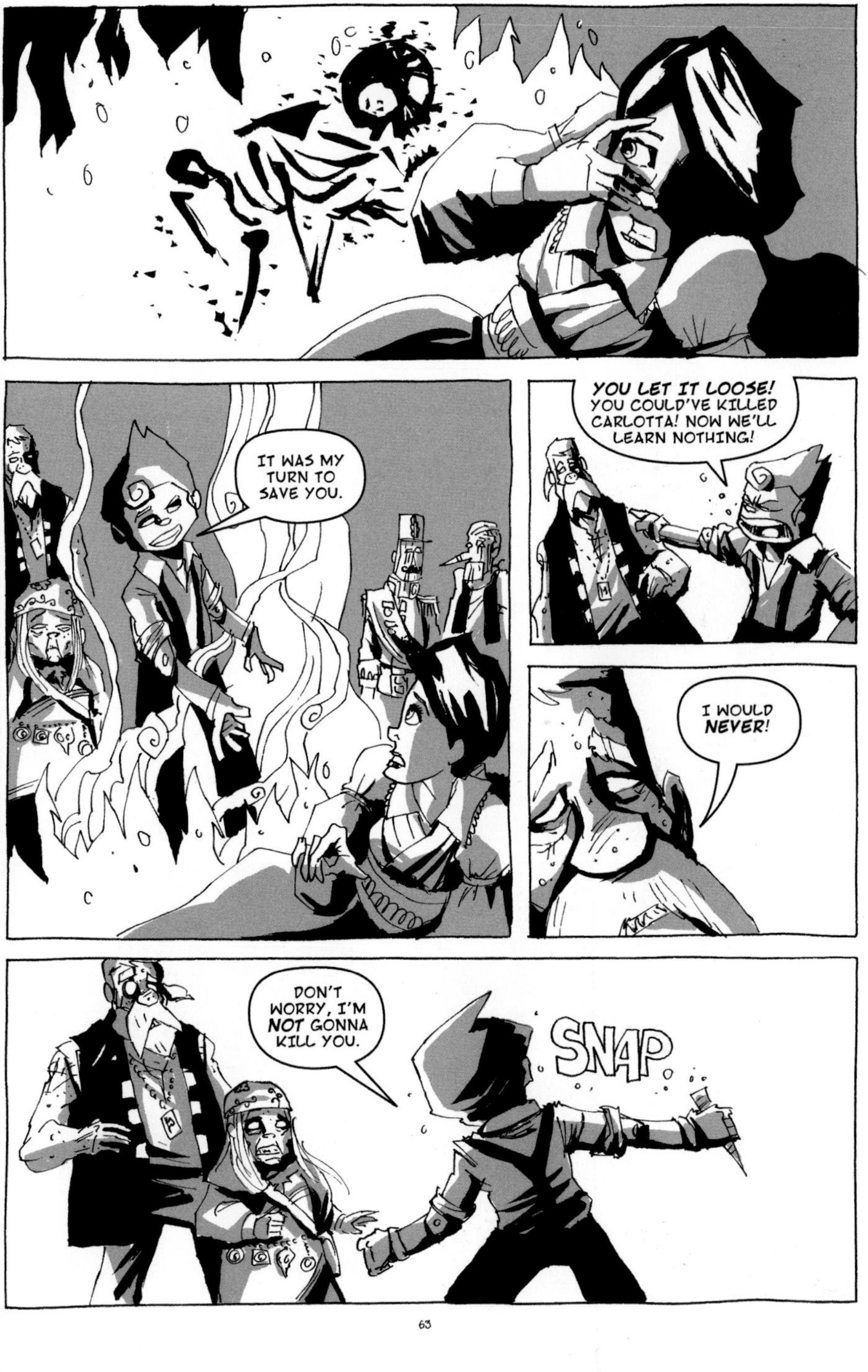
IT WAS MY TURN TO SAVE YOU.
YOU LET IT LOOSE! YOU COULD'VE KILLED CARLOTTA! NOW WE'LL LEARN NOTHING!
I WOULD NEVER!
DON'T WORRY, I'M NOT GONNA KILL YOU.
SNAP

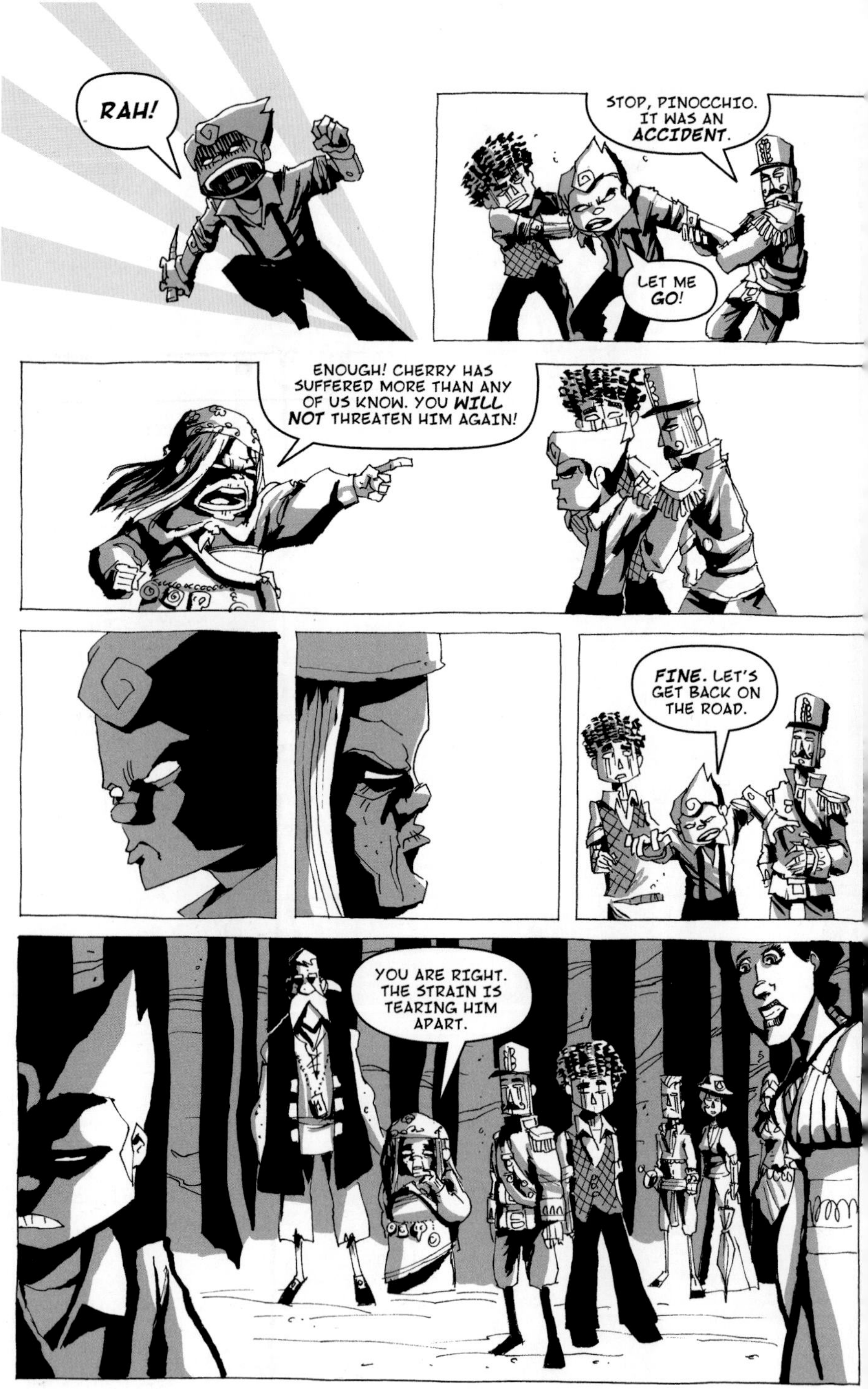
RAH!
STOP, PINOCCHIO. IT WAS AN ACCIDENT.
LET ME GO!
ENOUGH! CHERRY HAS SUFFERED MORE THAN ANY OF US KNOW. YOU WILL NOT THREATEN HIM AGAIN!
FINE. LET'S GET BACK ON THE ROAD.
YOU ARE RIGHT. THE STRAIN IS TEARING HIM APART.

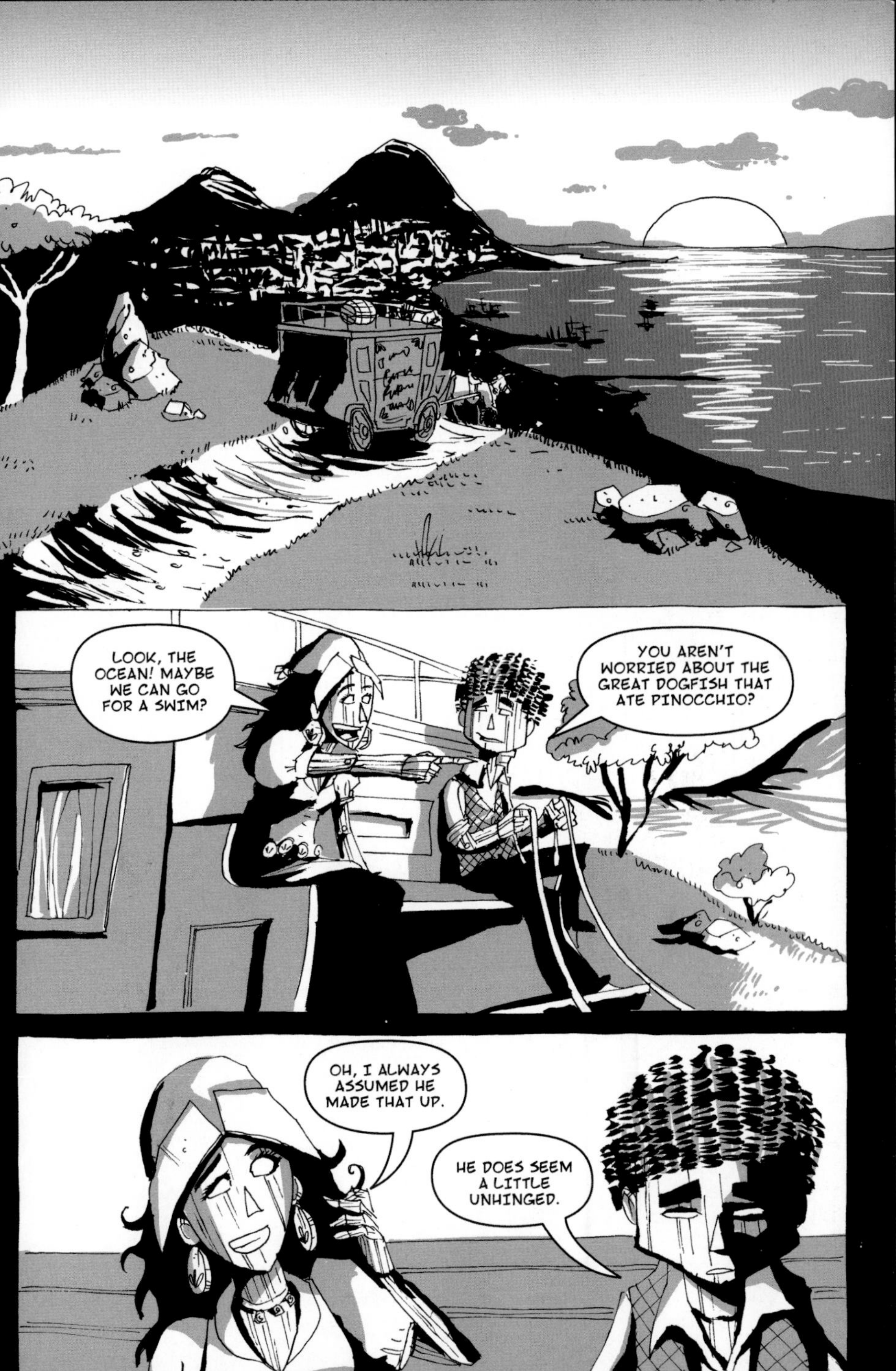
LOOK, THE OCEAN! MAYBE WE CAN GO FOR A SWIM?
YOU AREN'T WORRIED ABOUT THE GREAT DOGFISH THAT ATE PINOCCHIO?
OH, I ALWAYS ASSUMED HE MADE THAT UP.
HE DOES SEEM A LITTLE UNHINGED.

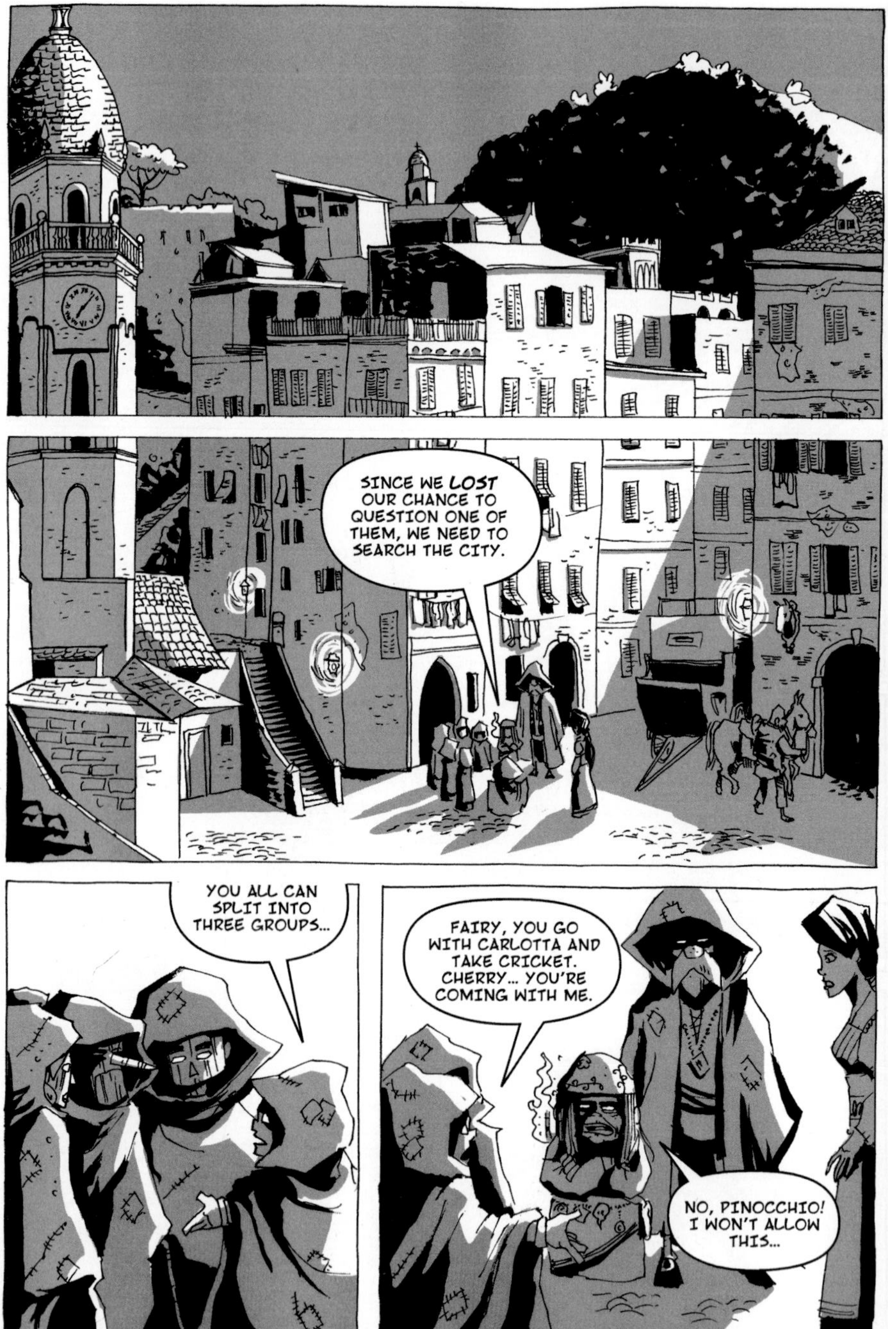
SINCE WE LOST OUR CHANCE TO QUESTION ONE OF THEM, WE NEED TO SEARCH THE CITY.
YOU ALL CAN SPLIT INTO THREE GROUPS...
FAIRY, YOU GO WITH CARLOTTA AND TAKE CRICKET. CHERRY... YOU'RE COMING WITH ME.
NO, PINOCCHIO! I WON'T ALLOW THIS...

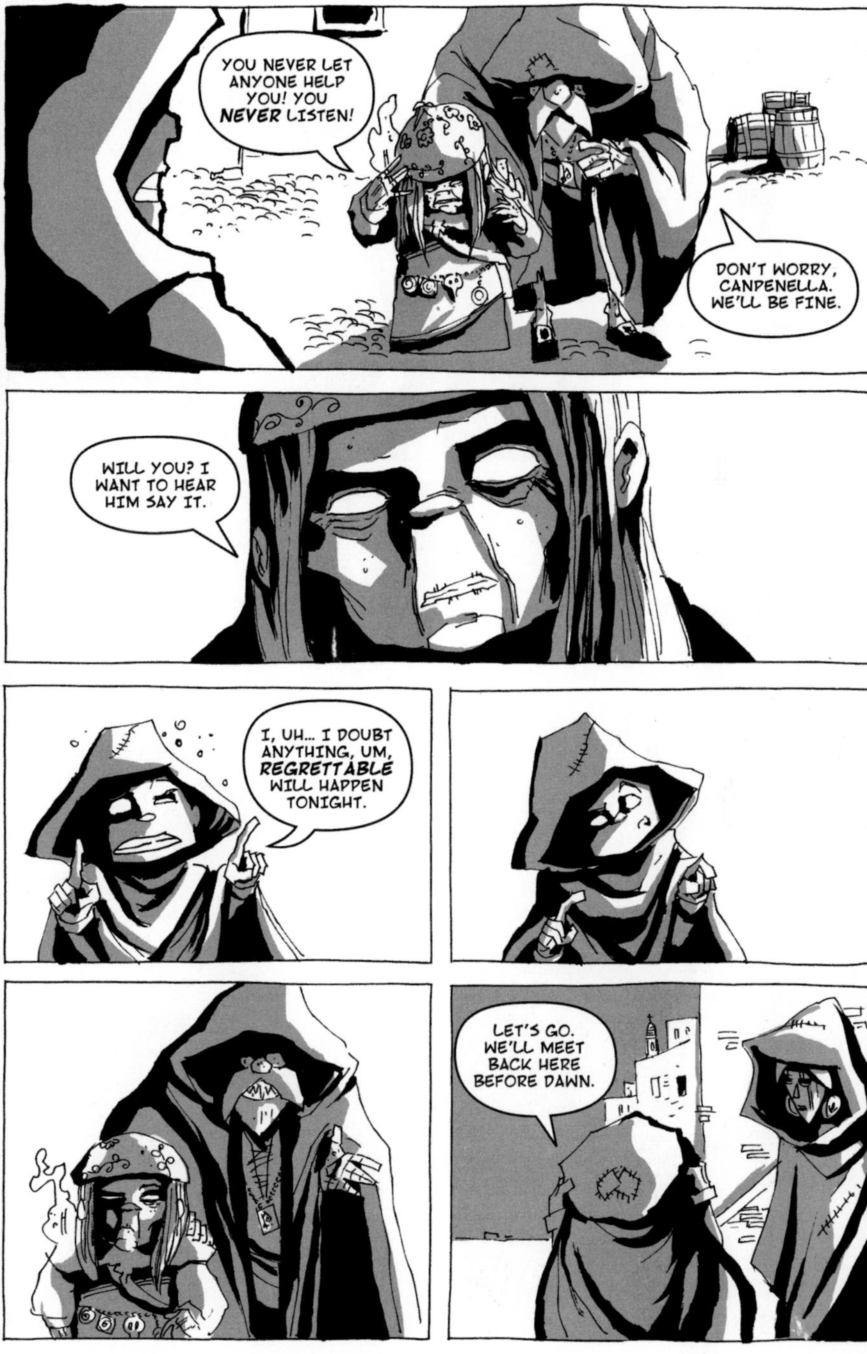
YOU NEVER LET ANYONE HELP YOU! YOU NEVER LISTEN!
DON'T WORRY, CANDENELLA. WE'LL BE FINE.
WILL YOU? I WANT TO HEAR HIM SAY IT.
I, UH... I DOUBT ANYTHING, UM, REGRETTABLE WILL HAPPEN TONIGHT.
LET'S GO. WE'LL MEET BACK HERE BEFORE DAWN.

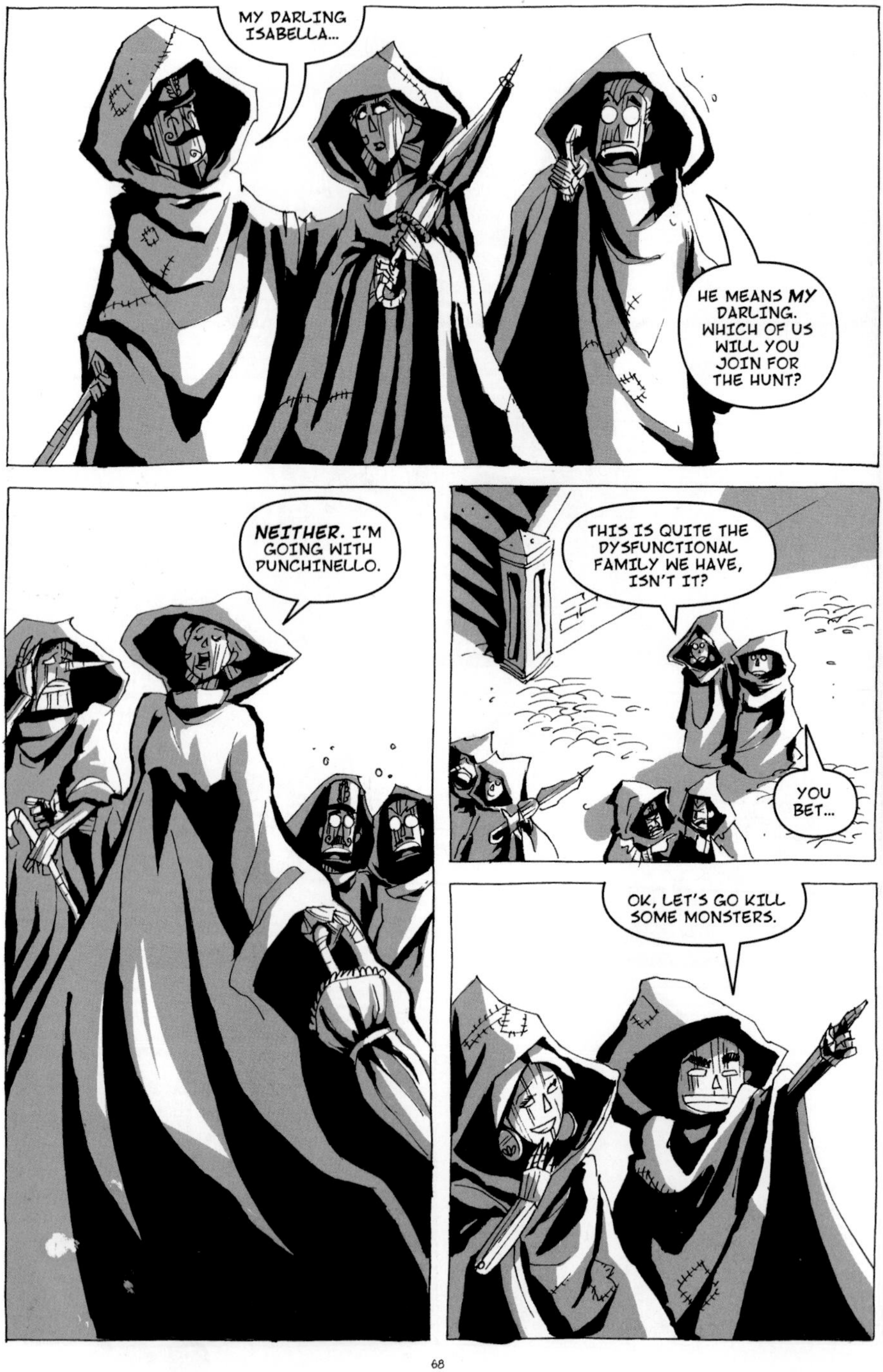
MY DARLING ISABELLA...
HE MEANS **MY** DARLING. WHICH OF US WILL YOU JOIN FOR THE HUNT?
NEITHER. I'M GOING WITH PUNCHINELLO.
THIS IS QUITE THE DYSFUNCTIONAL FAMILY WE HAVE, ISN'T IT?
YOU BET...
OK, LET'S GO KILL SOME MONSTERS.

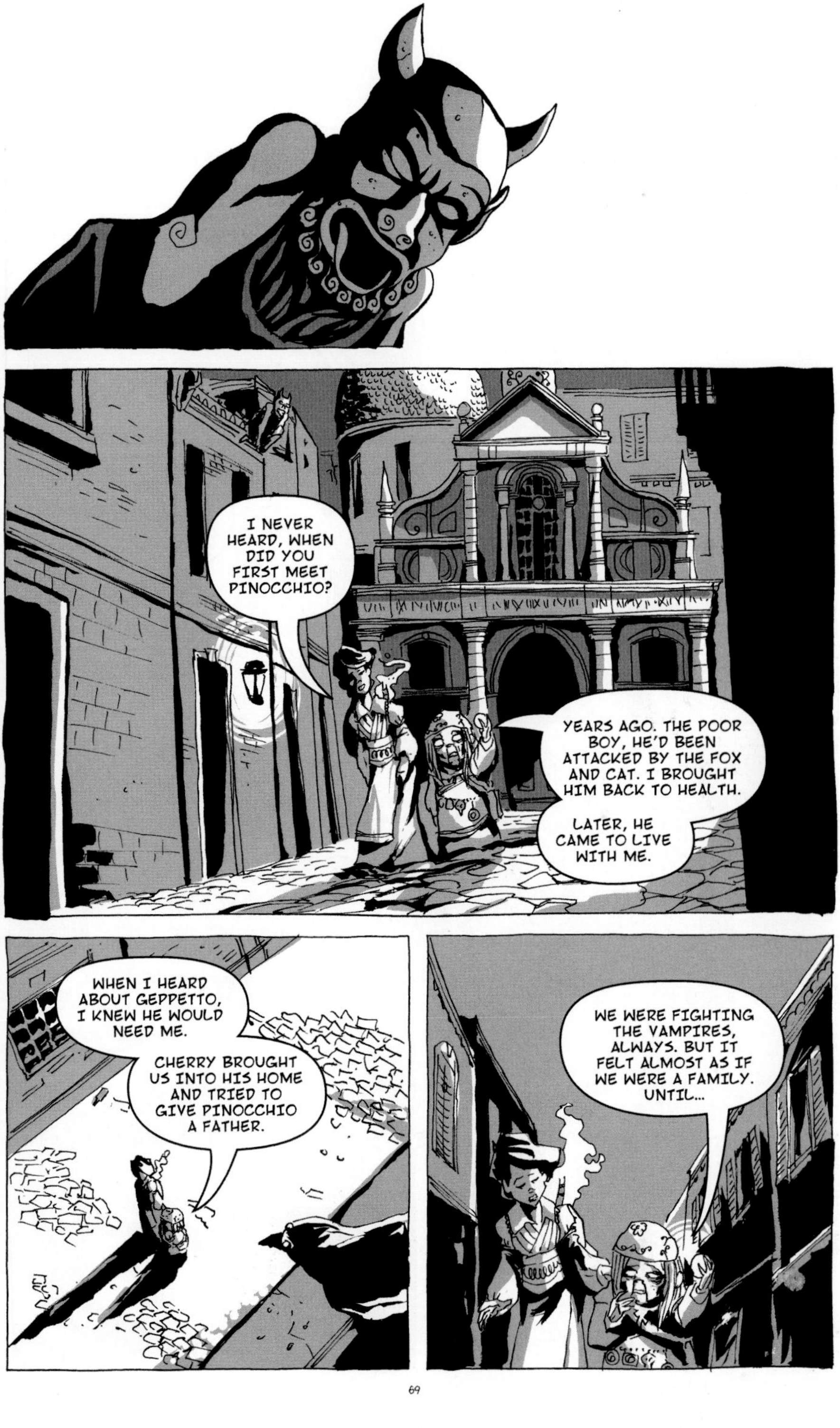
I NEVER HEARD, WHEN DID YOU FIRST MEET PINOCCHIO?
YEARS AGO. THE POOR BOY, HE'D BEEN ATTACKED BY THE FOX AND CAT. I BROUGHT HIM BACK TO HEALTH.
LATER, HE CAME TO LIVE WITH ME.
WHEN I HEARD ABOUT GEPPETTO, I KNEW HE WOULD NEED ME.
CHERRY BROUGHT US INTO HIS HOME AND TRIED TO GIVE PINOCCHIO A FATHER.
WE WERE FIGHTING THE VAMPIRES, ALWAYS. BUT IT FELT ALMOST AS IF WE WERE A FAMILY. UNTIL...

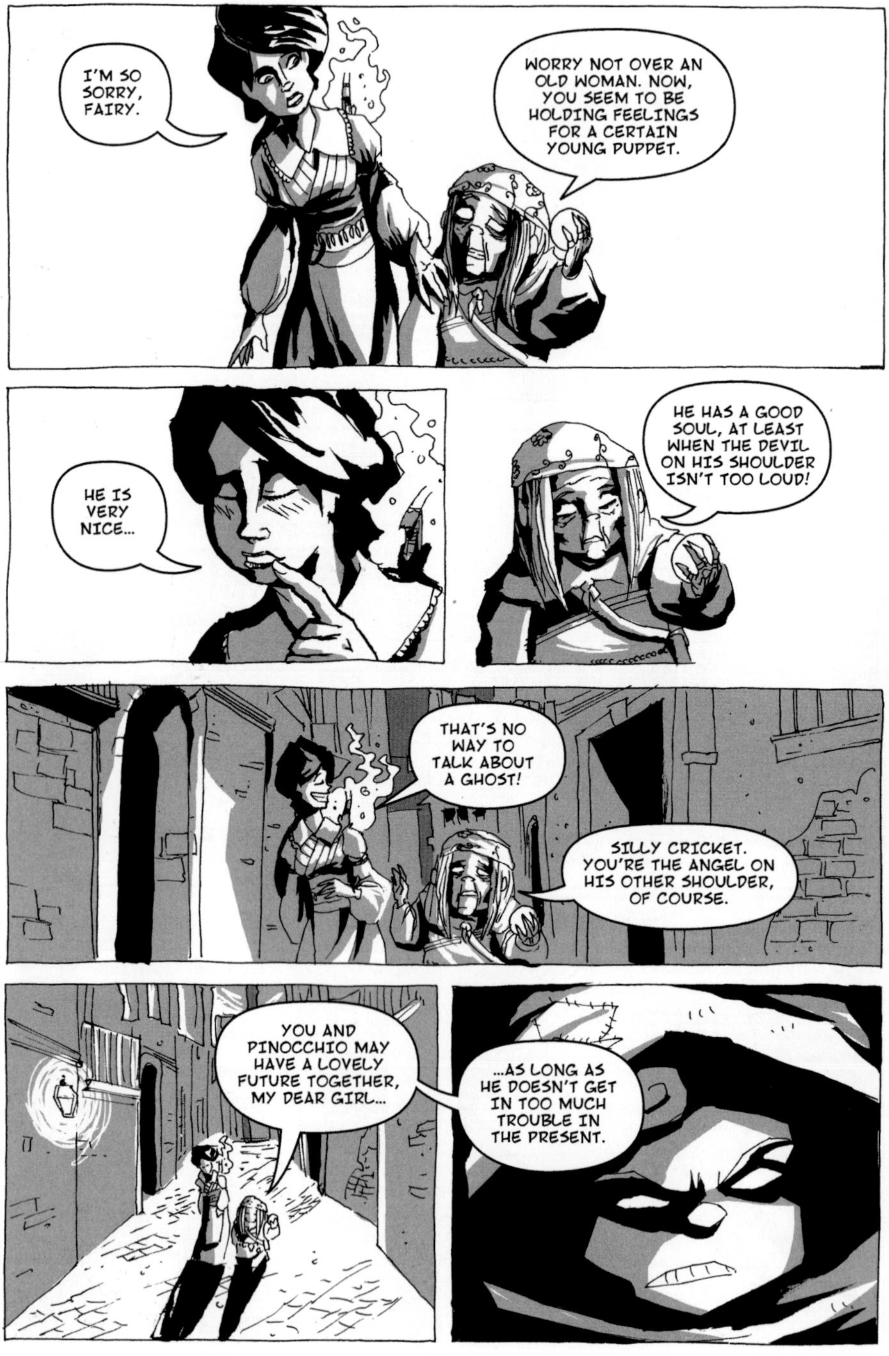
I'M SO SORRY, FAIRY.
WORRY NOT OVER AN OLD WOMAN. NOW, YOU SEEM TO BE HOLDING FEELINGS FOR A CERTAIN YOUNG PUPPET.
HE IS VERY NICE...
HE HAS A GOOD SOUL, AT LEAST WHEN THE DEVIL ON HIS SHOULDER ISN'T TOO LOUD!
THAT'S NO WAY TO TALK ABOUT A GHOST!
SILLY CRICKET. YOU'RE THE ANGEL ON HIS OTHER SHOULDER, OF COURSE.
YOU AND PINOCCHIO MAY HAVE A LOVELY FUTURE TOGETHER, MY DEAR GIRL...
...AS LONG AS HE DOESN'T GET IN TOO MUCH TROUBLE IN THE PRESENT.

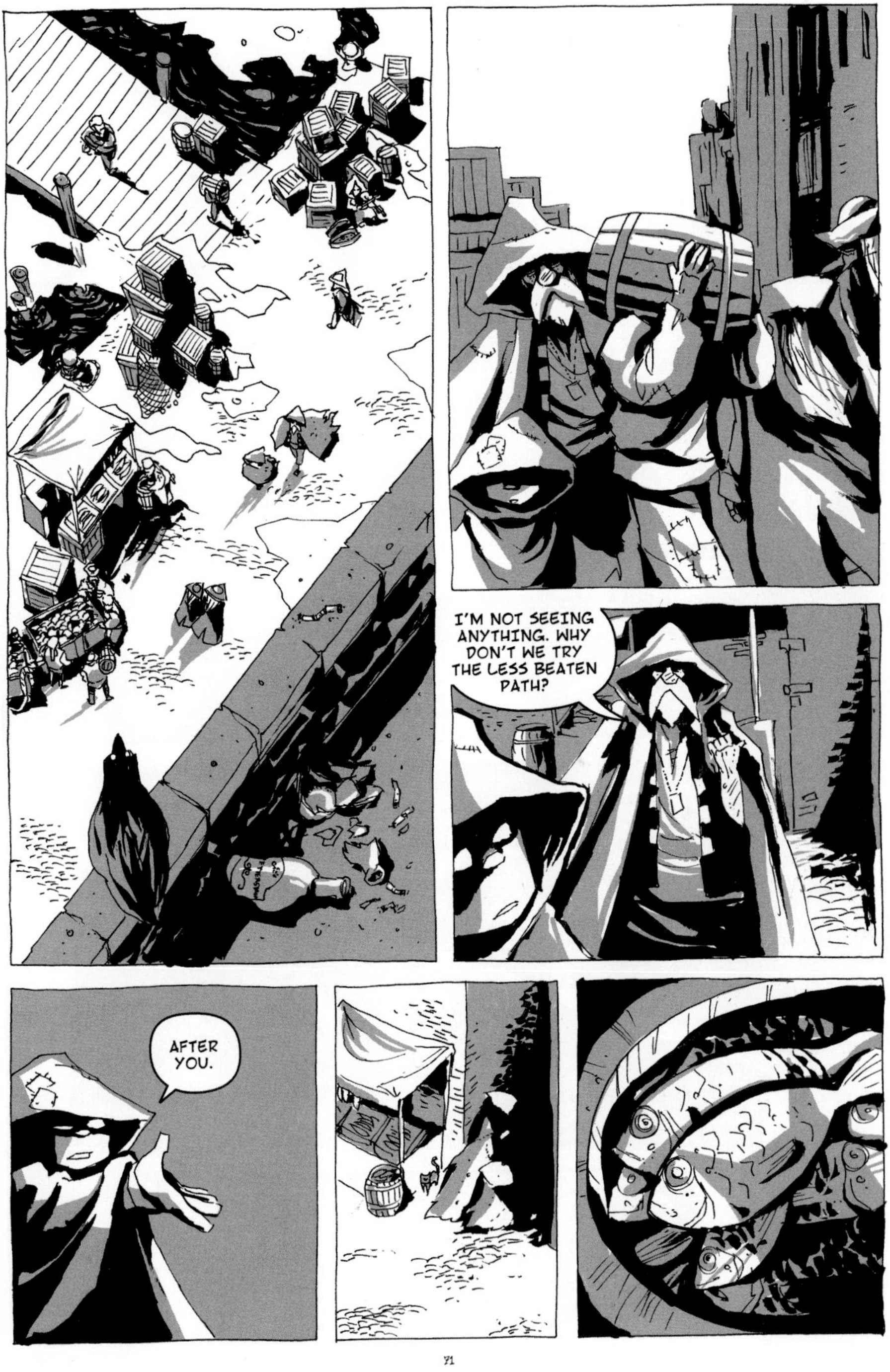
I'M NOT SEEING ANYTHING. WHY DON'T WE TRY THE LESS BEATEN PATH?
AFTER YOU.

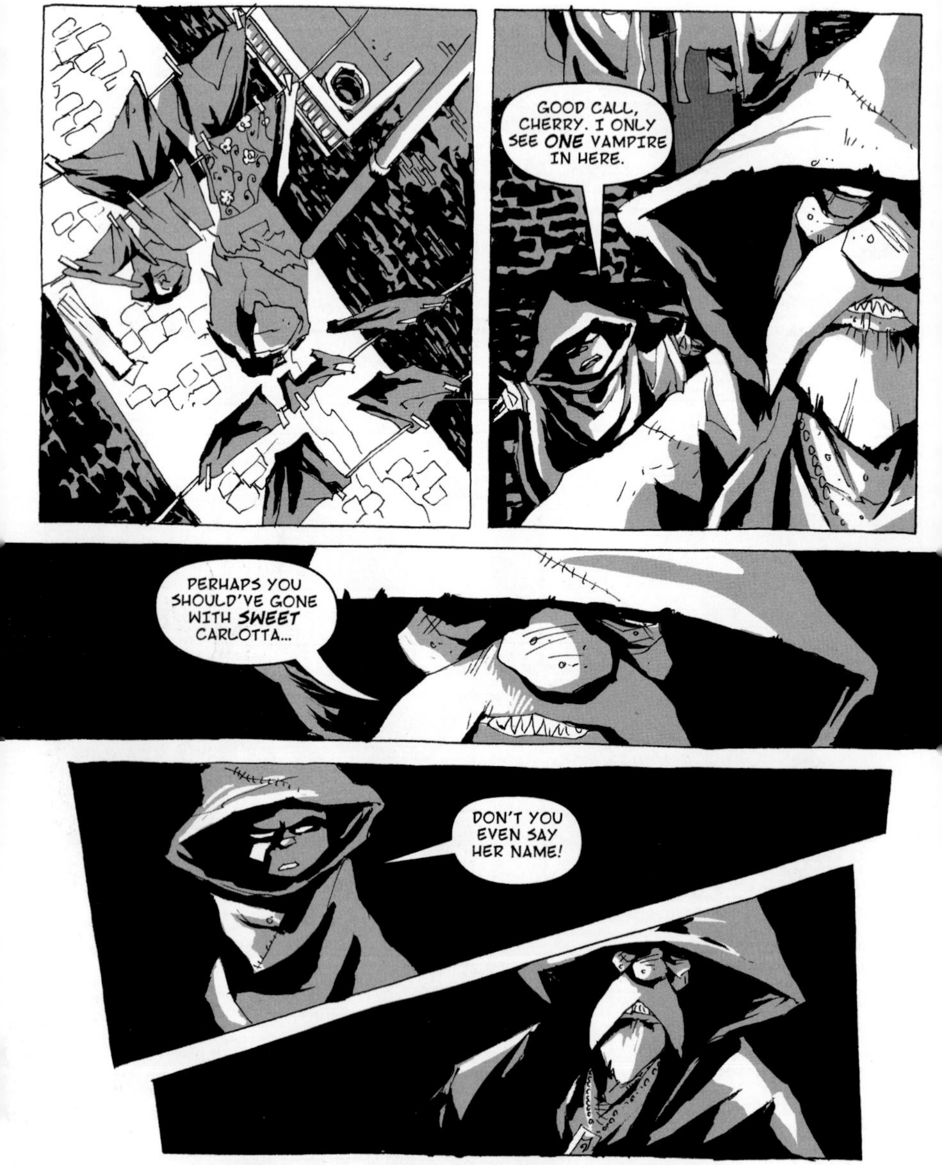
GOOD CALL, CHERRY. I ONLY SEE ONE VAMPIRE IN HERE.
PERHAPS YOU SHOULD'VE GONE WITH SWEET CARLOTTA...
DON'T YOU EVEN SAY HER NAME!
CARLOTTA...

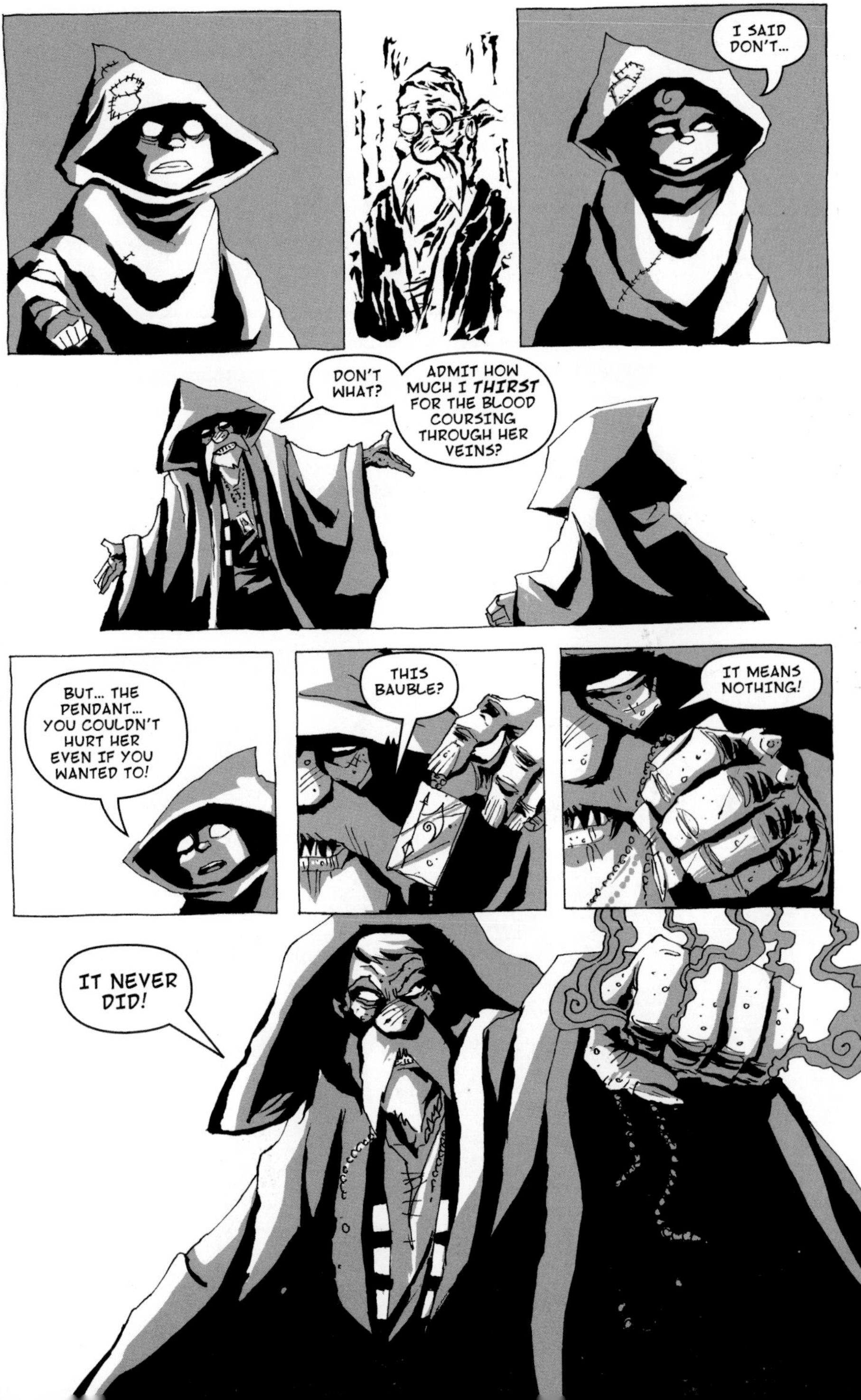
I SAID DON'T...
DON'T WHAT?
ADMIT HOW MUCH I THIRST FOR THE BLOOD COURSING THROUGH HER VEINS?
BUT... THE PENDANT... YOU COULDN'T HURT HER EVEN IF YOU WANTED TO!
THIS BAUBLE?
IT MEANS NOTHING!
IT NEVER DID!

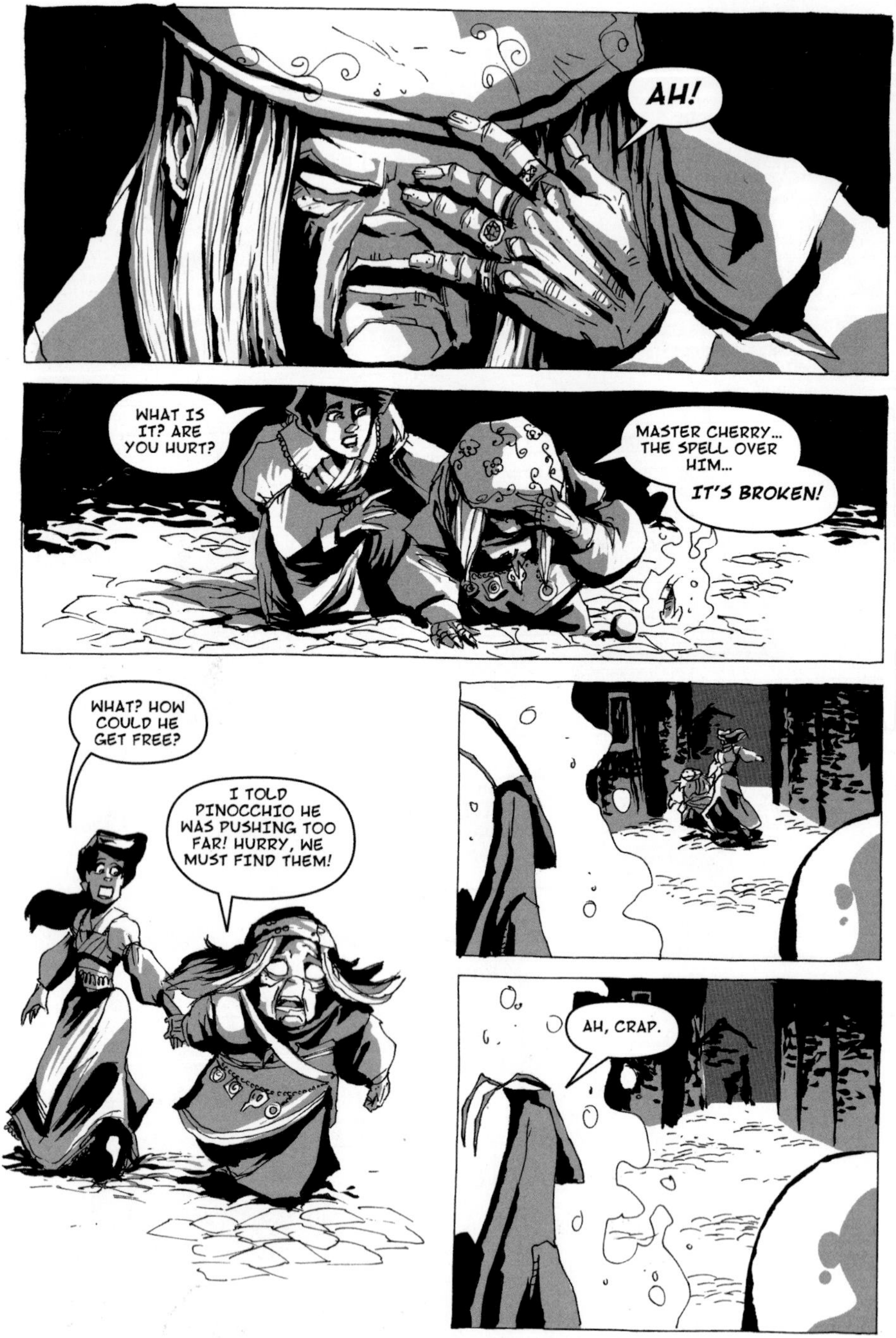
AH!
WHAT IS IT? ARE YOU HURT?
MASTER CHERRY... THE SPELL OVER HIM...
IT'S BROKEN!
WHAT? HOW COULD HE GET FREE?
I TOLD PINOCCHIO HE WAS PUSHING TOO FAR! HURRY, WE MUST FIND THEM!
AH, CRAP.

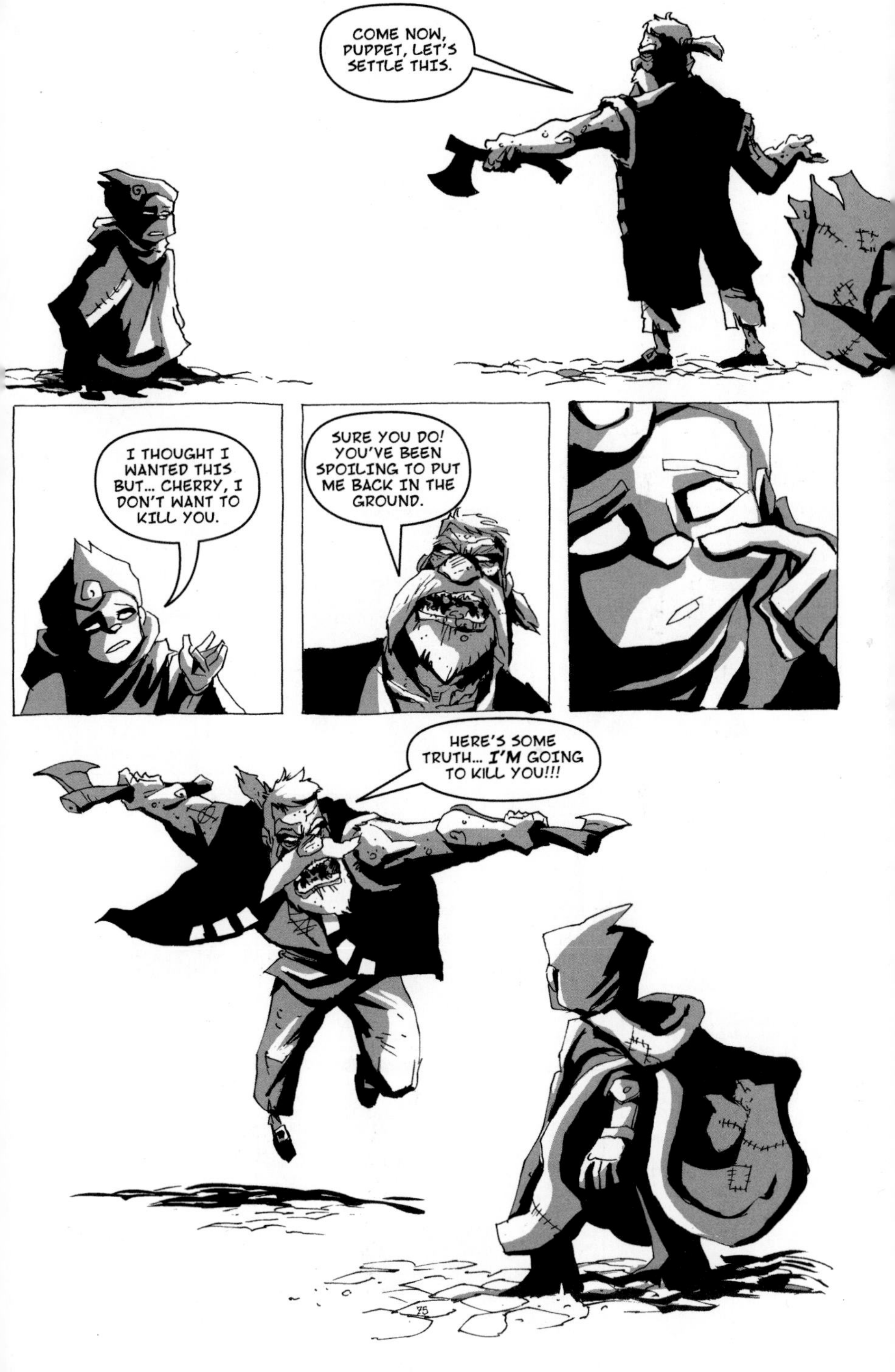
COME NOW, PUPPET, LET'S SETTLE THIS.
I THOUGHT I WANTED THIS BUT... CHERRY, I DON'T WANT TO KILL YOU.
SURE YOU DO! YOU'VE BEEN SPOILING TO PUT ME BACK IN THE GROUND.
HERE'S SOME TRUTH... I'M GOING TO KILL YOU!!!

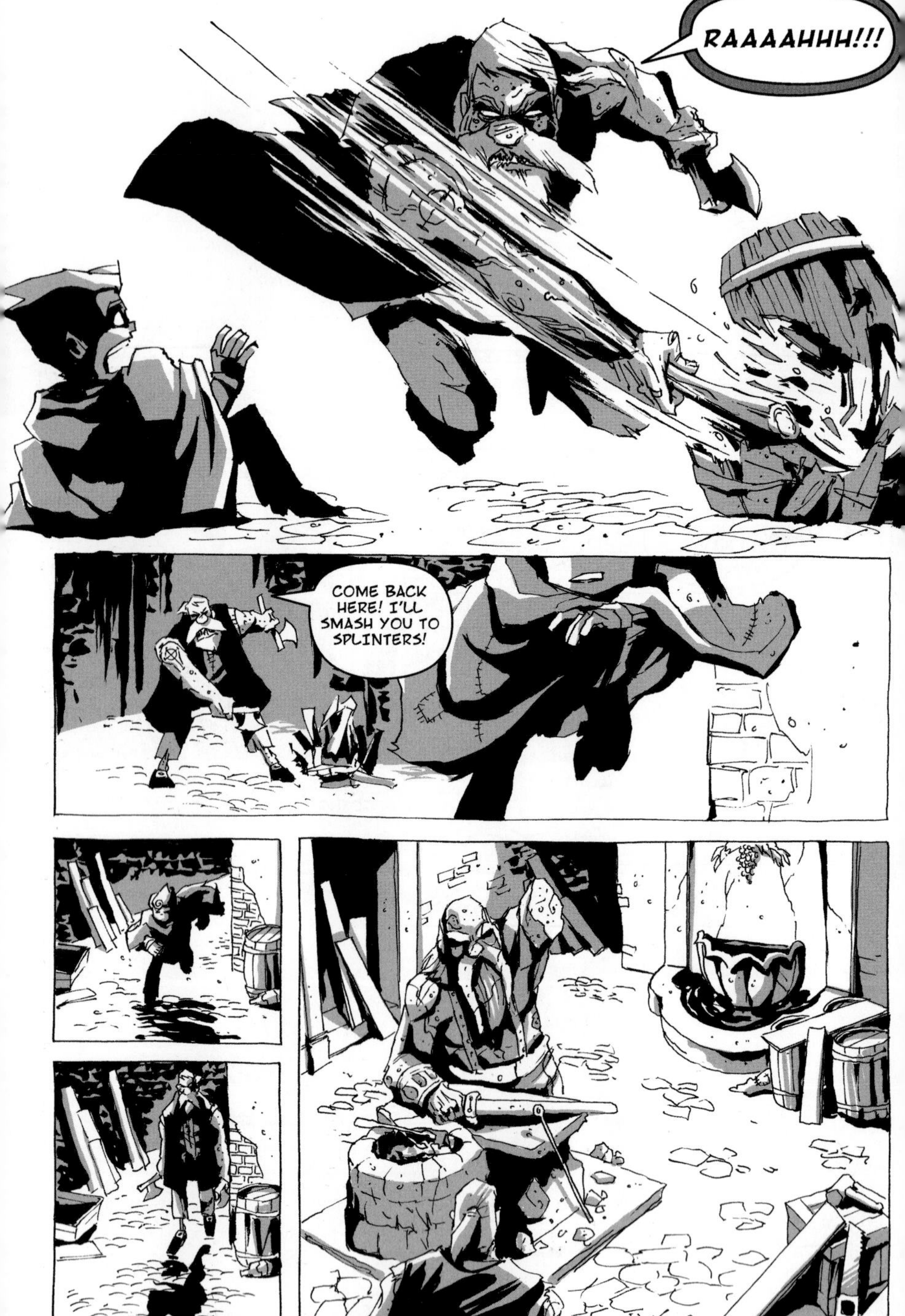
RAAAAHHH!!!
COME BACK HERE! I'LL SMASH YOU TO SPLINTERS!

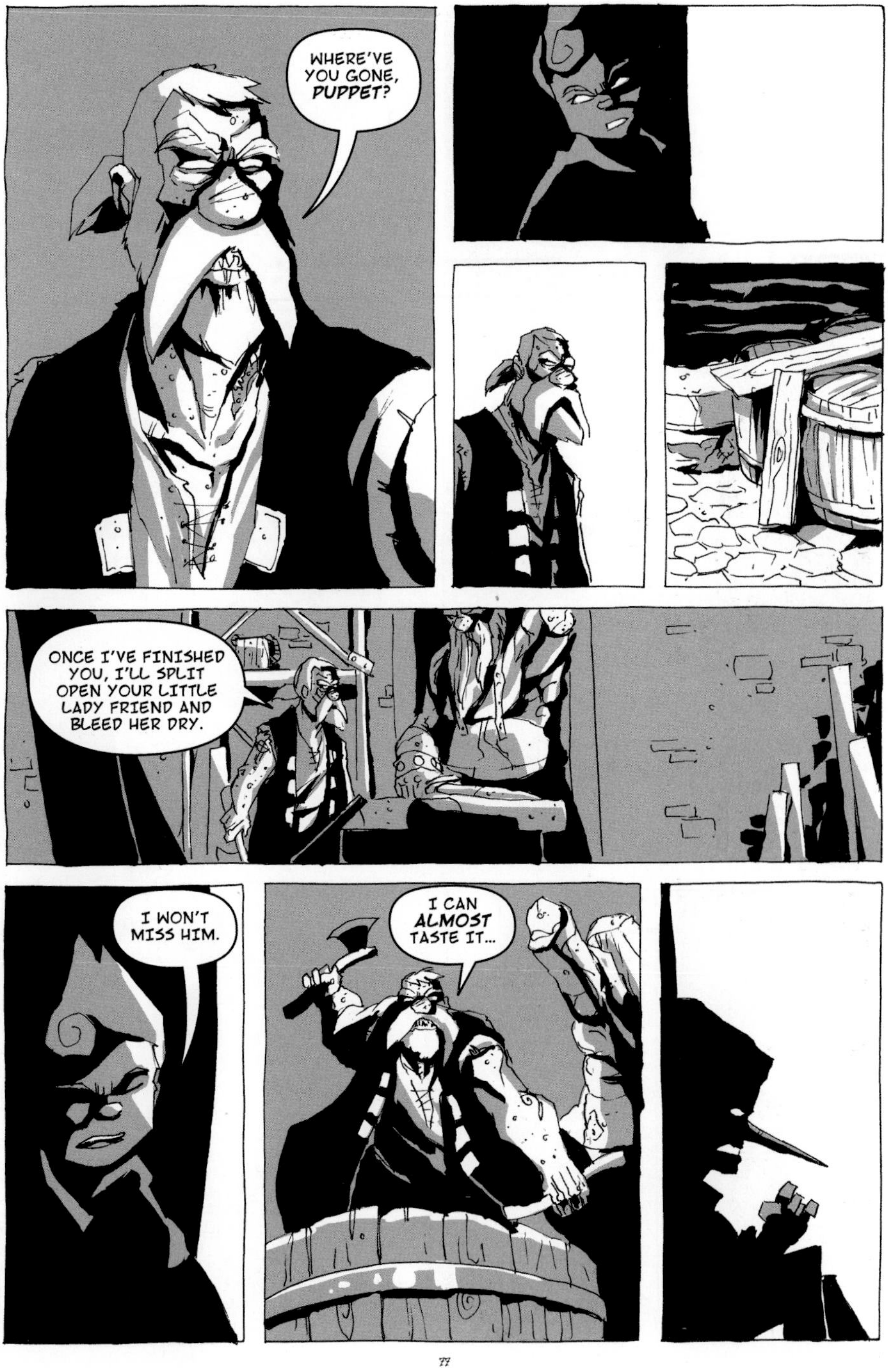

WHERE'VE YOU GONE, *PUPPET?*
ONCE I'VE FINISHED YOU, I'LL SPLIT OPEN YOUR LITTLE LADY FRIEND AND BLEED HER DRY.
I WON'T MISS HIM.
I CAN **ALMOST** TASTE IT...

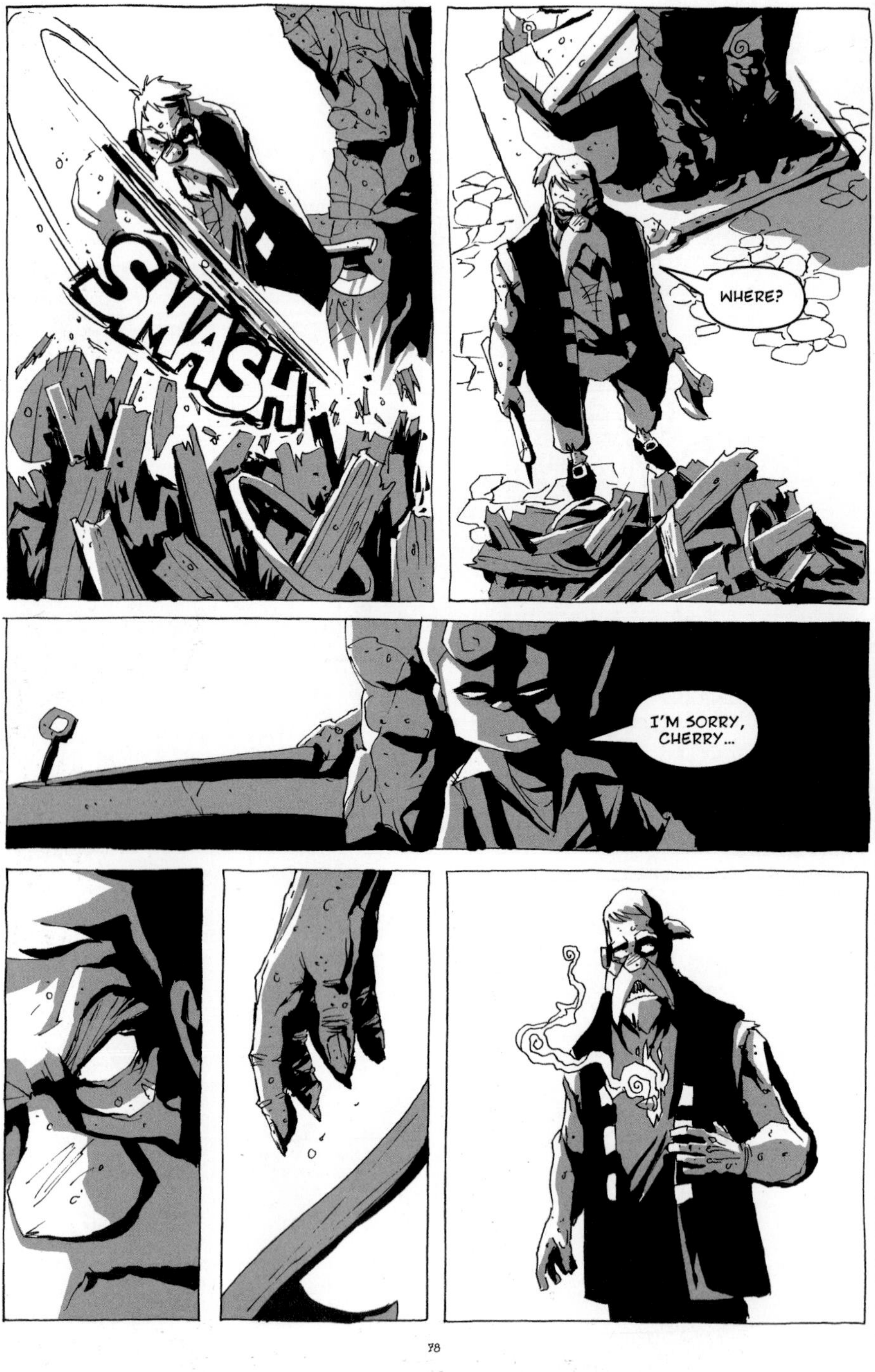
SMASH
WHERE?
I'M SORRY, CHERRY...

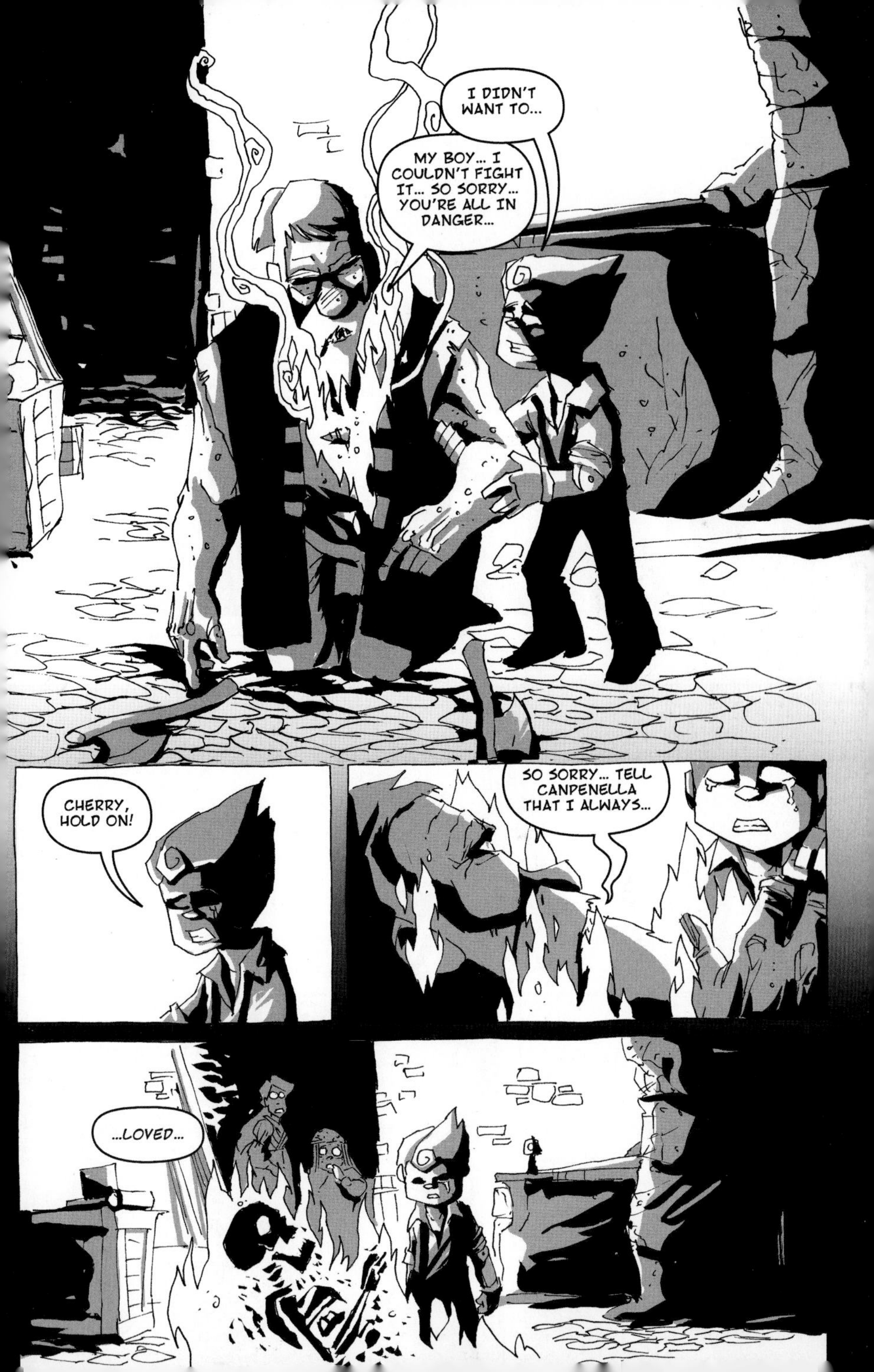
I DIDN'T WANT TO...
MY BOY... I COULDN'T FIGHT IT... SO SORRY... YOU'RE ALL IN DANGER...
CHERRY, HOLD ON!
SO SORRY... TELL CANDENELLA THAT I ALWAYS...
...LOVED...

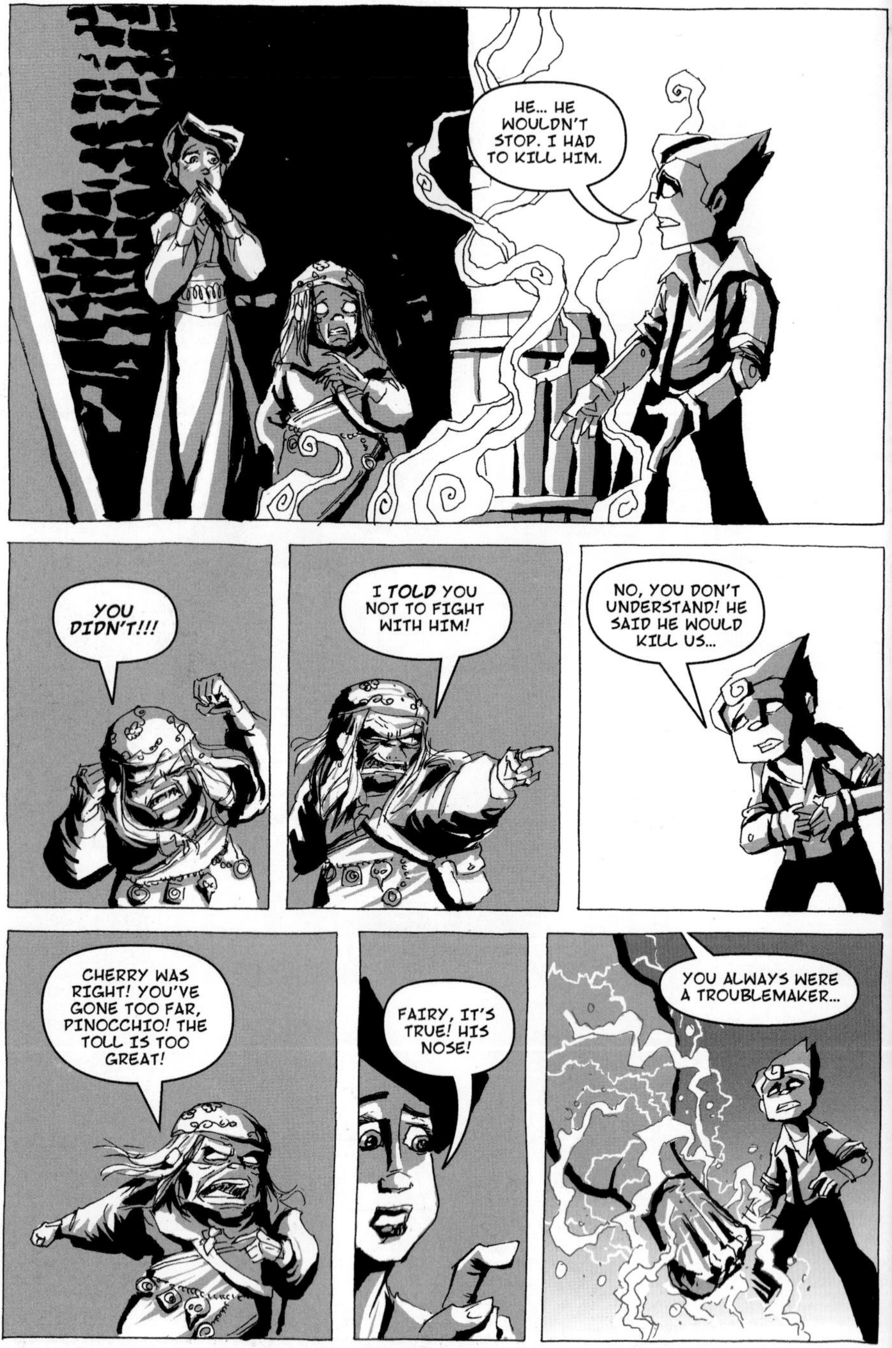

HE... HE WOULDN'T STOP. I HAD TO KILL HIM.
YOU DIDN'T!!!
I TOLD YOU NOT TO FIGHT WITH HIM!
NO, YOU DON'T UNDERSTAND! HE SAID HE WOULD KILL US...
CHERRY WAS RIGHT! YOU'VE GONE TOO FAR, PINOCCHIO! THE TOLL IS TOO GREAT!
FAIRY, IT'S TRUE! HIS NOSE!
YOU ALWAYS WERE A TROUBLEMAKER...

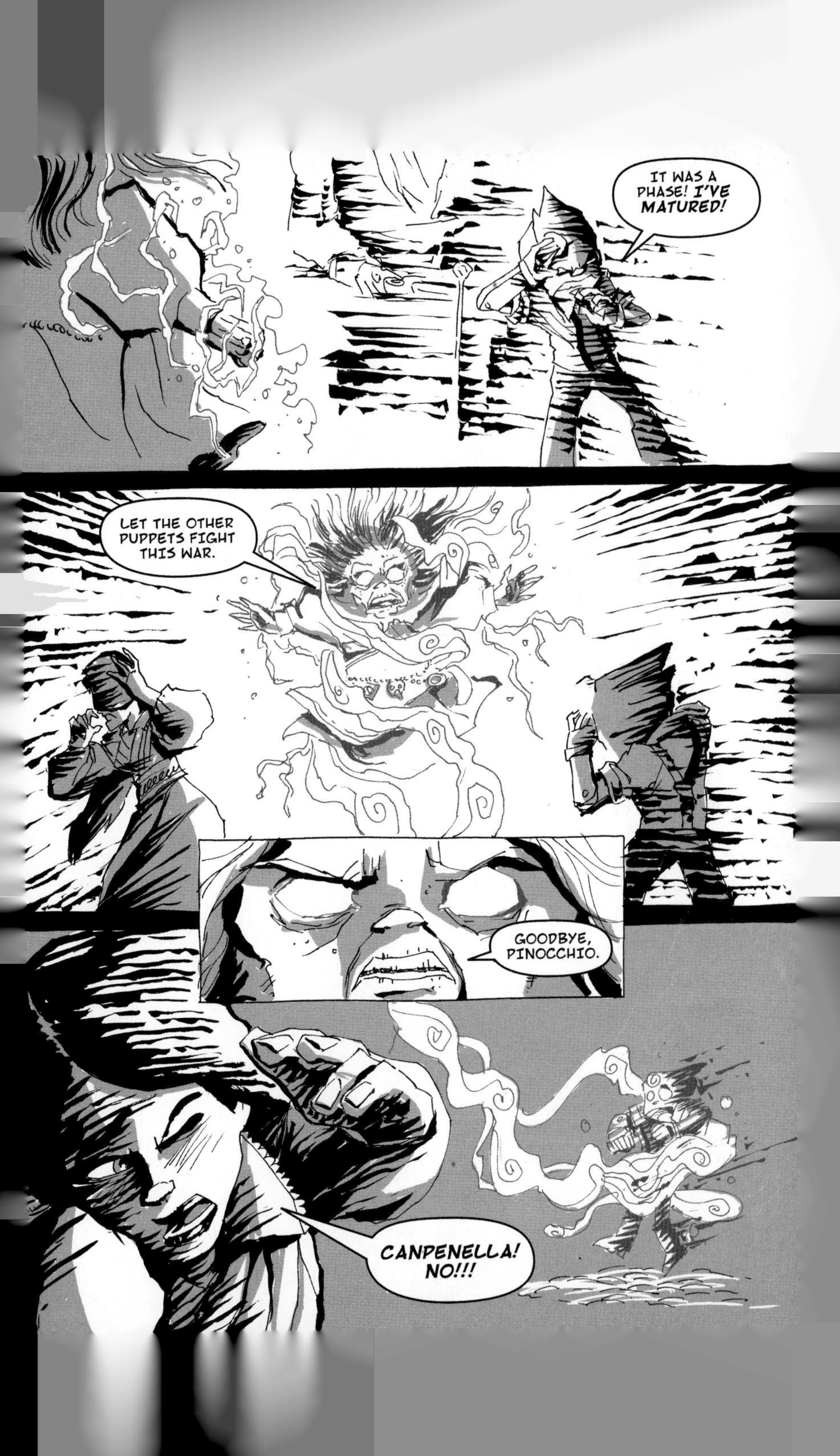
IT WAS A PHASE! I'VE MATURED!
LET THE OTHER PUPPETS FIGHT THIS WAR.
GOODBYE, PINOCCHIO.
CANPENELLA! NO!!!

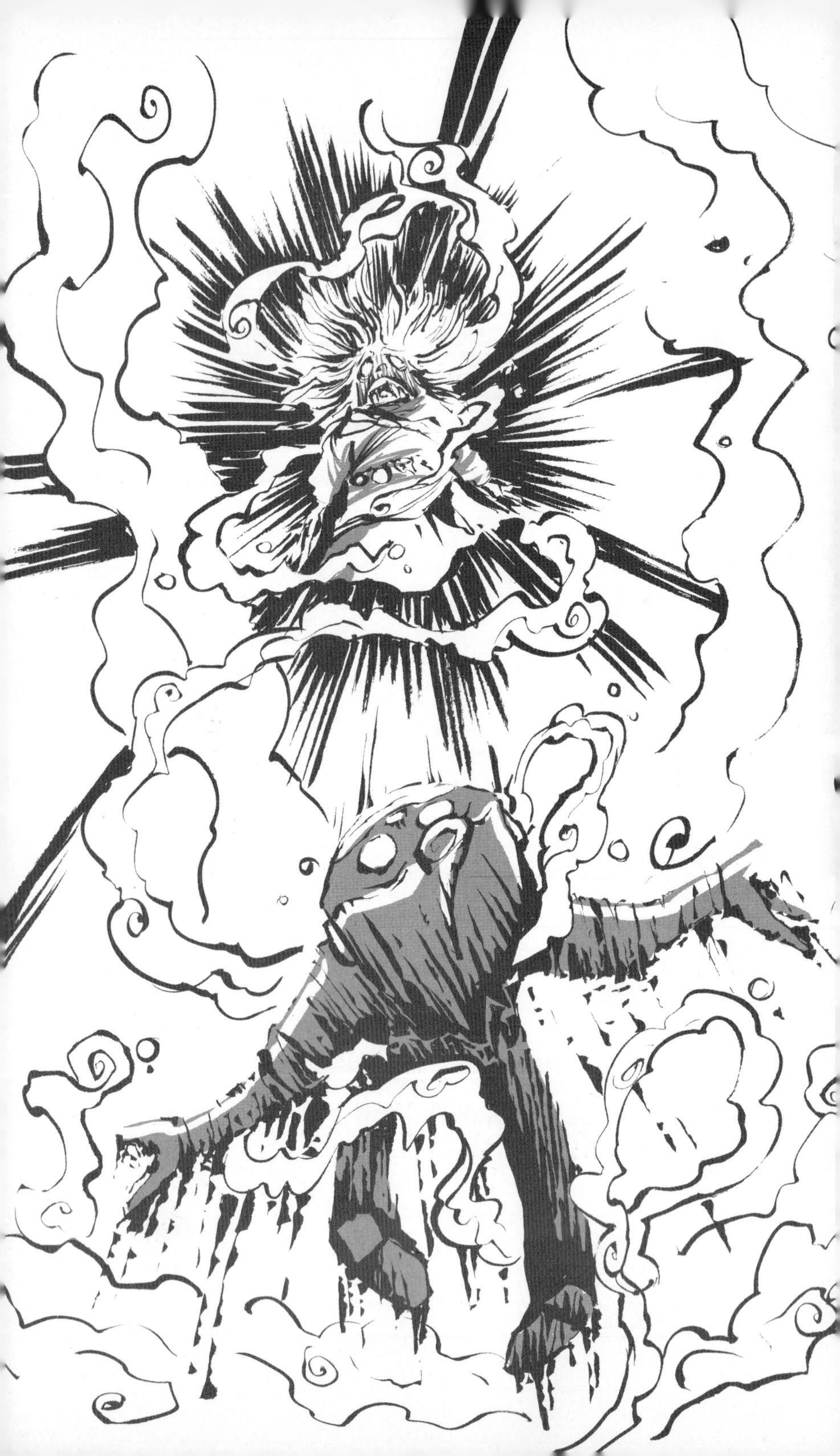

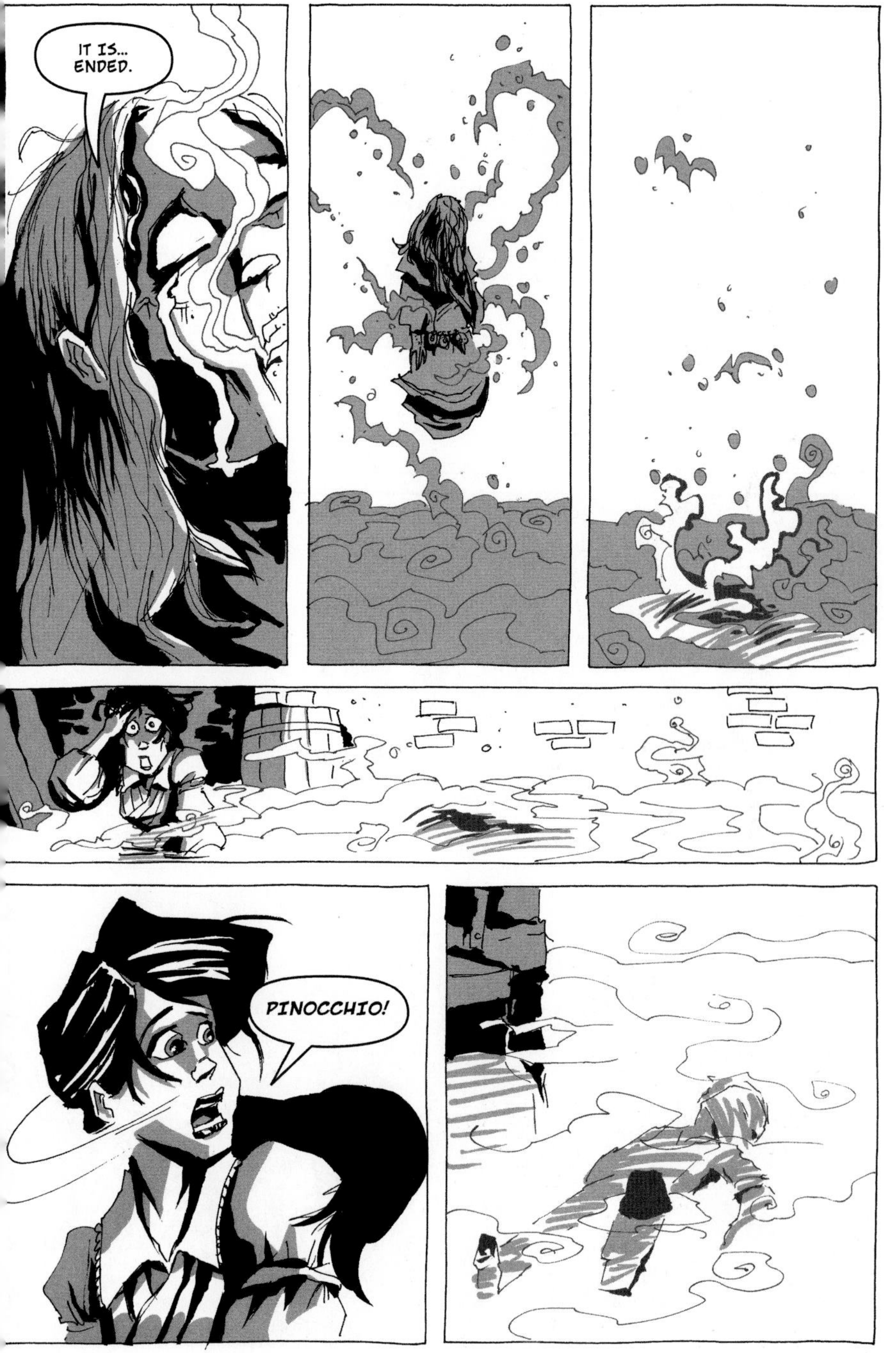
IT IS... ENDED.
PINOCCHIO!

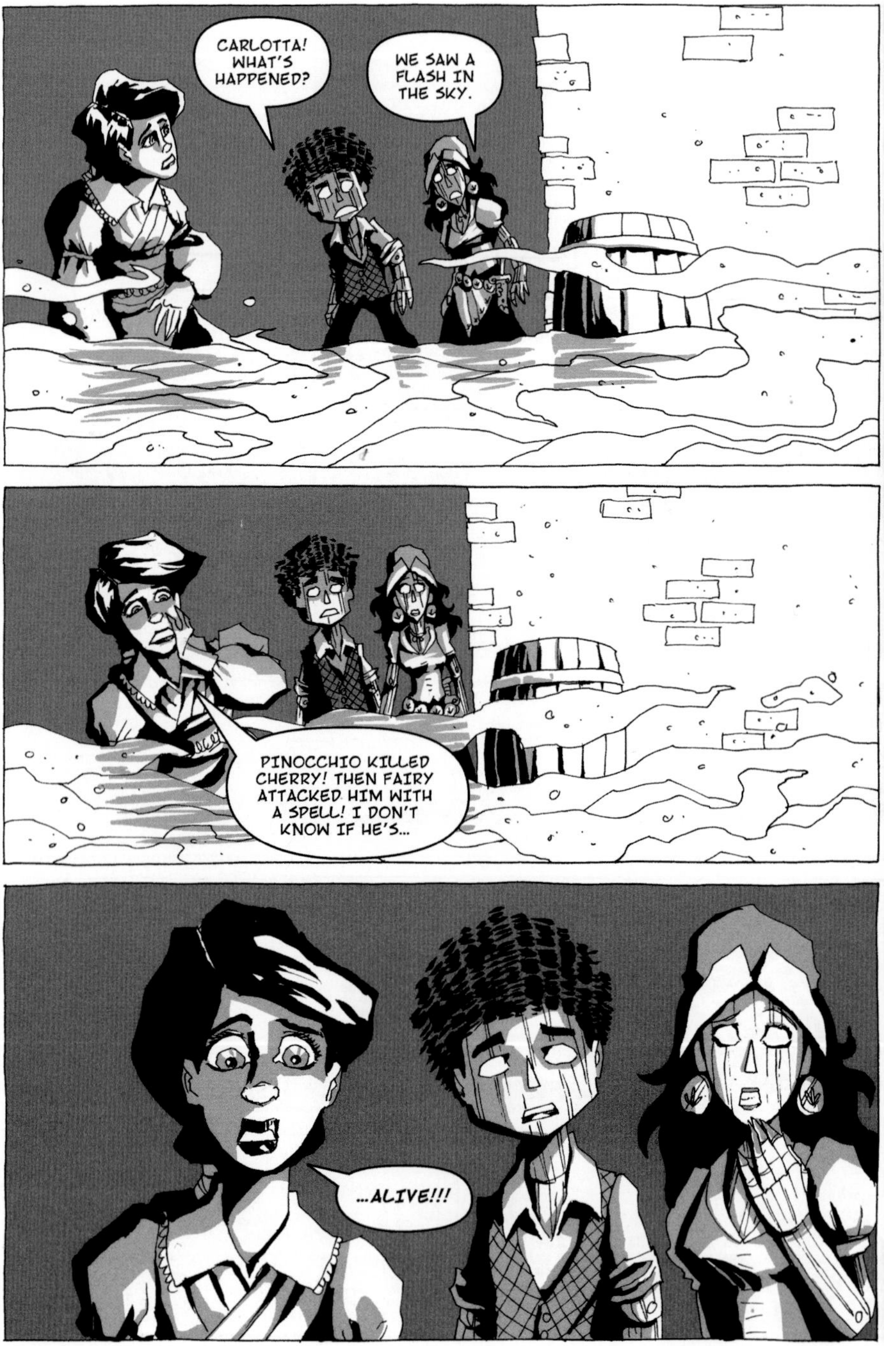
CARLOTTA! WHAT'S HAPPENED?
WE SAW A FLASH IN THE SKY.
PINOCCHIO KILLED CHERRY! THEN FAIRY ATTACKED HIM WITH A SPELL! I DON'T KNOW IF HE'S...
...ALIVE!!!

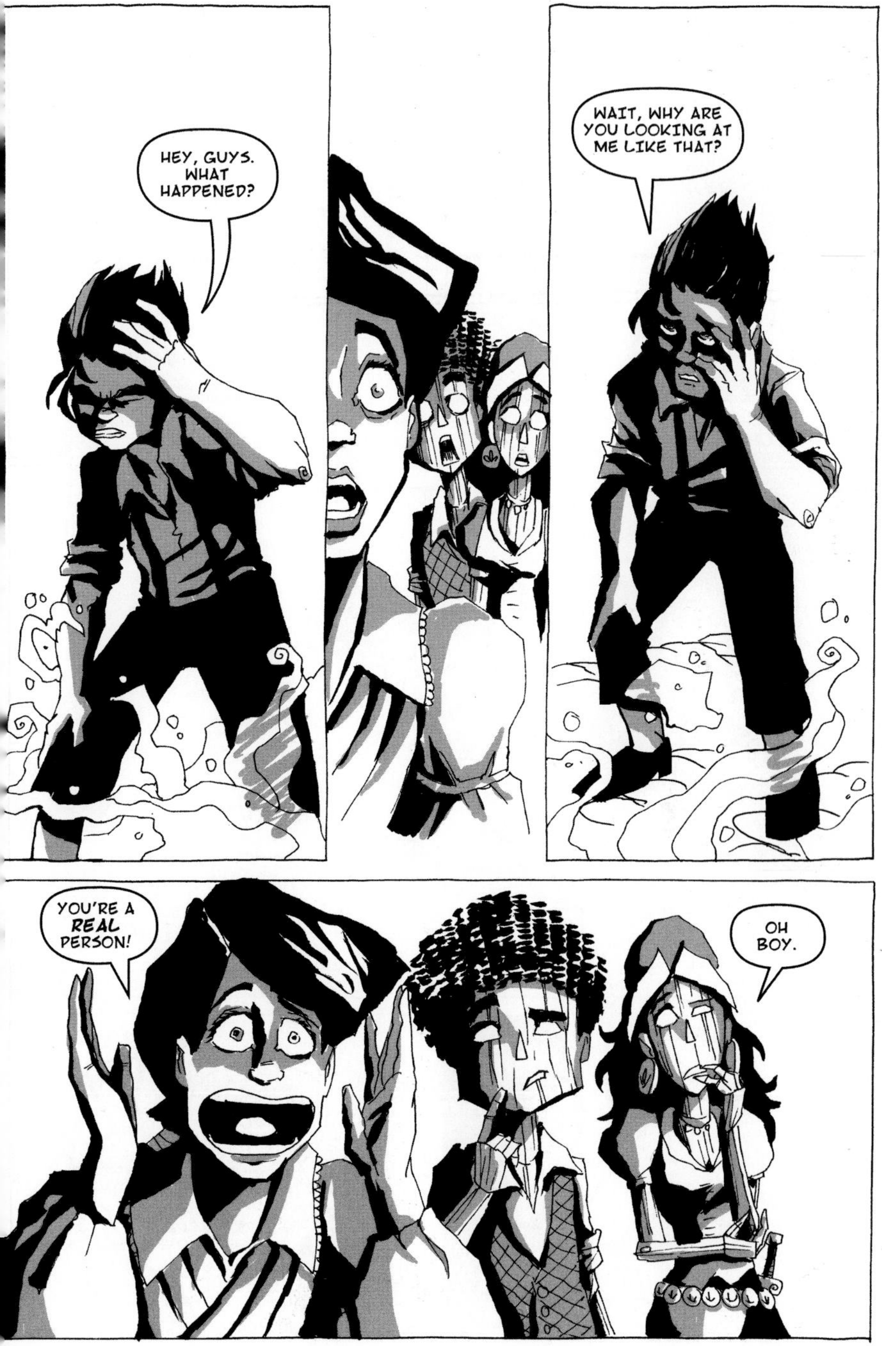
HEY, GUYS. WHAT HAPPENED?
WAIT, WHY ARE YOU LOOKING AT ME LIKE THAT?
YOU'RE A **REAL** PERSON!
OH BOY.

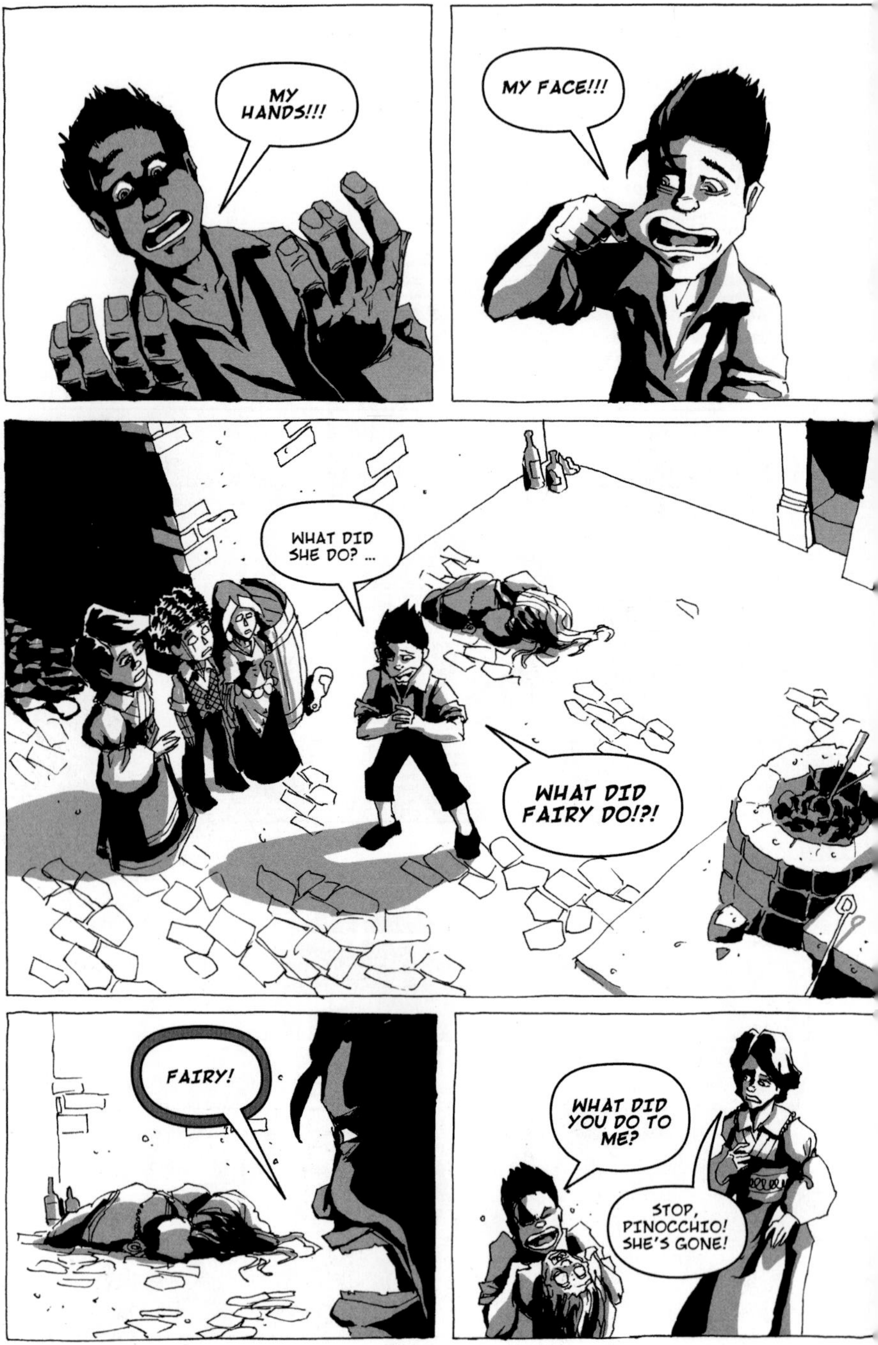
MY HANDS!!!
MY FACE!!!
WHAT DID SHE DO? ...
WHAT DID FAIRY DO!?!
FAIRY!
WHAT DID YOU DO TO ME?
STOP, PINOCCHIO! SHE'S GONE!

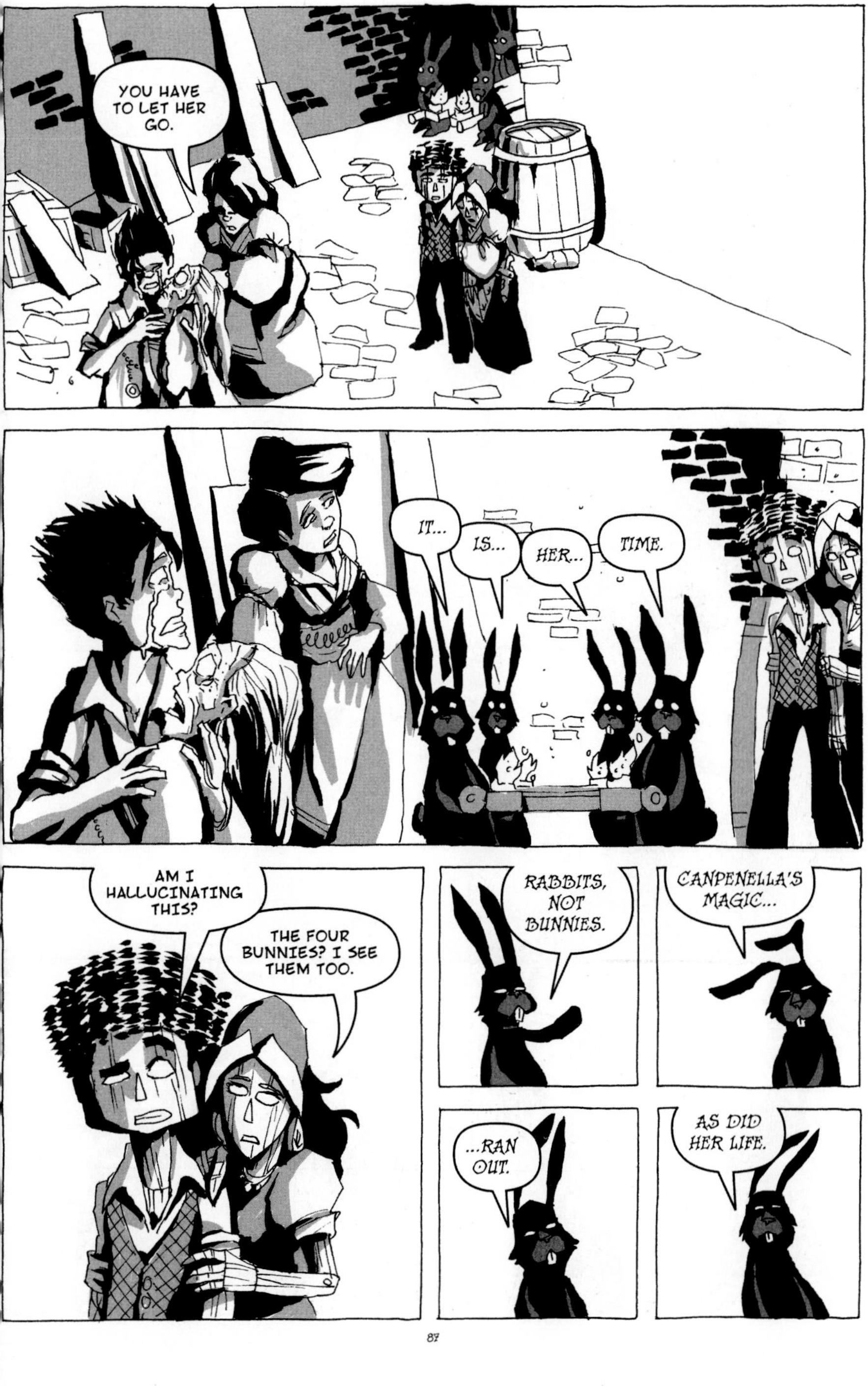
YOU HAVE TO LET HER GO.
IT...
IS...
HER...
TIME.
AM I HALLUCINATING THIS?
THE FOUR BUNNIES? I SEE THEM TOO.
RABBITS, NOT BUNNIES.
CANPENELLA'S MAGIC...
...RAN OUT.
AS DID HER LIFE.

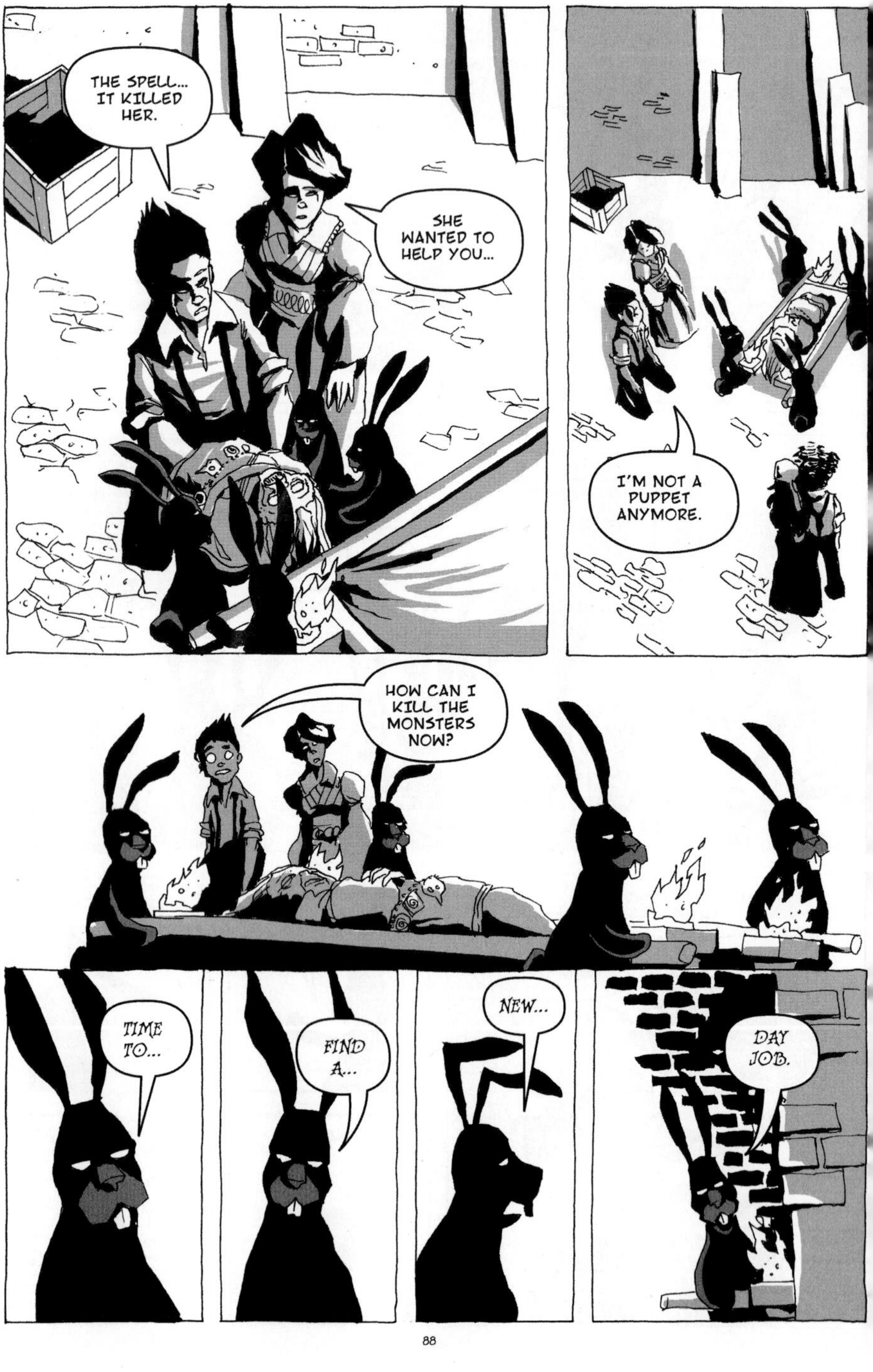
THE SPELL... IT KILLED HER.
SHE WANTED TO HELP YOU...
I'M NOT A PUPPET ANYMORE.
HOW CAN I KILL THE MONSTERS NOW?
TIME TO...
FIND A...
NEW...
DAY JOB.

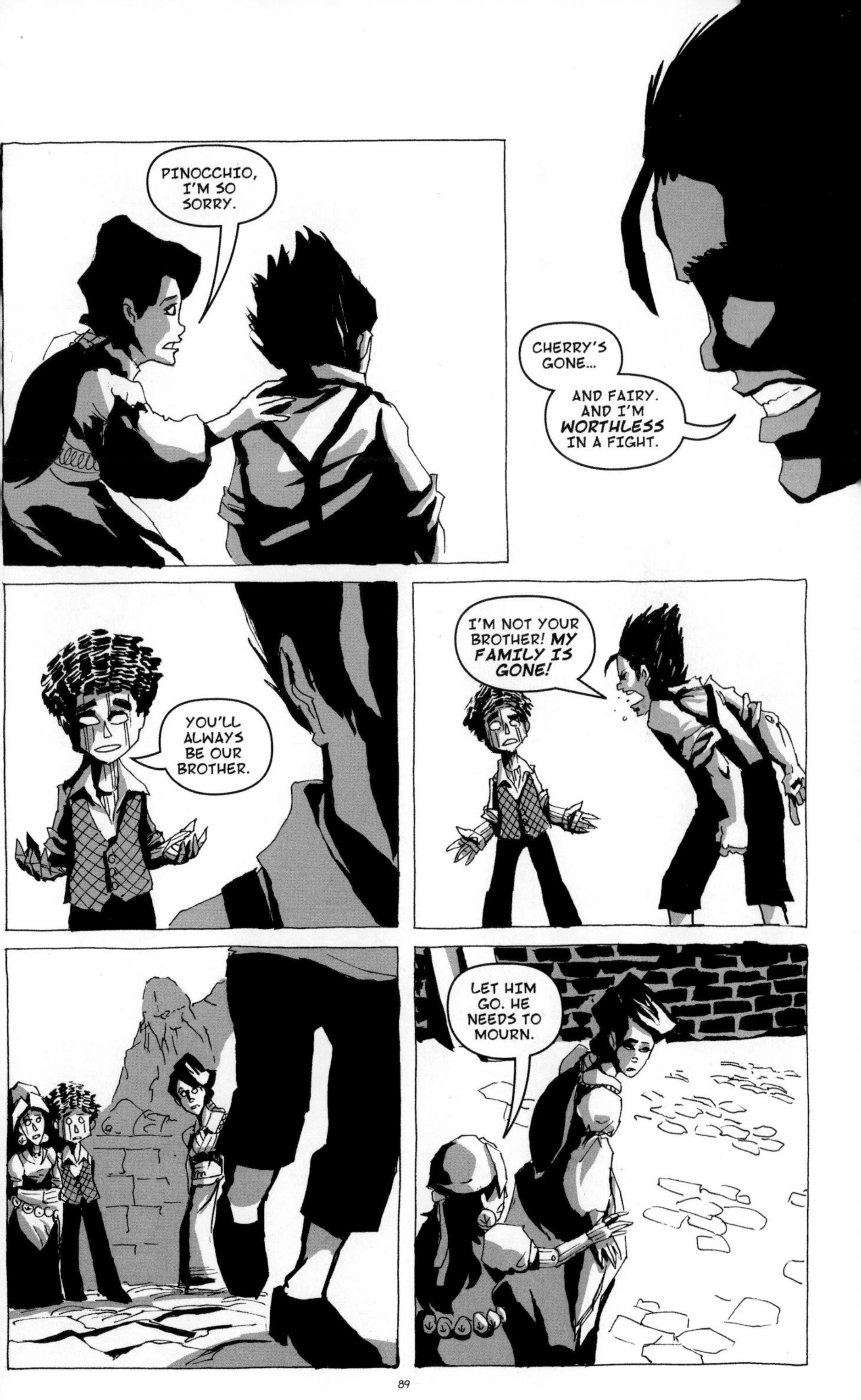
PINOCCHIO, I'M SO SORRY.
CHERRY'S GONE...
AND FAIRY. AND I'M **WORTHLESS** IN A FIGHT.
YOU'LL ALWAYS BE OUR BROTHER.
I'M NOT YOUR BROTHER! ***MY FAMILY IS GONE!***
LET HIM GO. HE NEEDS TO MOURN.

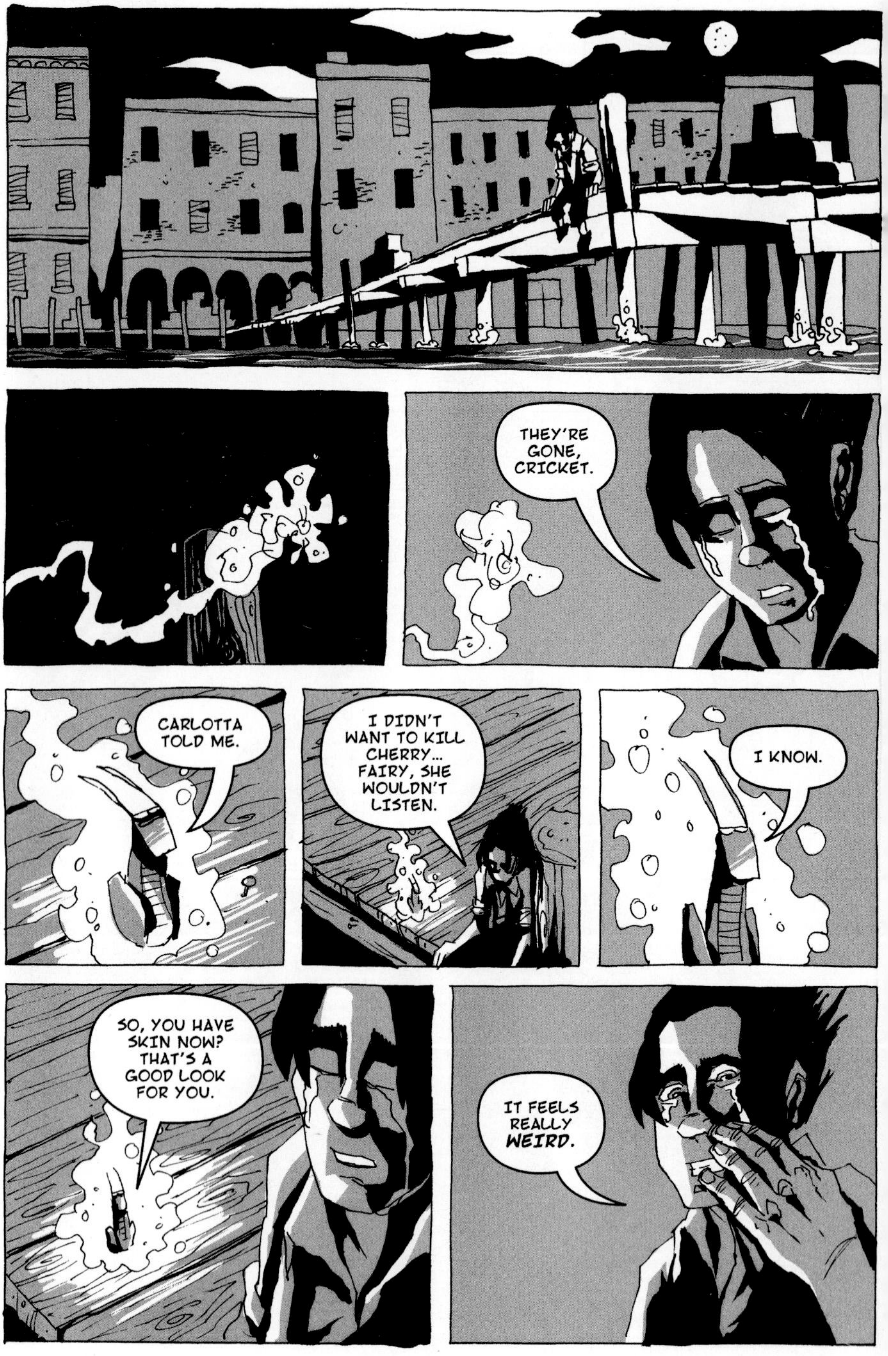
THEY'RE GONE, CRICKET.
CARLOTTA TOLD ME.
I DIDN'T WANT TO KILL CHERRY... FAIRY, SHE WOULDN'T LISTEN.
I KNOW.
SO, YOU HAVE SKIN NOW? THAT'S A GOOD LOOK FOR YOU.
IT FEELS REALLY **WEIRD**.

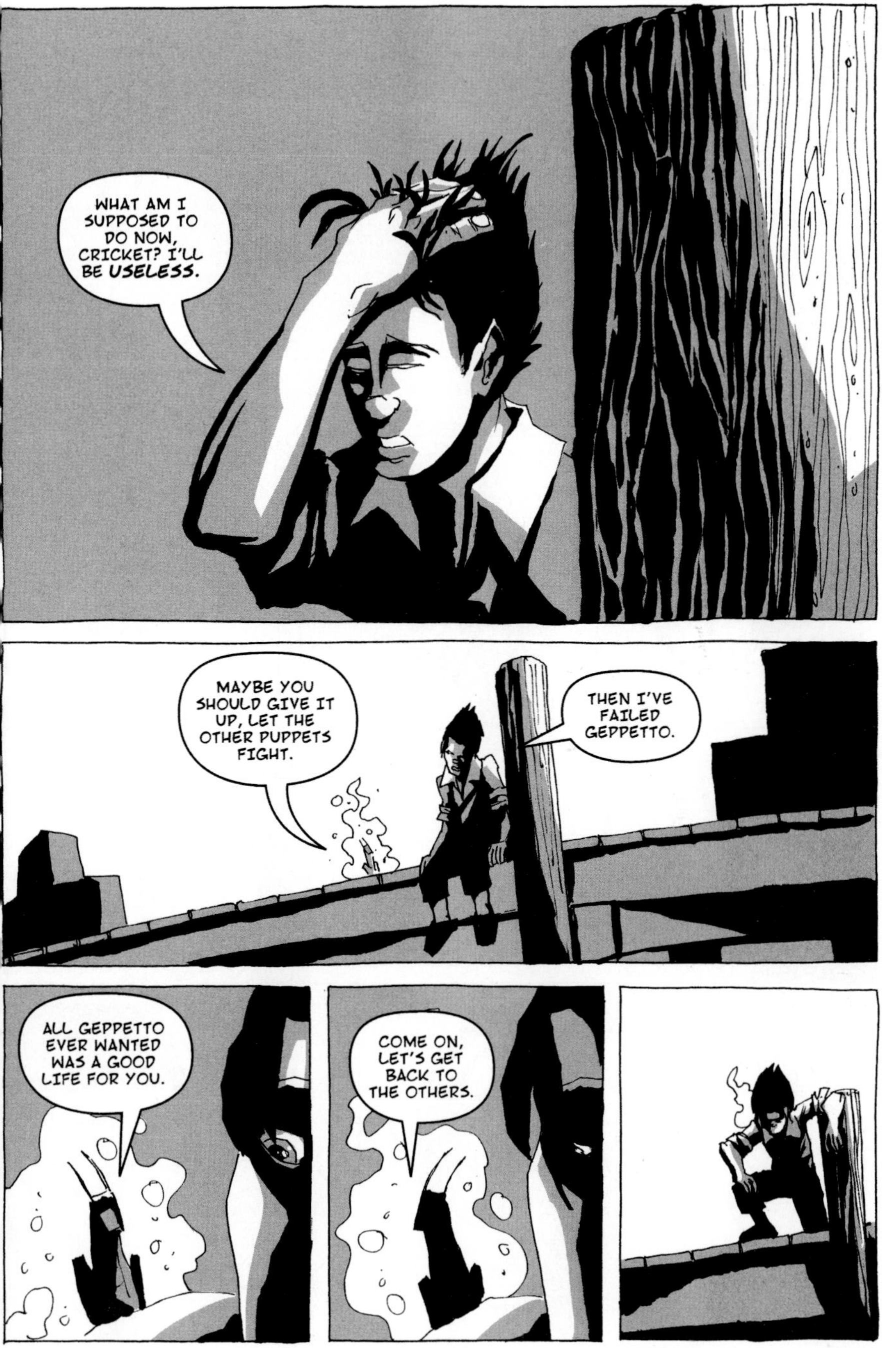
WHAT AM I SUPPOSED TO DO NOW, CRICKET? I'LL BE USELESS.
MAYBE YOU SHOULD GIVE IT UP, LET THE OTHER PUPPETS FIGHT.
THEN I'VE FAILED GEPPETTO.
ALL GEPPETTO EVER WANTED WAS A GOOD LIFE FOR YOU.
COME ON, LET'S GET BACK TO THE OTHERS.

ARE YOU DOING OK, MAN?

I'LL BE ALL RIGHT. SORRY I YELLED AT YOU.

WE'RE GOOD.

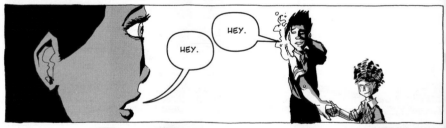

HEY.

HEY.

IT'S NEARLY DAWN. WHY DON'T YOU TWO HUMANS FIND SOME BREAKFAST. WE'LL MEET UP WITH THE REST OF THE GANG.

UM, OK. WE'LL MEET YOU BACK AT THE WAGON.

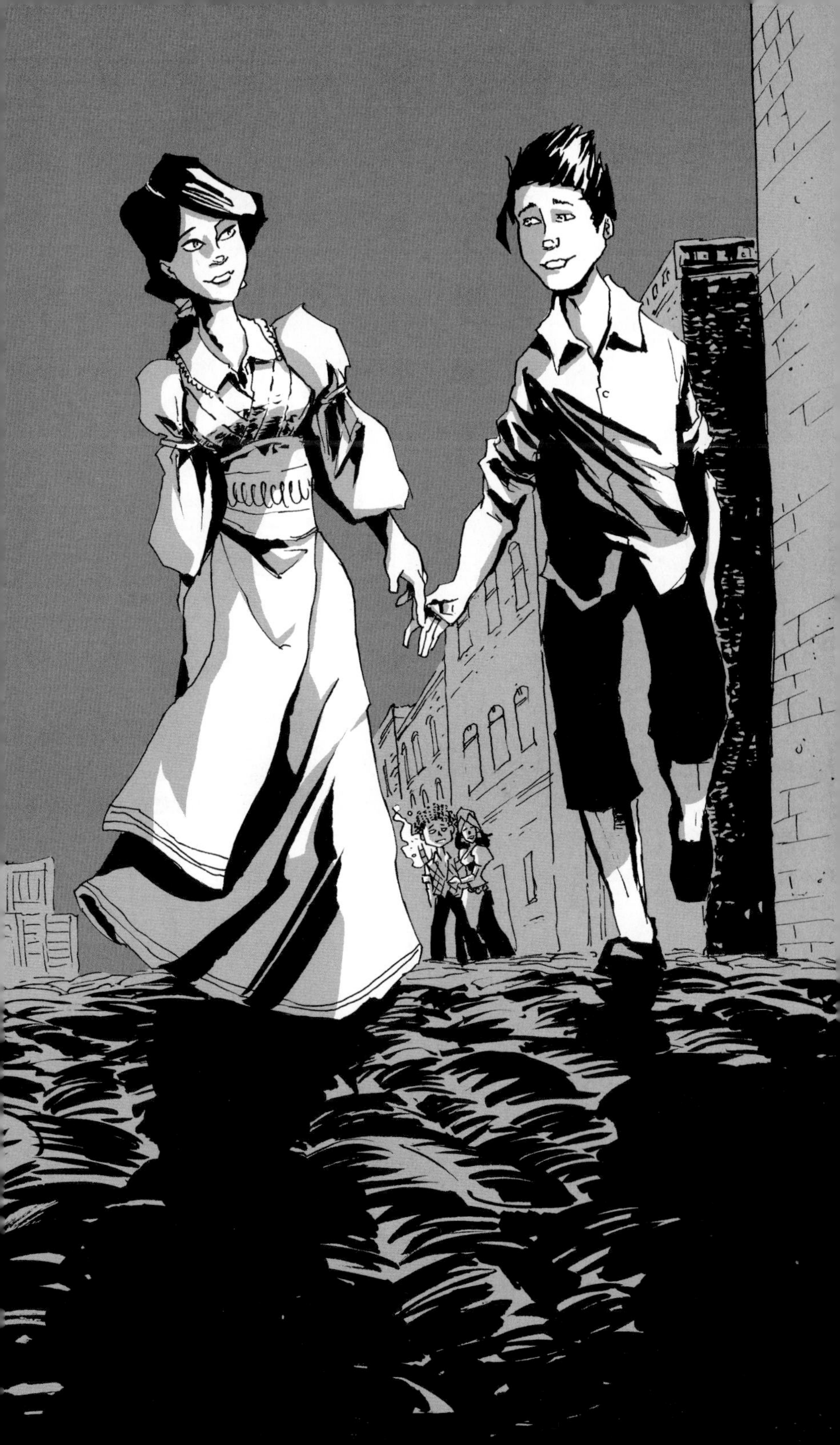

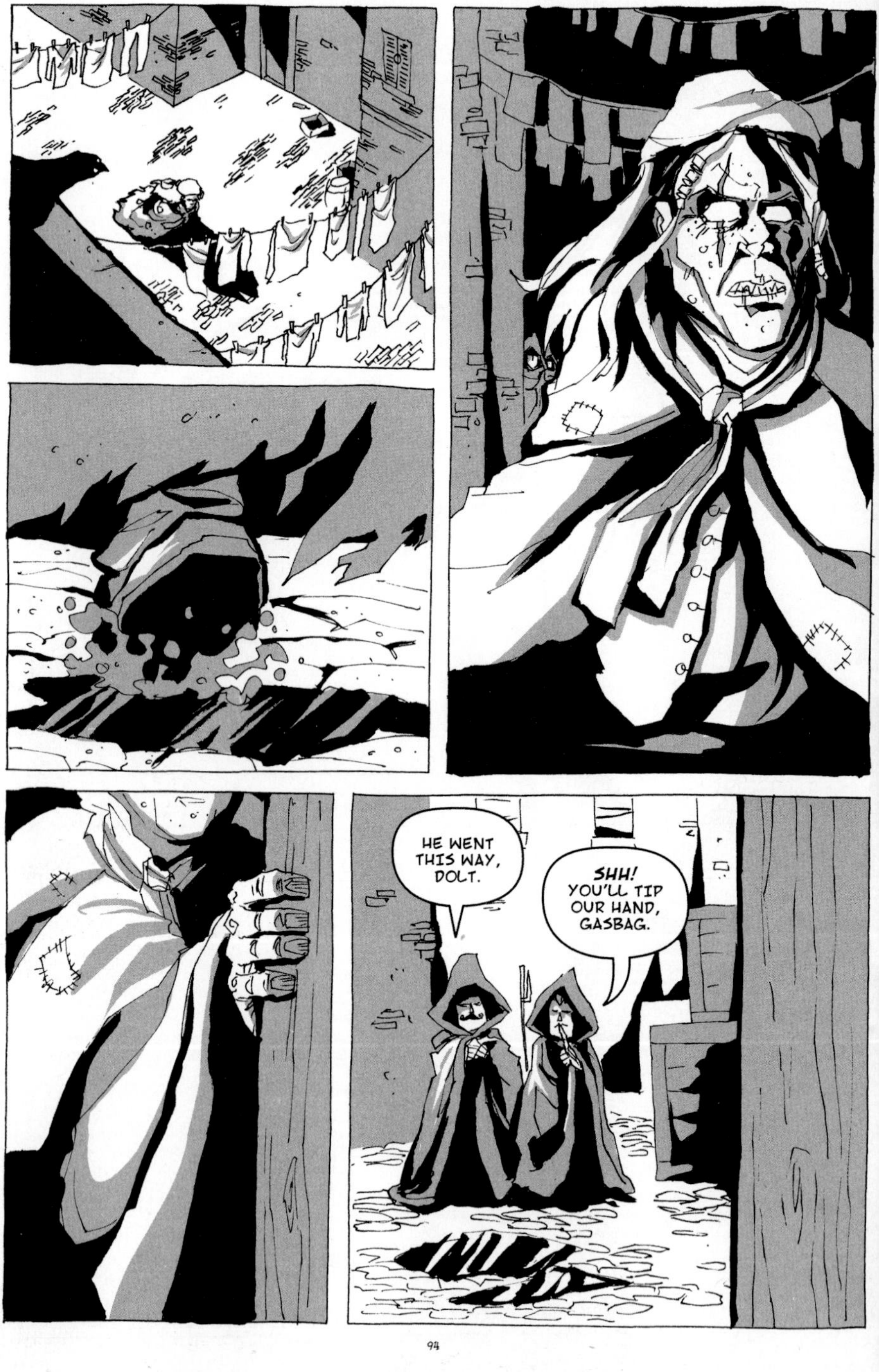
HE WENT THIS WAY, DOLT.
SHH! YOU'LL TIP OUR HAND, GASBAG.

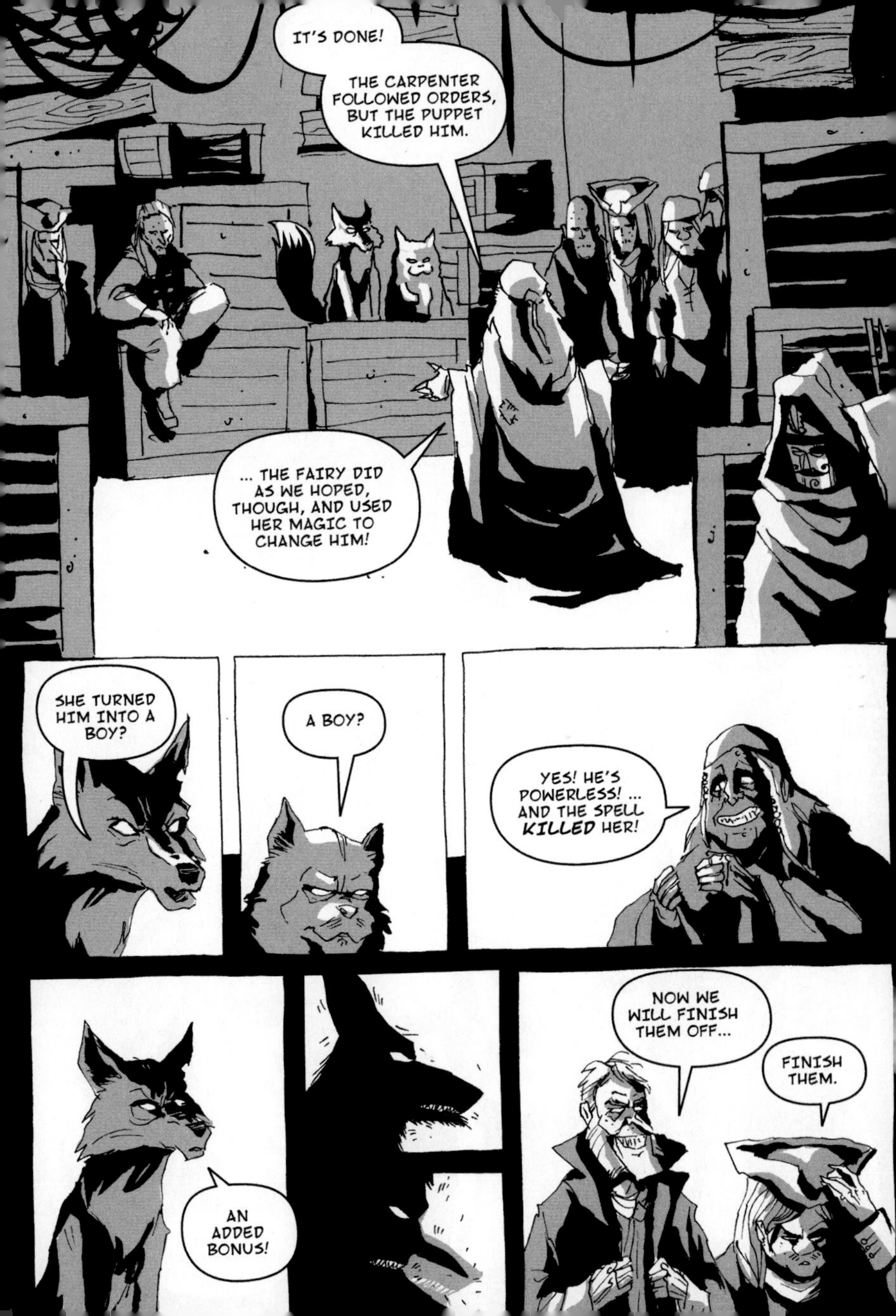
IT'S DONE!
THE CARPENTER FOLLOWED ORDERS, BUT THE PUPPET KILLED HIM.
... THE FAIRY DID AS WE HOPED, THOUGH, AND USED HER MAGIC TO CHANGE HIM!
SHE TURNED HIM INTO A BOY?
A BOY?
YES! HE'S POWERLESS! ... AND THE SPELL KILLED HER!
AN ADDED BONUS!
NOW WE WILL FINISH THEM OFF...
FINISH THEM.

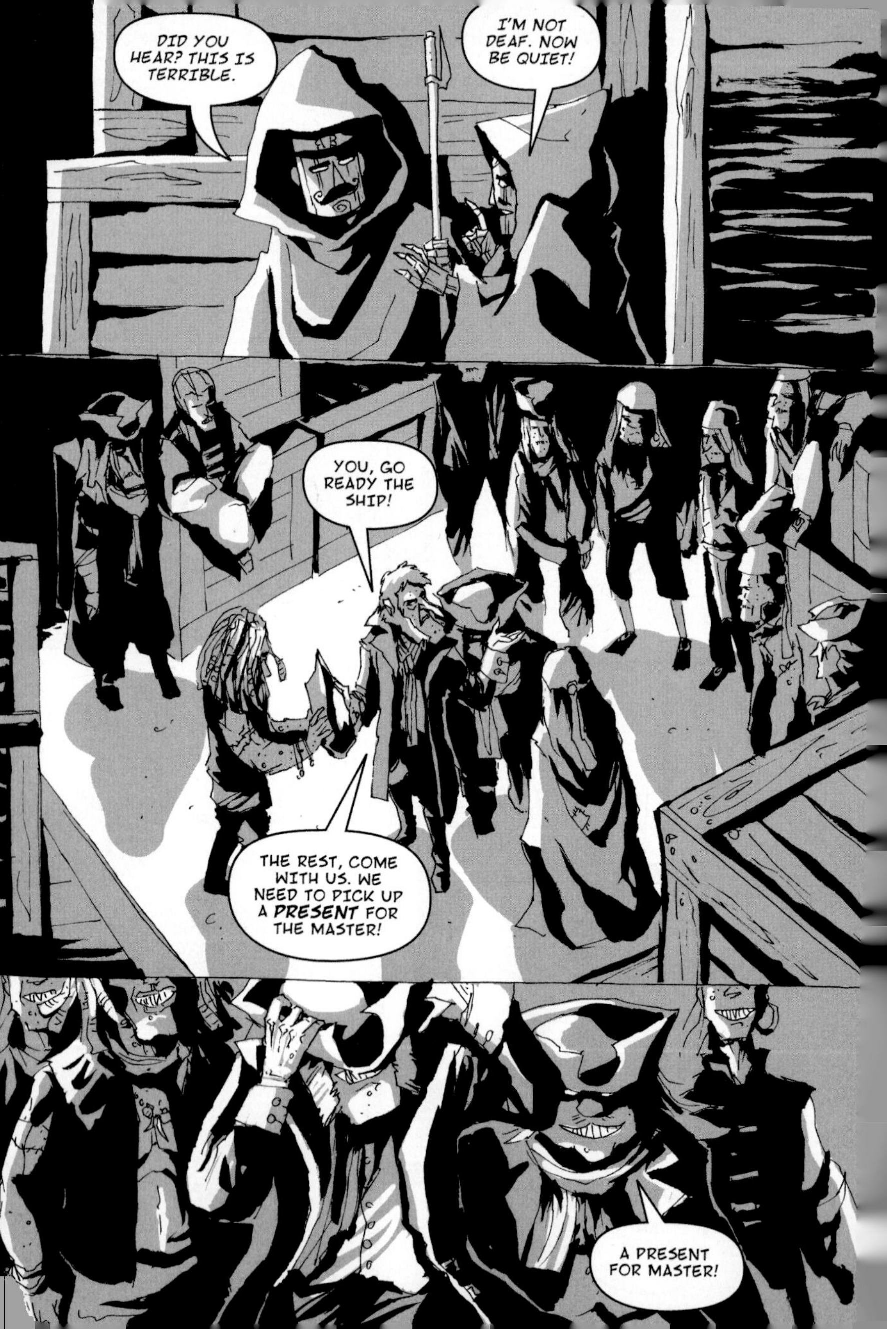
DID YOU HEAR? THIS IS TERRIBLE.
I'M NOT DEAF. NOW BE QUIET!
YOU, GO READY THE SHIP!
THE REST, COME WITH US. WE NEED TO PICK UP A PRESENT FOR THE MASTER!
A PRESENT FOR MASTER!

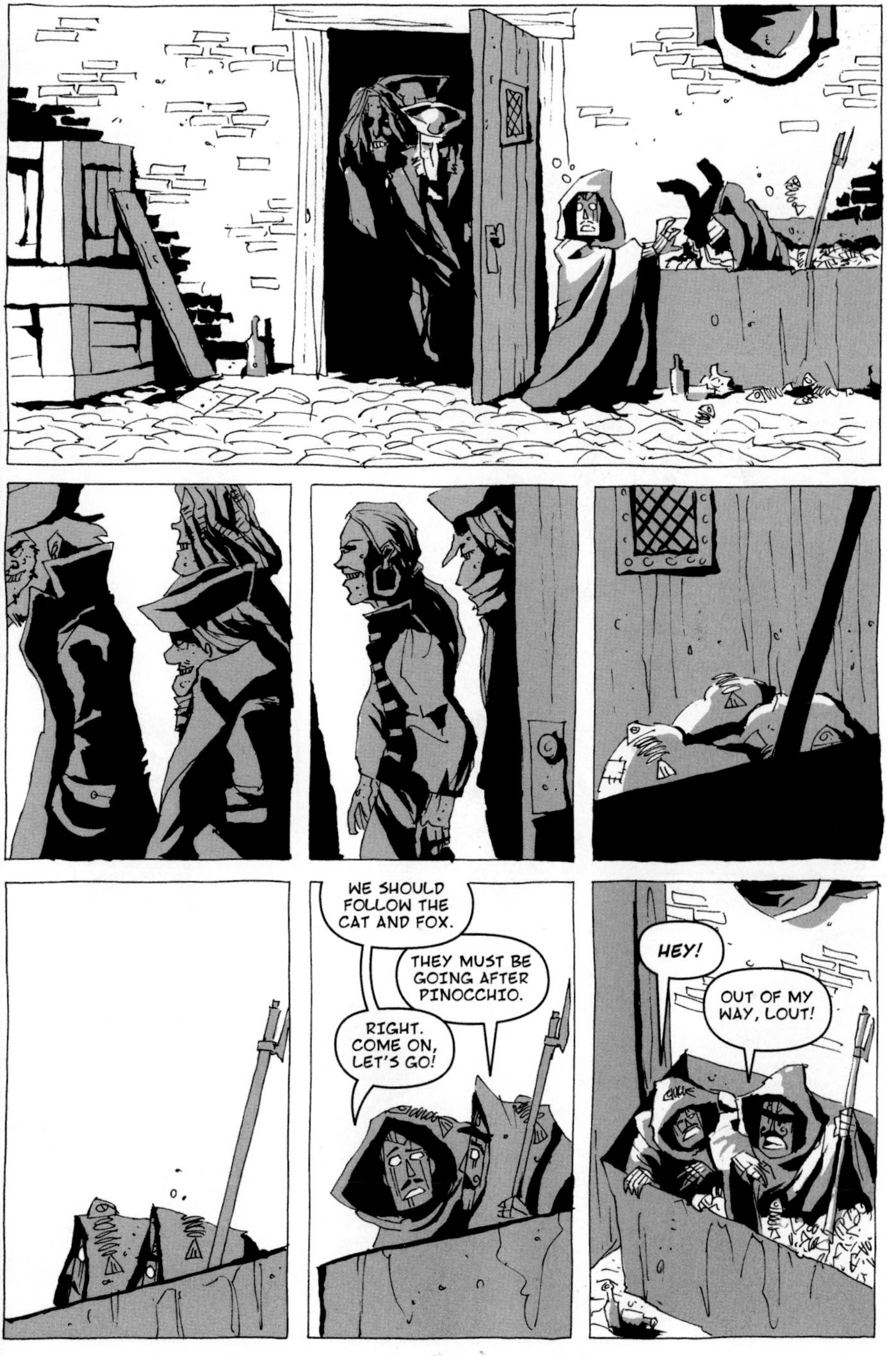
WE SHOULD FOLLOW THE CAT AND FOX.
THEY MUST BE GOING AFTER PINOCCHIO.
RIGHT. COME ON, LET'S GO!
HEY!
OUT OF MY WAY, LOUT!

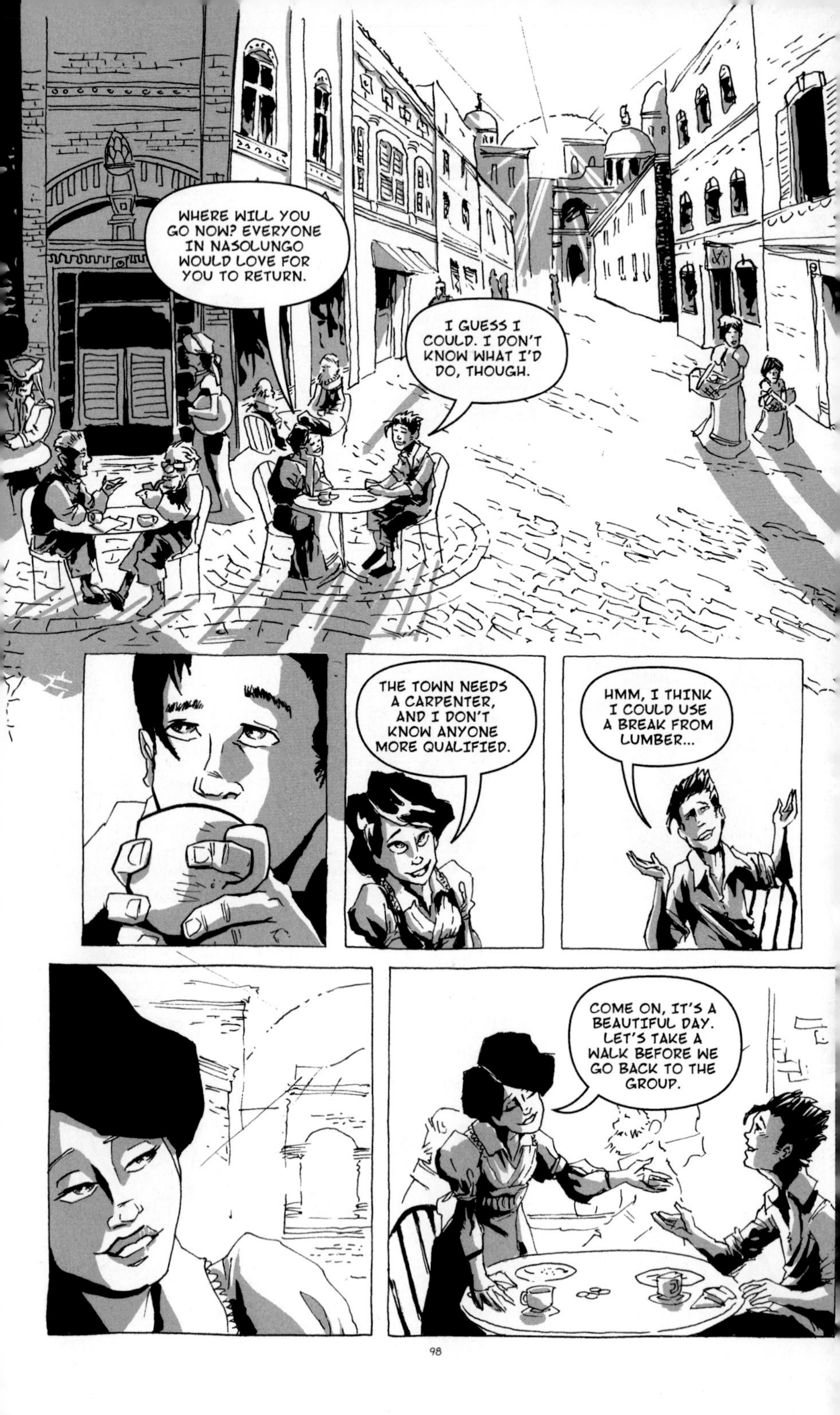
WHERE WILL YOU GO NOW? EVERYONE IN NASOLUNGO WOULD LOVE FOR YOU TO RETURN.
I GUESS I COULD. I DON'T KNOW WHAT I'D DO, THOUGH.
THE TOWN NEEDS A CARPENTER, AND I DON'T KNOW ANYONE MORE QUALIFIED.
HMM, I THINK I COULD USE A BREAK FROM LUMBER...
COME ON, IT'S A BEAUTIFUL DAY. LET'S TAKE A WALK BEFORE WE GO BACK TO THE GROUP.

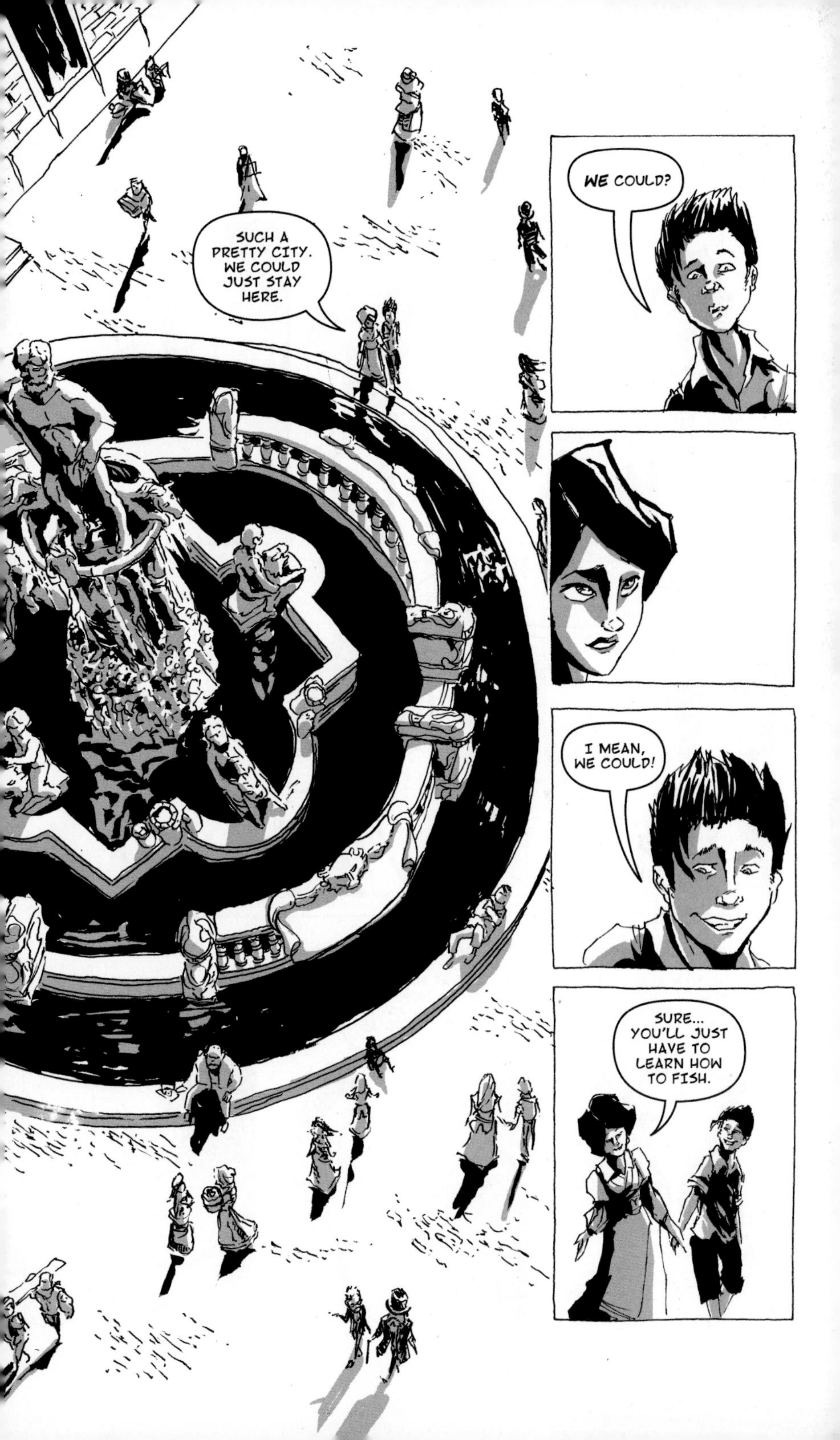
SUCH A PRETTY CITY. WE COULD JUST STAY HERE.
WE COULD?
I MEAN, WE COULD!
SURE... YOU'LL JUST HAVE TO LEARN HOW TO FISH.

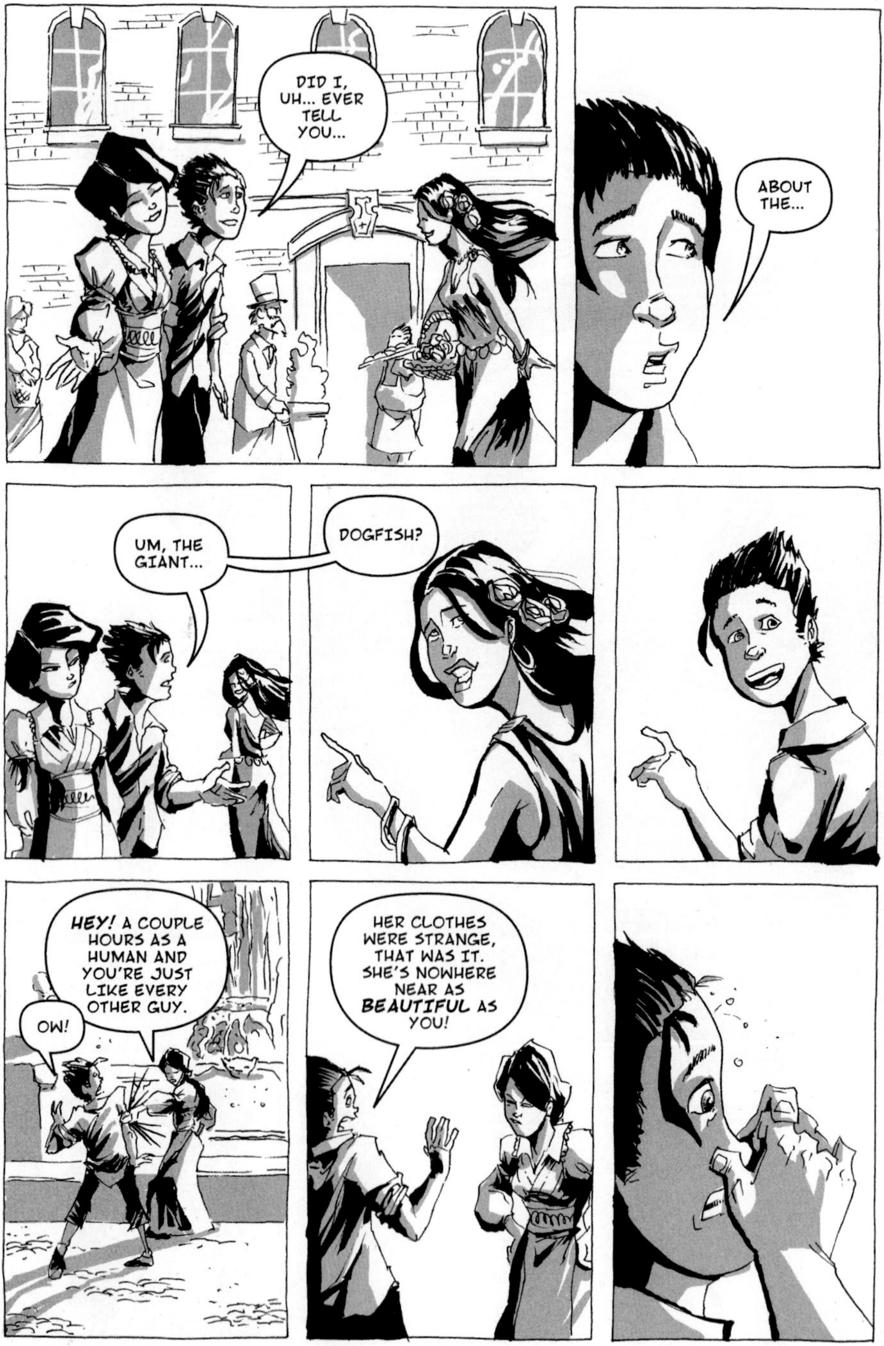
DID I, UH... EVER TELL YOU...
ABOUT THE...
UM, THE GIANT...
DOGFISH?
HEY! A COUPLE HOURS AS A HUMAN AND YOU'RE JUST LIKE EVERY OTHER GUY.
OW!
HER CLOTHES WERE STRANGE, THAT WAS IT. SHE'S NOWHERE NEAR AS BEAUTIFUL AS YOU!

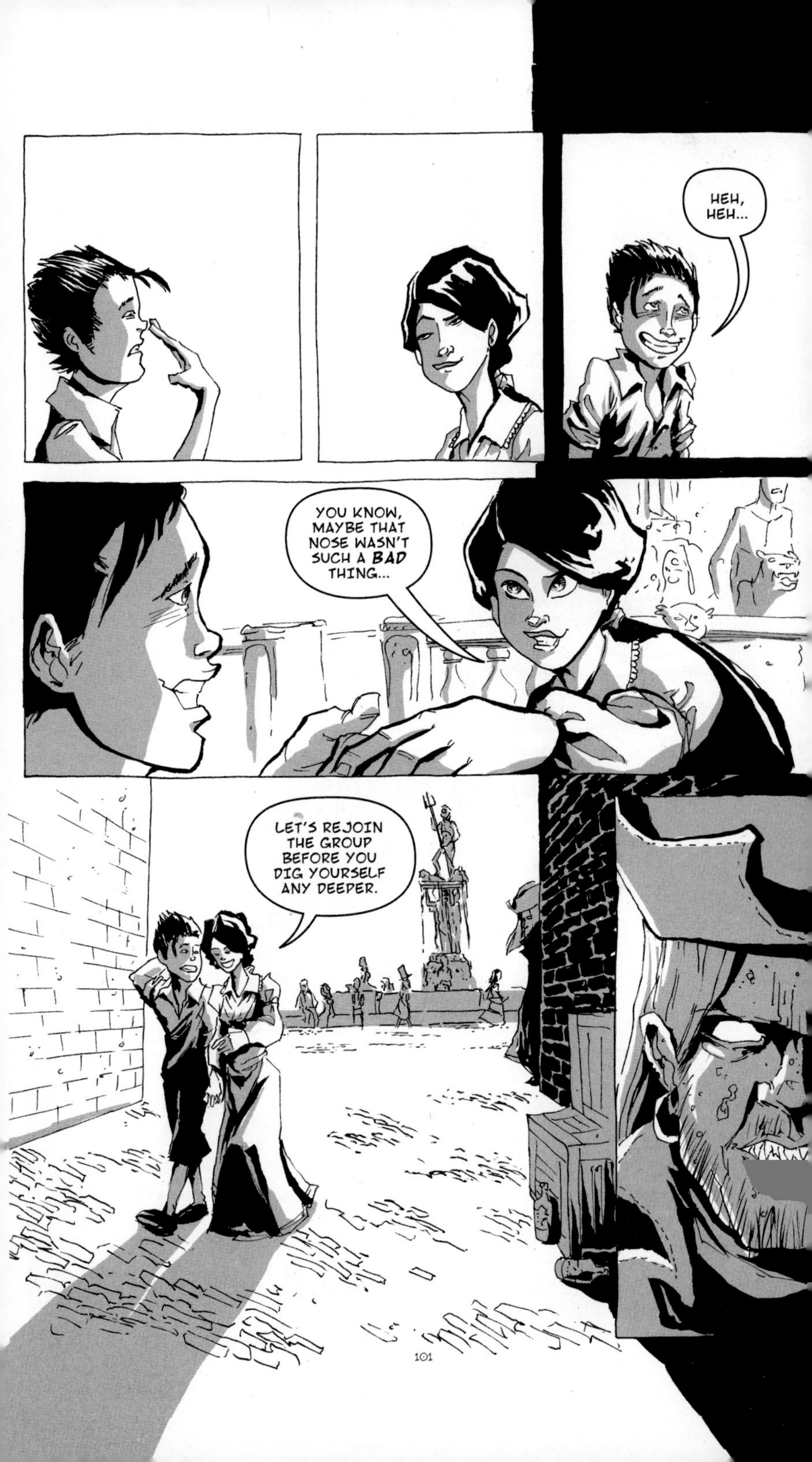
HEH,
HEH...
YOU KNOW, MAYBE THAT NOSE WASN'T SUCH A **BAD** THING...
LET'S REJOIN THE GROUP BEFORE YOU DIG YOURSELF ANY DEEPER.

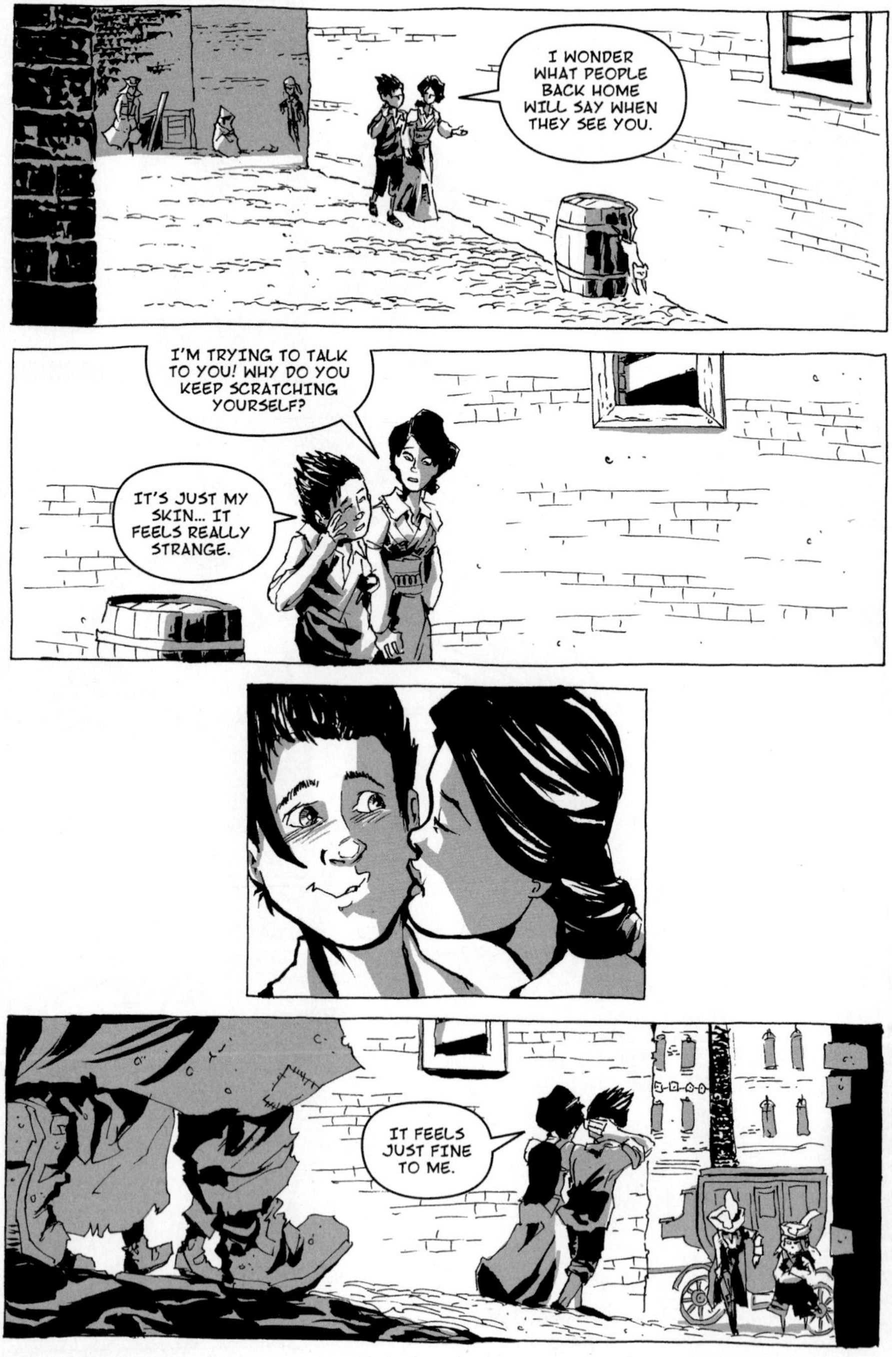
I WONDER WHAT PEOPLE BACK HOME WILL SAY WHEN THEY SEE YOU.
I'M TRYING TO TALK TO YOU! WHY DO YOU KEEP SCRATCHING YOURSELF?
IT'S JUST MY SKIN... IT FEELS REALLY STRANGE.
IT FEELS JUST FINE TO ME.

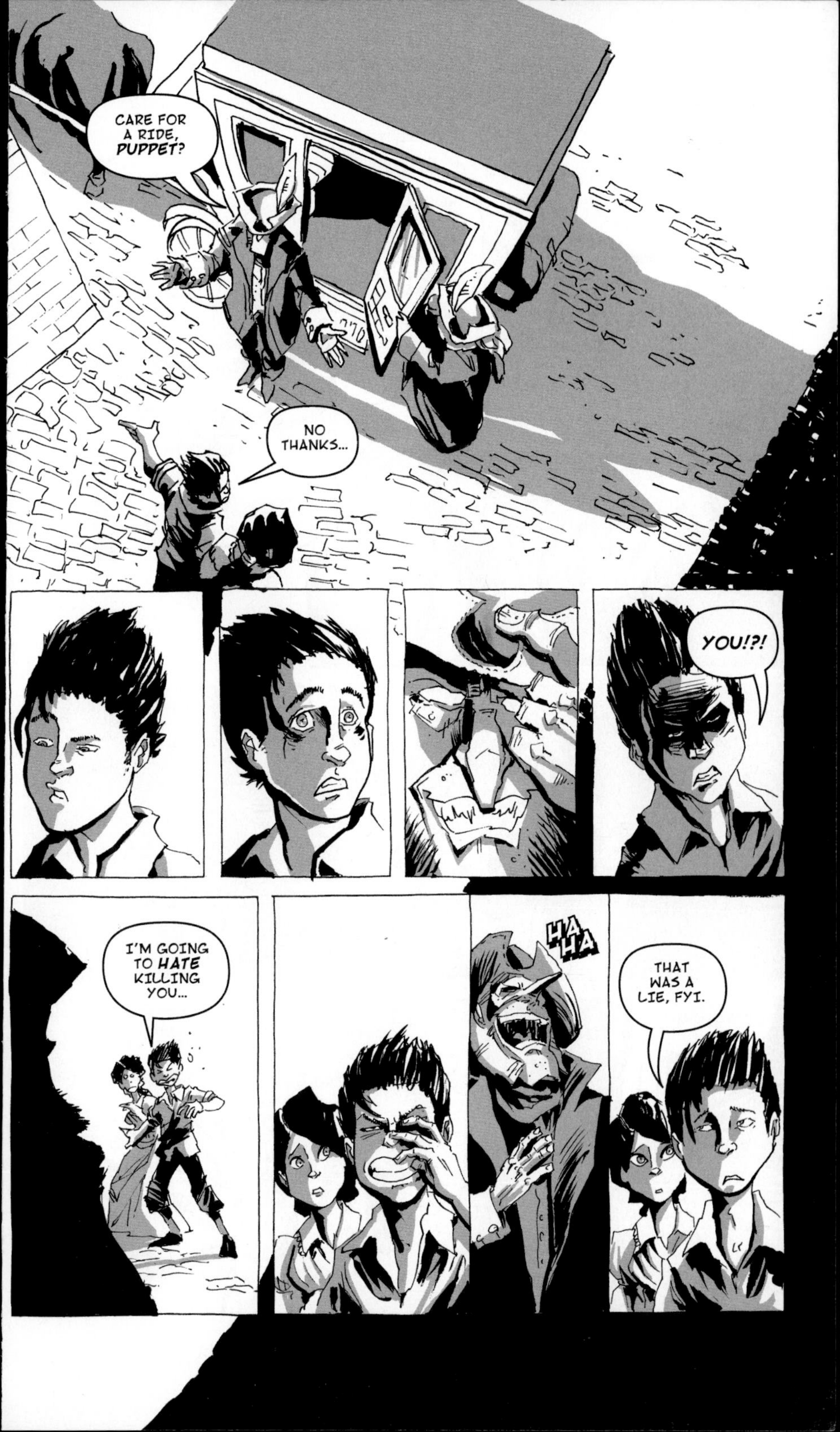
CARE FOR A RIDE, *PUPPET*?
NO THANKS...
YOU!?!
I'M GOING TO *HATE* KILLING YOU...
HA HA
THAT WAS A LIE, FYI.

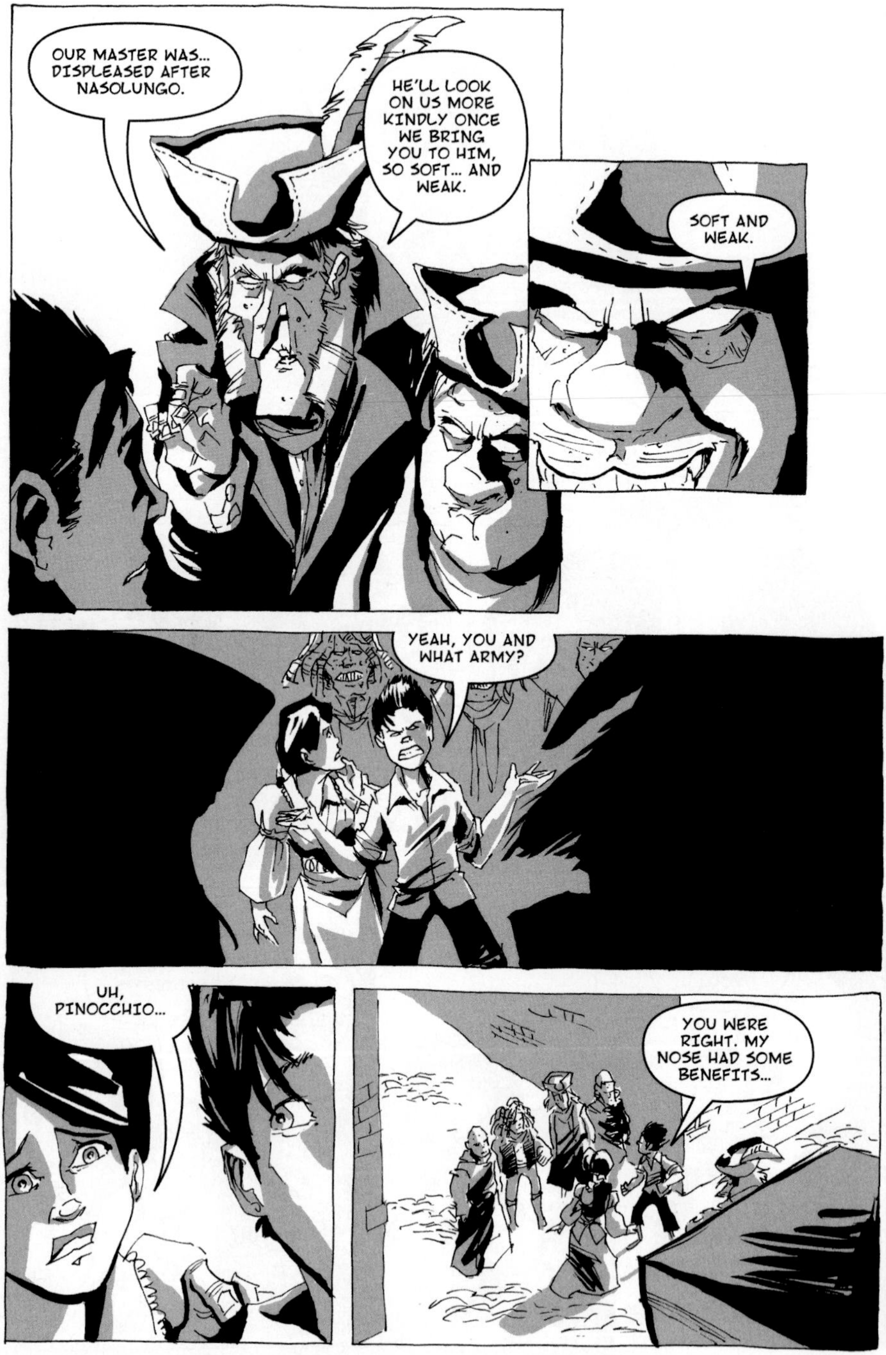

OUR MASTER WAS... DISPLEASED AFTER NASOLUNGO.
HE'LL LOOK ON US MORE KINDLY ONCE WE BRING YOU TO HIM, SO SOFT... AND WEAK.
SOFT AND WEAK.
YEAH, YOU AND WHAT ARMY?
UH, PINOCCHIO...
YOU WERE RIGHT. MY NOSE HAD SOME BENEFITS...

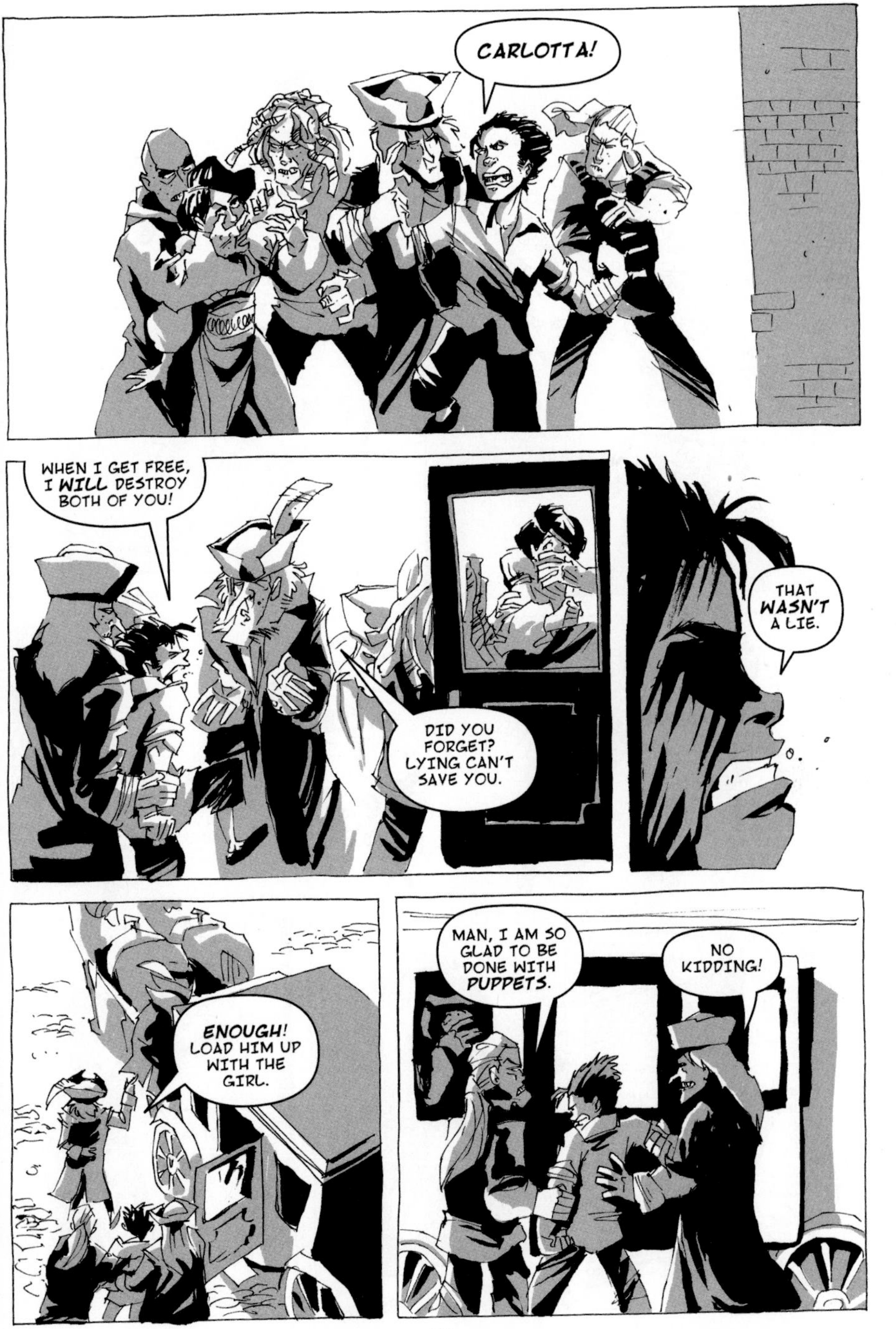

CARLOTTA!
WHEN I GET FREE, I WILL DESTROY BOTH OF YOU!
DID YOU FORGET? LYING CAN'T SAVE YOU.
THAT WASN'T A LIE.
ENOUGH! LOAD HIM UP WITH THE GIRL.
MAN, I AM SO GLAD TO BE DONE WITH PUPPETS.
NO KIDDING!

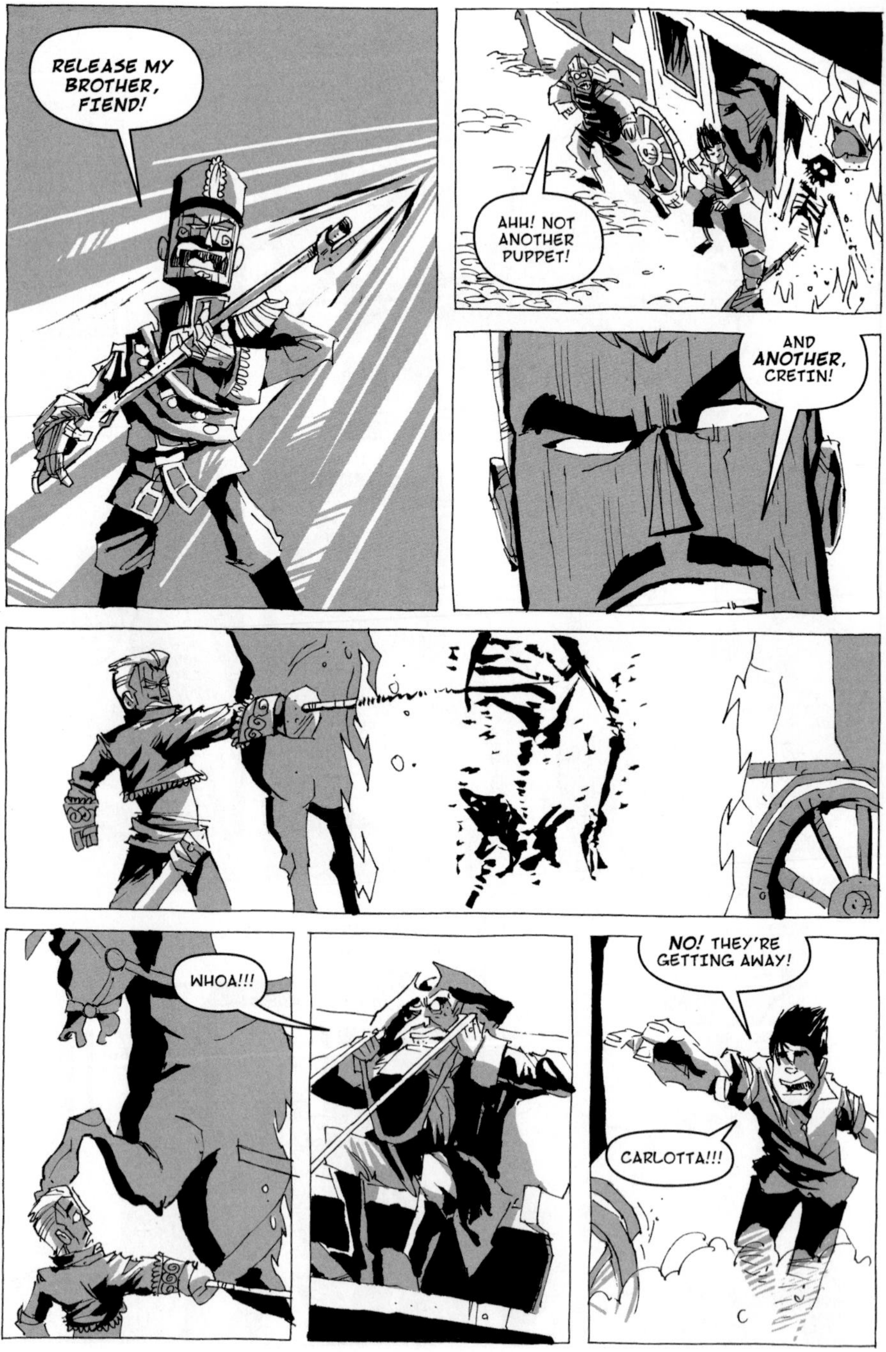
RELEASE MY BROTHER, FIEND!
AHH! NOT ANOTHER PUPPET!
AND ANOTHER, CRETIN!
WHOA!!!
NO! THEY'RE GETTING AWAY!
CARLOTTA!!!

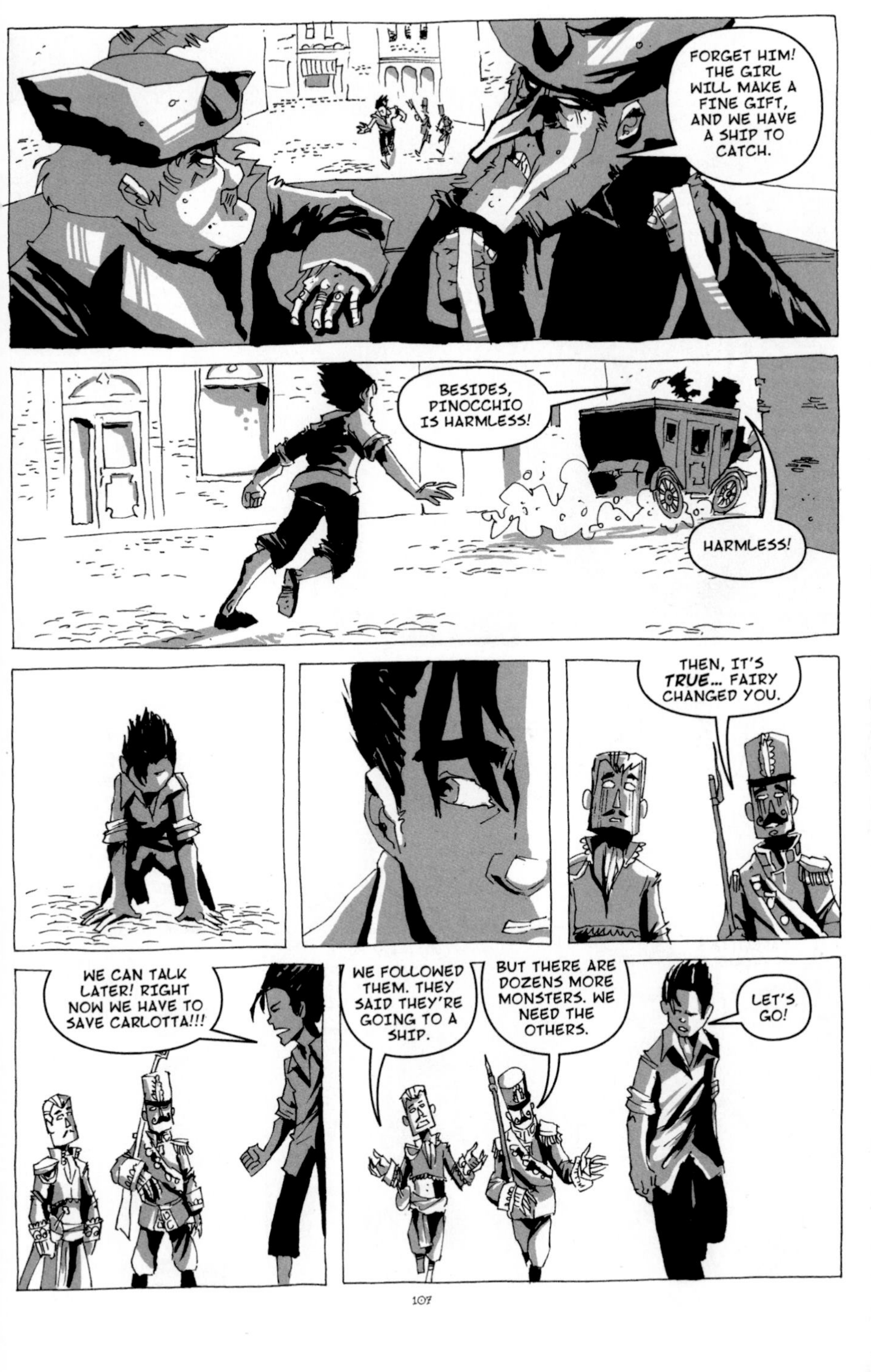
FORGET HIM! THE GIRL WILL MAKE A FINE GIFT, AND WE HAVE A SHIP TO CATCH.
BESIDES, PINOCCHIO IS HARMLESS!
HARMLESS!
THEN, IT'S TRUE... FAIRY CHANGED YOU.
WE CAN TALK LATER! RIGHT NOW WE HAVE TO SAVE CARLOTTA!!!
WE FOLLOWED THEM. THEY SAID THEY'RE GOING TO A SHIP.
BUT THERE ARE DOZENS MORE MONSTERS. WE NEED THE OTHERS.
LET'S GO!

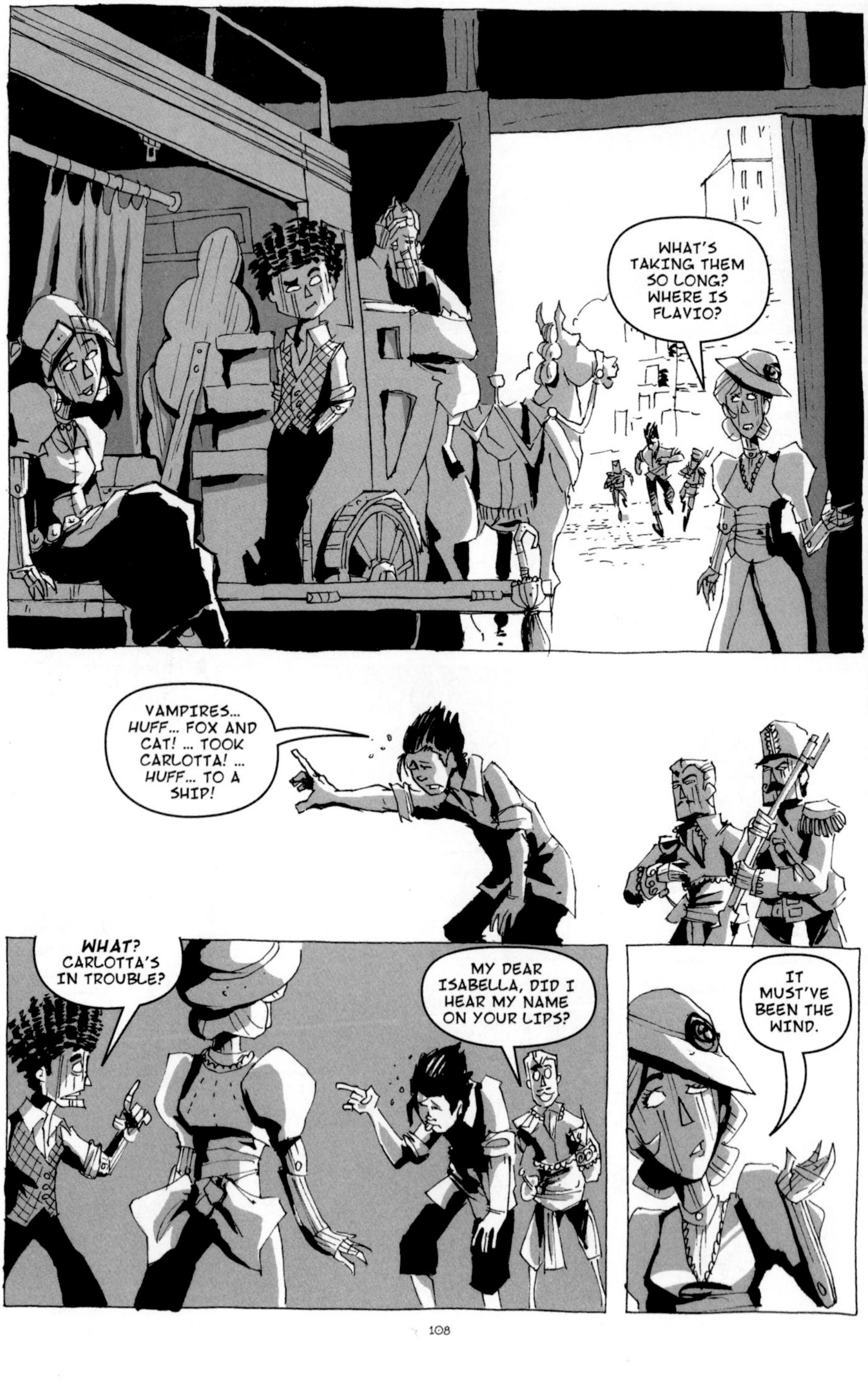
WHAT'S TAKING THEM SO LONG? WHERE IS FLAVIO?
VAMPIRES... HUFF... FOX AND CAT! ... TOOK CARLOTTA! ... HUFF... TO A SHIP!
WHAT? CARLOTTA'S IN TROUBLE?
MY DEAR ISABELLA, DID I HEAR MY NAME ON YOUR LIPS?
IT MUST'VE BEEN THE WIND.

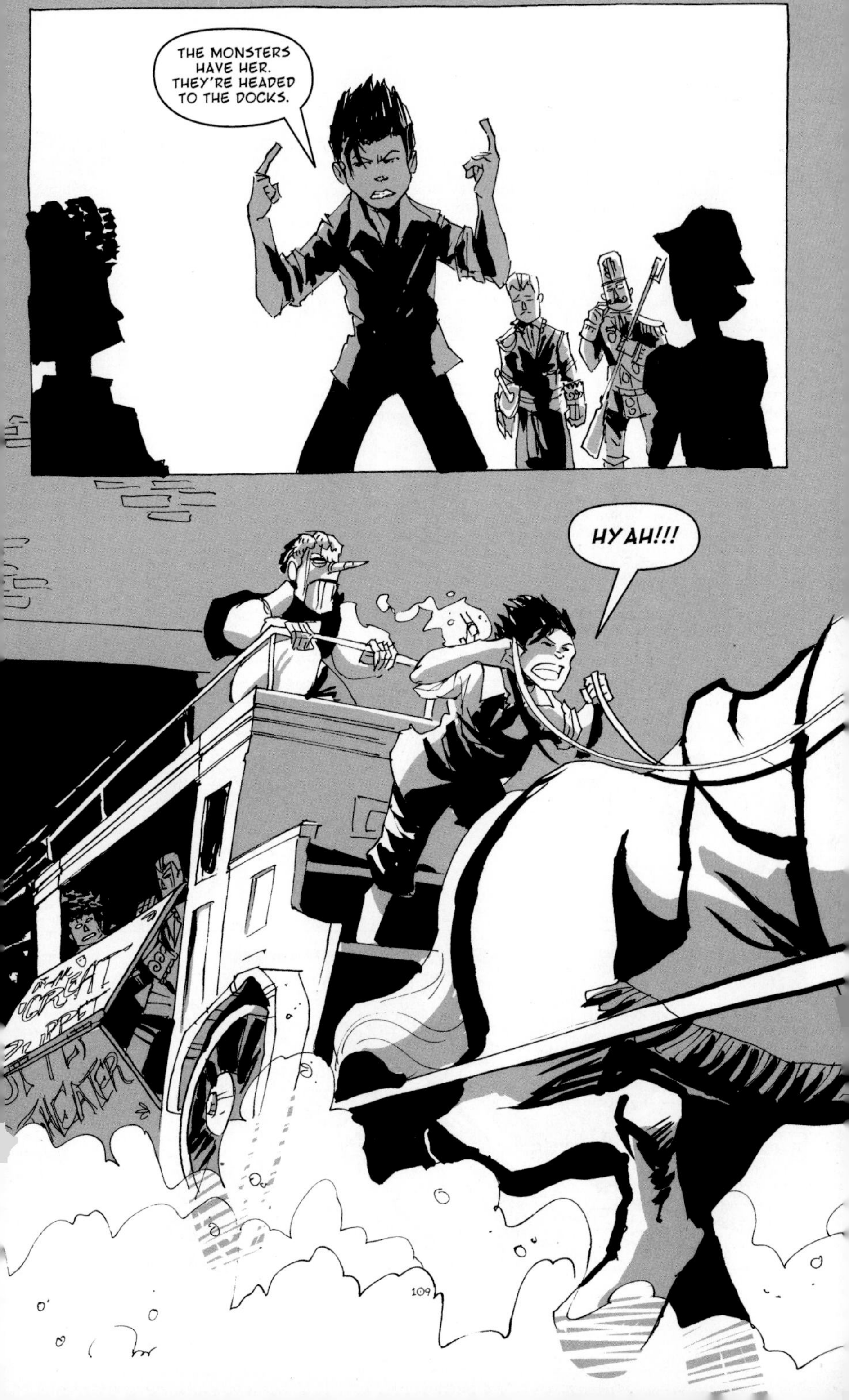
THE MONSTERS HAVE HER. THEY'RE HEADED TO THE DOCKS.
HYAH!!!

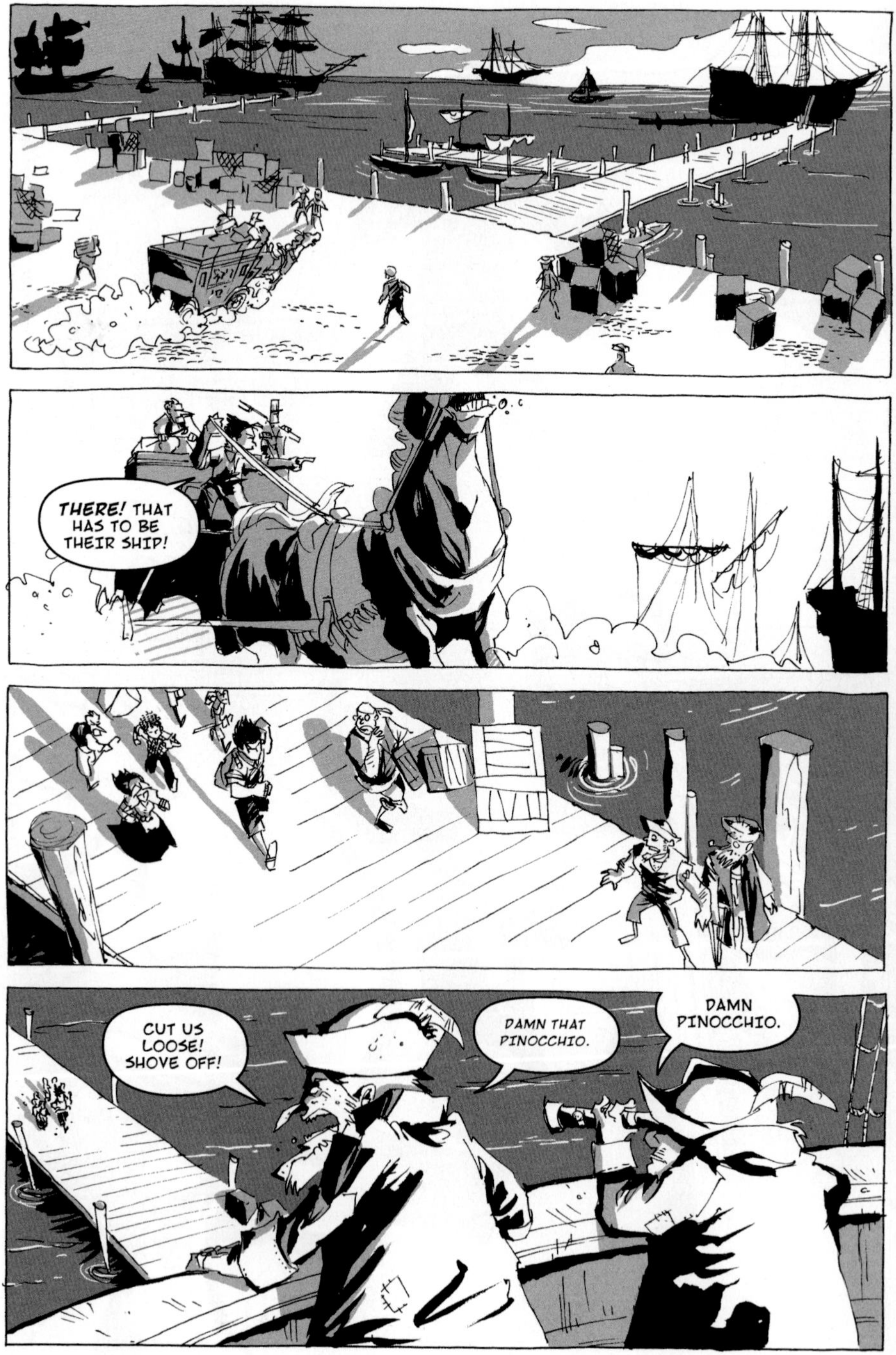
THERE! THAT HAS TO BE THEIR SHIP!
CUT US LOOSE! SHOVE OFF!
DAMN THAT PINOCCHIO.
DAMN PINOCCHIO.

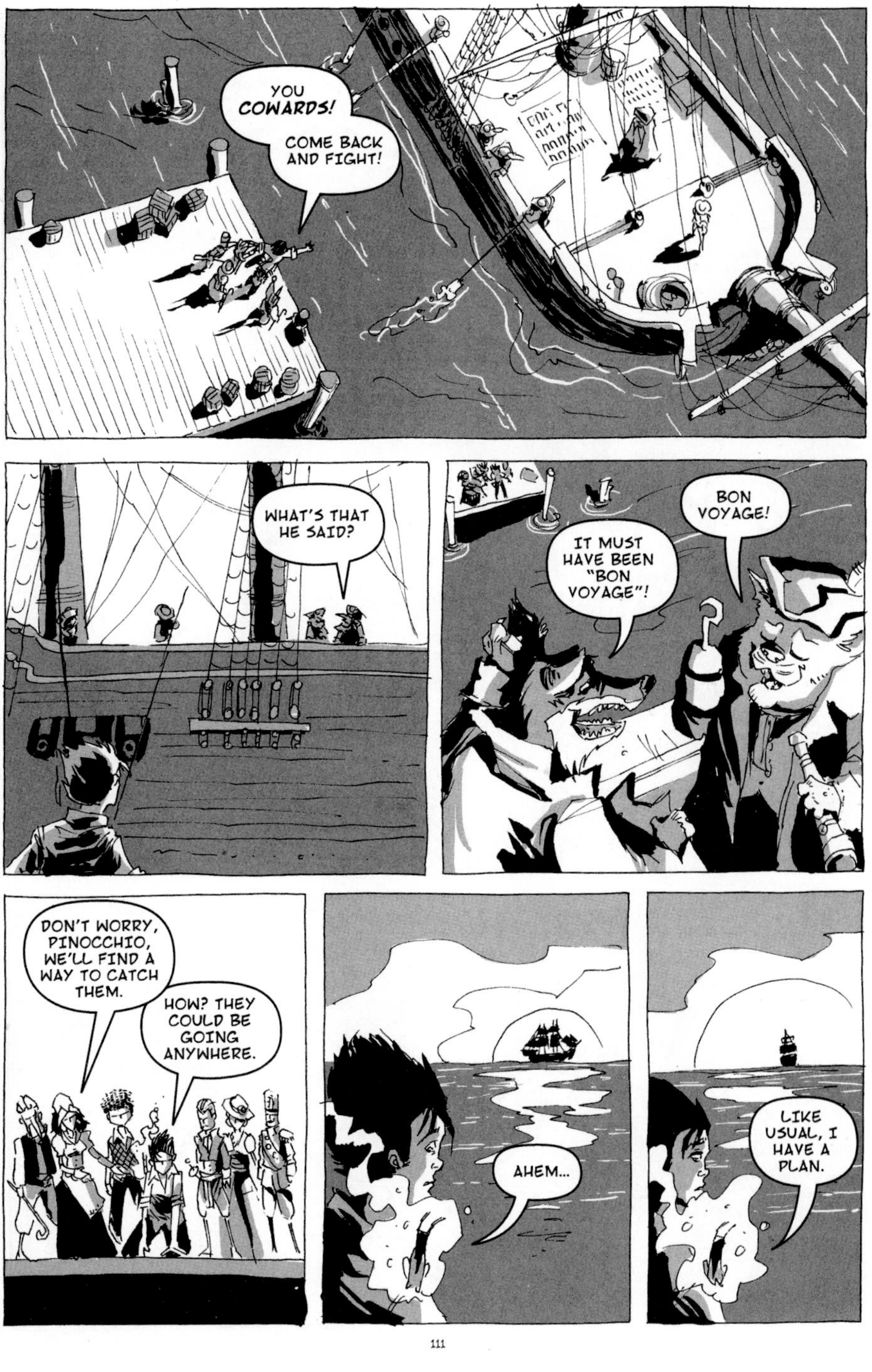
YOU COWARDS!
COME BACK AND FIGHT!
WHAT'S THAT HE SAID?
BON VOYAGE!
IT MUST HAVE BEEN "BON VOYAGE"!
DON'T WORRY, PINOCCHIO, WE'LL FIND A WAY TO CATCH THEM.
HOW? THEY COULD BE GOING ANYWHERE.
AHEM...
LIKE USUAL, I HAVE A PLAN.

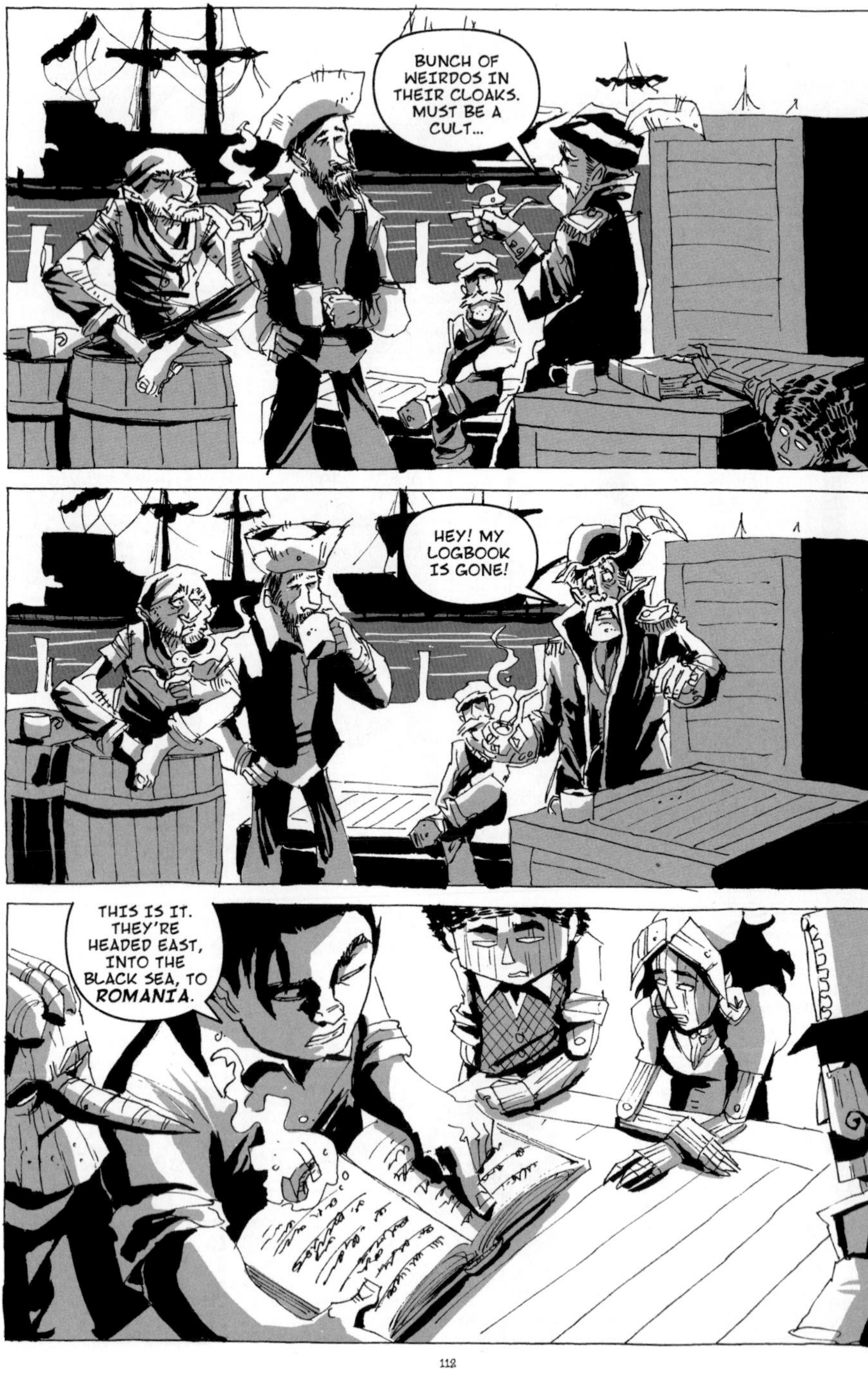
BUNCH OF WEIRDOS IN THEIR CLOAKS. MUST BE A CULT...
HEY! MY LOGBOOK IS GONE!
THIS IS IT. THEY'RE HEADED EAST, INTO THE BLACK SEA, TO **ROMANIA**.

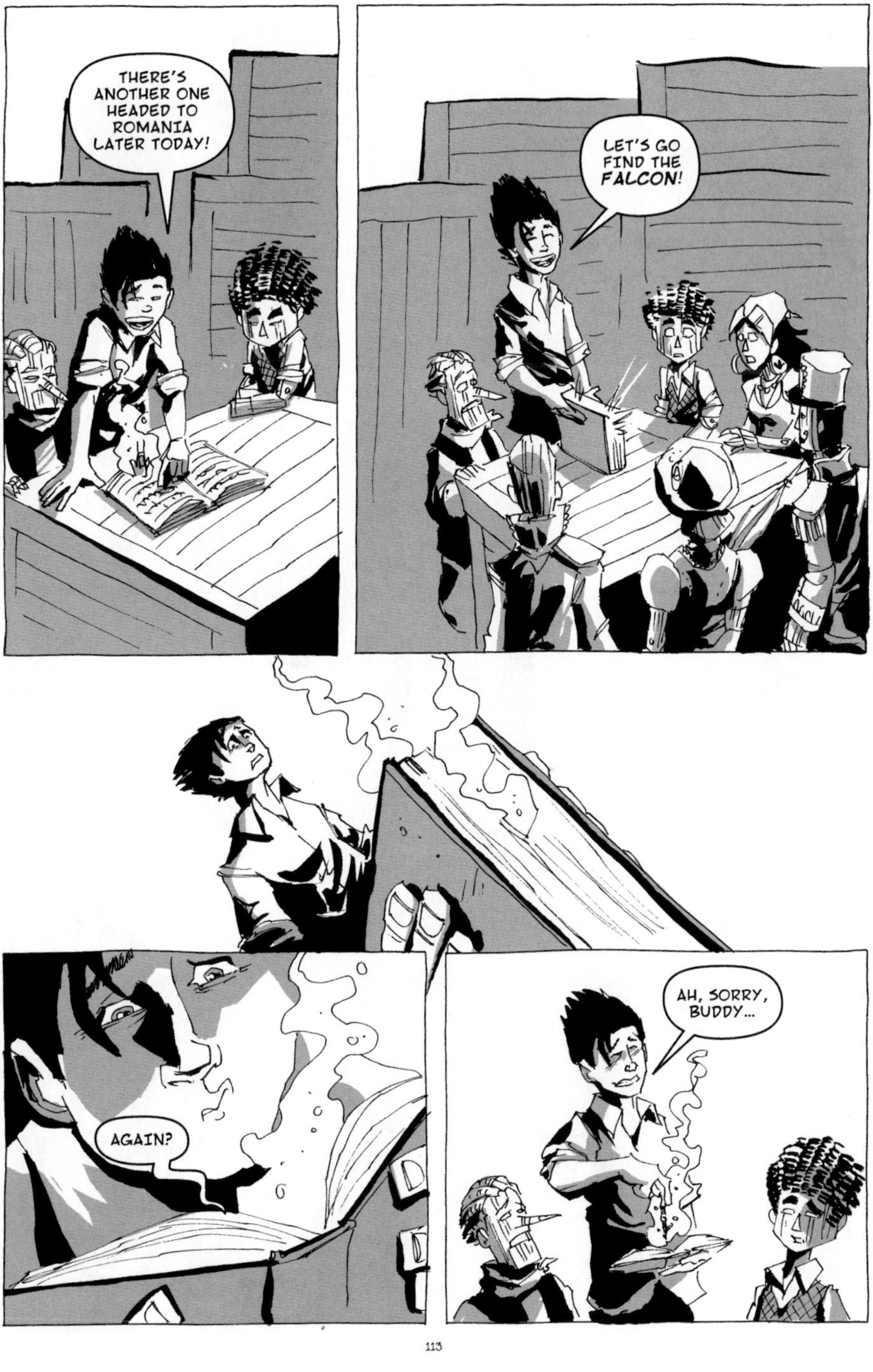
THERE'S ANOTHER ONE HEADED TO ROMANIA LATER TODAY!
LET'S GO FIND THE FALCON!
AGAIN?
AH, SORRY, BUDDY...

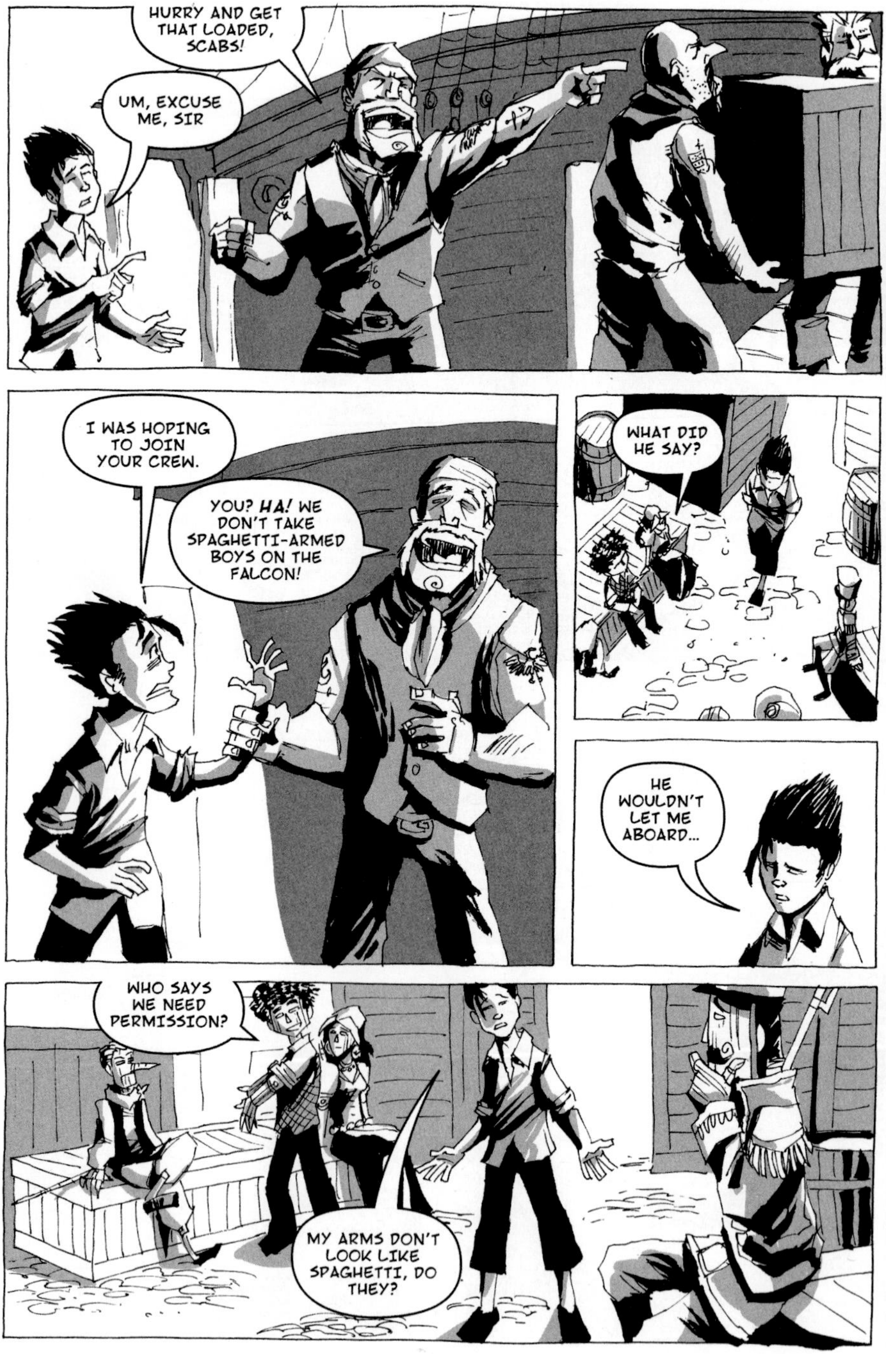
HURRY AND GET THAT LOADED, SCABS!
UM, EXCUSE ME, SIR
I WAS HOPING TO JOIN YOUR CREW.
YOU? HA! WE DON'T TAKE SPAGHETTI-ARMED BOYS ON THE FALCON!
WHAT DID HE SAY?
HE WOULDN'T LET ME ABOARD...
WHO SAYS WE NEED PERMISSION?
MY ARMS DON'T LOOK LIKE SPAGHETTI, DO THEY?

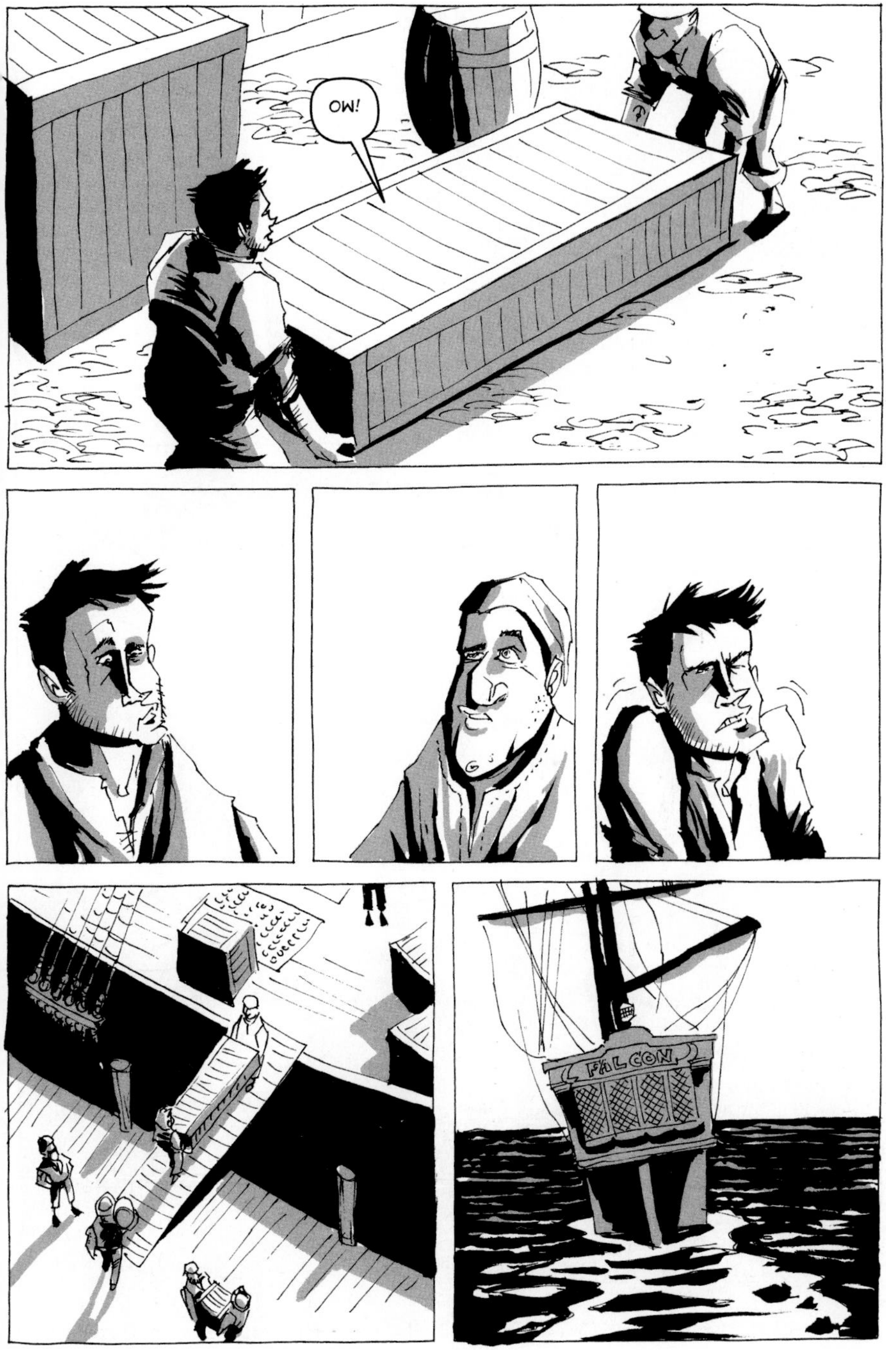
OW!
FALCON

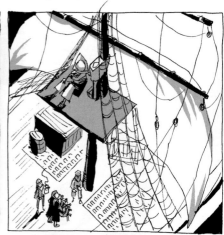

WHO IS STICKING THEIR KNEE IN MY BACK?

GREAT PLAN, CRICKET!

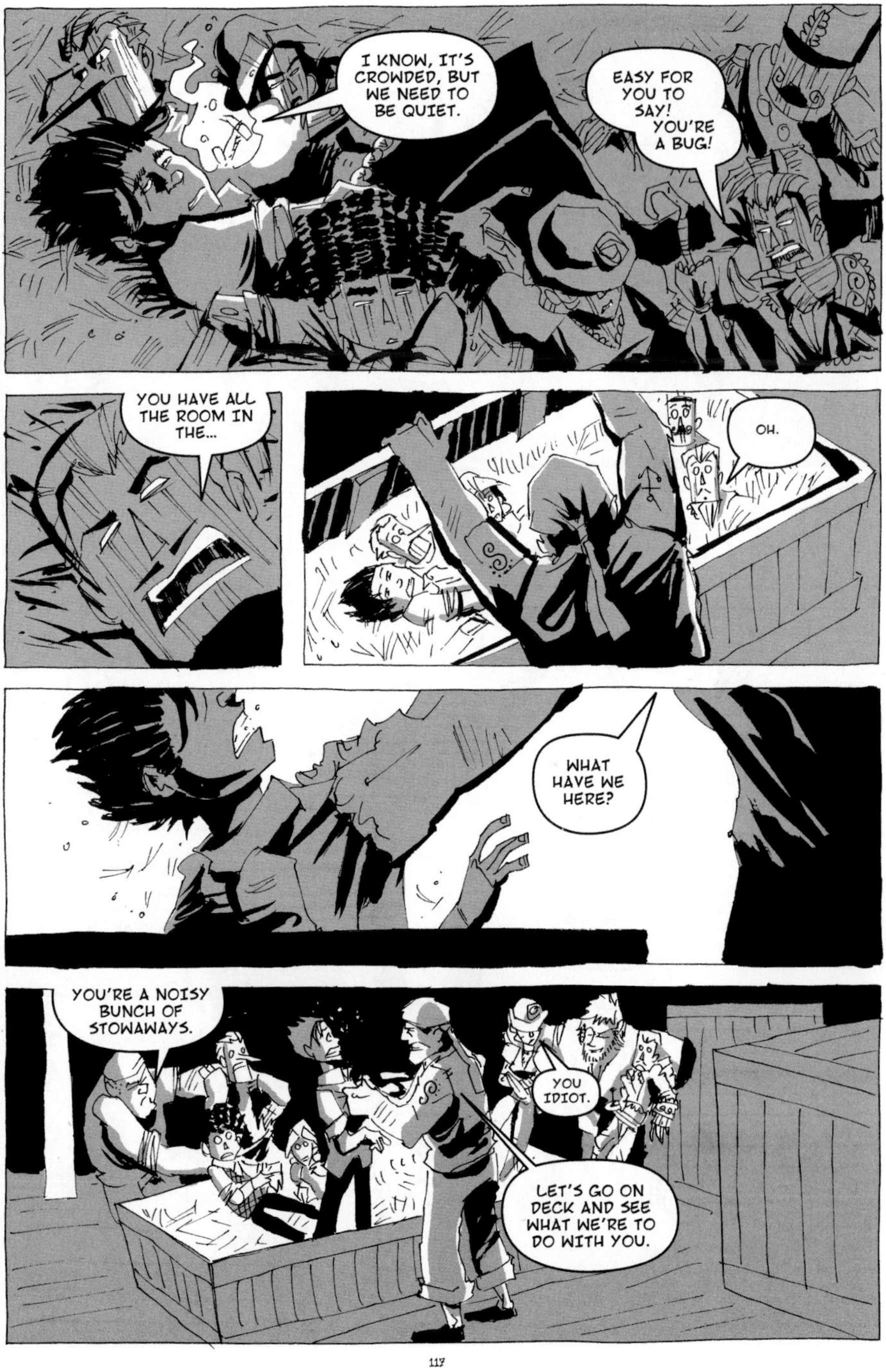
I KNOW, IT'S CROWDED, BUT WE NEED TO BE QUIET.
EASY FOR YOU TO SAY! YOU'RE A BUG!
YOU HAVE ALL THE ROOM IN THE...
OH.
WHAT HAVE WE HERE?
YOU'RE A NOISY BUNCH OF STOWAWAYS.
YOU IDIOT.
LET'S GO ON DECK AND SEE WHAT WE'RE TO DO WITH YOU.

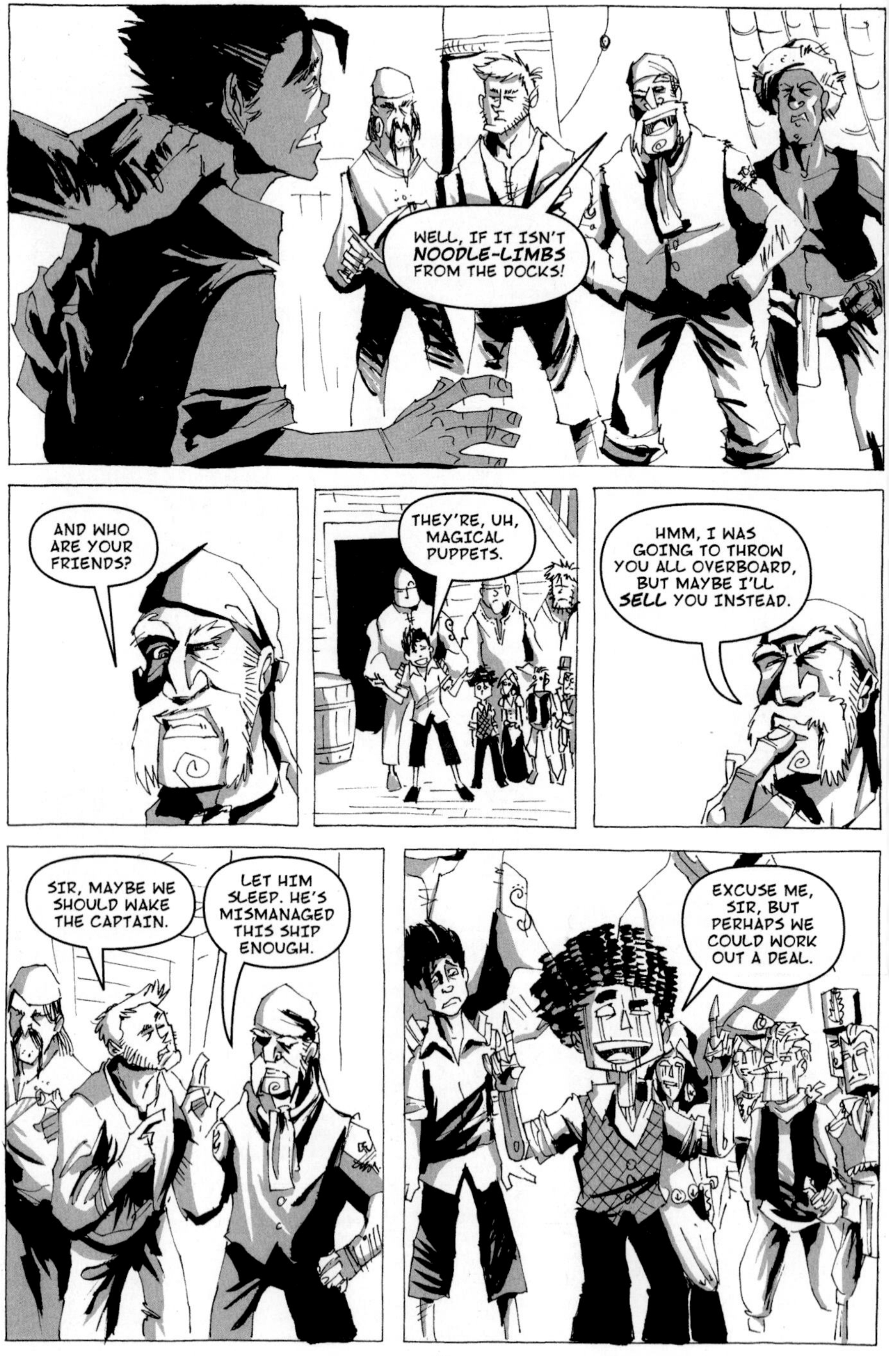
WELL, IF IT ISN'T NOODLE-LIMBS FROM THE DOCKS!
AND WHO ARE YOUR FRIENDS?
THEY'RE, UH, MAGICAL PUPPETS.
HMM, I WAS GOING TO THROW YOU ALL OVERBOARD, BUT MAYBE I'LL SELL YOU INSTEAD.
SIR, MAYBE WE SHOULD WAKE THE CAPTAIN.
LET HIM SLEEP. HE'S MISMANAGED THIS SHIP ENOUGH.
EXCUSE ME, SIR, BUT PERHAPS WE COULD WORK OUT A DEAL.

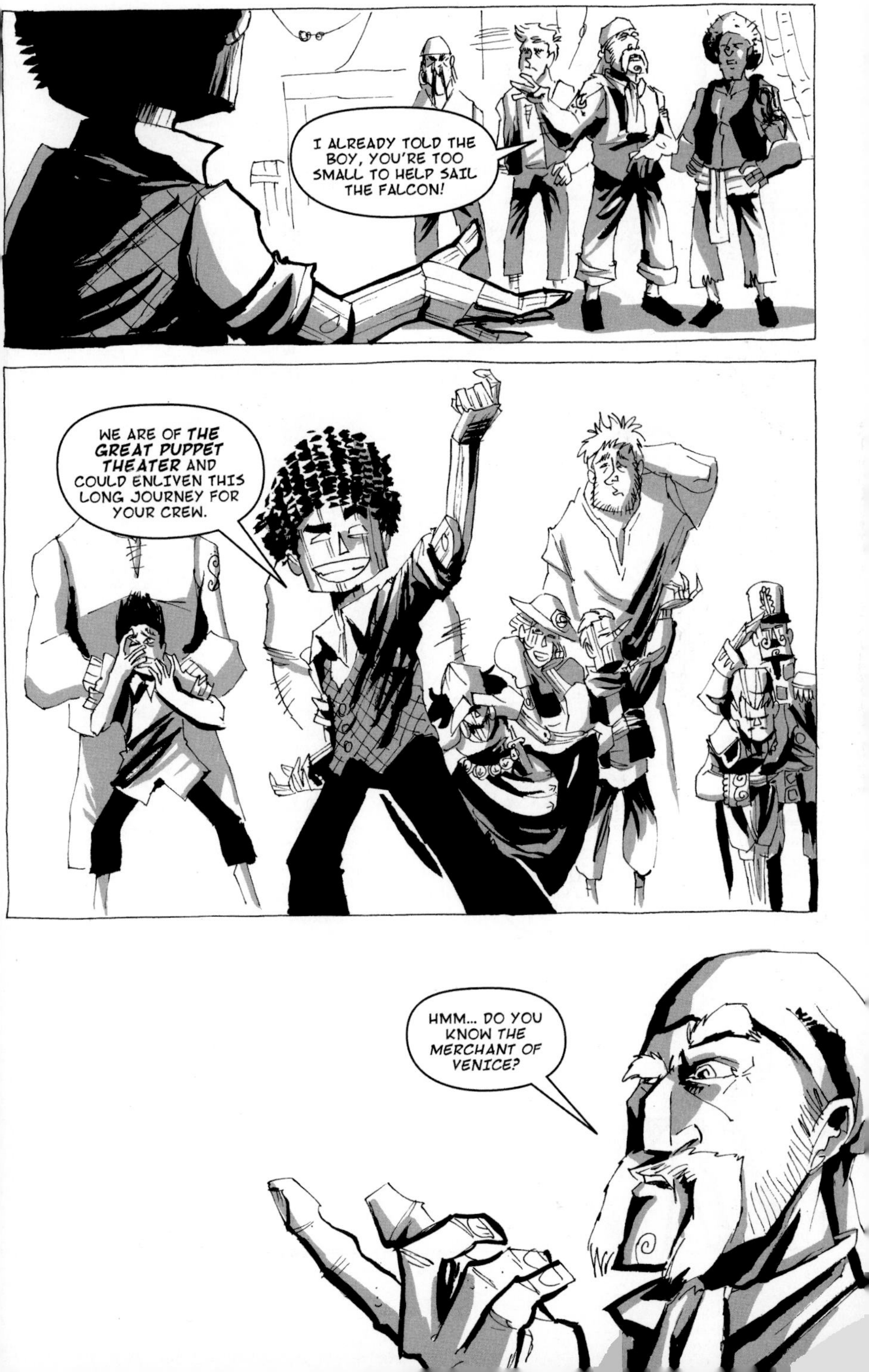
I ALREADY TOLD THE BOY, YOU'RE TOO SMALL TO HELP SAIL THE FALCON!
WE ARE OF **THE GREAT PUPPET THEATER** AND COULD ENLIVEN THIS LONG JOURNEY FOR YOUR CREW.
HMM... DO YOU KNOW *THE MERCHANT OF VENICE?*

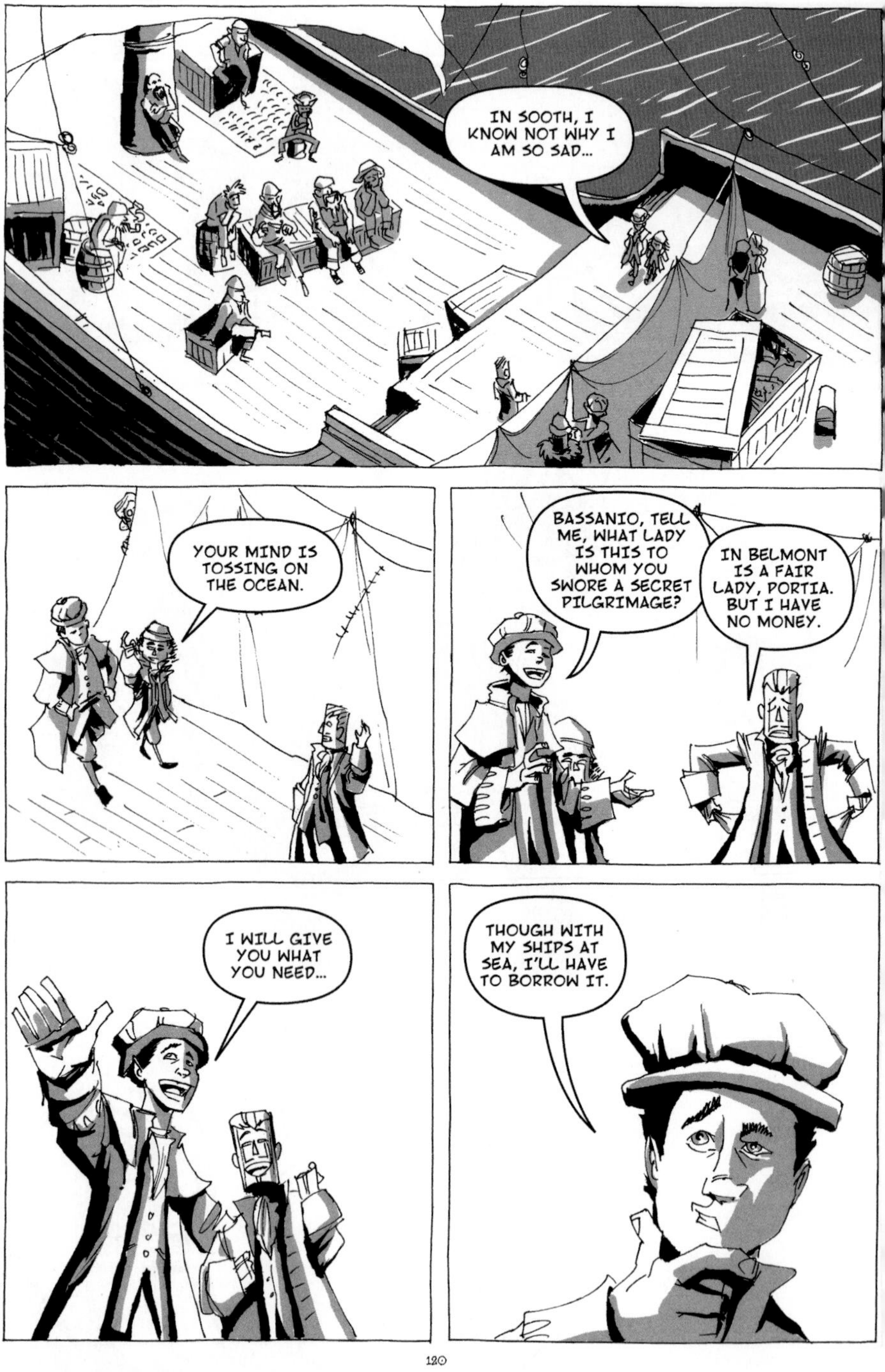
IN SOOTH, I KNOW NOT WHY I AM SO SAD...
YOUR MIND IS TOSSING ON THE OCEAN.
BASSANIO, TELL ME, WHAT LADY IS THIS TO WHOM YOU SWORE A SECRET PILGRIMAGE?
IN BELMONT IS A FAIR LADY, PORTIA. BUT I HAVE NO MONEY.
I WILL GIVE YOU WHAT YOU NEED...
THOUGH WITH MY SHIPS AT SEA, I'LL HAVE TO BORROW IT.

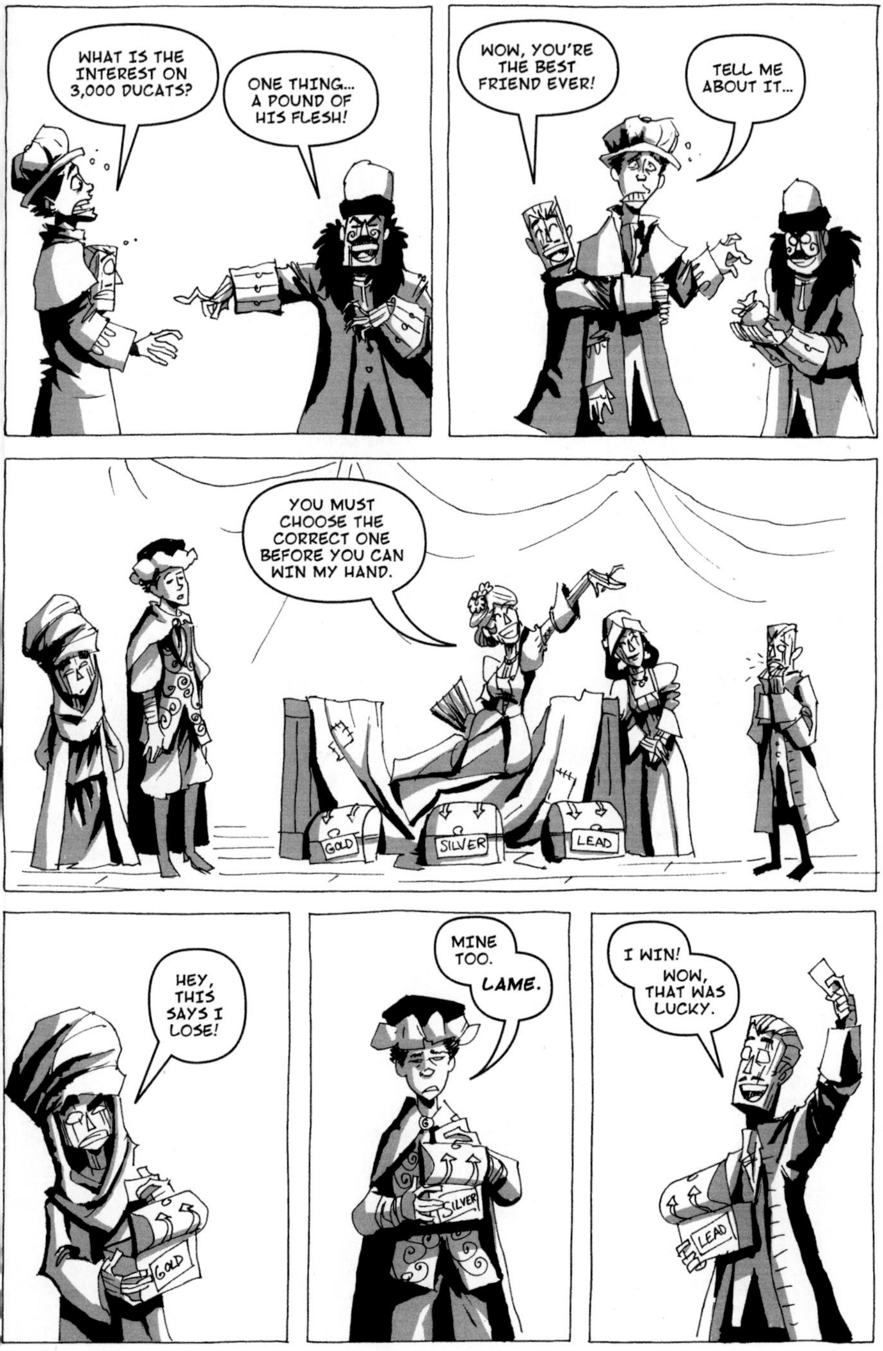
WHAT IS THE INTEREST ON 3,000 DUCATS?
ONE THING... A POUND OF HIS FLESH!
WOW, YOU'RE THE BEST FRIEND EVER!
TELL ME ABOUT IT...
YOU MUST CHOOSE THE CORRECT ONE BEFORE YOU CAN WIN MY HAND.
GOLD
SILVER
LEAD
HEY, THIS SAYS I LOSE!
GOLD
MINE TOO.
LAME.
SILVER
I WIN!
WOW, THAT WAS LUCKY.
LEAD

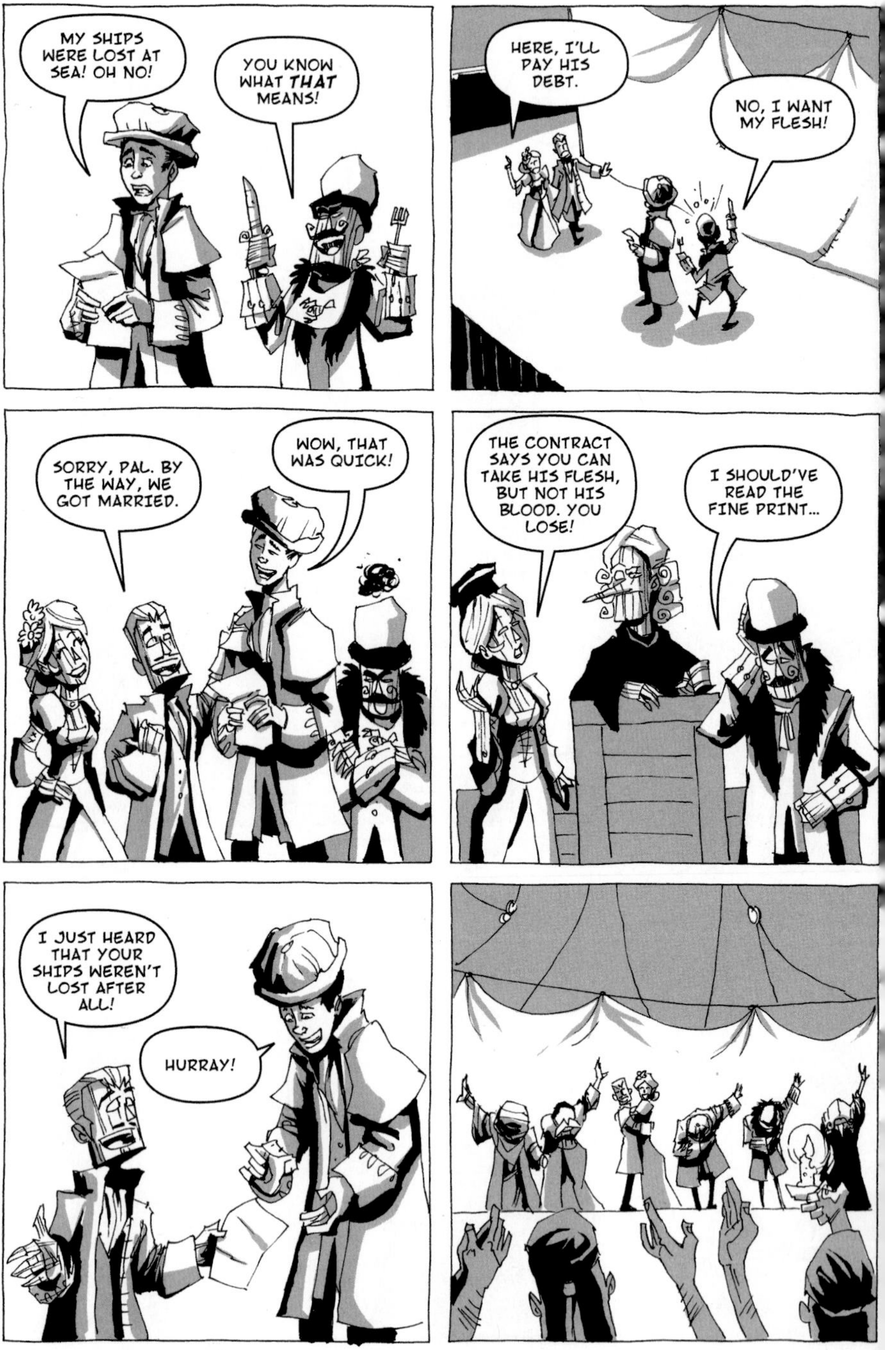
MY SHIPS WERE LOST AT SEA! OH NO!
YOU KNOW WHAT *THAT* MEANS!
HERE, I'LL PAY HIS DEBT.
NO, I WANT MY FLESH!
SORRY, PAL. BY THE WAY, WE GOT MARRIED.
WOW, THAT WAS QUICK!
THE CONTRACT SAYS YOU CAN TAKE HIS FLESH, BUT NOT HIS BLOOD. YOU LOSE!
I SHOULD'VE READ THE FINE PRINT...
I JUST HEARD THAT YOUR SHIPS WEREN'T LOST AFTER ALL!
HURRAY!

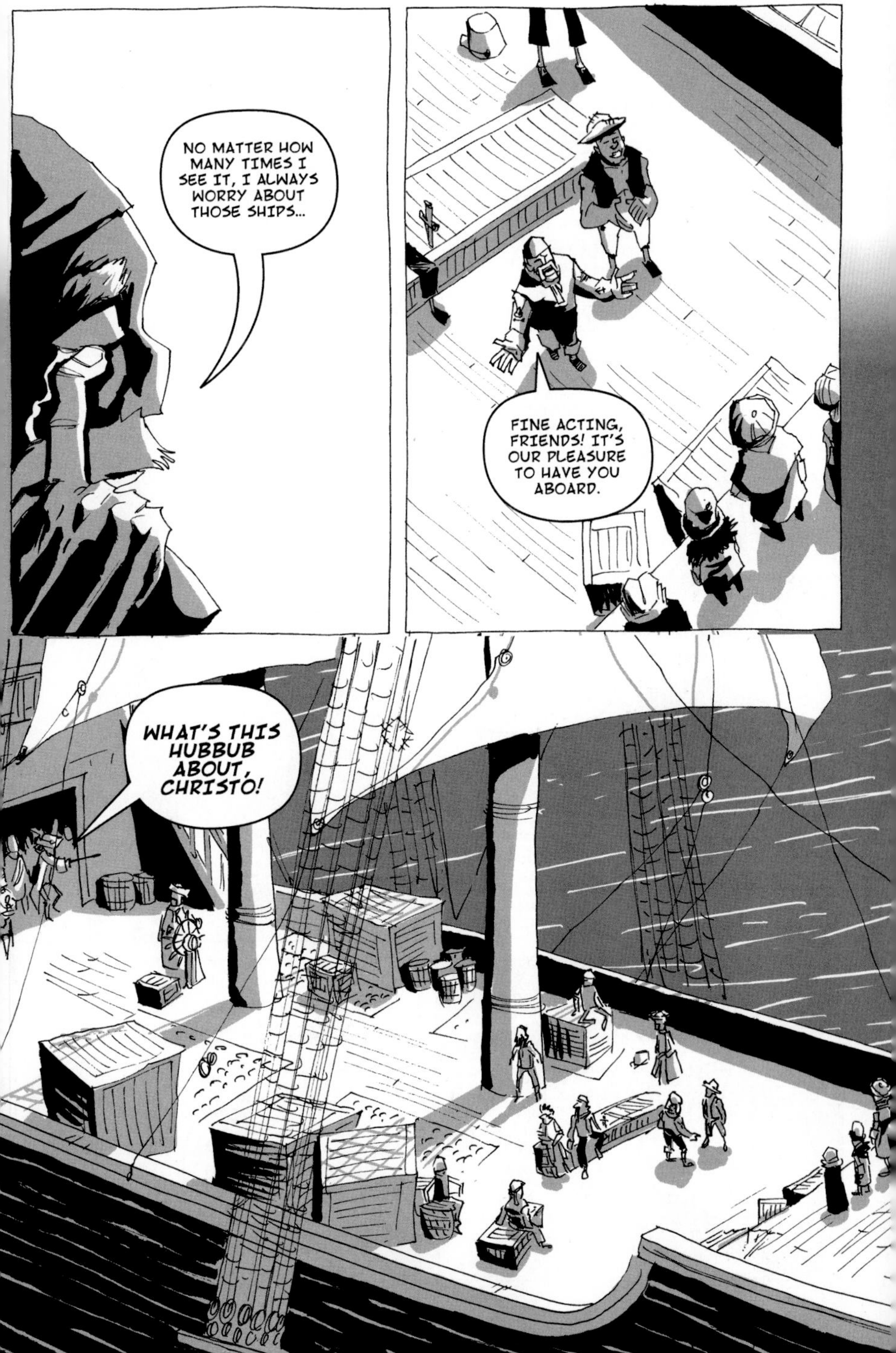
NO MATTER HOW MANY TIMES I SEE IT, I ALWAYS WORRY ABOUT THOSE SHIPS...
FINE ACTING, FRIENDS! IT'S OUR PLEASURE TO HAVE YOU ABOARD.
WHAT'S THIS HUBBUB ABOUT, CHRISTO!

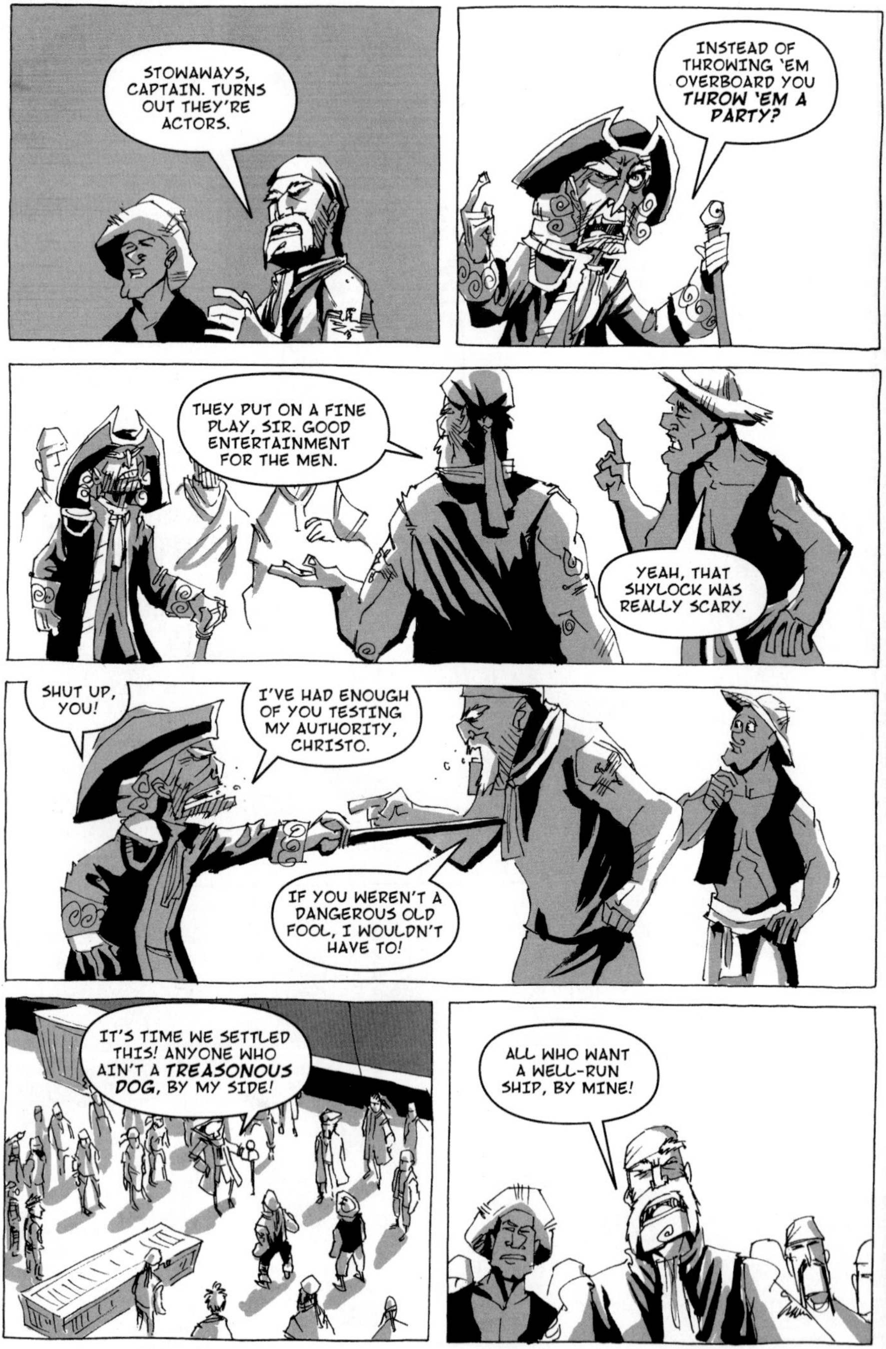
STOWAWAYS, CAPTAIN. TURNS OUT THEY'RE ACTORS.
INSTEAD OF THROWING 'EM OVERBOARD YOU THROW 'EM A PARTY?
THEY PUT ON A FINE PLAY, SIR. GOOD ENTERTAINMENT FOR THE MEN.
YEAH, THAT SHYLOCK WAS REALLY SCARY.
SHUT UP, YOU!
I'VE HAD ENOUGH OF YOU TESTING MY AUTHORITY, CHRISTO.
IF YOU WEREN'T A DANGEROUS OLD FOOL, I WOULDN'T HAVE TO!
IT'S TIME WE SETTLED THIS! ANYONE WHO AIN'T A TREASONOUS DOG, BY MY SIDE!
ALL WHO WANT A WELL-RUN SHIP, BY MINE!

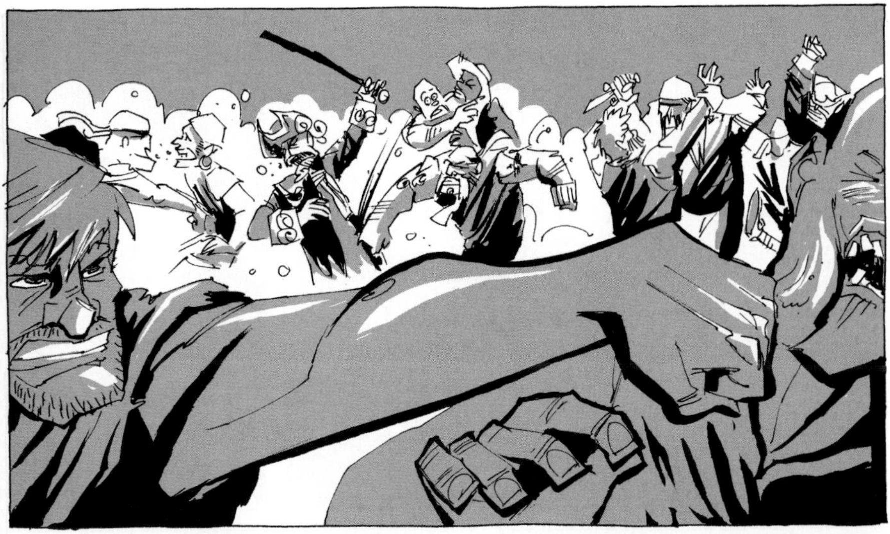

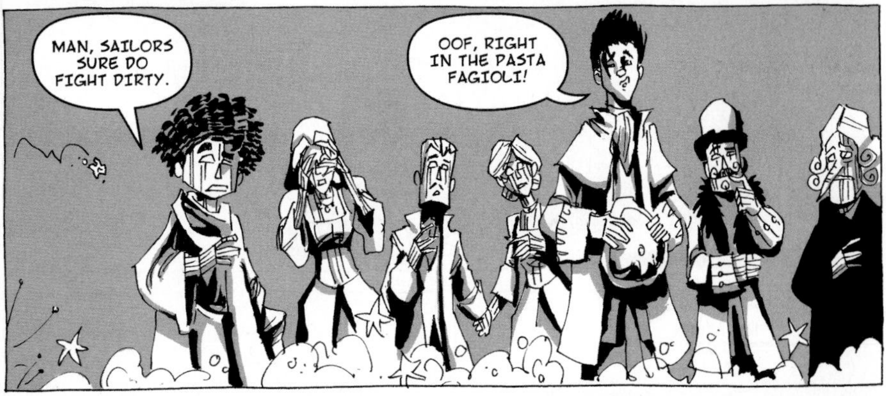
MAN, SAILORS SURE DO FIGHT DIRTY.
OOF, RIGHT IN THE PASTA FAGIOLI!

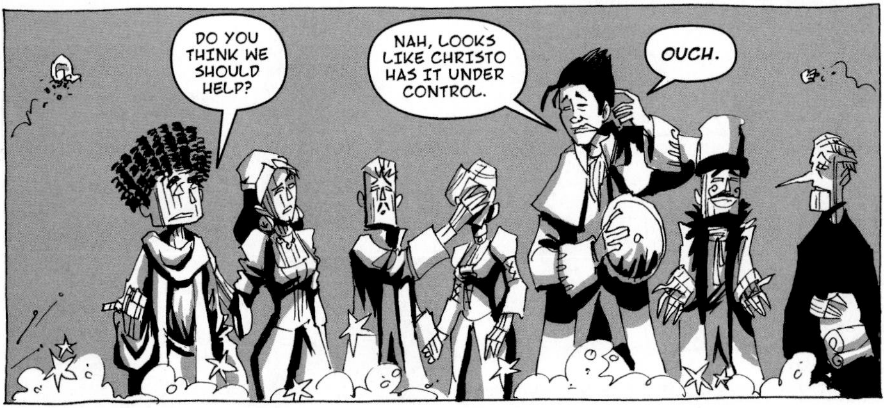
DO YOU THINK WE SHOULD HELP?
NAH, LOOKS LIKE CHRISTO HAS IT UNDER CONTROL.
OUCH.

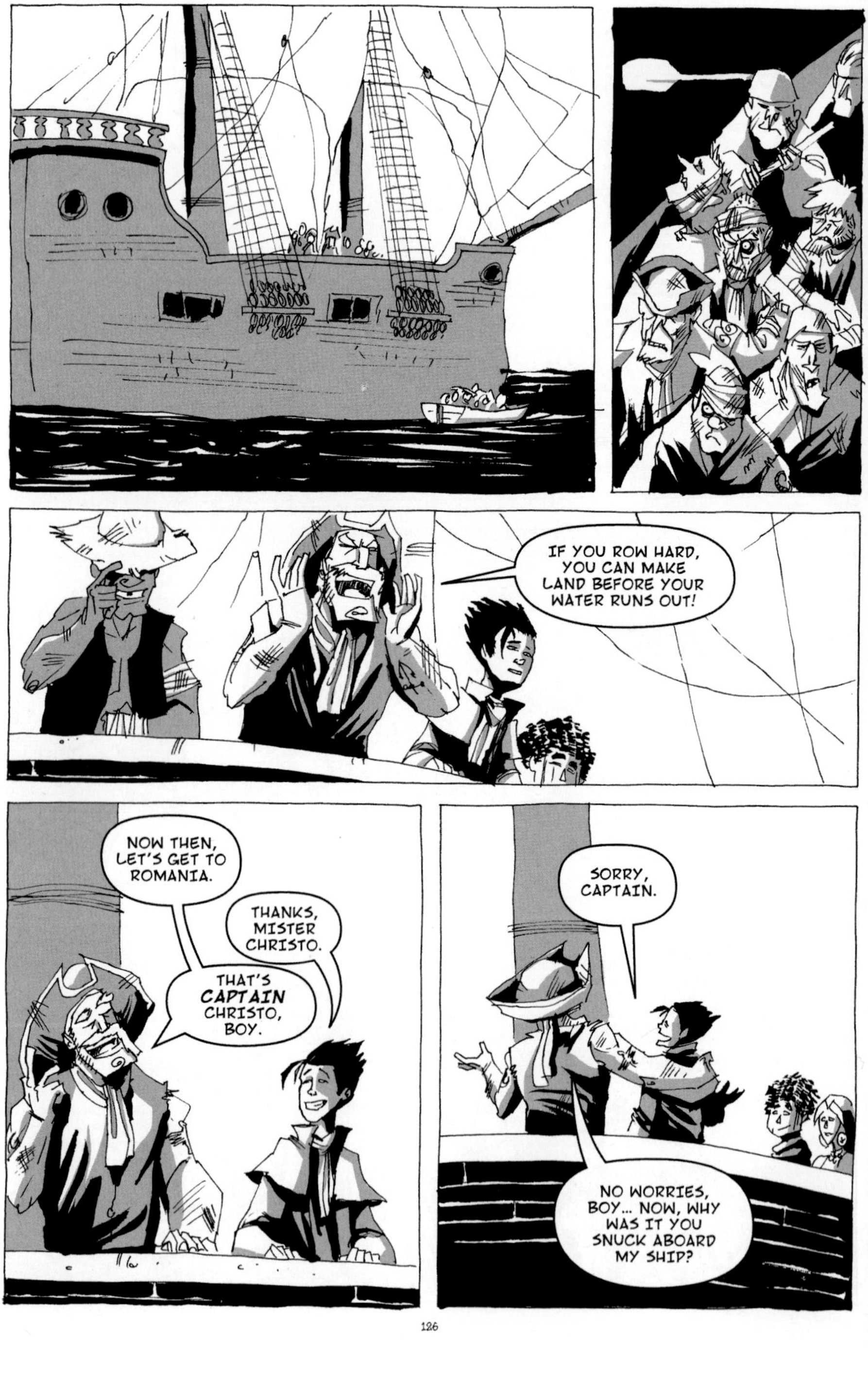
IF YOU ROW HARD, YOU CAN MAKE LAND BEFORE YOUR WATER RUNS OUT!
NOW THEN, LET'S GET TO ROMANIA.
THANKS, MISTER CHRISTO.
THAT'S *CAPTAIN* CHRISTO, BOY.
SORRY, CAPTAIN.
NO WORRIES, BOY... NOW, WHY WAS IT YOU SNUCK ABOARD MY SHIP?

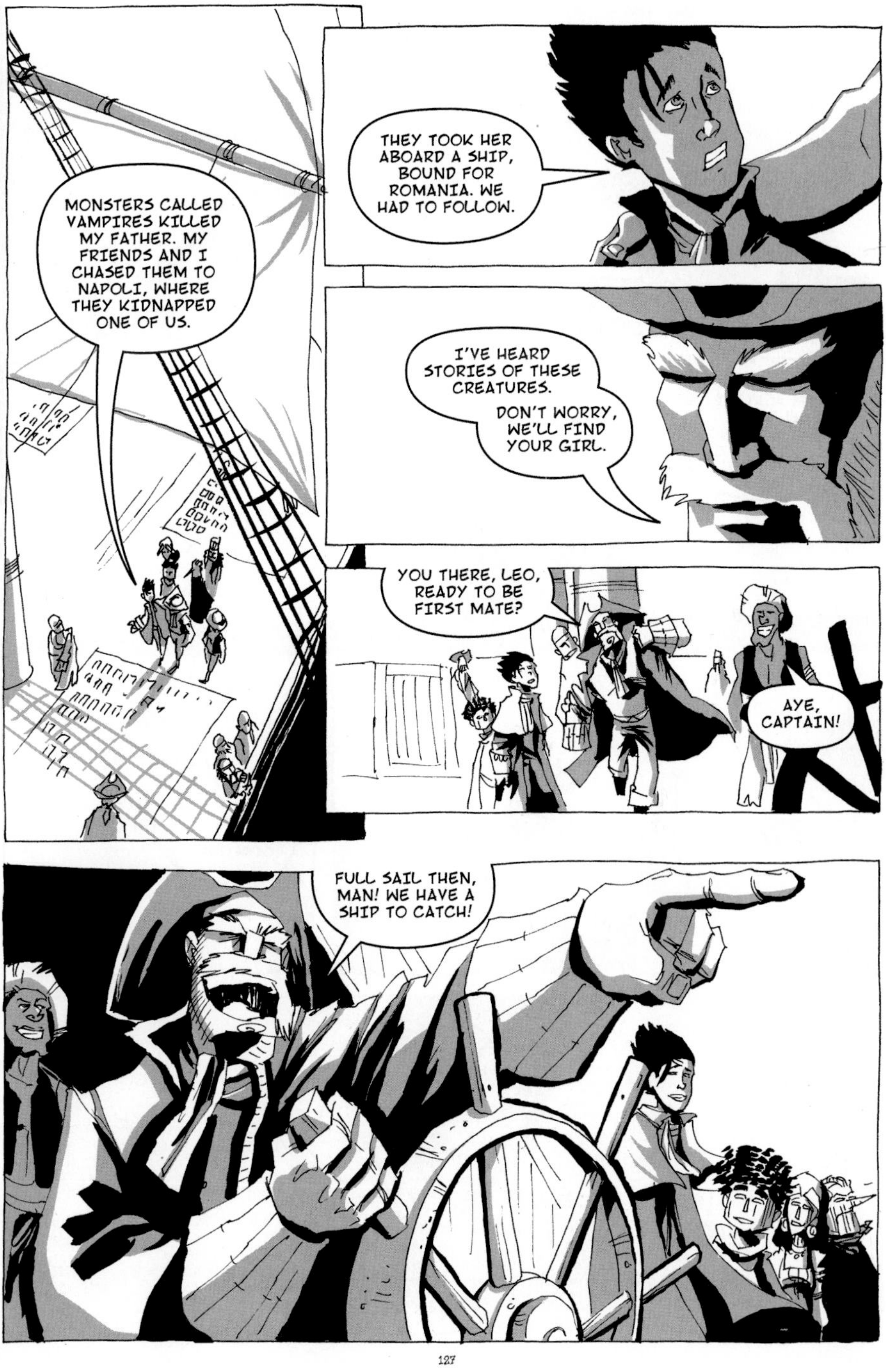
MONSTERS CALLED VAMPIRES KILLED MY FATHER. MY FRIENDS AND I CHASED THEM TO NAPOLI, WHERE THEY KIDNAPPED ONE OF US.
THEY TOOK HER ABOARD A SHIP, BOUND FOR ROMANIA. WE HAD TO FOLLOW.
I'VE HEARD STORIES OF THESE CREATURES.
DON'T WORRY, WE'LL FIND YOUR GIRL.
YOU THERE, LEO, READY TO BE FIRST MATE?
AYE, CAPTAIN!
FULL SAIL THEN, MAN! WE HAVE A SHIP TO CATCH!

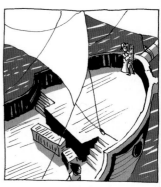

I'M SORRY I HELD YOU AWAY SO LONG. OF COURSE I LOVE YOU.

MY DEAR, THAT'S ALL I EVER WANTED IN THE WORLD.

DON'T WORRY. I'M COMING.

SIGH...

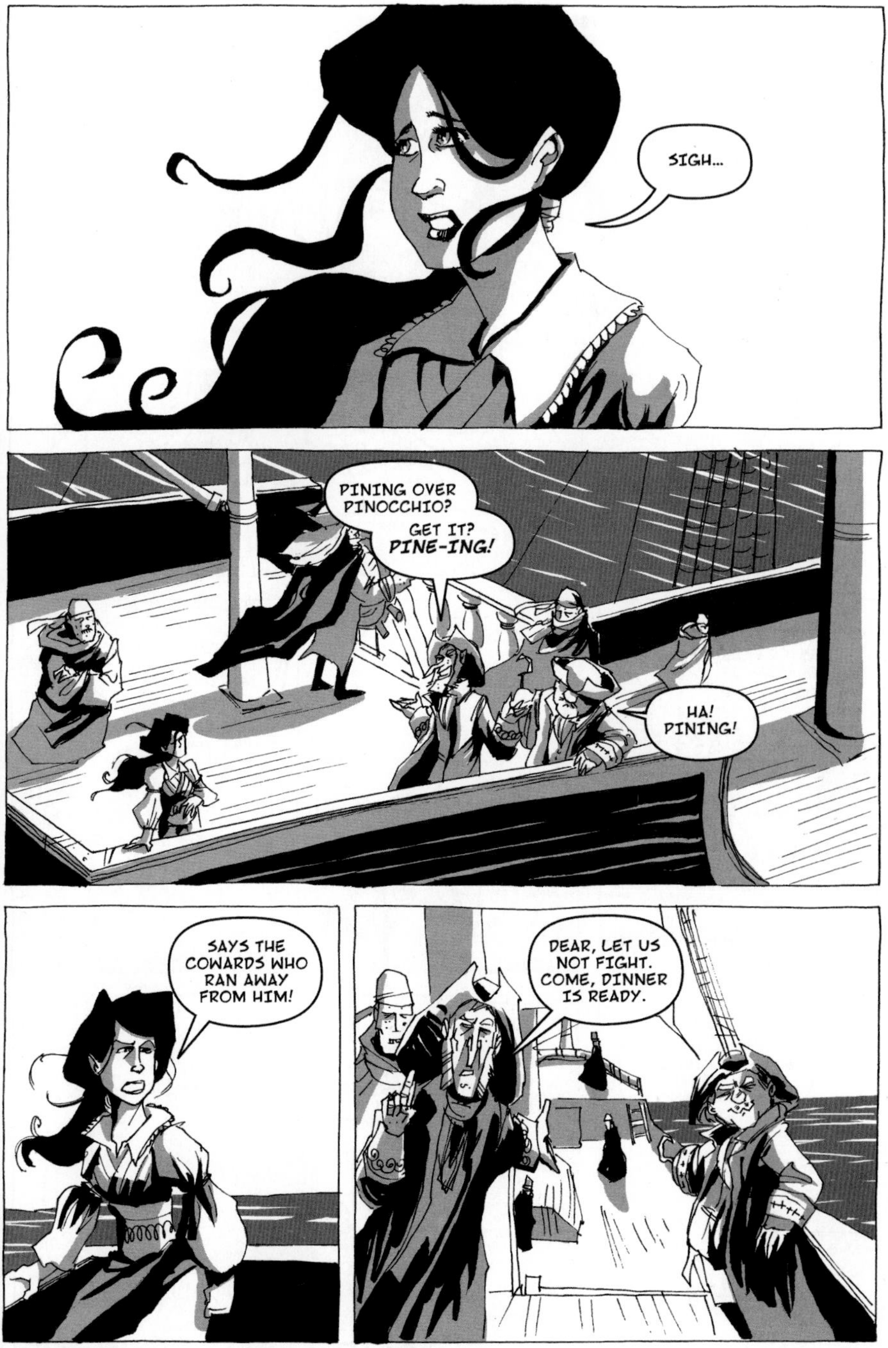
SIGH...
PINING OVER PINOCCHIO?
GET IT? PINE-ING!
HA! PINING!
SAYS THE COWARDS WHO RAN AWAY FROM HIM!
DEAR, LET US NOT FIGHT. COME, DINNER IS READY.

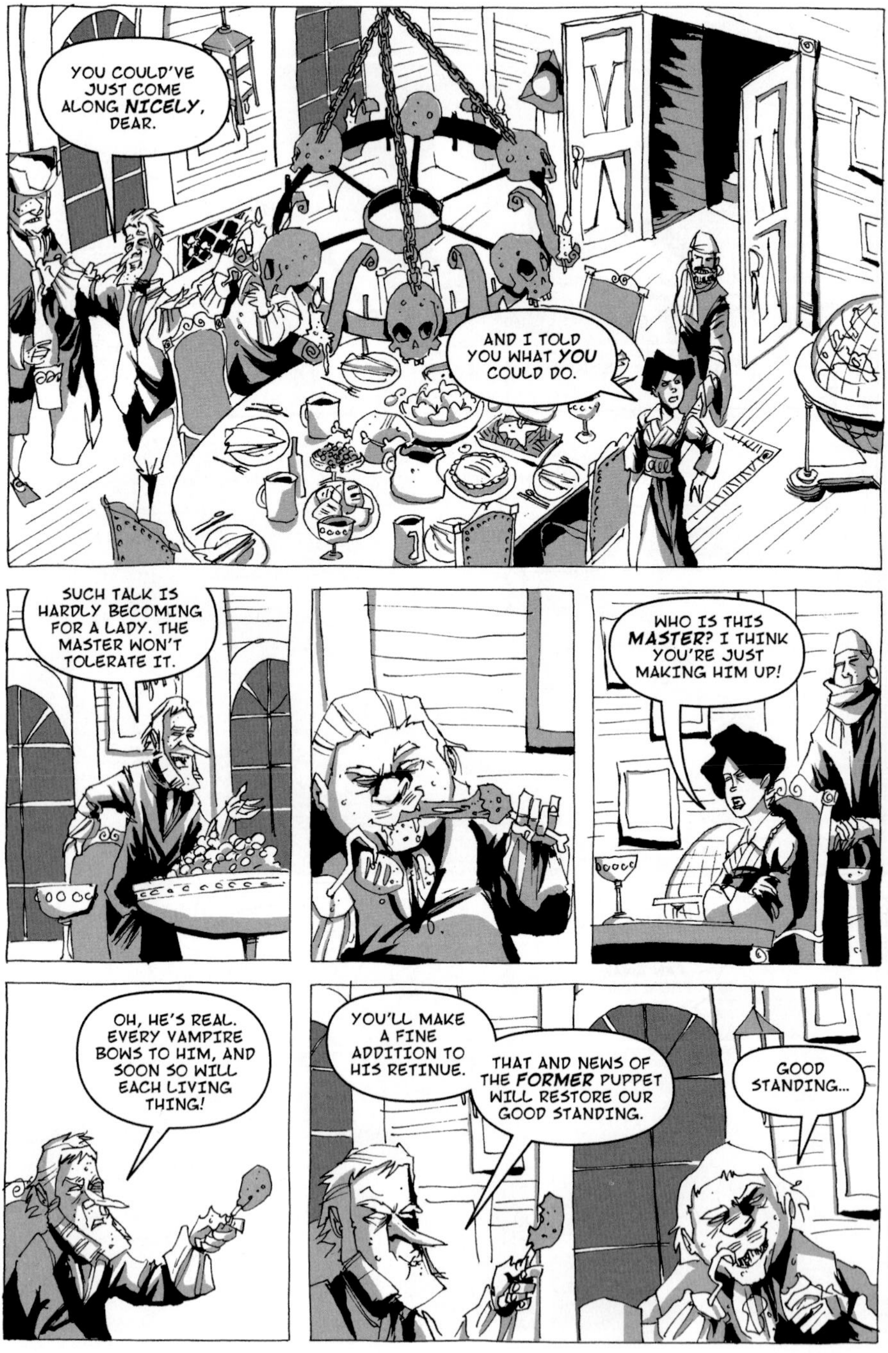

YOU COULD'VE JUST COME ALONG NICELY, DEAR.
AND I TOLD YOU WHAT YOU COULD DO.
SUCH TALK IS HARDLY BECOMING FOR A LADY. THE MASTER WON'T TOLERATE IT.
WHO IS THIS MASTER? I THINK YOU'RE JUST MAKING HIM UP!
OH, HE'S REAL. EVERY VAMPIRE BOWS TO HIM, AND SOON SO WILL EACH LIVING THING!
YOU'LL MAKE A FINE ADDITION TO HIS RETINUE.
THAT AND NEWS OF THE FORMER PUPPET WILL RESTORE OUR GOOD STANDING.
GOOD STANDING...

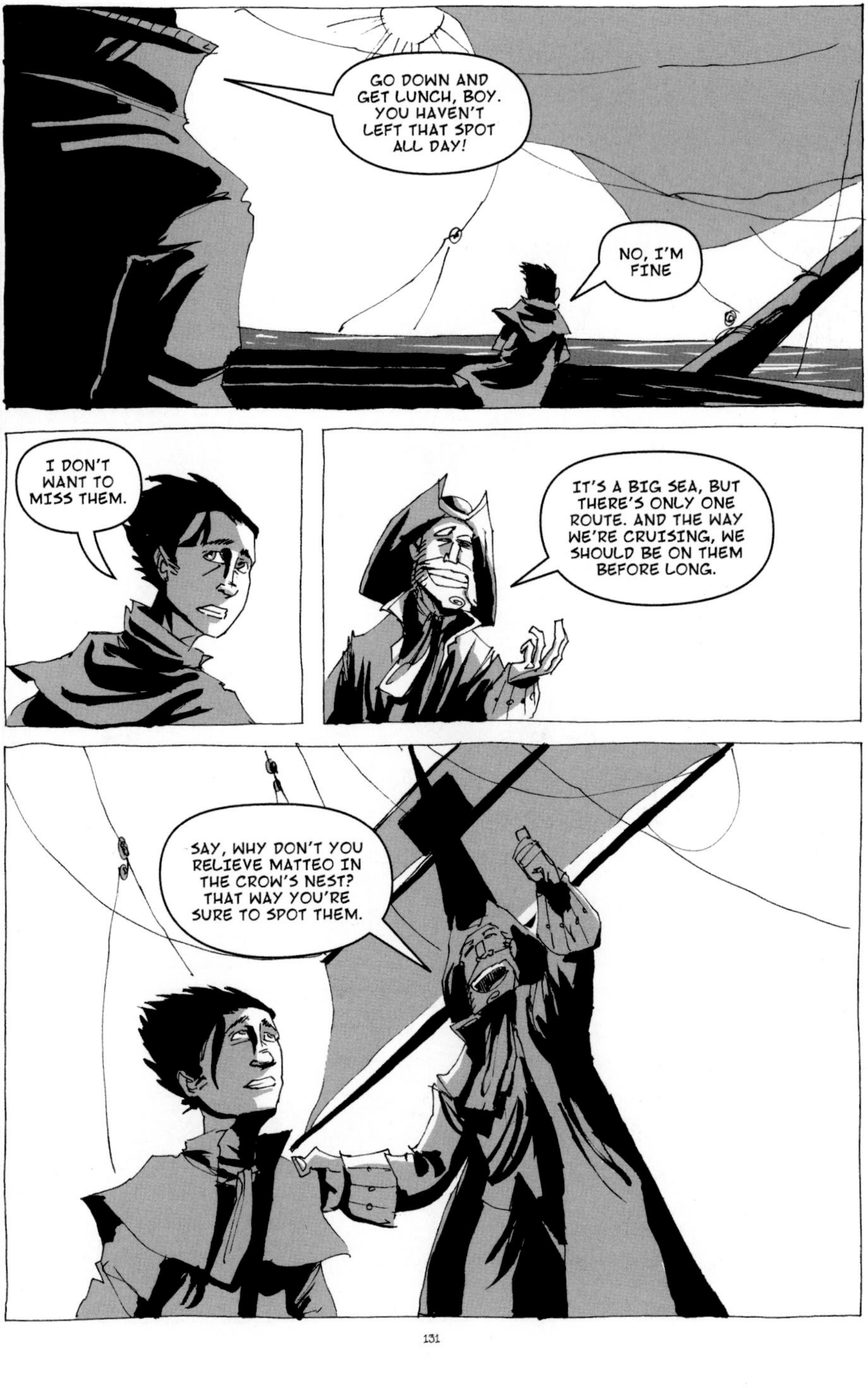
GO DOWN AND GET LUNCH, BOY. YOU HAVEN'T LEFT THAT SPOT ALL DAY!
NO, I'M FINE
I DON'T WANT TO MISS THEM.
IT'S A BIG SEA, BUT THERE'S ONLY ONE ROUTE. AND THE WAY WE'RE CRUISING, WE SHOULD BE ON THEM BEFORE LONG.
SAY, WHY DON'T YOU RELIEVE MATTEO IN THE CROW'S NEST? THAT WAY YOU'RE SURE TO SPOT THEM.

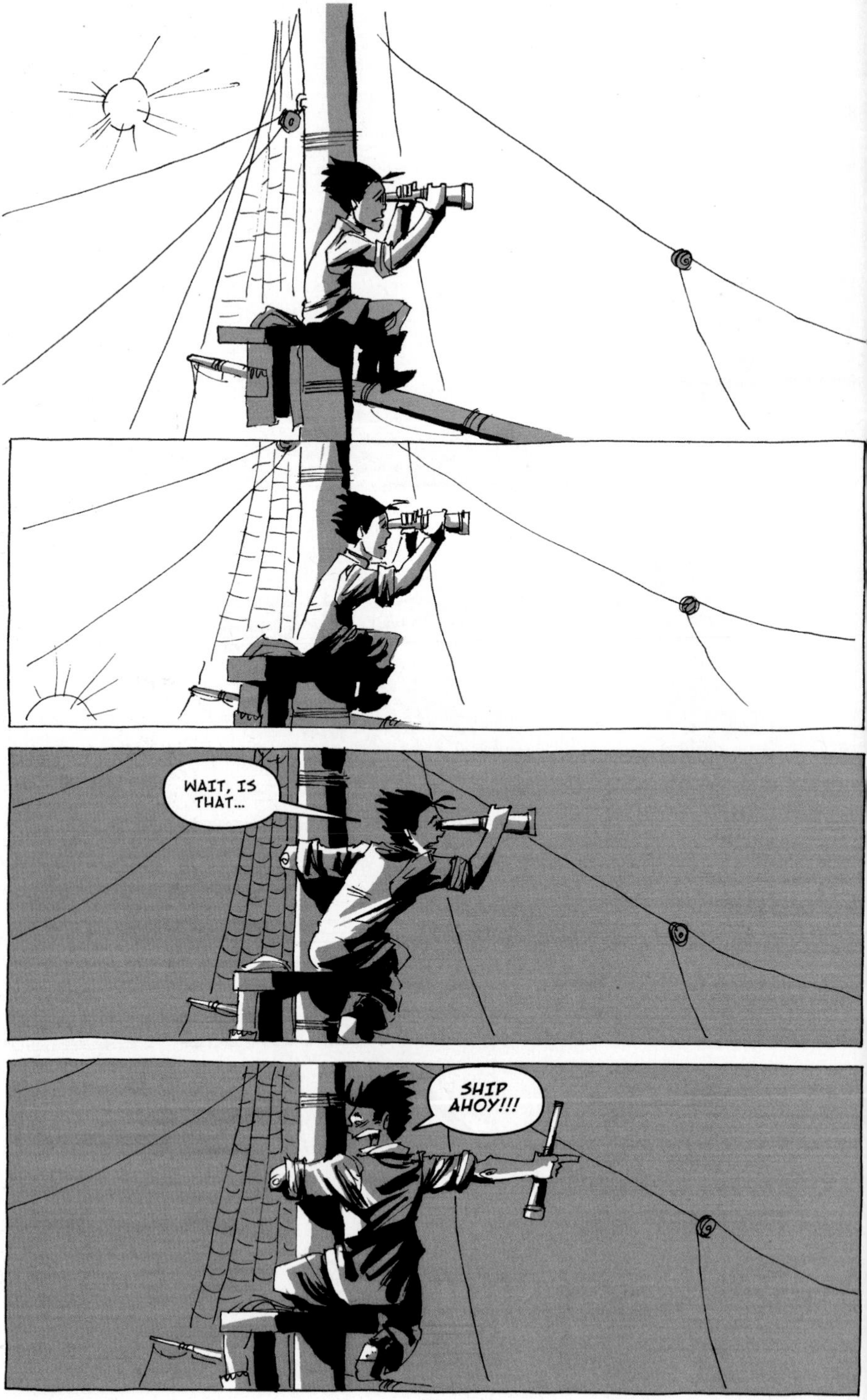
WAIT, IS THAT...
SHIP AHOY!!!

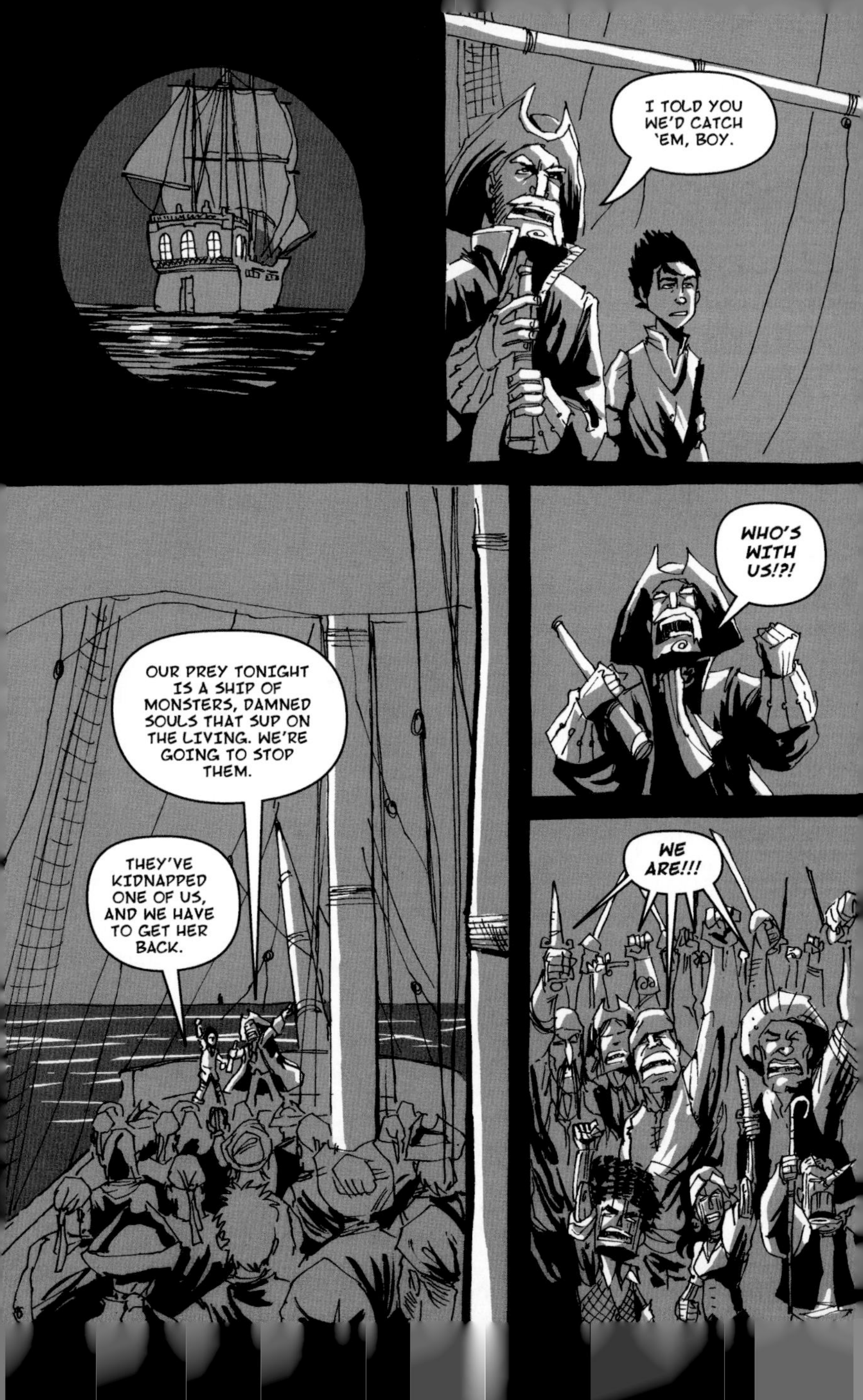
I TOLD YOU WE'D CATCH 'EM, BOY.
OUR PREY TONIGHT IS A SHIP OF MONSTERS, DAMNED SOULS THAT SUP ON THE LIVING. WE'RE GOING TO STOP THEM.
THEY'VE KIDNAPPED ONE OF US, AND WE HAVE TO GET HER BACK.
WHO'S WITH US!?!
WE ARE!!!

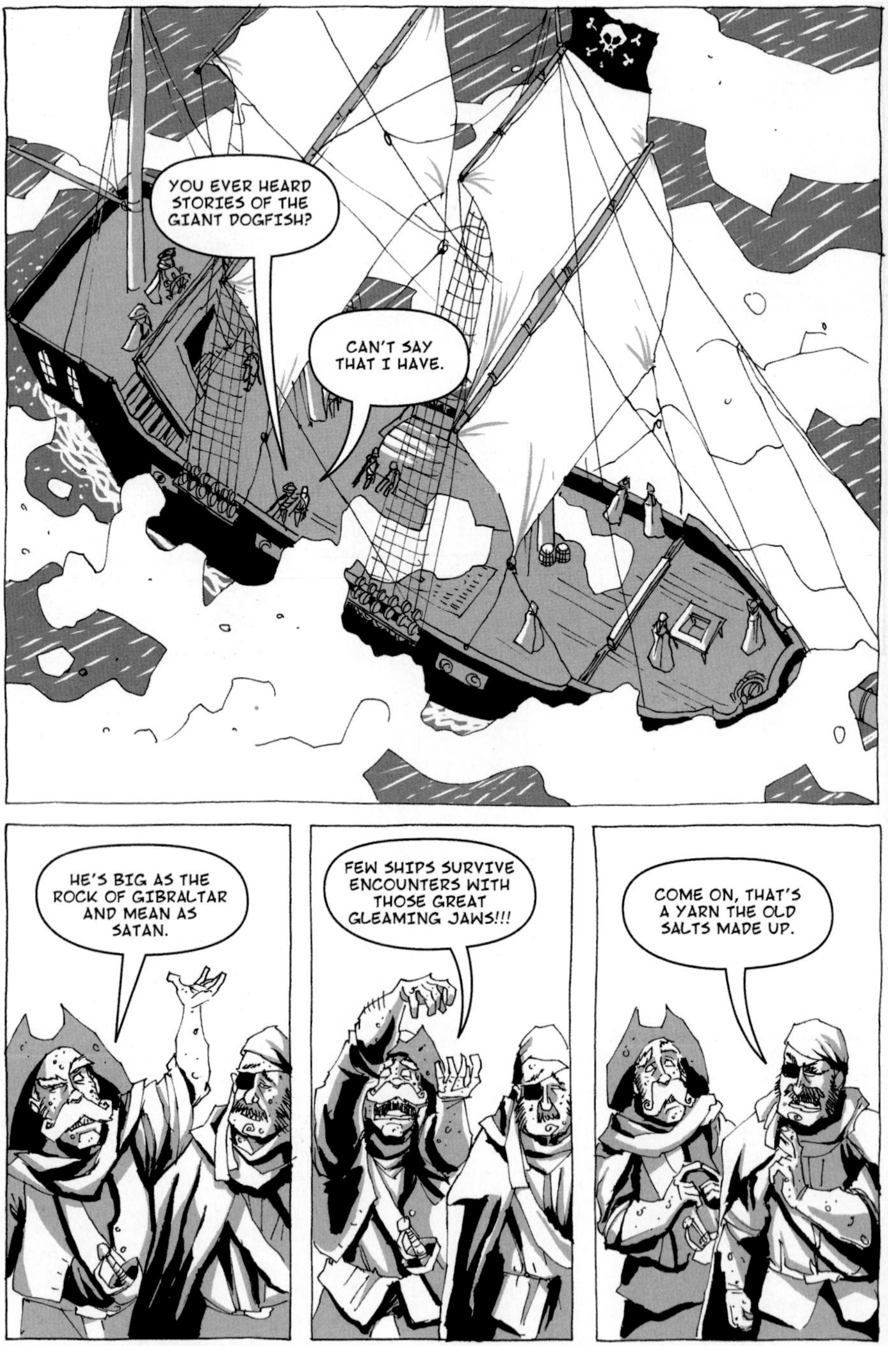
YOU EVER HEARD STORIES OF THE GIANT DOGFISH?
CAN'T SAY THAT I HAVE.
HE'S BIG AS THE ROCK OF GIBRALTAR AND MEAN AS SATAN.
FEW SHIPS SURVIVE ENCOUNTERS WITH THOSE GREAT GLEAMING JAWS!!!
COME ON, THAT'S A YARN THE OLD SALTS MADE UP.

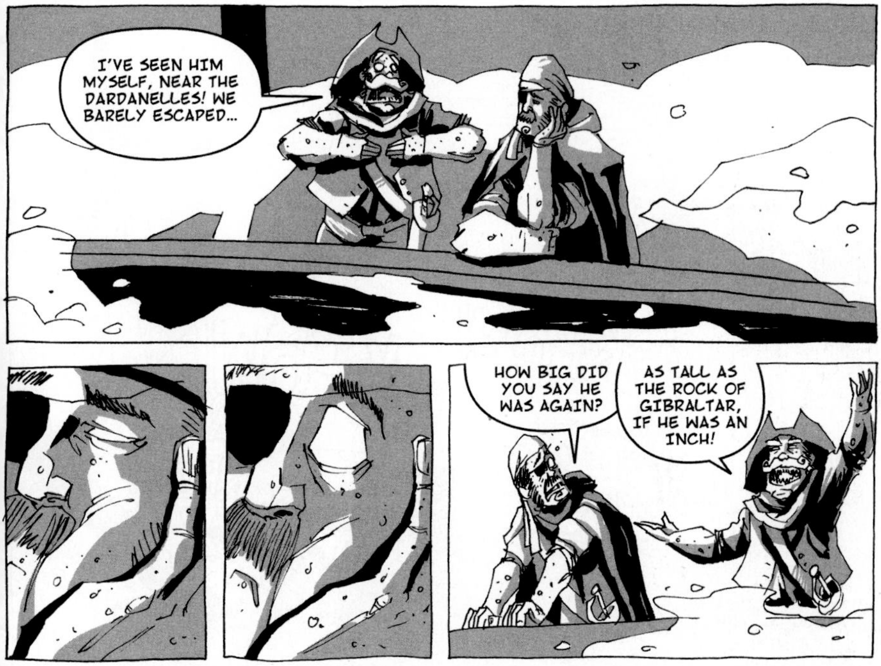
I'VE SEEN HIM MYSELF, NEAR THE DARDANELLES! WE BARELY ESCAPED...
HOW BIG DID YOU SAY HE WAS AGAIN?
AS TALL AS THE ROCK OF GIBRALTAR, IF HE WAS AN INCH!

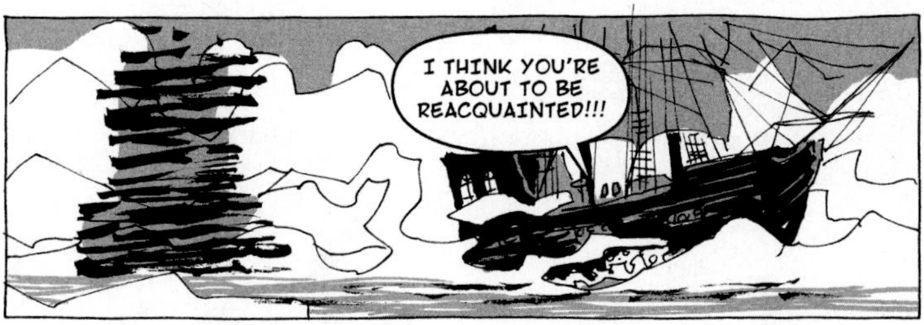
I THINK YOU'RE ABOUT TO BE REACQUAINTED!!!

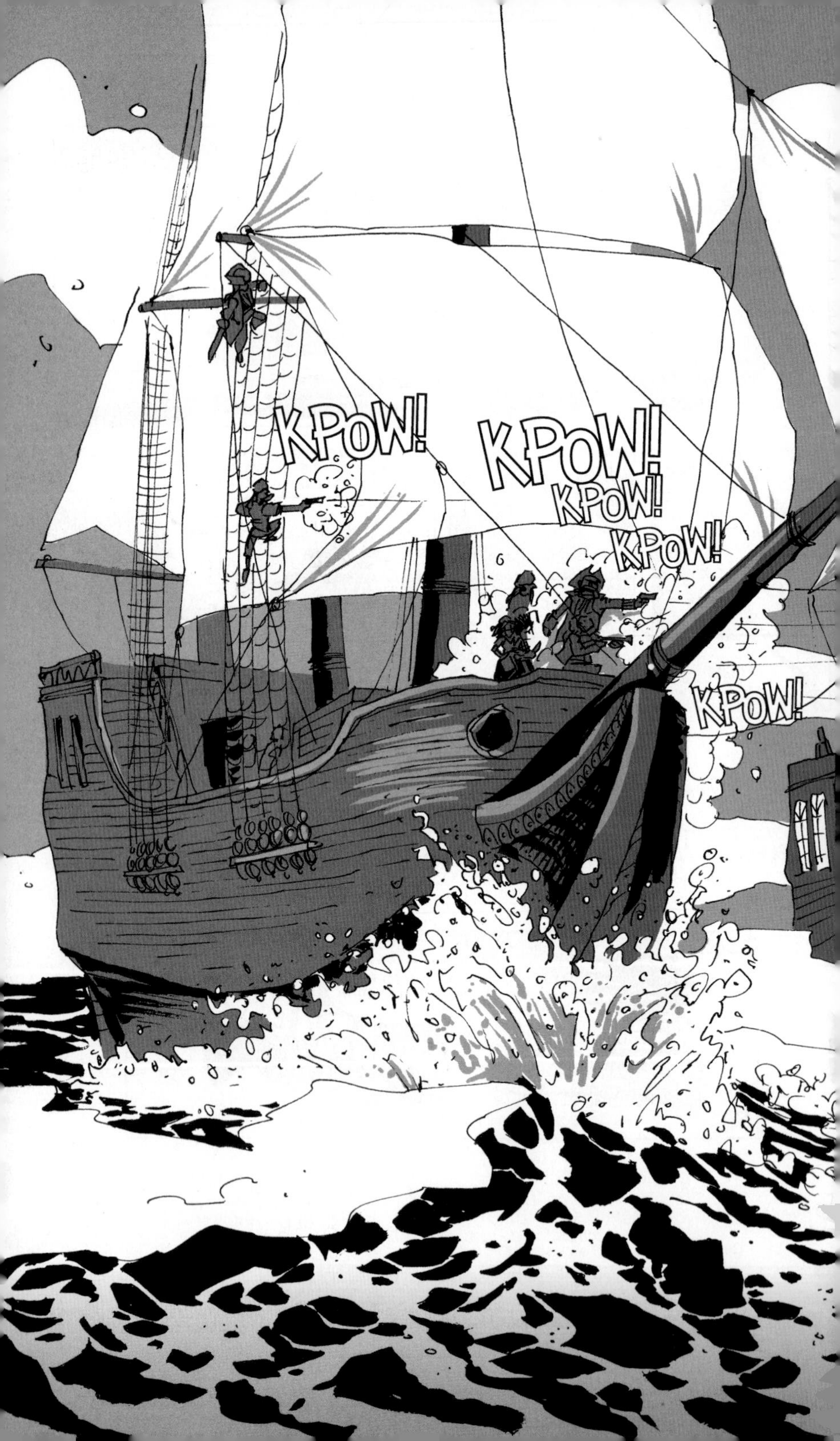
KPOW!
KPOW!
KPOW!
KPOW!
KPOW!

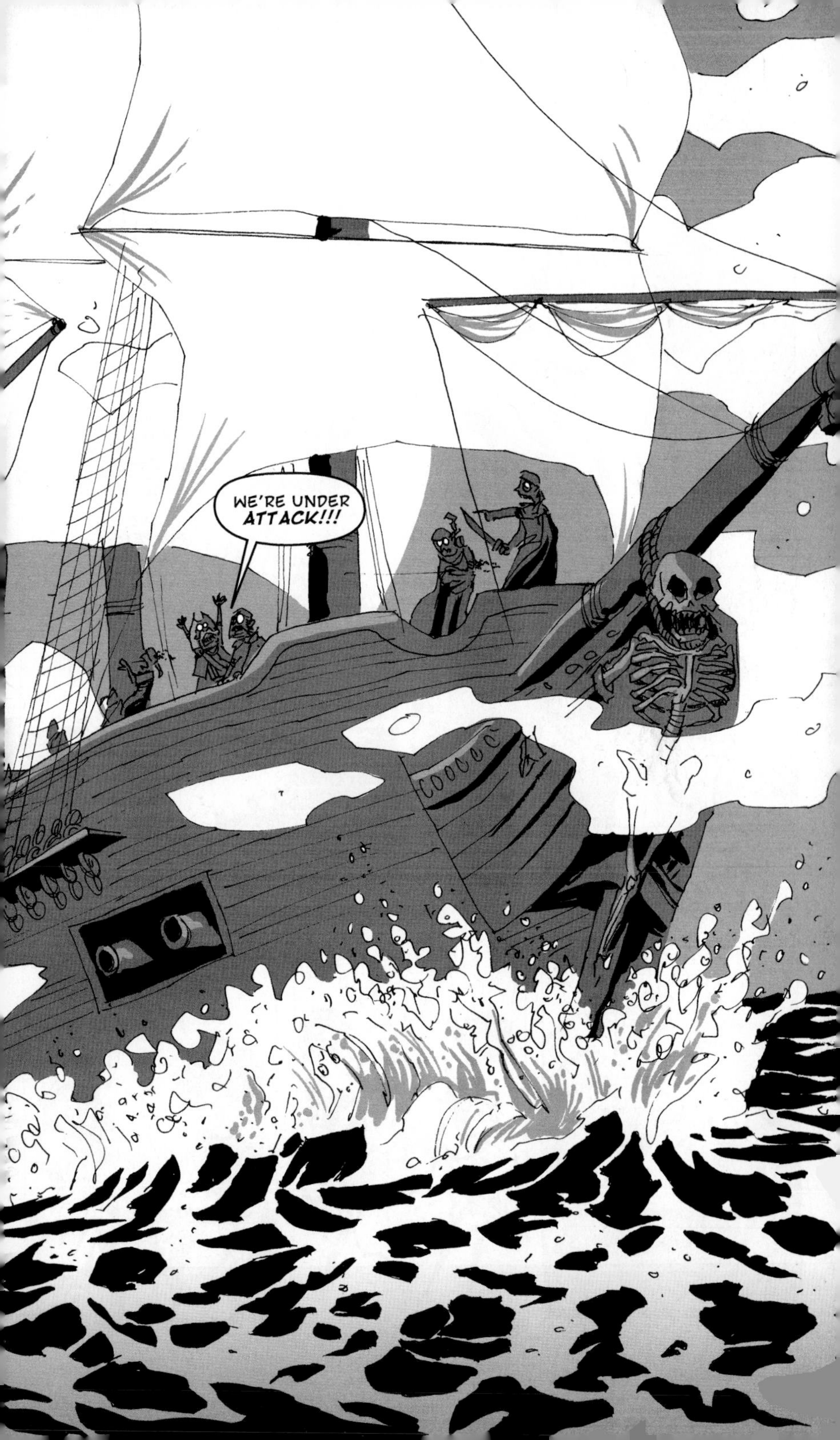
WE'RE UNDER ATTACK!!!

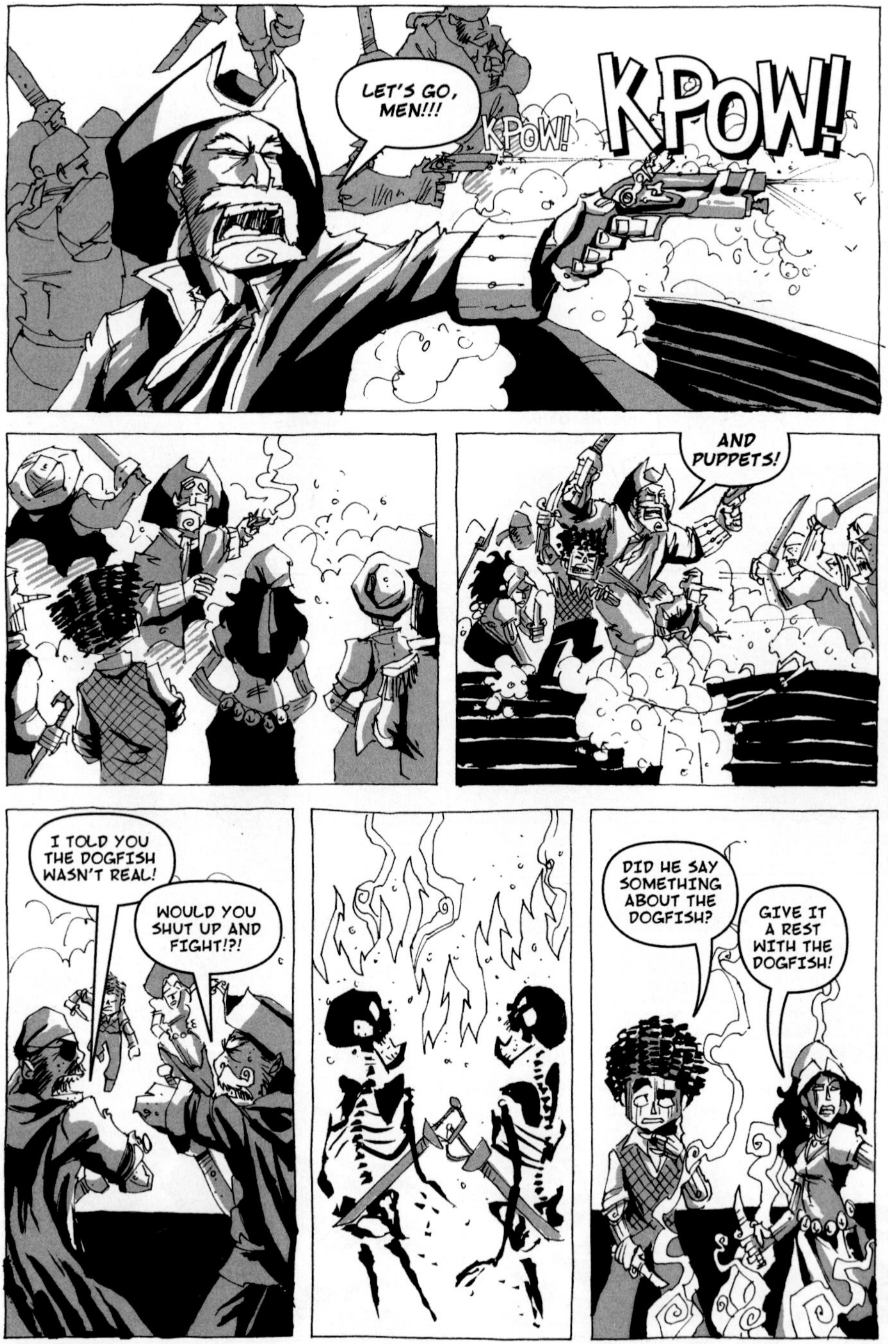
LET'S GO, MEN!!!
KPOW!
KPOW!
AND PUPPETS!
I TOLD YOU THE DOGFISH WASN'T REAL!
WOULD YOU SHUT UP AND FIGHT!?!
DID HE SAY SOMETHING ABOUT THE DOGFISH?
GIVE IT A REST WITH THE DOGFISH!

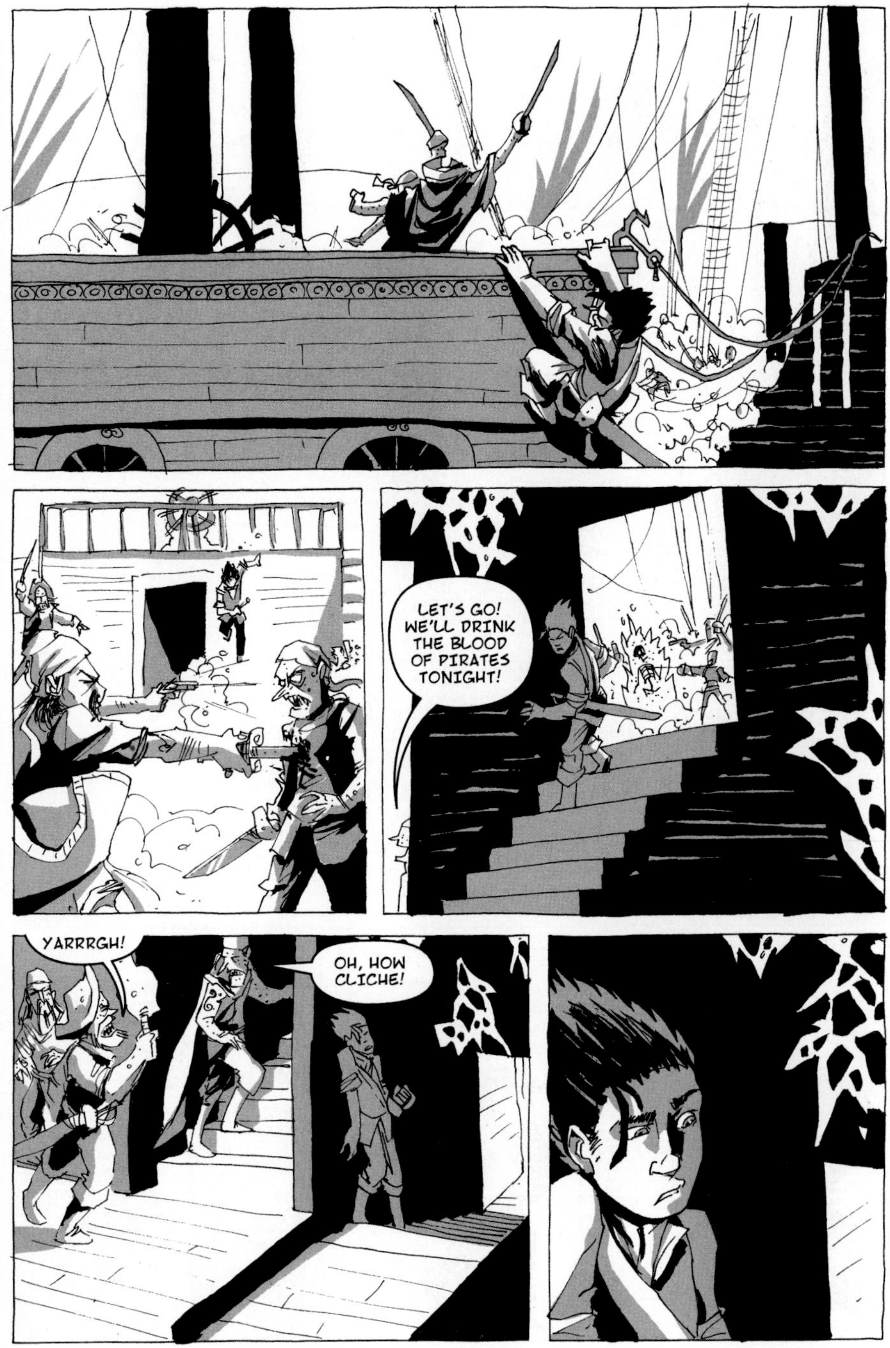
LET'S GO! WE'LL DRINK THE BLOOD OF PIRATES TONIGHT!
YARRRGH!
OH, HOW CLICHE!

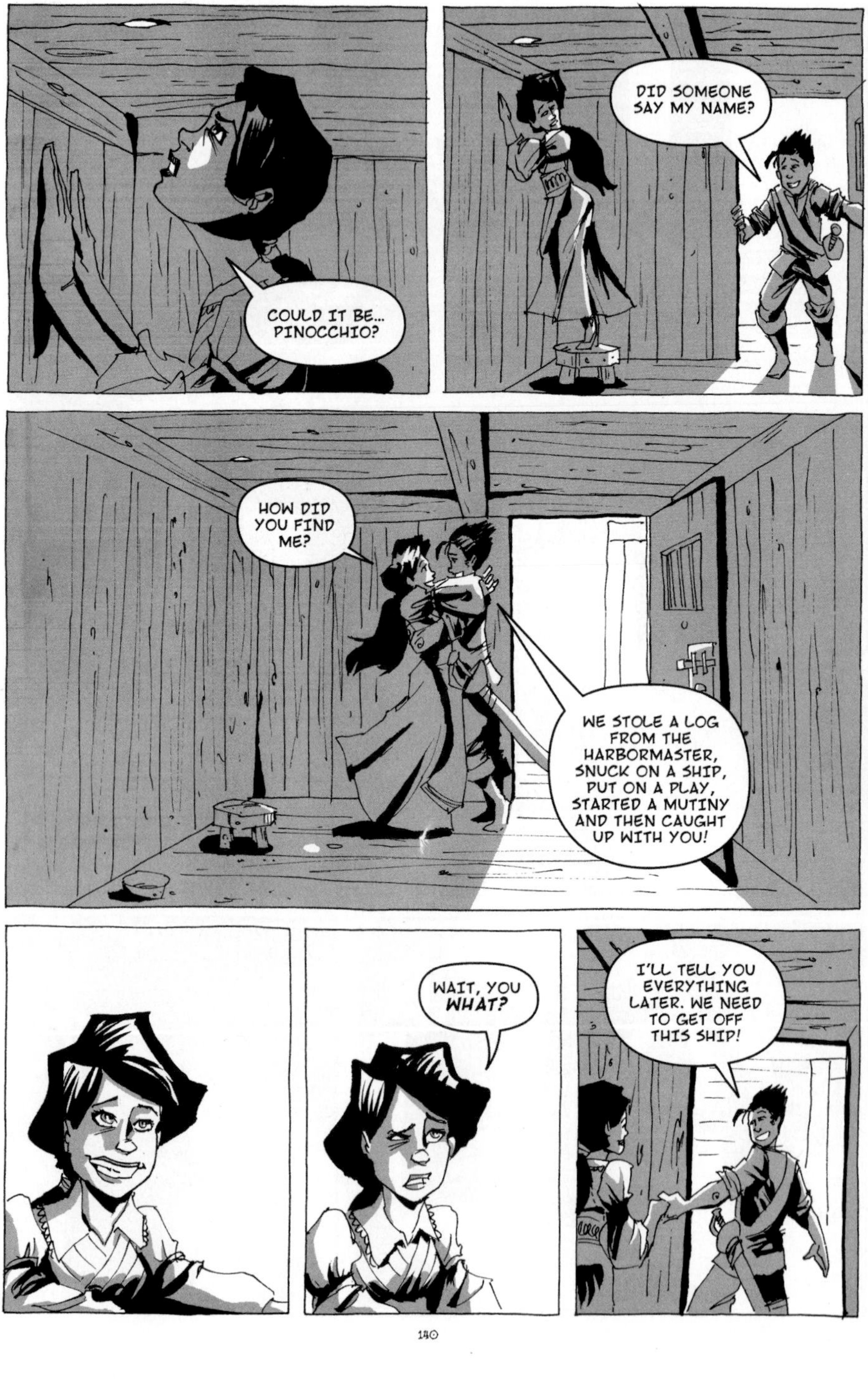
COULD IT BE... PINOCCHIO?
DID SOMEONE SAY MY NAME?
HOW DID YOU FIND ME?
WE STOLE A LOG FROM THE HARBORMASTER, SNUCK ON A SHIP, PUT ON A PLAY, STARTED A MUTINY AND THEN CAUGHT UP WITH YOU!
WAIT, YOU **WHAT?**
I'LL TELL YOU EVERYTHING LATER. WE NEED TO GET OFF THIS SHIP!

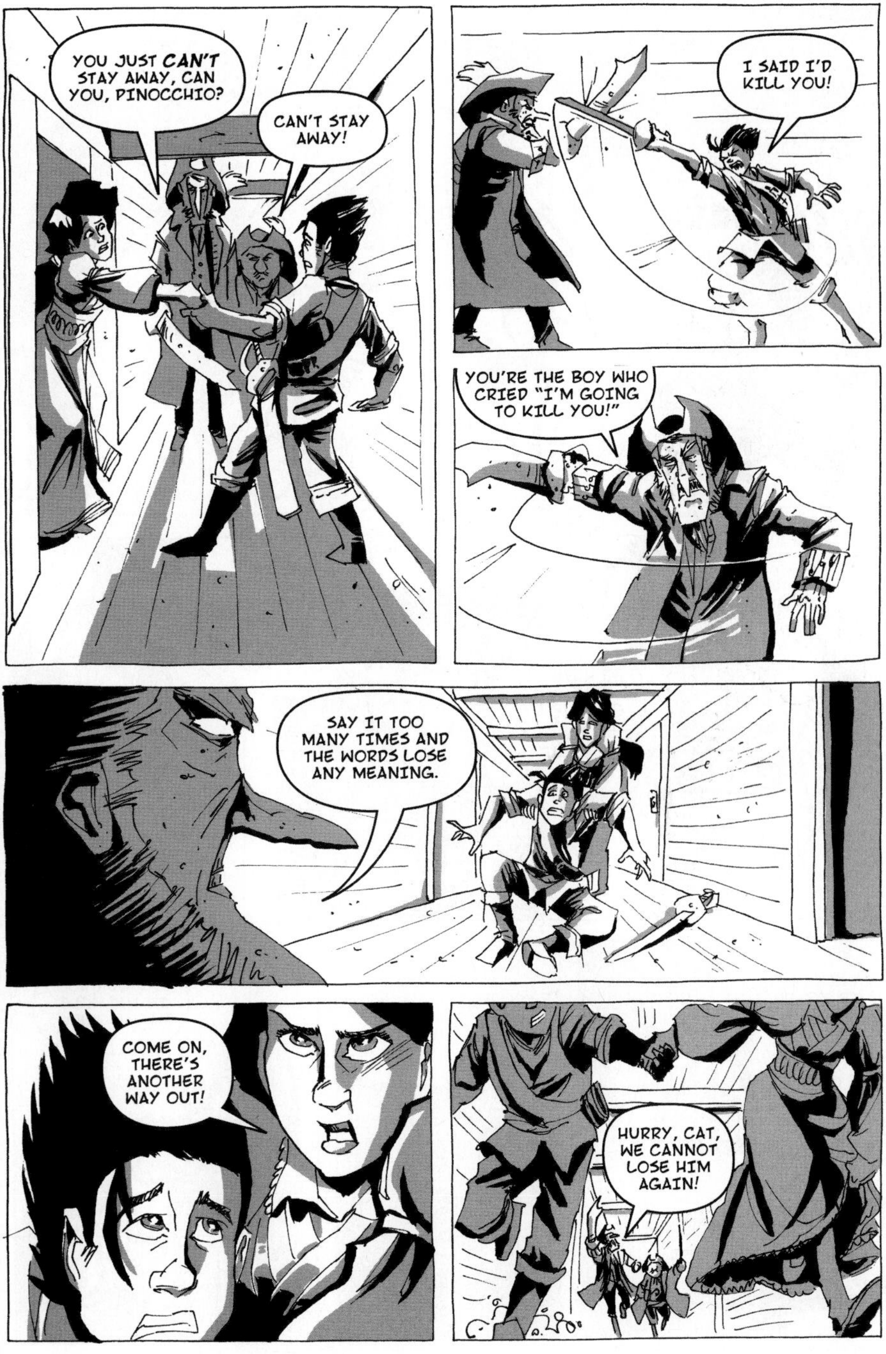
YOU JUST CAN'T STAY AWAY, CAN YOU, PINOCCHIO?
CAN'T STAY AWAY!
I SAID I'D KILL YOU!
YOU'RE THE BOY WHO CRIED "I'M GOING TO KILL YOU!"
SAY IT TOO MANY TIMES AND THE WORDS LOSE ANY MEANING.
COME ON, THERE'S ANOTHER WAY OUT!
HURRY, CAT, WE CANNOT LOSE HIM AGAIN!

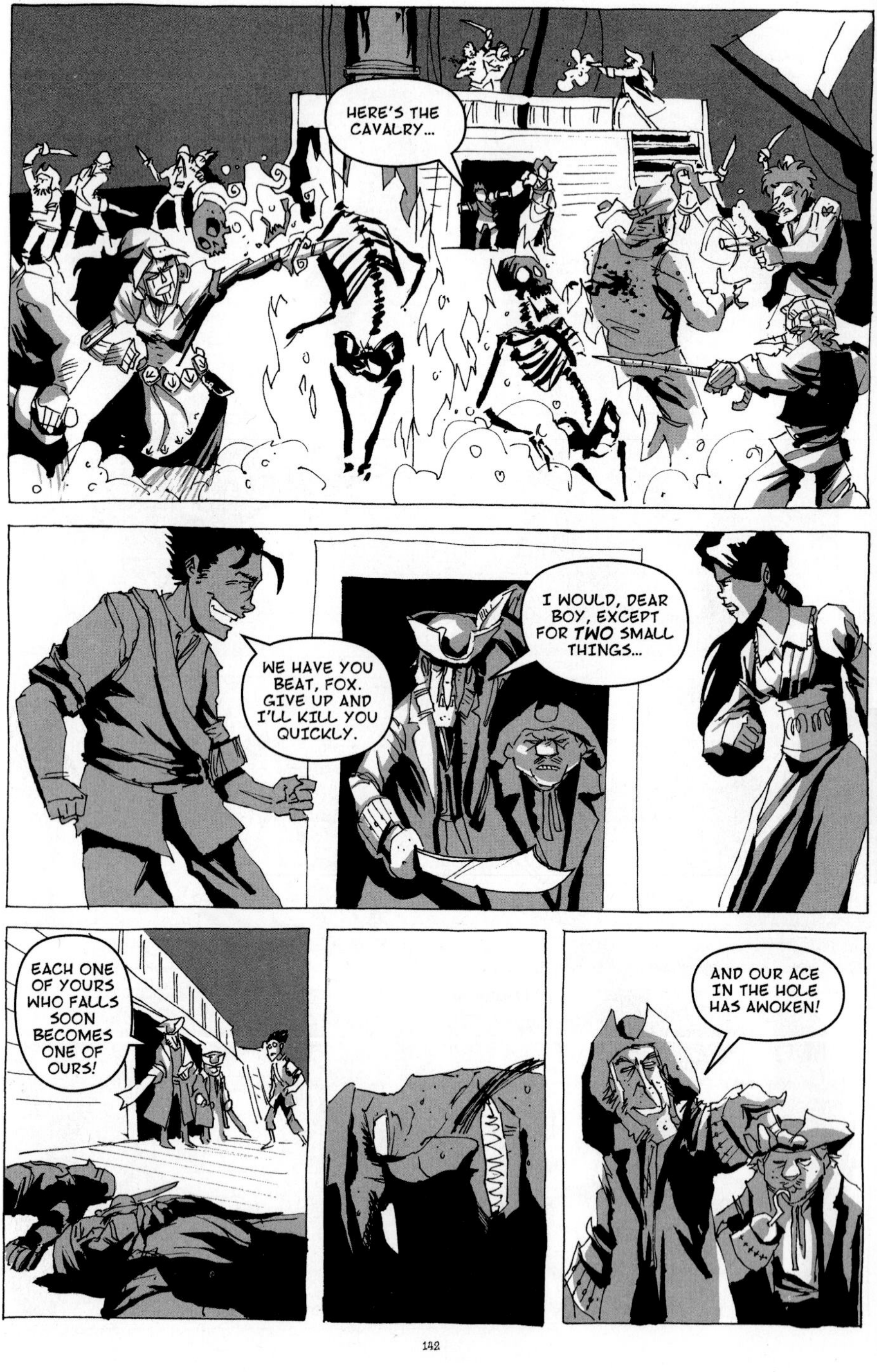
HERE'S THE CAVALRY...
WE HAVE YOU BEAT, FOX. GIVE UP AND I'LL KILL YOU QUICKLY.
I WOULD, DEAR BOY, EXCEPT FOR *TWO* SMALL THINGS...
EACH ONE OF YOURS WHO FALLS SOON BECOMES ONE OF OURS!
AND OUR ACE IN THE HOLE HAS AWOKEN!

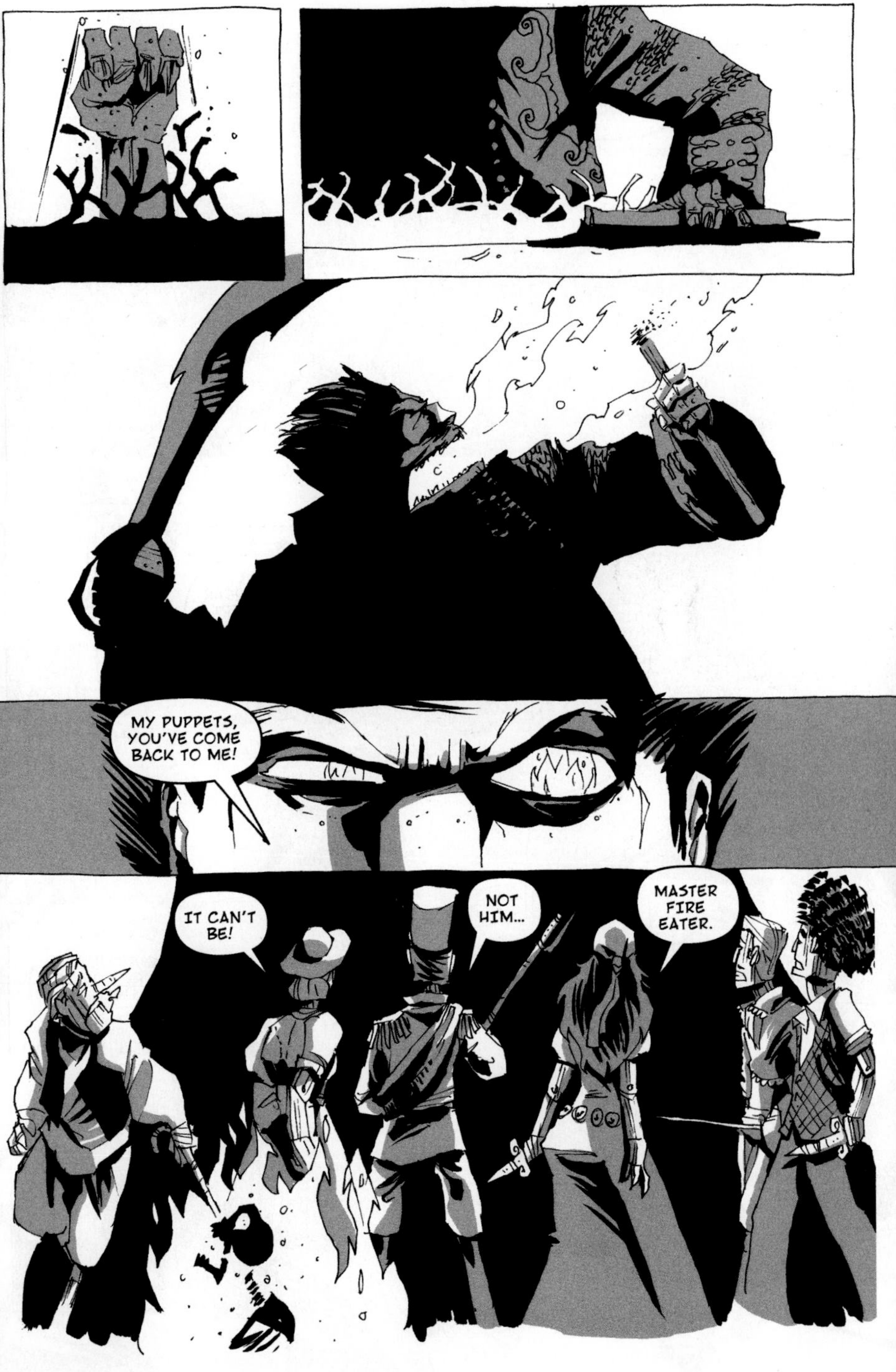
MY PUPPETS, YOU'VE COME BACK TO ME!
IT CAN'T BE!
NOT HIM...
MASTER FIRE EATER.

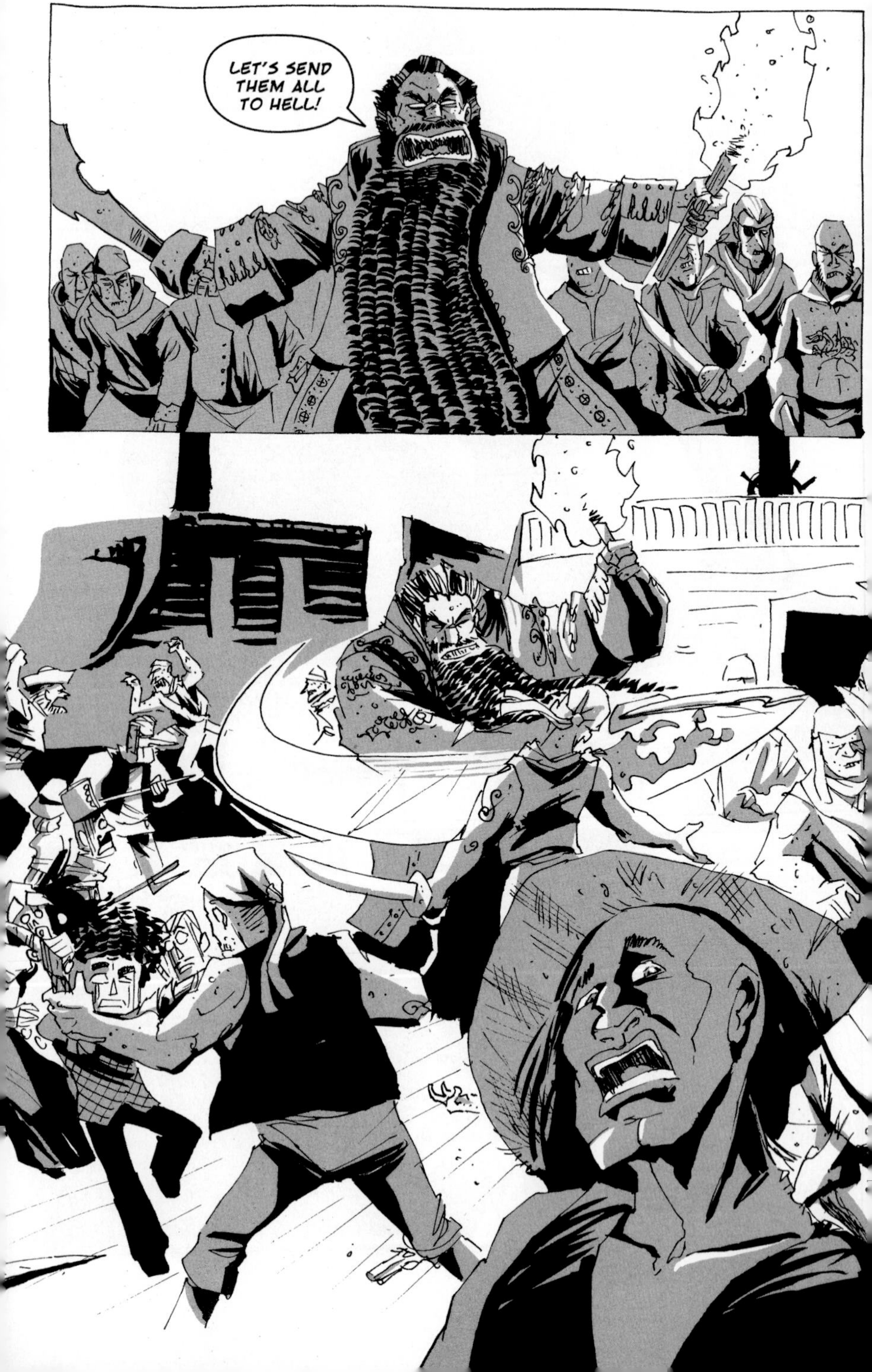
LET'S SEND THEM ALL TO HELL!

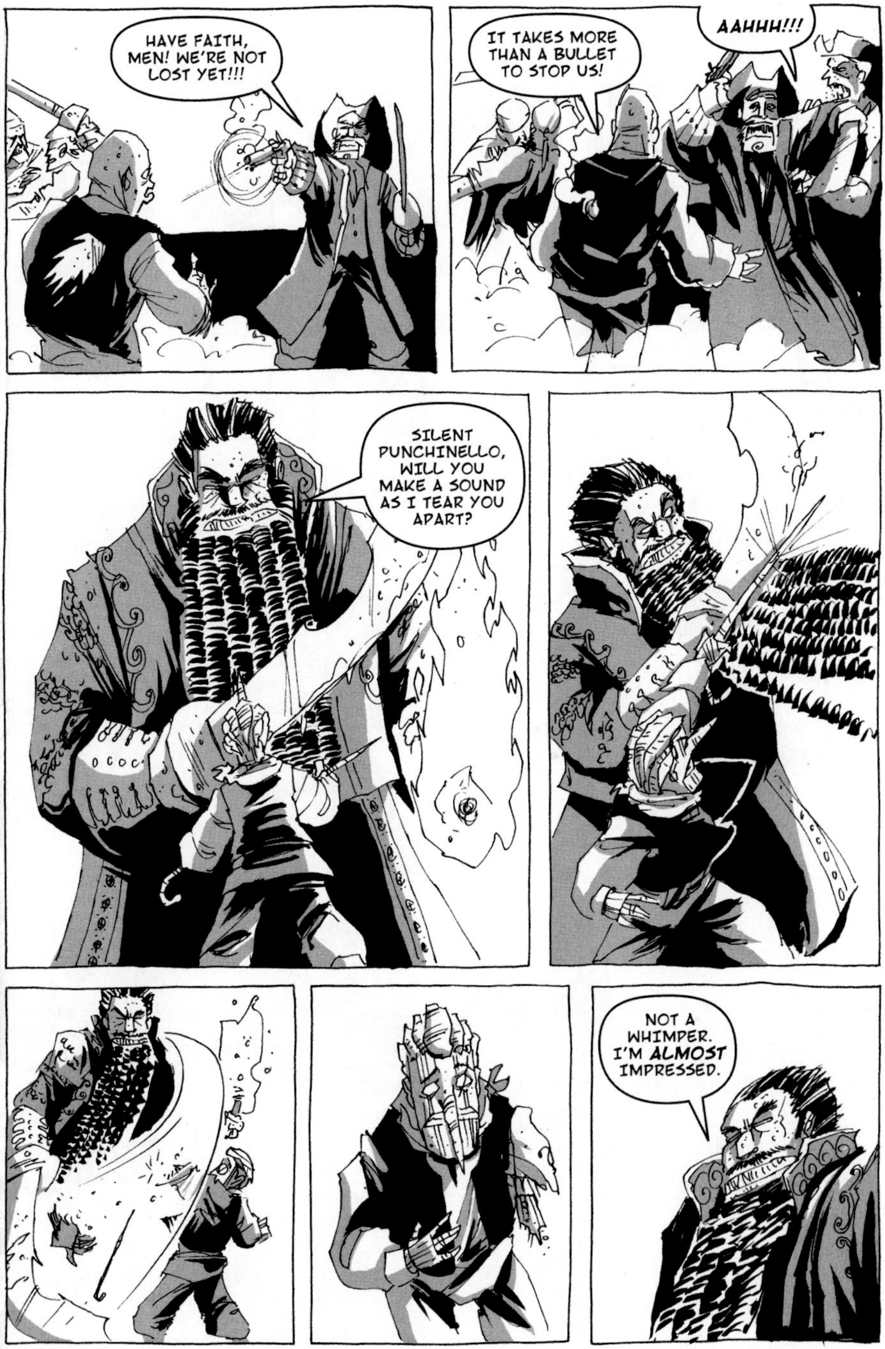
HAVE FAITH, MEN! WE'RE NOT LOST YET!!!
IT TAKES MORE THAN A BULLET TO STOP US!
AAHHH!!!
SILENT PUNCHINELLO, WILL YOU MAKE A SOUND AS I TEAR YOU APART?
NOT A WHIMPER. I'M ALMOST IMPRESSED.

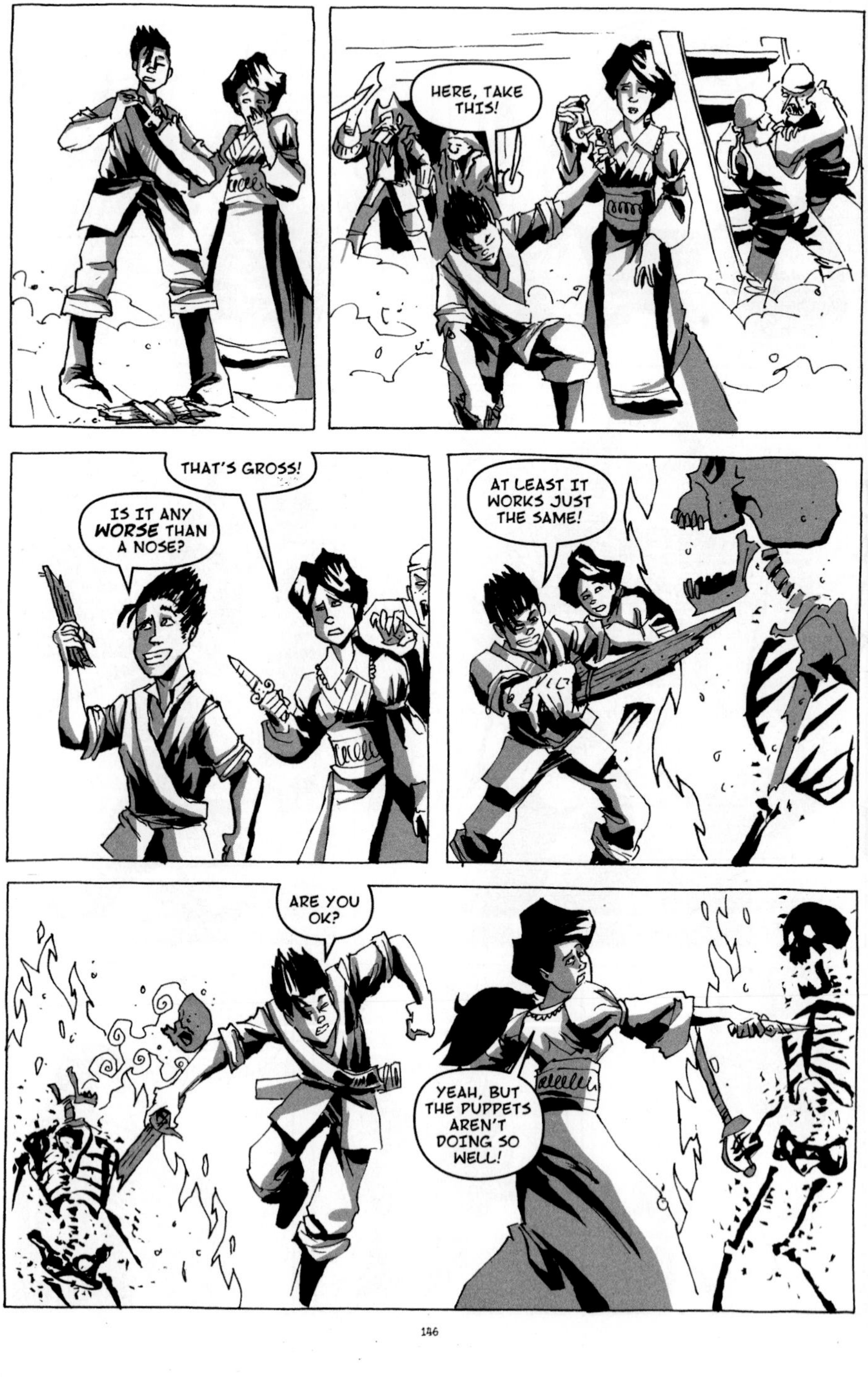
HERE, TAKE THIS!
IS IT ANY WORSE THAN A NOSE?
THAT'S GROSS!
AT LEAST IT WORKS JUST THE SAME!
ARE YOU OK?
YEAH, BUT THE PUPPETS AREN'T DOING SO WELL!

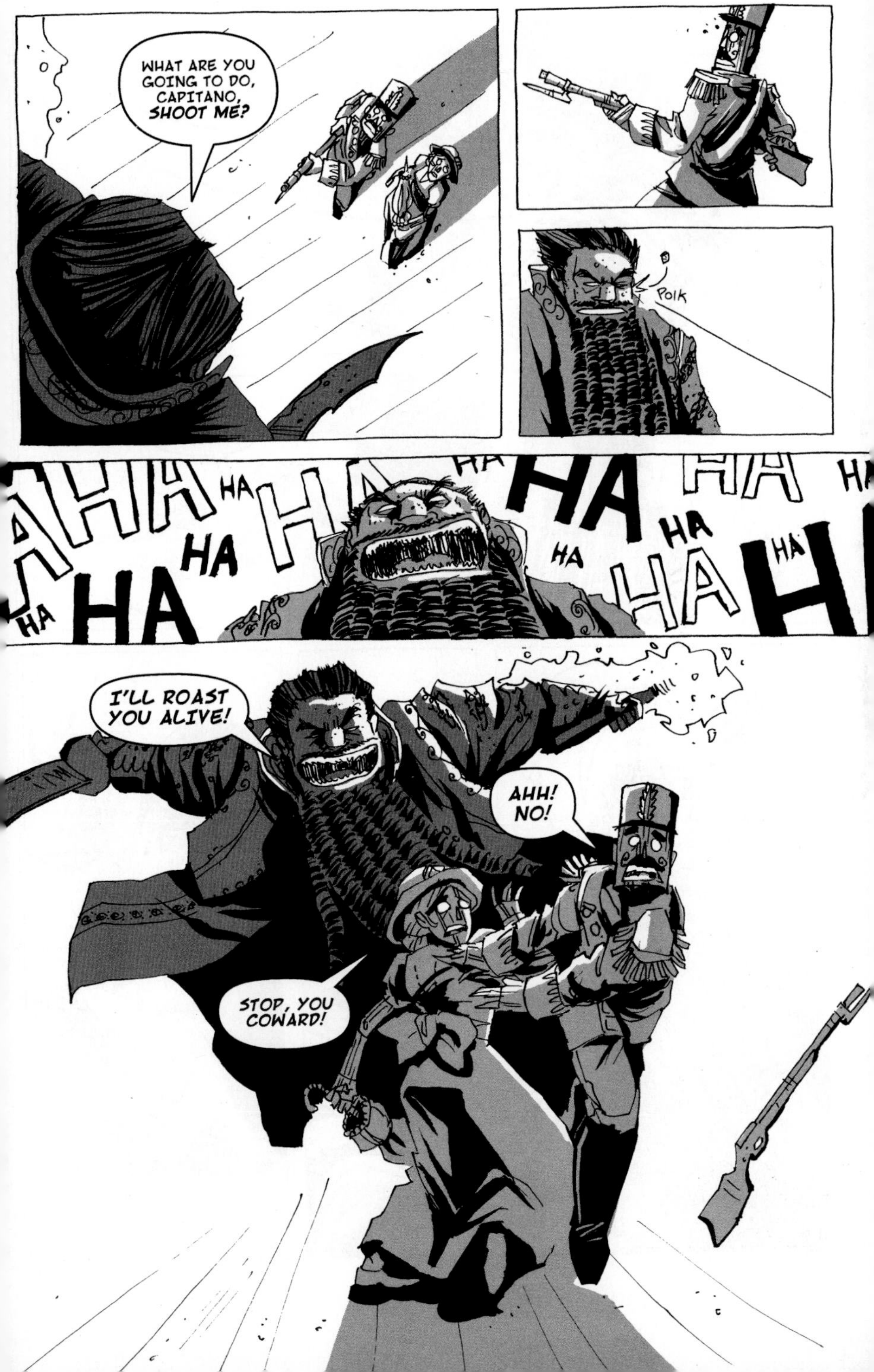
WHAT ARE YOU GOING TO DO, CAPITANO, SHOOT ME?
POIK
HA HA HA HA HA HA HA HA HA HA HA HA HA
I'LL ROAST YOU ALIVE!
AHH! NO!
STOP, YOU COWARD!

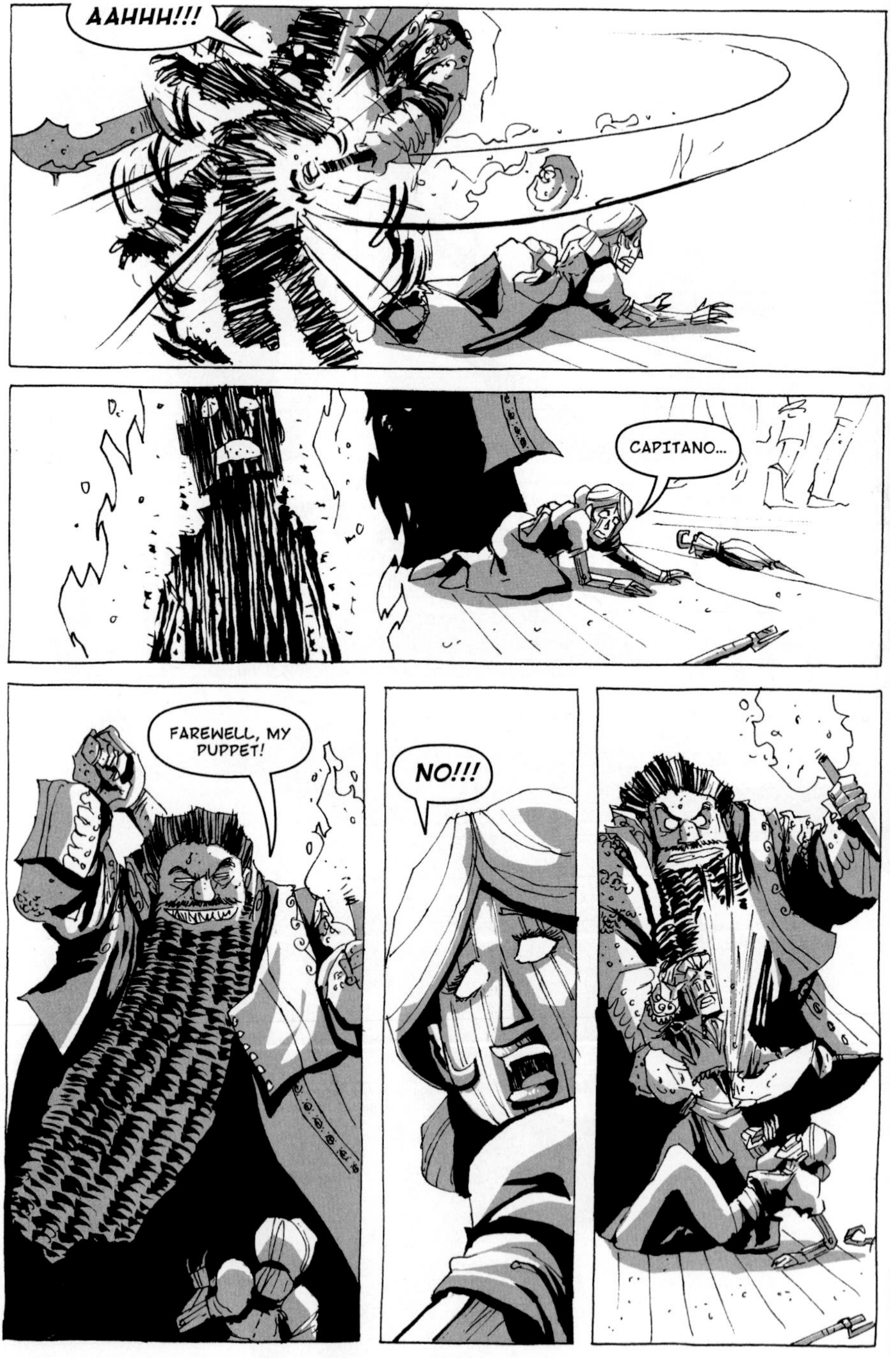
AAHHH!!!
CAPITANO...
FAREWELL, MY PUPPET!
NO!!!

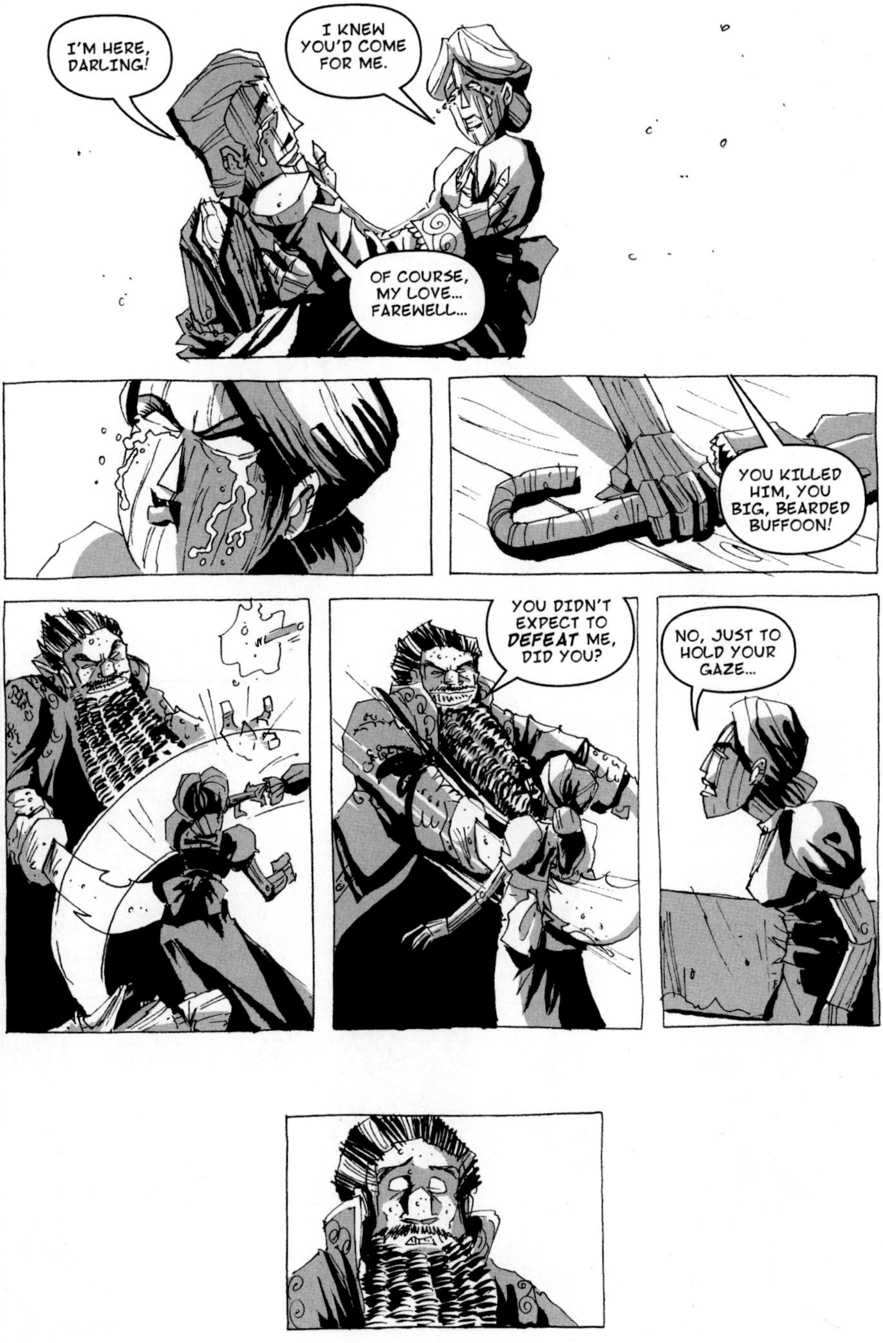
I'M HERE, DARLING!
I KNEW YOU'D COME FOR ME.
OF COURSE, MY LOVE... FAREWELL...
YOU KILLED HIM, YOU BIG, BEARDED BUFFOON!
YOU DIDN'T EXPECT TO DEFEAT ME, DID YOU?
NO, JUST TO HOLD YOUR GAZE...

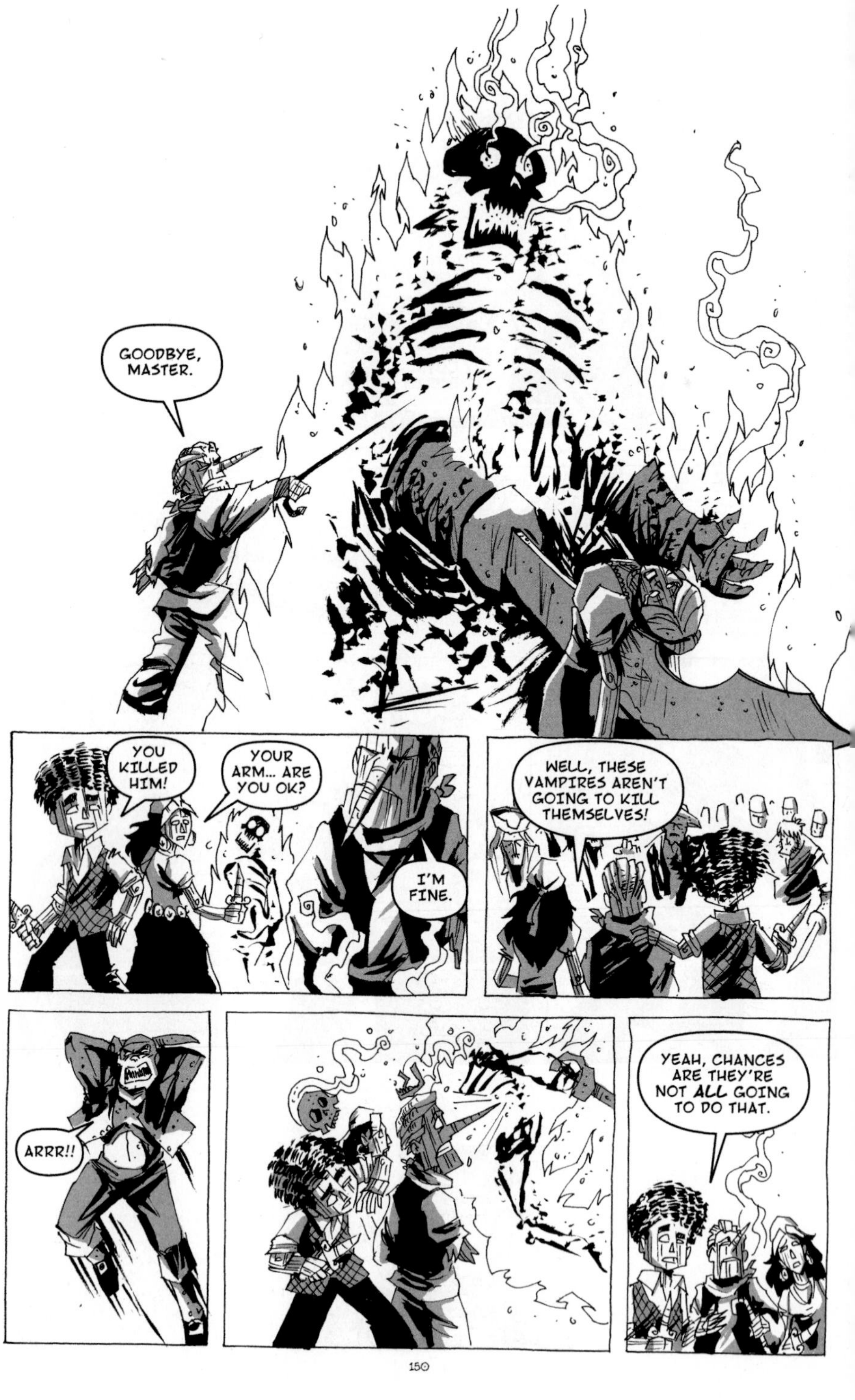

GOODBYE, MASTER.
YOU KILLED HIM!
YOUR ARM... ARE YOU OK?
I'M FINE.
WELL, THESE VAMPIRES AREN'T GOING TO KILL THEMSELVES!
ARRR!!
YEAH, CHANCES ARE THEY'RE NOT **ALL** GOING TO DO THAT.

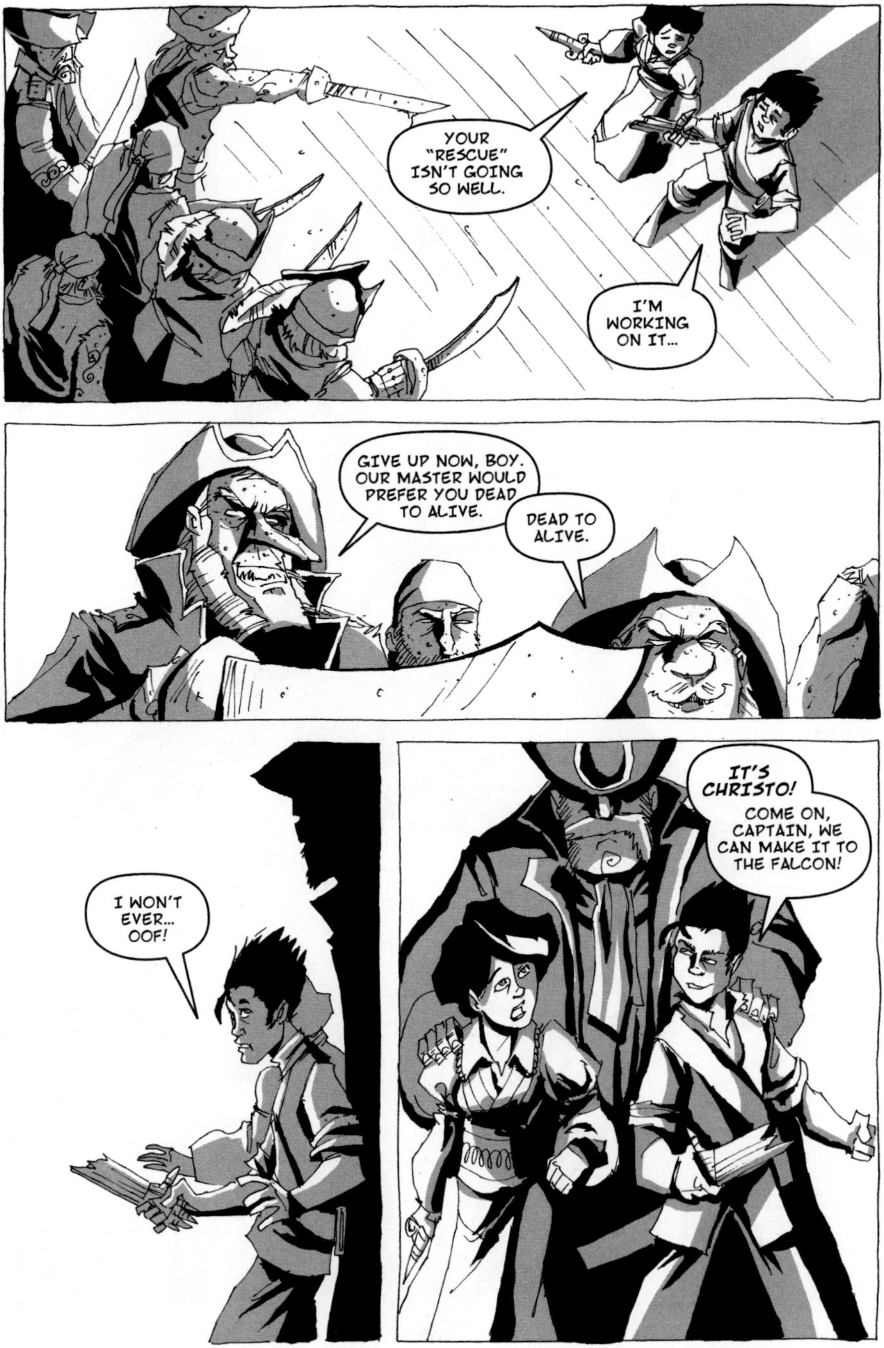
YOUR "RESCUE" ISN'T GOING SO WELL.
I'M WORKING ON IT...
GIVE UP NOW, BOY. OUR MASTER WOULD PREFER YOU DEAD TO ALIVE.
DEAD TO ALIVE.
I WON'T EVER... OOF!
IT'S CHRISTO!
COME ON, CAPTAIN, WE CAN MAKE IT TO THE FALCON!

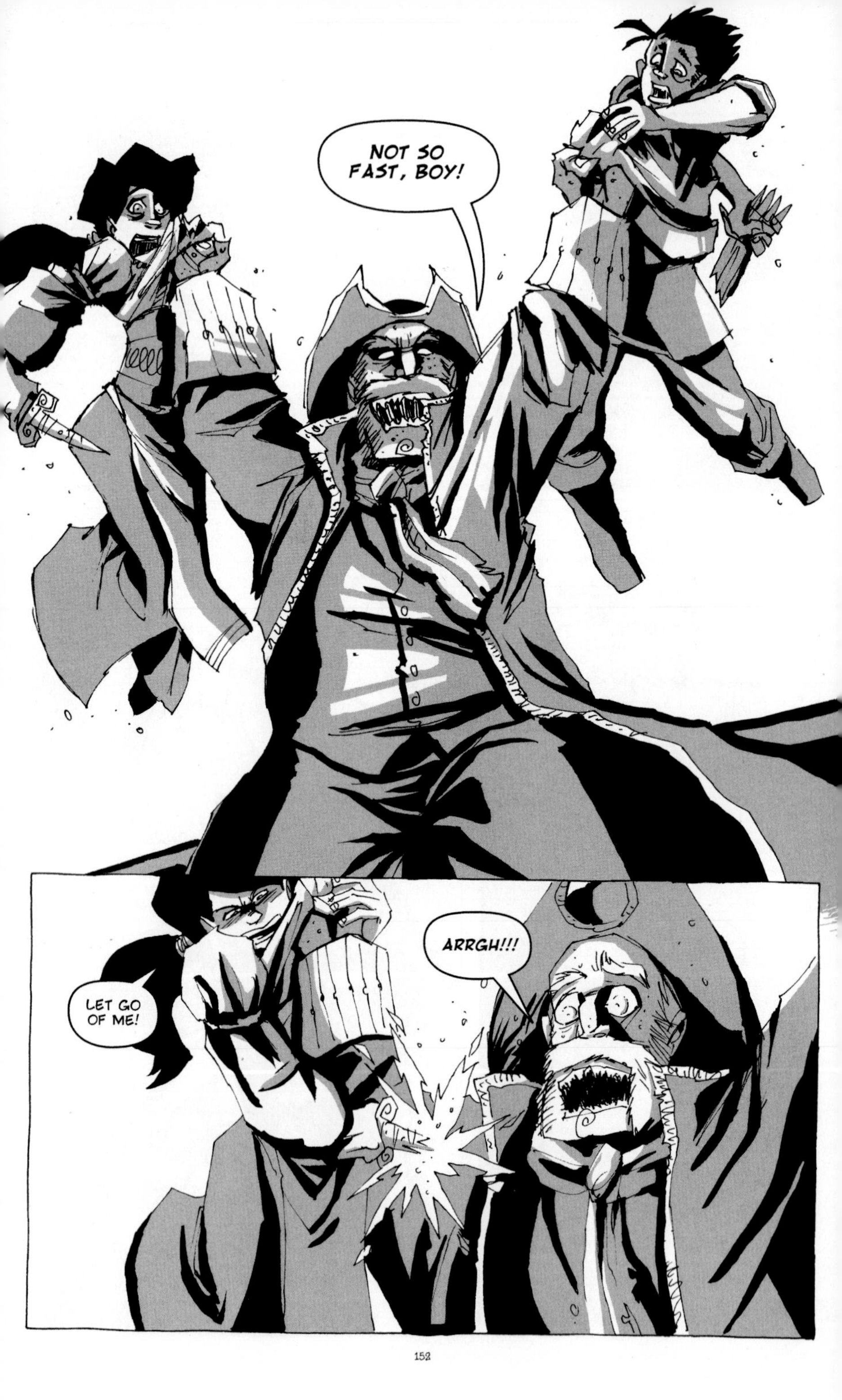
NOT SO FAST, BOY!
LET GO OF ME!
ARRGH!!!

GOOD WORK, CARLOTTA! YOU SAVED...

US?

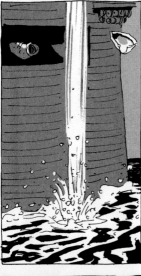

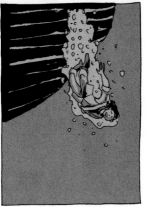

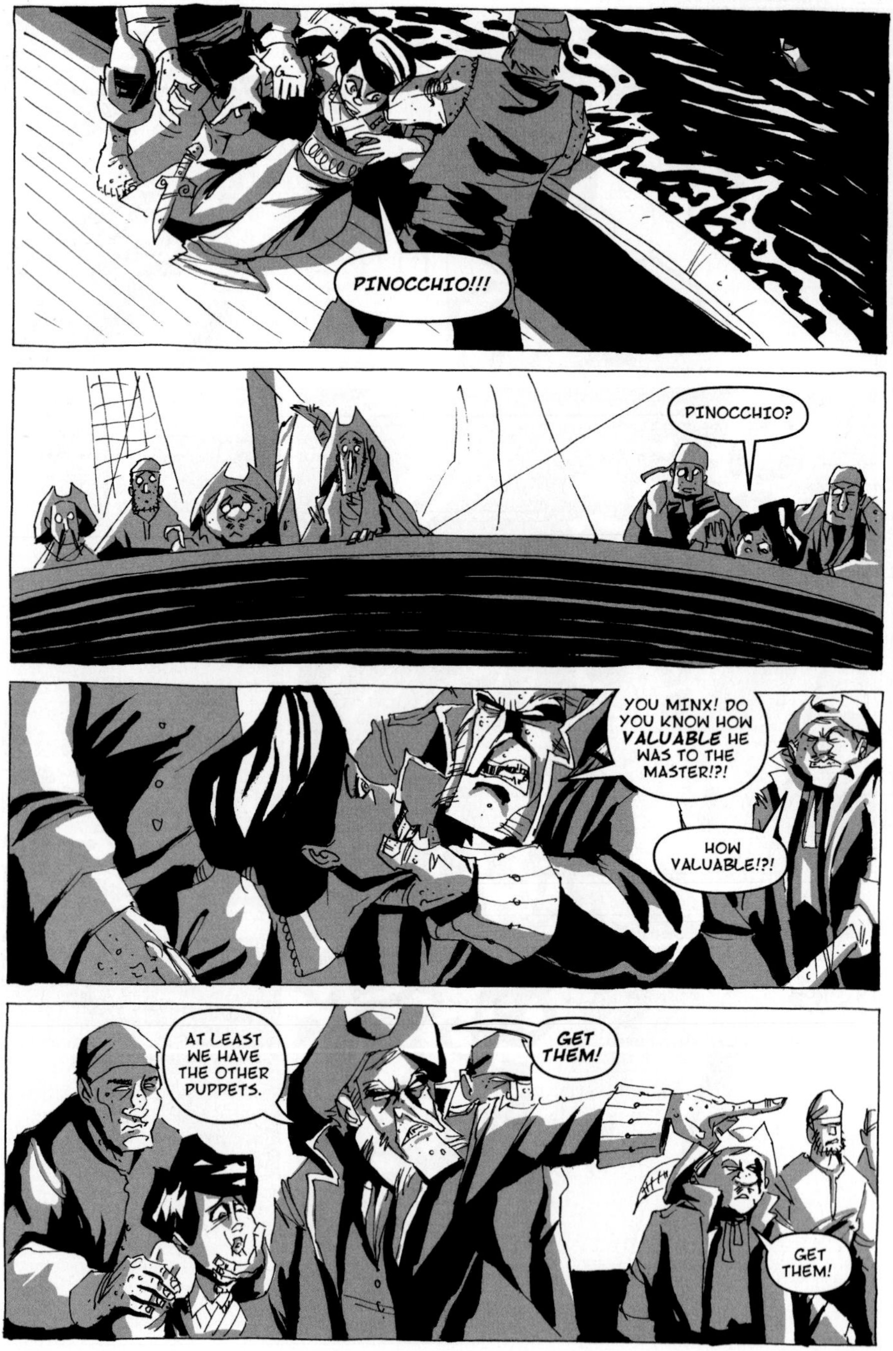
PINOCCHIO!!!
PINOCCHIO?
YOU MINX! DO YOU KNOW HOW VALUABLE HE WAS TO THE MASTER!?!
HOW VALUABLE!?!
AT LEAST WE HAVE THE OTHER PUPPETS.
GET THEM!
GET THEM!

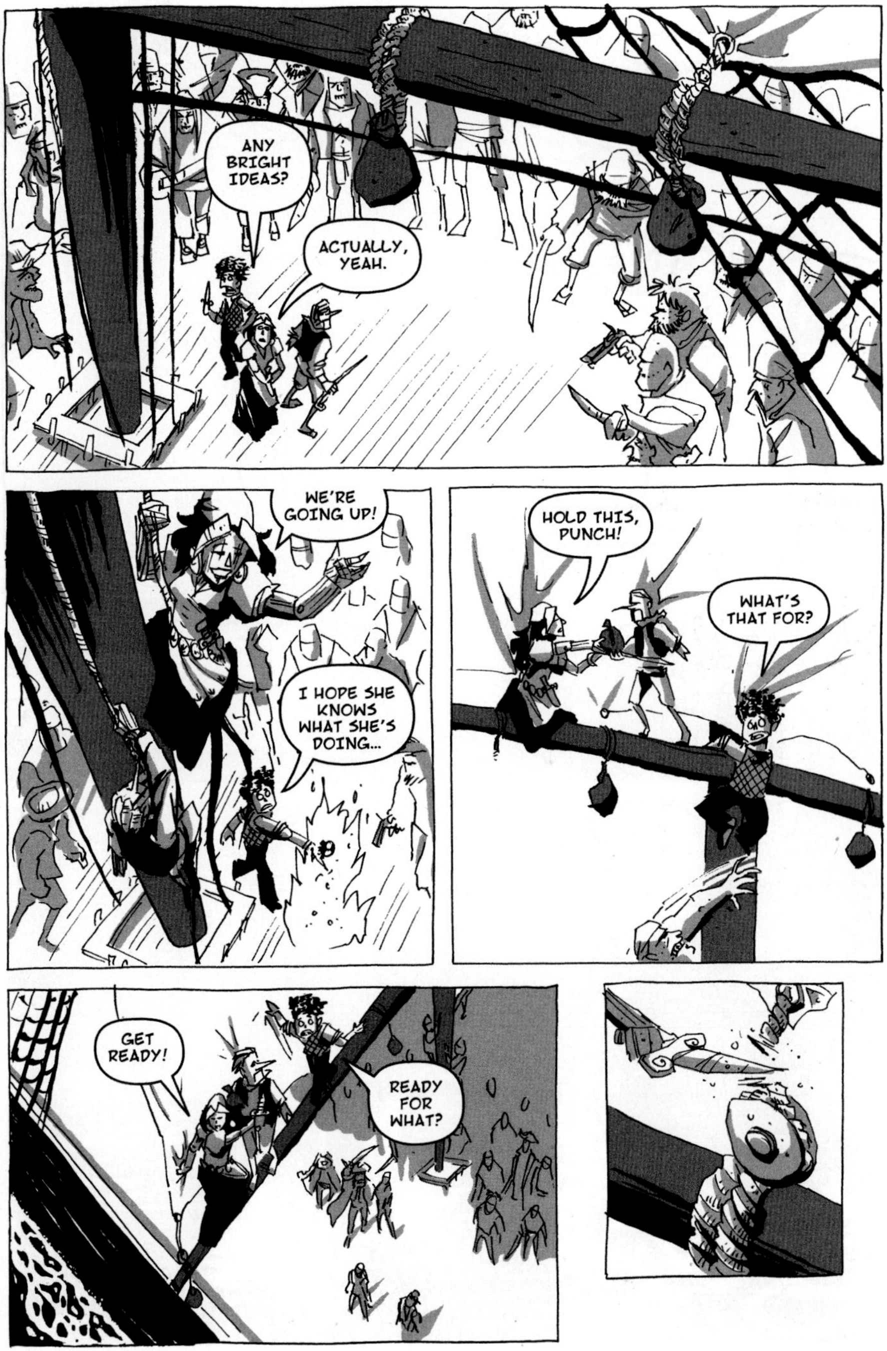
ANY BRIGHT IDEAS?
ACTUALLY, YEAH.
WE'RE GOING UP!
I HOPE SHE KNOWS WHAT SHE'S DOING...
HOLD THIS, PUNCH!
WHAT'S THAT FOR?
GET READY!
READY FOR WHAT?

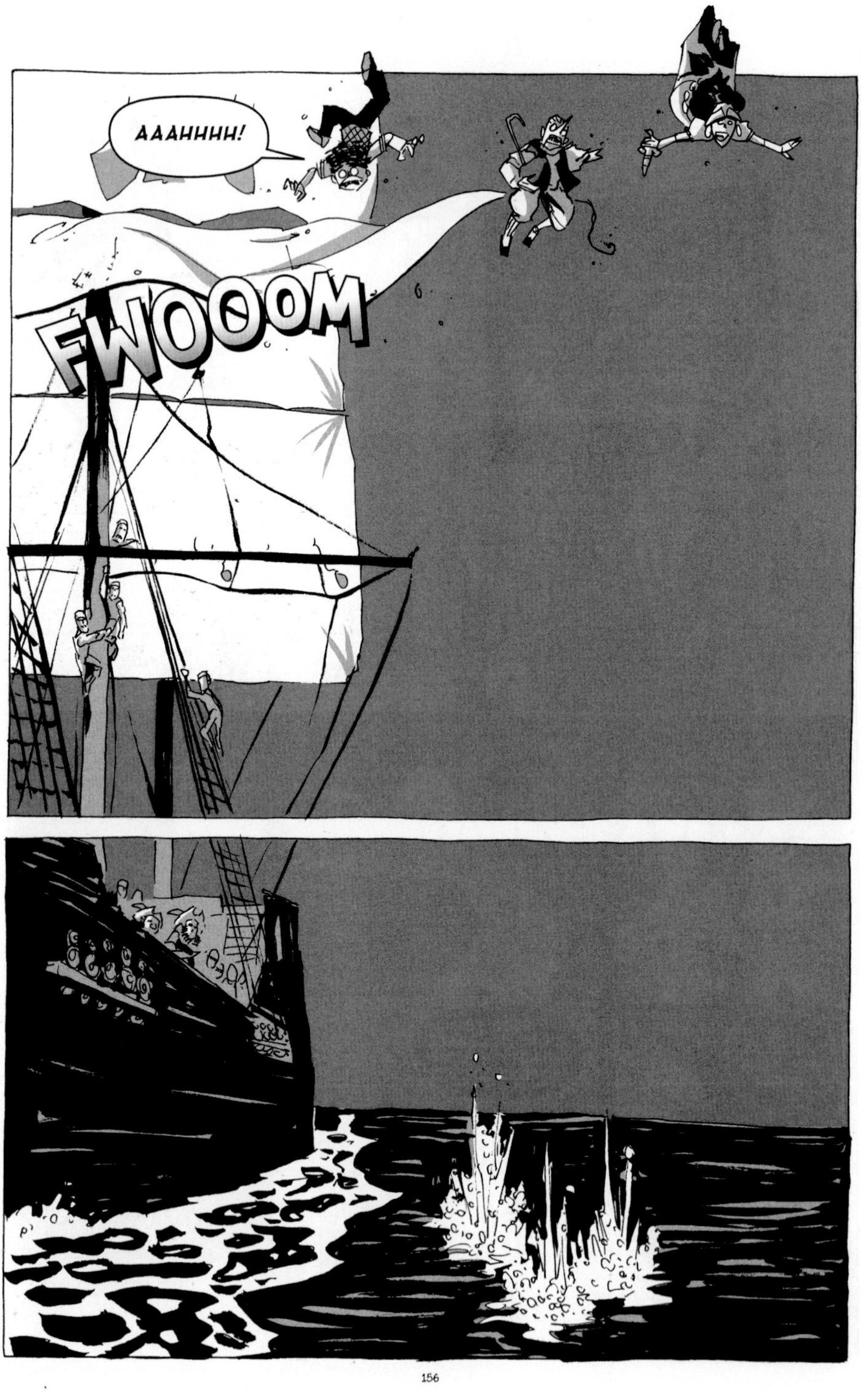
AAAHHHH!
FWOOOM

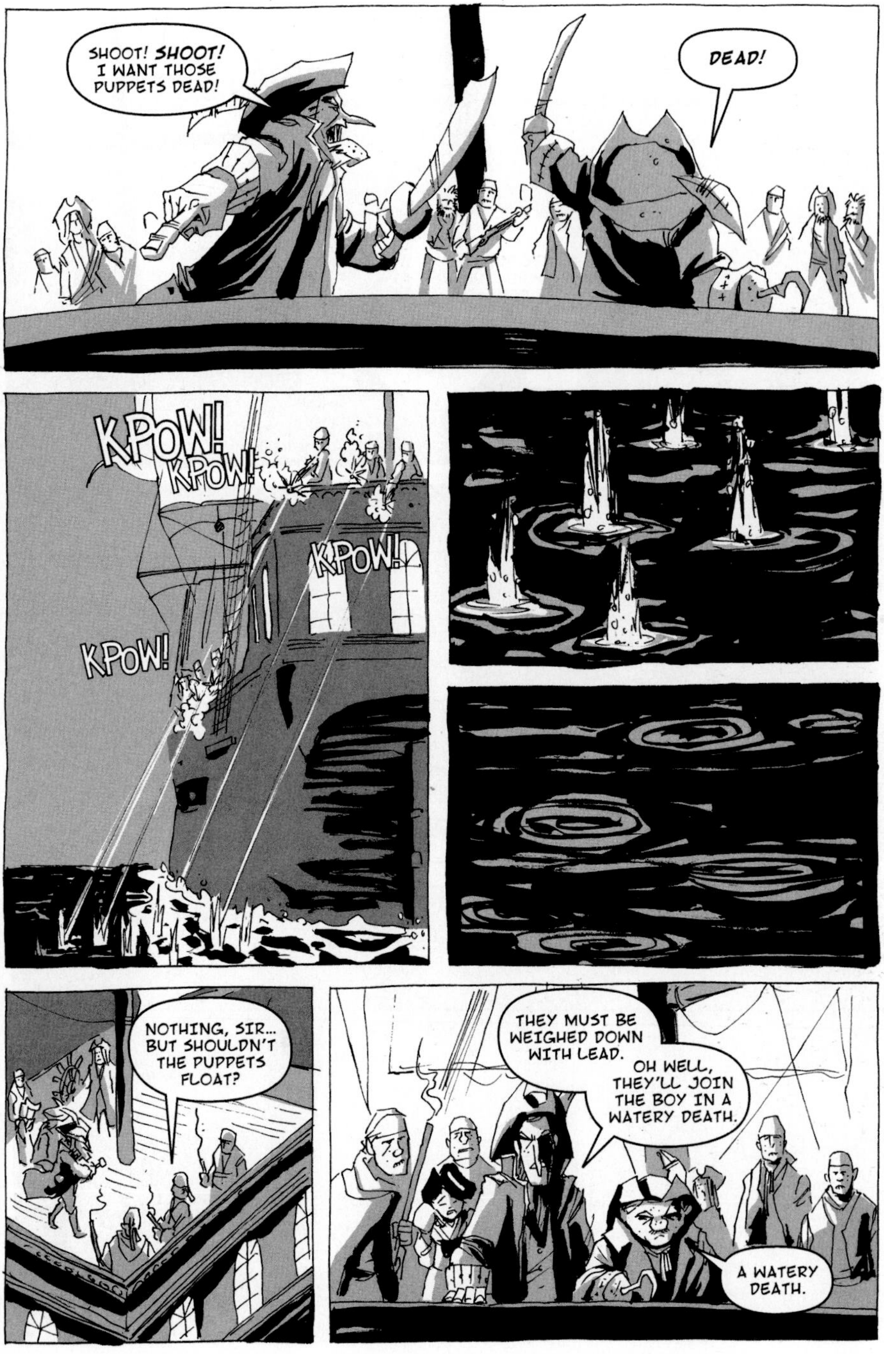
SHOOT! SHOOT! I WANT THOSE PUPPETS DEAD!
DEAD!
KPOW! KPOW!
KPOW!
KPOW!
NOTHING, SIR... BUT SHOULDN'T THE PUPPETS FLOAT?
THEY MUST BE WEIGHED DOWN WITH LEAD.
OH WELL, THEY'LL JOIN THE BOY IN A WATERY DEATH.
A WATERY DEATH.

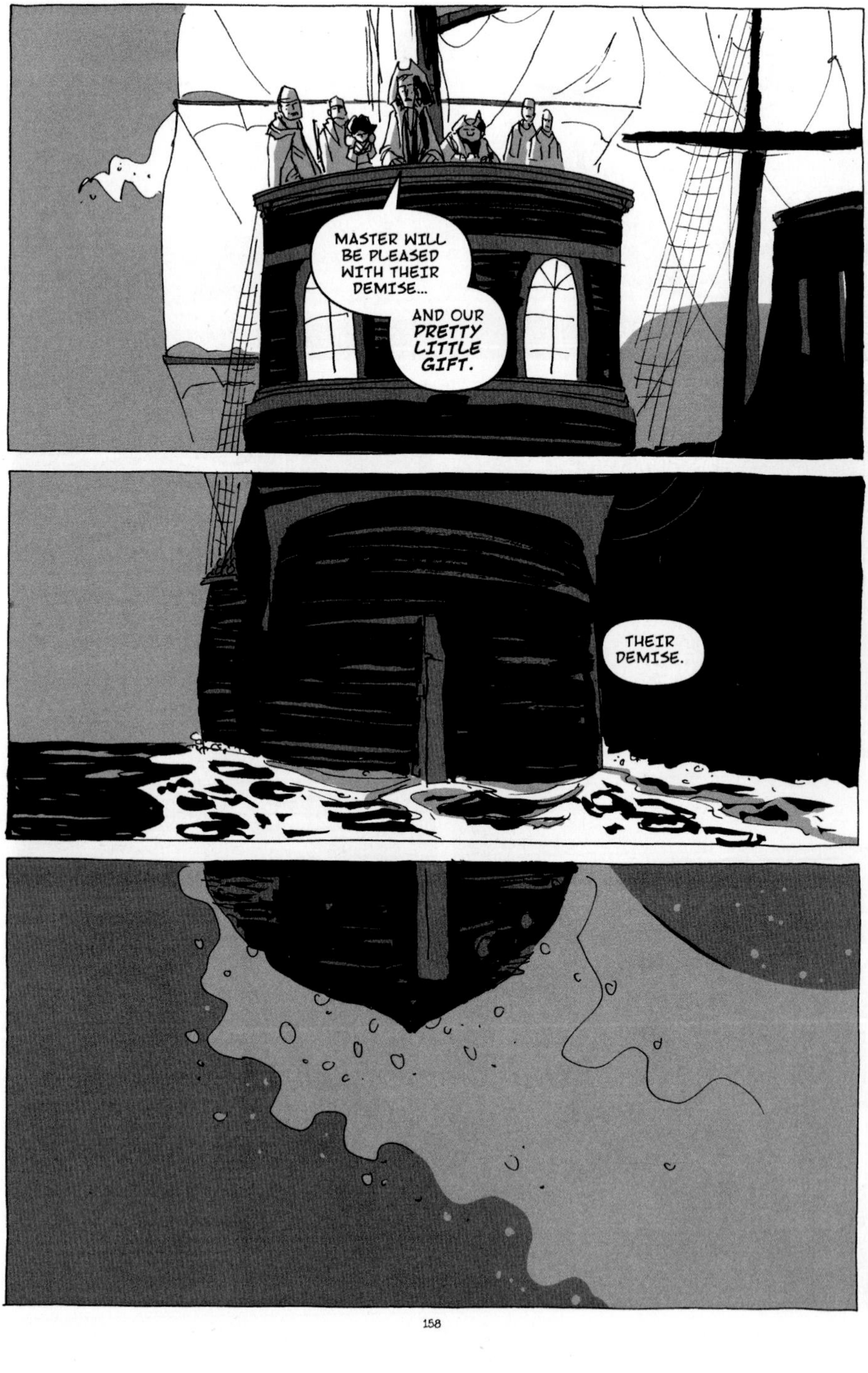
MASTER WILL BE PLEASED WITH THEIR DEMISE...
AND OUR PRETTY LITTLE GIFT.
THEIR DEMISE.

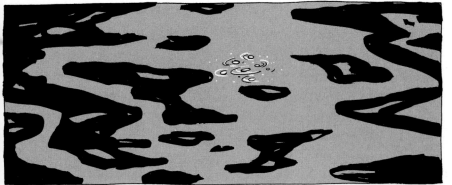

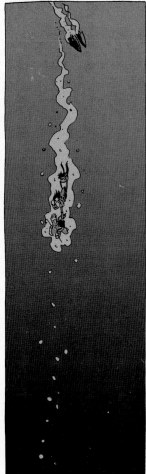

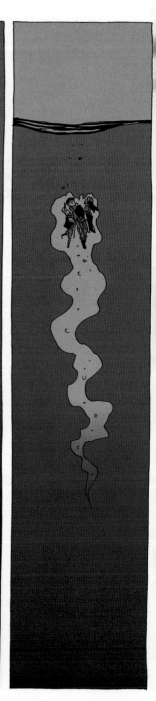

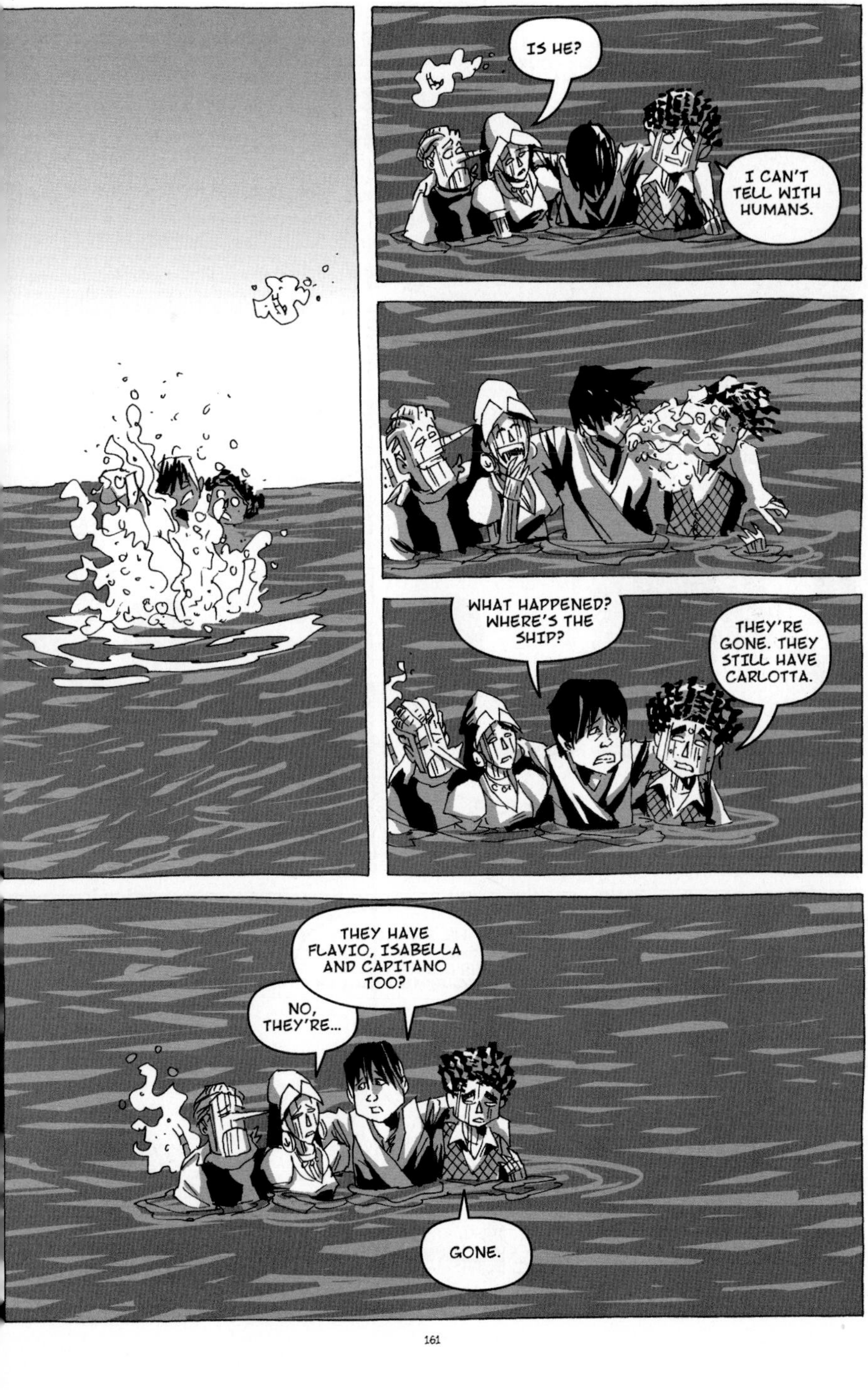
IS HE?
I CAN'T TELL WITH HUMANS.
WHAT HAPPENED? WHERE'S THE SHIP?
THEY'RE GONE. THEY STILL HAVE CARLOTTA.
THEY HAVE FLAVIO, ISABELLA AND CAPITANO TOO?
NO, THEY'RE...
GONE.

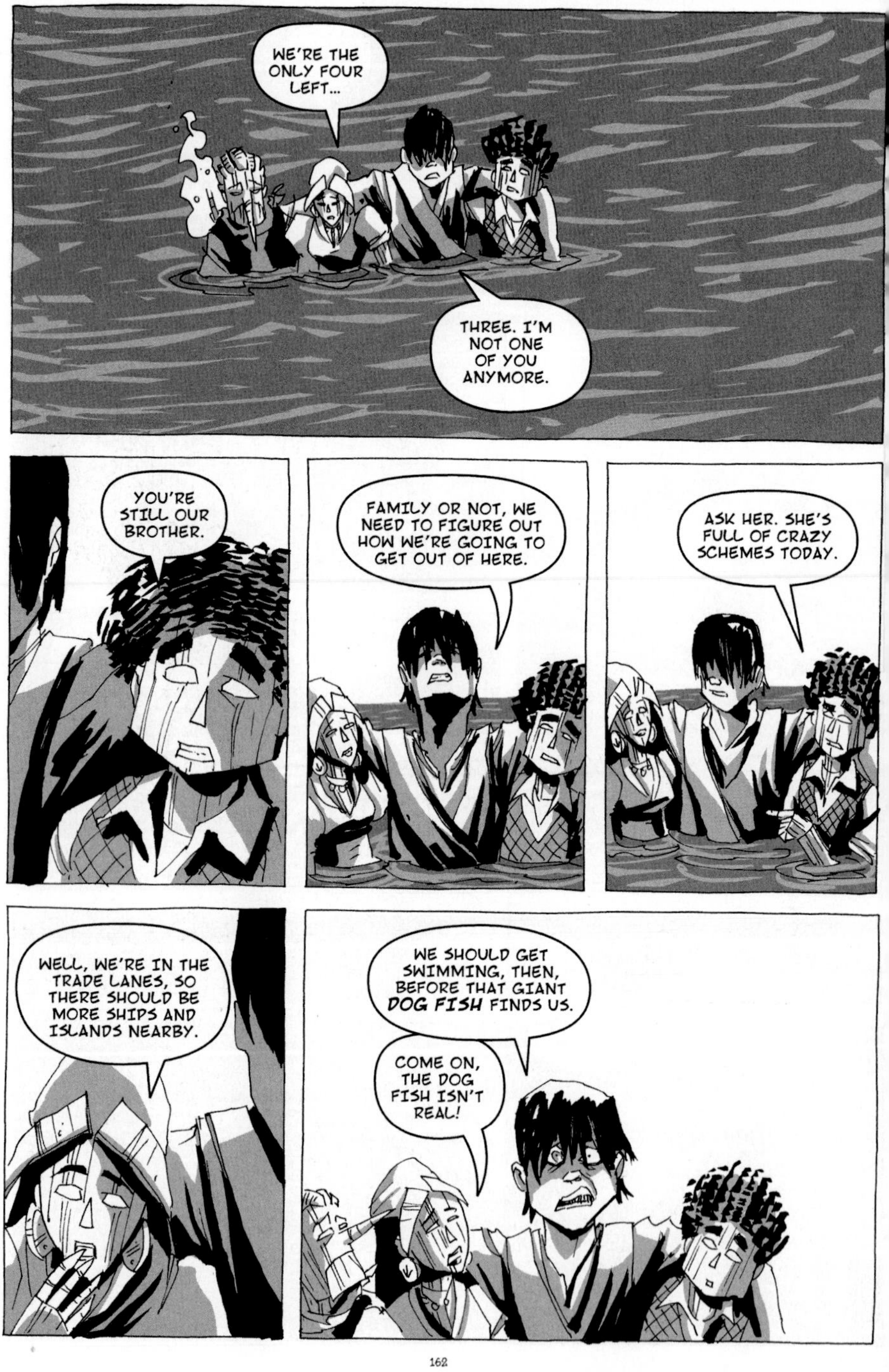
WE'RE THE ONLY FOUR LEFT...
THREE. I'M NOT ONE OF YOU ANYMORE.
YOU'RE STILL OUR BROTHER.
FAMILY OR NOT, WE NEED TO FIGURE OUT HOW WE'RE GOING TO GET OUT OF HERE.
ASK HER. SHE'S FULL OF CRAZY SCHEMES TODAY.
WELL, WE'RE IN THE TRADE LANES, SO THERE SHOULD BE MORE SHIPS AND ISLANDS NEARBY.
WE SHOULD GET SWIMMING, THEN, BEFORE THAT GIANT *DOG FISH* FINDS US.
COME ON, THE DOG FISH ISN'T REAL!

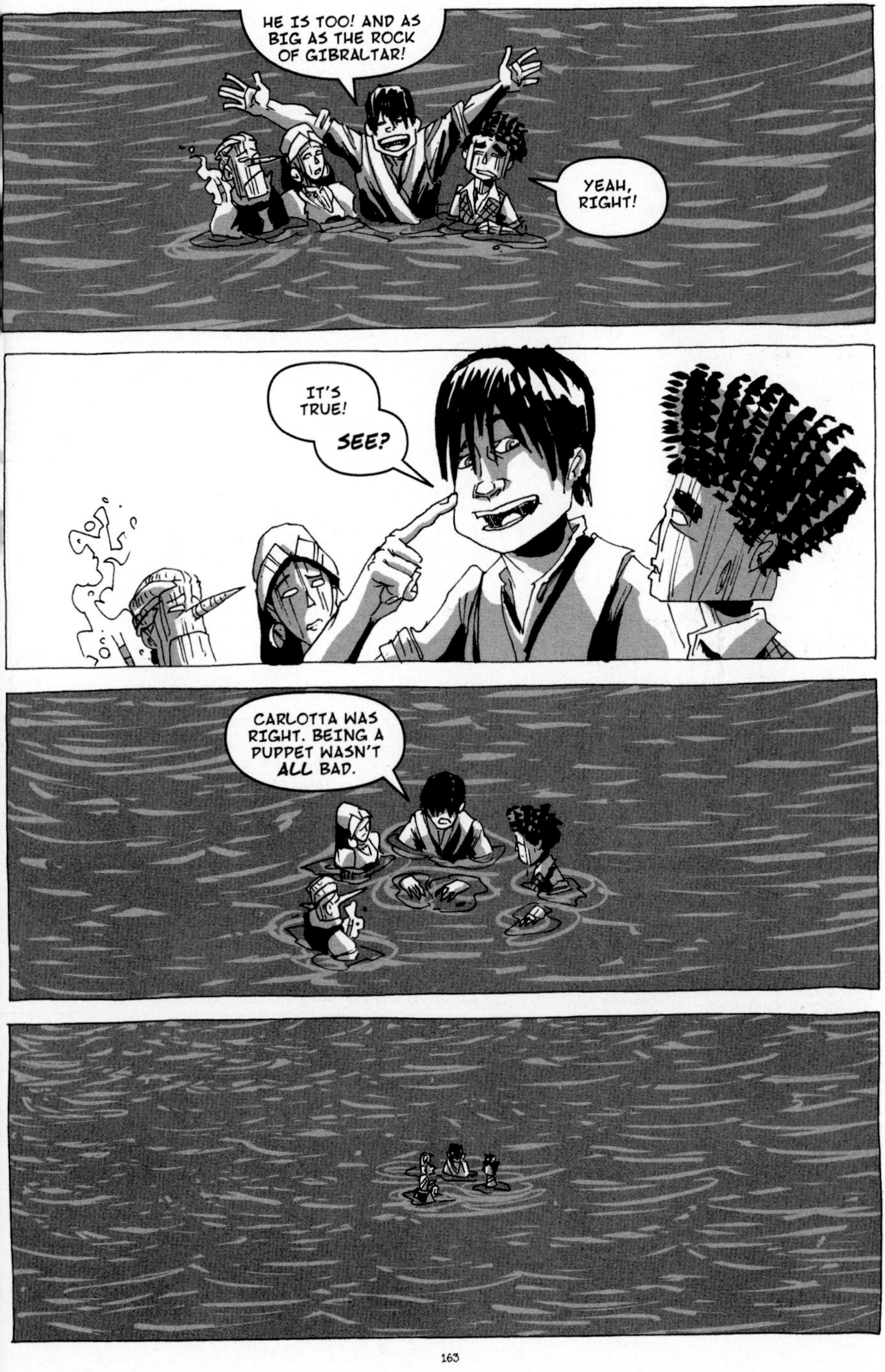
HE IS TOO! AND AS BIG AS THE ROCK OF GIBRALTAR!
YEAH, RIGHT!
IT'S TRUE! SEE?
CARLOTTA WAS RIGHT. BEING A PUPPET WASN'T ALL BAD.

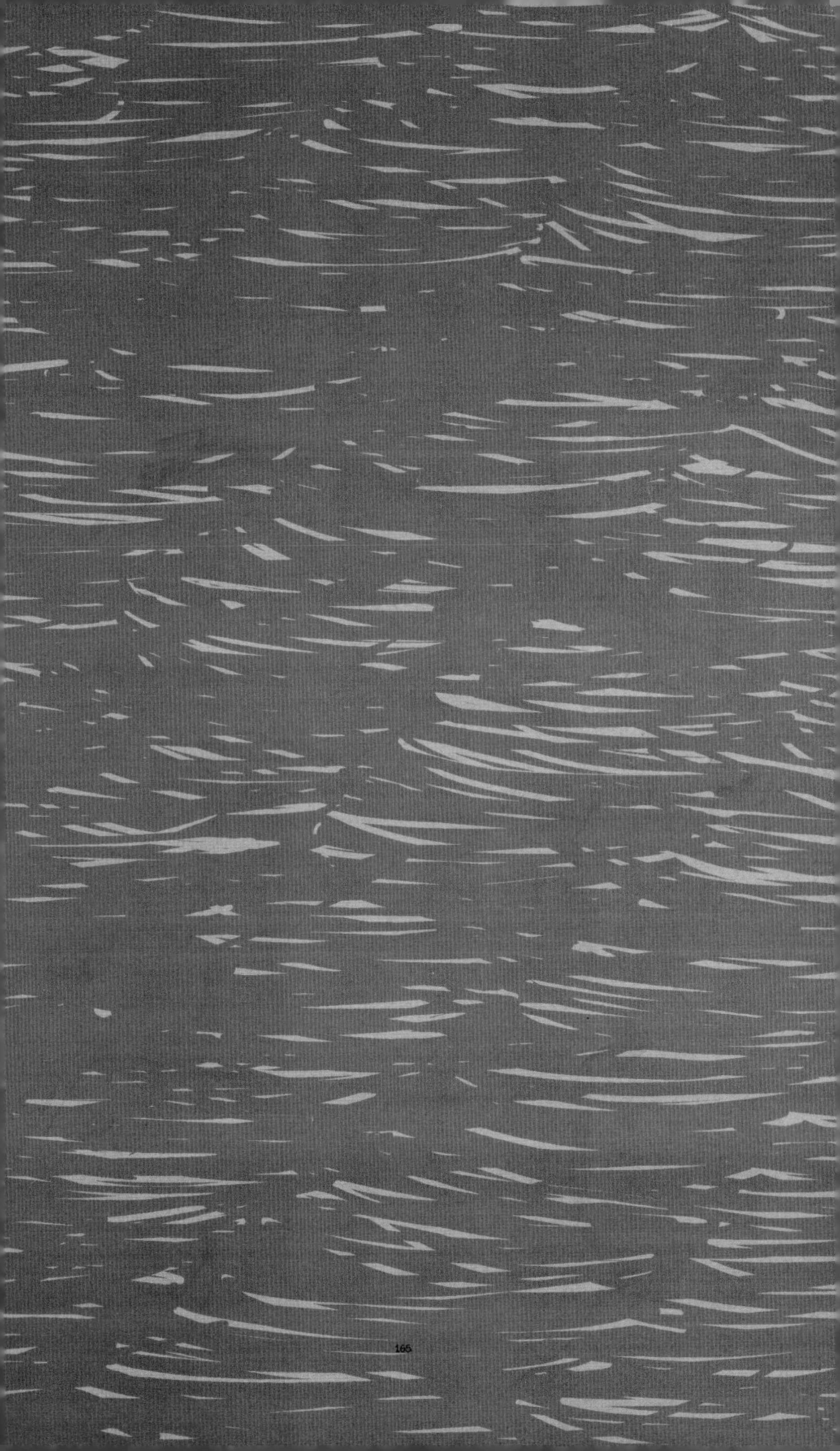

Van Jensen

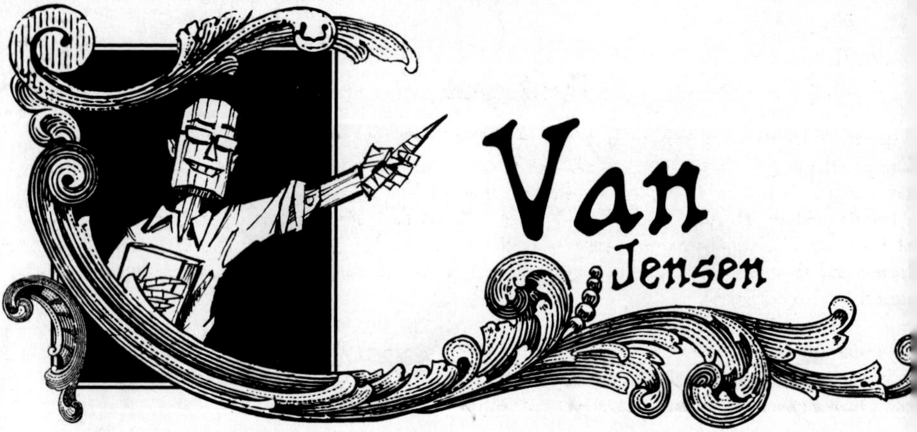

Van Jensen is an award-winning journalist and the writer of Pinocchio, Vampire Slayer and its sequel. Prior to working in comics, Jensen was a crime reporter at the Arkansas Democrat-Gazette. In his spare time, Jensen writes and draws the mini-comic series Nebraska, retelling true stories from growing up in a town of 300 in western Nebraska. He lives in Atlanta with his wife, Amy, and their mutt, Chase.

Dusty Higgins

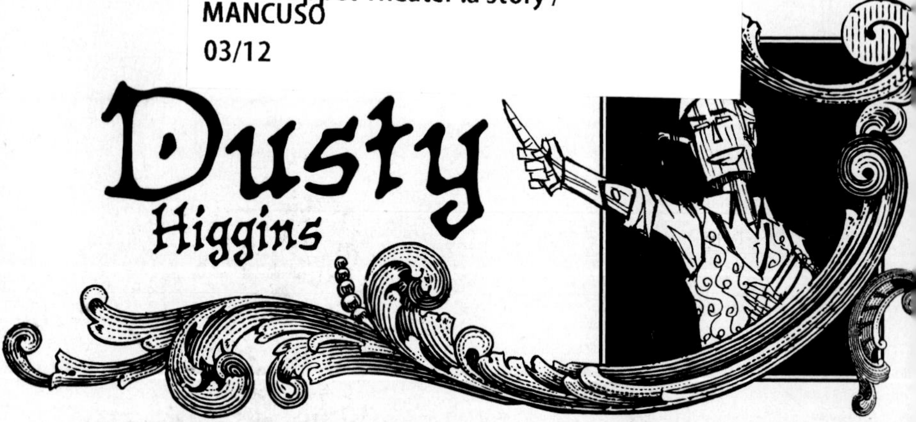

In 2005, if you had told Dusty Higgins he would be drawing not just a few pages, but *hundreds* of pages for a graphic novel about a vampire slaying puppet he would've laughed... then slapped you in the face. It's amazing what can happen in five years. *Pinocchio, Vampire Slayer* began as a short funny story to give Higgins a little taste of what working on a graphic novel might be like before he began work on what he thought would be much longer, more involved stories. He is now preparing to work on the *third* volume of *Pinocchio, Vampire Slayer* while that pile of other ideas gets taller and taller.

Higgins lives in Bryant, Arkansas with his wonderful wife, Kristin, beautiful baby daughter, Kahlan, and neurotic dog, Starbuck.